AS Level Applied Business for EDEXCEL

Single award

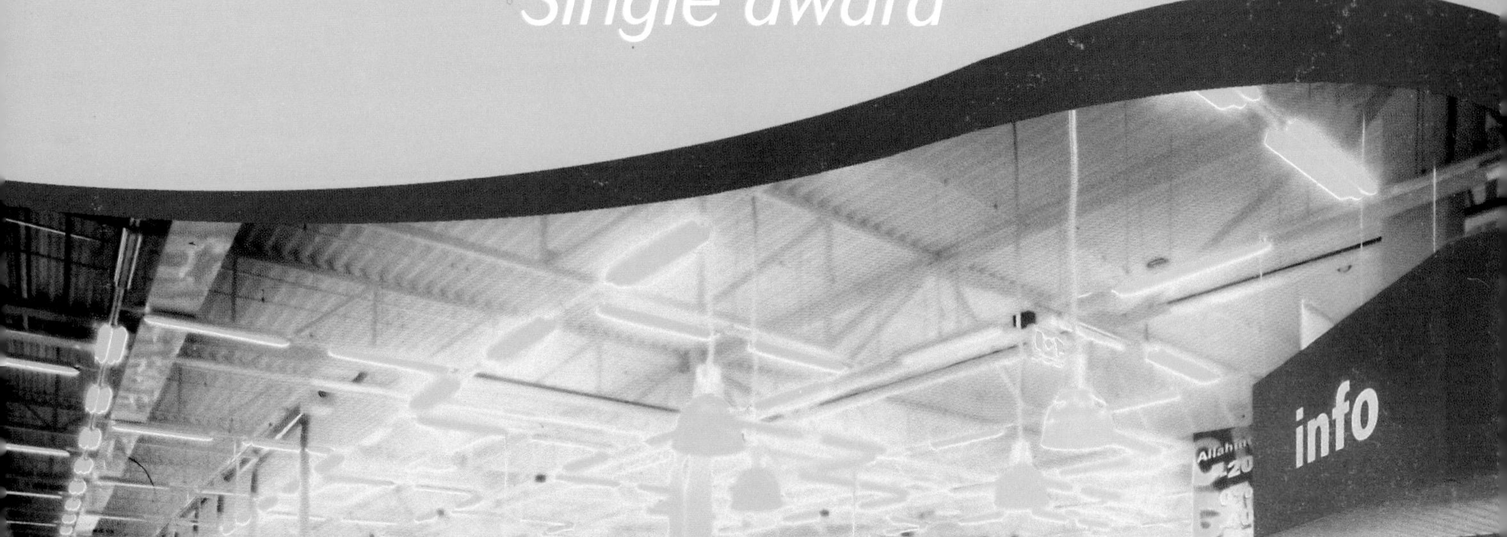

John Evans-Pritchard • Rob Jones
Alan Mansfield • Dave Gray

CU00901022

endorsed by edexcel

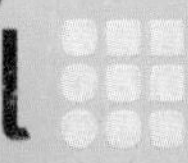

Acknowledgements

Dedication

To Sheila, Amanda Jane, Chris and Alf, Jan, Natalie, Holly and Ellen.

Cover design by Caroline Waring-Collins. Illustration © Tiit Veermae/Alamy.
Graphics by Caroline Waring-Collins.
Photography by Andrew Allen and Dave Gray.
Proof reading by Sue Oliver.
Reviewer - Stuart Kneller.
Typing - Ingrid Hamer

Acknowledgements

The publishers would like to thank the following for the use of photographs and copyright material. Other copyright material is acknowledged at source. Campbell/TopFoto p88; Corel pp75, 84; Digital Stock pp60, 79; Digital Vision pp22(r), 48, 96, 105, 115, 117, 164; Ilpo Musto/Rex Features p37; Jane Haralambos p129; John Tickner/Rex Features p47; PhotoDisc pp25, 30, 43, 44, 59, 64(t), 70(t,b), 86(t,b), 93, 97(t,b), 101(t,b), 104, 105, 114, 134, 177, 187; Photofusion pp123, 142; Rex Features pp8, 61; Shout/Rex Features p46; Stockbyte pp22(l), 35, 50(b), 120, 128, 163; TopFoto/EMPICS pp20, 41, 179, 188; TopFoto/ImageWorks pp50(t), 55, 109, 147; TopFoto/National p178; TopFoto/UPPA p145; Topham/PA pp54, 69.

Office for National Statisitics material is Crown Copyright, reproduced here with the permission of Her Majesty's Stationery Office.

Every effort has been made to locate the copyright owners of material used in this book. Any errors and omissions brought to the notice of the publisher are regretted and will be credited in subsequent printings.

British Library Cataloguing in Publication Data
A catalogue record for this book is available from the British Library.

ISBN 978-1-4058-2114-8

Contribution © John Evans-Pritchard, Rob Jones, Alan Mansfield, Dave Gray

Pearson Education
Edinburgh Gate
Harlow
Essex
CM20 2JE
First published 2005
Third impression 2008

Typesetting by Caroline Waring-Collins, Waring Collins Ltd.

Printed and bound in China WC/03

Contents

Unit 1 Investigating people at work

Unit 2 Investigating business

Unit 3 Investigating marketing

Preface

AS Level Applied Business for EDEXCEL (Single award) is one of a series of books written to follow the EDEXCEL Advanced Subsidiary GCE and Advanced GCE in Applied Business (Single and double awards). Other books in the series include:

- **AS Level Applied Business for EDEXCEL (Double award)** containing Units 1-7.
- **A2 Level Applied Business for EDEXCEL (Single and double awards)** containing Units 8-14;
- **Applied Business for EDEXCEL Teachers' Guide**.

AS Level Applied Business for EDEXCEL (Single award) contains Units 1-3 of the specification. Units have the following features.

Content coverage Units provide comprehensive coverage of 'What you need to learn' in Units 1-3 of the EDEXCEL specification. They give the content knowledge for Unit 1 external assessment and essential background information for internally assessed Units 2 and 3.

Meeting the assessment criteria Unit 1 contains sample questions in the style of the external examination, with sample marks. They clearly show the expected answers and how marks are allocated in the externally assessed examination. Understanding how questions are answered and marked will enable students to achieve examination success. Units 2 and 3 provide suggested student responses in internal assessment at Mark Bands 1, 2 and 3. Understanding the type of response required for different Mark Bands will allow students to meet the assessement criteria effectively. Answers are not meant to be comprehensive, reflecting all of a student's internal assessment, just the part that relates to the content covered in that section.

Examination practice Unit 1 provides sample questions which reflect the style of question asked in the externally assessed examination. Completing all the examination practice questions will allow students to practise and develop the skills for examination success.

Portfolio practice Units 2 and 3 provide questions which allow students to practise the knowledge, application, analysis and evaluation skills which they need to demonstrate in internal assessment.

Research activity Units 2 and 3 provide suggested research and investigation activities. They allow students to practise the research skills required for their internal assessment.

Business examples Many examples are given of actual businesses to illustrate how their operations relate to the EDEXCEL specification.

The publication has been endorsed by EDEXCEL.

Author team for the series

- **John Evans-Pritchard** is Chief Examiner with a major awarding body and an experienced author and teacher.
- **Margaret Hancock** is Principal Examiner with a major awarding body and an experienced author and education consultant for Business Studies.
- **Rob Jones** is an Examiner with a major awarding body and an experienced author and teacher.
- **Alan Mansfield** is Principal Examiner with a major awarding body and an experienced business and education consultant.
- **Dave Gray** is an experienced author and teacher.

The authors would like to thank Stuart Kneller for acting as a reviewer and for his comments and advice in the development and production of the series of books.

1 Business aims and objectives

Aims and objectives

All businesses have something that they are trying to achieve which explains the purpose of the businesses and why they are here. For many businesses the long-run purpose is to make profits for their owners, but there are many other purposes as explained below. First it is necessary to distinguish between aims and objectives.

There is a difference in the meaning and use of the two words, although in some cases businesses may not make any distinction between them. The words do, after all, both indicate the purpose of what is being done.

The technical difference and the one that will be used for this unit is:

- an aim is what the business is trying to achieve in the end - what the final target is;
- an objective is what needs to be done in order to achieve this aim.

This is illustrated in Figure 1.

Identifying a business's aims and objectives

Sometimes a business will state what its aims and objectives are, but often the real aims and objectives are hidden away. In other cases the business will state what its aims and objectives are to mislead people and only careful research will reveal what the actual aims and objective of the business are.

Companies often openly publish their main aims and objectives, sometimes as part of their 'mission statement'. A mission statement states the basic fundamental purpose of a business and so it should include what the main aims are. Unfortunately, it is sometimes used to try to convince customers that the business is only interested in what is good for the customer.

Major business aims

The major aims of businesses will depend on why they are in business and what they are producing. Businesses in the public and private sectors tend to have different reasons for being in business and, therefore, different aims. These differences are considered in section 2. Section 1 considers general aims and objectives and how they can differ depending on what is being produced and sold. Some examples are shown in Figures 1 and 2.

Figure 2 *Business aims*

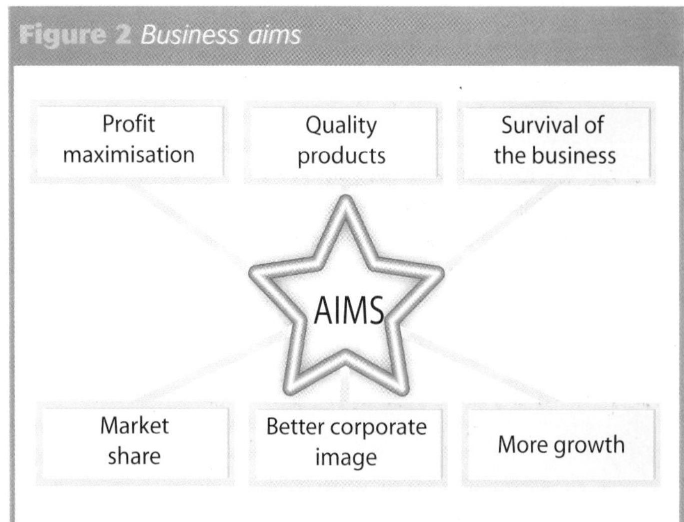

Making sales and profit

For most businesses selling their products is vital, otherwise they will not have the money necessary to buy raw materials, pay their employees and stay in business. For many businesses the primary aim is to make profits for their owners. In reality it may be difficult to find a business that will state that making profit is its major aim. Making the maximum profit, profit maximisation, is often a major aim although some businesses are prepared to 'satisfice' and make only satisfactory profits.

For example, *The Independent* reported in April 2001 that:

Figure 1 *Aims and objectives*

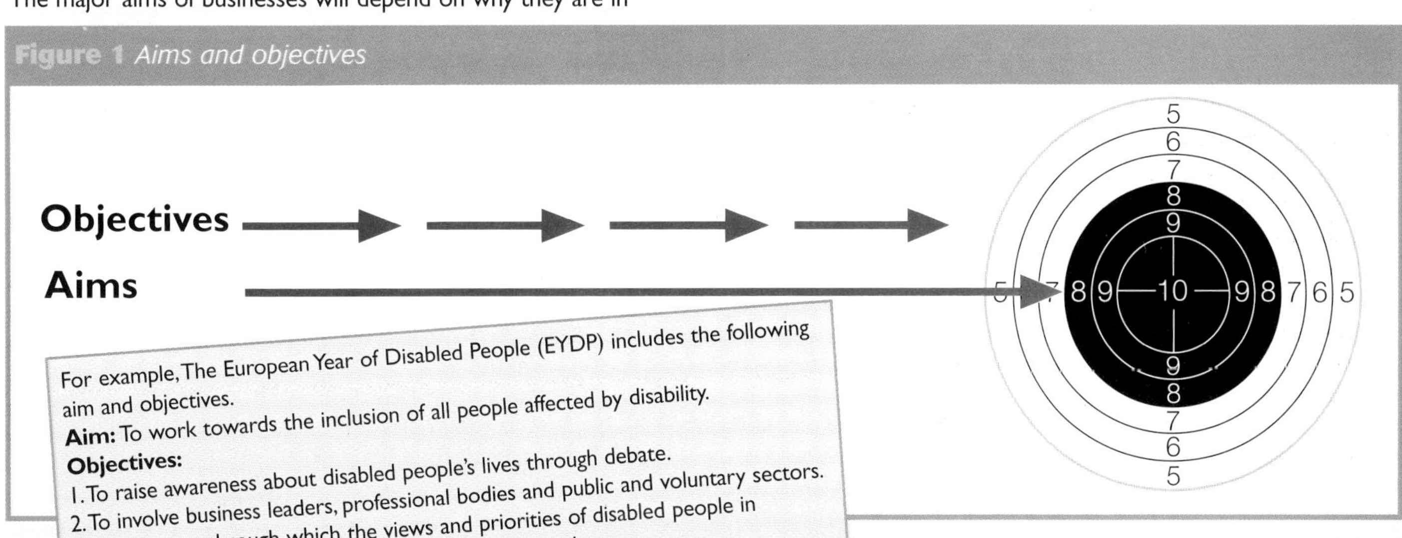

'Tesco broke through the £1bn profit barrier for the first time yesterday but was immediately criticised by farming groups for making 'obscene' returns while the industry is in crisis and the foot-and-mouth outbreak continues'. Some objectives needed to achieve profit maximisation are shown in Table 1.

Table 1 *Profit maximisation*

Business aim	Typical objectives needed to meet that aim
Profit maximisation and high sales	Find new markets through effective market research.
	Increase promotion through media such as the Internet.
	Revise pricing policies to meet customers' expectations.
	Improve customer service through better complaints procedures.
	Set performance targets for all employees.
	Reduce costs wherever this can be done without affecting quality or performance.

Growth

The easiest way for a business to increase it sales and its profits is to get bigger. This can be done in a number of ways.

- Internal growth, where the business grows simply by selling more products to more customers, increasing the number of outlets and building new factories.
- Moving into new markets, e.g. abroad.
- Diversifying by selling different products.
- Taking over other businesses.

Some objectives needed to achieve growth are shown in Table 2. Figure 3 shows how Caffè Nero has grown.

Table 2 *Growth*

Business aim	Typical objectives needed to meet that aim
Growth	All of those listed for maximising profits and sales.
	Achieve a wider customer base.
	Research and develop new products to replace declining products.
	Ensure that additional funds are available to meet any increase in demand.
	Establish the business name as a market leader, perhaps by creating a brand.

Gaining market share

When businesses enter a new market it is important that they gain market share so that their product is recognised and the business can expand. Gaining market share may also be a way in which existing businesses expand.

Many markets, such as basic groceries and food, have relatively fixed total sales, so the only way to expand is by taking market share from other businesses. There is another benefit of gaining market share. When businesses become market leaders or even monopolies this gives them great power, which in the long run will allow them to earn higher profits.

For example, in 2005 the supermarket group J Sainsbury took over 114 convenience stores from Jacksons. Convenience stores are now recognised as one of the key growth areas in UK retailing and Sainsbury is keen to attract a greater share of the market for those consumers wishing to shop locally. Some objectives needed to gain market share are shown in Table 3.

Table 3 *Market share*

Business aim	Typical objectives needed to meet that aim
Gaining market share	All of those listed for maximising profits and sales.
	Achieve annual growth in sales of (say) 5-15%.
	Ensure that prices are set at levels equal to or below those of competitors.
	Reduce the number of competitors in the market through takeover or merger.
	Use aggressive promotion to show the strengths of the business's products and the weaknesses of competitors' products.

Figure 3 *Caffè Nero growth*

Caffè Nero Group Plc founded in only 1997 was, by 2004, the largest independent coffee retailer in the UK, with over 198 outlets. This expansion has come from setting up new outlets, and buying competitors' outlets.

- March 2001 – Raises £7.5m from Stock Exchange flotation to fund expansion.
- Feb. 2001 – Buys 26 of its Aroma coffee bars from McDonald's for £3.5m, taking the Caffè Nero chain to more than 100.
- June 2001 – Opens first coffee bar at easyInternet Cafe's High Street Kensington branch in London.
- Aug. 2002 – Aimed to open up to four coffee bars a month over the next 12 months, having secured a new £7m funding facility.
- Feb. 2003 – Announces plans to expand its chain of 111 coffee bars to 125 during 2004.
- Sept. 2003 – Announces plans to expand its chain of 131 coffee bars to 150 by January 2004 and to 300 within five years. Target increased to 400 in Feb. 2004.
- June 2004 – acquired eight stores in the south of England from Coffee Republic for £0.7m, taking its chain to 171 sites.

Source: adapted from www.caffenero.com.

Quality goods and services

For many businesses the quality of the good produced or service provided will determine how successful they are. This is especially true in competitive markets. Being ranked as the best in the business is a very powerful marketing factor.

Many businesses achieve this aim through modifying and improving their products. Others achieve this through branding their products. If the branding is very strong there will be no other business in the market and their product will therefore, automatically, be the best. Branding is discussed in section 32.

For example, the Soil Association checks UK farms to ensure a farm that claims to be producing organic arable or livestock products meets the customers' expectations. Its requirements are the highest in the world. Aberhyddnant Farm in the Brecon Beacons National Park is an example or a farm that sticks rigidly to this standard as it produces organic beef and lamb. Some objectives needed to achieve quality products are shown in Table 4. Figure 4 shows how Denby Pottery ensures quality.

Table 4 *Quality goods and servcies*

Business aim	Typical objectives needed to meet that aim
Better quality goods and services	Carry out market research to find out what customers really want.
	Carry out research and development into new products.
	Set internal minimum quality standards.
	Seek external recognition of quality as with the BS 7000 and ISO 9000.
	Provide customers with fast and effective solutions whenever products fail to match their expected quality.

Figure 4 *Denby Pottery quality*

- Started in 1806 because of the quality of the clay at Denby in Derbyshire.
- Expanded through its international reputation for quality bottles and jars.
- As glass production became cheaper Denby changed to producing quality kitchenware.
- In the 1930s Denby introduced classic giftware ranges.
- In the 1950s Denby changed to producing high quality tableware, employing the best designers.
- In the 1970s Denby introduced its revolutionary oven-to-tableware.

Why is Denby unique? Its mark of quality is shown through:
- versatile and stylish tableware for entertaining and everyday use;
- distinctive shapes and rich colours to create a unique look;
- practical tableware that goes from the oven to the table - effortlessly,
- the highest standards of English craftwork for nearly 200 years;
- exceptionally durable and safe for use in the oven, microwave, freezer or dishwasher.

Source: adapted from www.denbypottery.co.uk.

Improving the corporate image

Corporate image is about how a business is seen by its customers and the general public. In today's highly competitive world of business it is often not enough just to have a high quality product available at a competitive price. More and more, customers are beginning to question how businesses behave and how what they do affects not just their direct customers, but also society, the environment and their employees. Businesses need to provide good publicity and avoid negative publicity.

Businesses use the following ways to ensure a positive public image.
- Having environmentally friendly products and methods of production.
- Treating employees fairly, with no discrimination.
- Contributing to charity.
- Supporting the local community through sponsorship.
- Providing customers with top of the range products at a fair price.
- Becoming the market leader that all other businesses try to copy.

Some objectives needed to improve corporate image are shown in Table 5. Figure 5 shows how Red Bull has attempted to improve its image.

Table 5 *Corporate image*

Business aim	Typical objectives needed to meet that aim
Improving the corporate image	Create a meaningful corporate aim in the form of a mission statement.
	Assess the general public's expectations of the business.
	Ensure all government requirements in terms of environmental, social and ethical standards are met and surpassed.
	Raise public awareness of the business through press releases and sponsorships.
	Engender a feeling of corporate identity in all members of staff.

Survival

For some businesses survival can become the most important aim. This can occur as the business is first launched into a competitive market and struggles to make a name for itself against established competitors. It also regularly happens to established businesses and even very well known ones. There are many reasons why demand for a business's products might decline and make survival the primary aim.

- Out of date products.
- The entry into the market of major competitors.
- A downturn in the business cycles.
- Negative publicity about the business or its products.
- Poor management of costs.

Some objectives needed to achieve survival are shown in Table 6. Table 7 shows the number of incorporated companies closing in Great Britain over a six month period. Mainly these are companies which have failed to meet their primary aim of survival. There are even more sole trader businesses that had to close in the same period.

Figure 5 *Red Bull's sponsorship and corporate image*

On the 6th March 2005 Red Bull hit a major part of the sporting big time as Red Bull Racing competed in Formula 1 for the first time. Scotsman David Coultard secured 4th place in the first race of the season, but the smaller events have not been forgotten.

From the 5th to 10th of April the Zed Rooms at The Old Truman Brewery in East London will be hosting the 'Red Bull Art of Can' exhibition. Here 'cans will imitate art'. The entries will be displayed for a week and judged by artist Tracey Emin, presenter Sara Cox, art critic Nick Hackworth and fashion designers Basso & Brooke.

Source: adapted from http://www.redbull.co.uk/ which shows the ranges of events that Red Bull supports.

Examination practice · Dasani

Dasani was launched by Coca-Cola in the UK in 2004 to offer a healthy alternative to their standard Coca-Cola products. It boasted pure water based on a 'highly sophisticated purification system'.

The press then reported that the water was simply being piped in from Thames water, put through a similar purification system to that found in many houses and the price being raised from 0.03p/litre to 95p/litre. Bromide was then added and oxidised into bromate at twice the legal limit, making it very much less healthy than ordinary tap water.

Coca-Cola had to recall all of the bottles of Dasani but claimed that the incident would not affect the brand name of Dasani or Coca-Cola.

Source: adapted from various sources.

(a) Suggest an aim which Coca-Cola was trying to achieve by launching Dasani. Justify your answer. (3 marks)

(b) Suggest another aim which Coca-Cola should have been trying to achieve, yet failed to achieve. Explain your answer. (3 marks)

(c) This incident affected the reputation of Coca-Cola in the UK. List and justify actions that the company should have taken in order to ensure that its reputation would not have been affected in the long run. (6 marks)

(d) Explain the effects that this incident may have had on UK employees working in the Coca-Cola bottling plant. (4 marks)

Table 6 *Survival*

Business aim	Typical objectives needed to meet that aim
Survival	Establish the cause of the loss of sales.
	Reduce costs to allow effective competition.
	Secure long term financial backing.
	Change or improve the product if this is felt to be sub-standard.
	Implement an effective marketing strategy.

Table 7 *Company Liquidations (Great Britain)*

Month	Total
Jan 2005	1,104
Dec 2004	1,886
Nov 2004	1,324
Oct 2004	1,492
Sep 2004	1,367
Aug 2004	1,375
6 month total	**8,548**

Source: adapted from Companies House.

Meeting the assessment criteria

When Stuart Rose, Marks & Spencer's Chief Executive, looked at the problems of falling sales facing the company in 2004 he identified, amongst many other problems, that it has let rivals steal its core business.

His solution was that M&S needed to win back the 35 to 55 year-old women shoppers from cheaper clothes chains and supermarkets and that this should be done by getting the right goods on the shelves, in terms of style and quality, at the right price. For the food business he stressed that M&S needed to focus on quality and innovation as they had done in the past.

Source: adapted from *The Guardian*, July 2004.

(a) From Stuart Rose's comments identify **ONE** aim that M&S has for the future and list **TWO** objectives that would help to meet this aim. **(3 marks)**

Exemplar responses

- *Gain back market share from competitors (aim) – win back 35-55 year olds (objective) – set the right price (objective).*
- *Increase sales of food items (aim) – ensure quality is what customers expect (objective) – find new innovative products (objective).*

Mark allocation

1 mark for identifying aim.
1 mark for each related objective. **(3 marks)**

(b) Stuart Rose identified rival firms stealing M&S's business as a major cause of the company's problems. How important, therefore, is it to:
(i) 'win back the 35 to 55 year old women shoppers'?
(ii) 'get the right goods in terms of style and quality'?
(6 marks)

Exemplar responses

(i) Rivals taking away core customers – the core customers are the 35 to 55 year old women so the problem is major – winning back these customers should, therefore, have a major positive effect on M&S's sales and profits.

(ii) M&S has lost customers because its styles and quality are not considered adequate by customers – supermarkets are making inroads on M&S's sales (e.g. George) – improving style and quality will help to make M&S appeal to its core customers so that they reject the competitors.

Mark allocation

1 mark for recognising the problem (should be different for (i) and (ii)).
1 mark for quantifying the problem (it asked for 'how important').
1 mark for how the suggested strategy helps to solve the problem.
(1 + 1 + 1) x 3
(6 marks)

2 Types of ownership

Ownership

The aims and objectives that a business has will depend on a variety of factors. Some of these have been covered in section 1. The organisational structure and functions will be covered in sections 3 and 4. This section considers the effects of three main factors and also what impact they may have on such aspects as the size of the business. The three main factors are:

- what sector of industry the business is in;
- whether it is profit making, non-profit making or a not-for-profit business;
- what type of ownership it has.

Industrial sectors

Businesses in different sectors of industry operate in very different ways. Whilst most will share the same basic aims of making profits, increasing market share and survival some aims and many objectives will be different.

Primary Industry Primary industry is involved with directly using what nature has provided in order to produce goods.

- **Farming or agriculture.** The UK has a wide range of agricultural businesses including arable farming, livestock farming, organic farming and horticulture. All of these require use of land, so having the right kind of land, improving the land the business has and ensuring that is it not polluted, become vital objectives.

  For example, www.organicfarmfoods.co.uk states that 'The aim of every organic farmer is to produce the highest possible quality of food in optimum quantity and seeks to co-exist and work with nature rather than to dominate it'. Each of the needs shown in Table 1 will create its own objective for the business involved.
- **Fishing.** This covers two main sectors of business - sea fishing, for example in the North Sea, and fish farming, such as trout and salmon farms. The major requirements and objectives here include ensuring sufficient stocks for the future, reducing water pollution, working within EU restrictions on fishing and marketing the benefits of fish over other food.

Table 1 *Aims and objectives in primary industry*

Type of farming	Examples of aims and objectives
Arable	Good soil, good seeds, right climate, sufficient water.
Livestock	Good pedigree, correct feed, shelter, virus protection.
Organic	Unpolluted soil/livestock, customer awareness.
Horticulture	Fertile soil, local markets, new strains of plants.

- **Forestry.** Specific concerns here may be what type of trees to grow, as they grow at different rates and have widely differing values, what the market value will be in the future, as they take so long to grow, and what government support is available
- **Mining.** These tend to be large scale operations and ones that require high expenditure before anything is produced. Concerns may involve where the funds will come from, the effects of cheaper imports and what responsibilities the owners have when the mines are finally closed down.

Secondary Industry Secondary industry covers all manufacturing and construction businesses. Here businesses are using raw materials from the primary sector to produce a very wide range of goods. Businesses are likely to have different aims depending on what is being produced.

For example, in the highly competitive world of vacuum cleaners Dyson has, yet again, come up with another innovation, meeting its aim to stay ahead of the field. Instead of the conventional wheels, Dyson is using a single ball which is designed to make the vacuum cleaner easier to handle and to move into and out of confined spaces.

Some examples of industries are shown in Table 2.

Table 2 *Aims and objectives in secondary industry*

Type of industry	Examples of aims and objectives
Chemical industry	Ensuring harmful waste products are disposed of safely.
Car industry	Developing a cost effective alternative to petrol driven vehicles.
Tobacco industry	Diversifying into new non-tobacco products as smoking in public places is banned.
House building industry	Planning to build more smaller houses as the government raises the stamp duty threshold to £120,000.

Tertiary Industry Tertiary industry provides services to both the general public and to other businesses. This is now the largest sector of UK production and includes a very wide range of services' from personal services such as hairdressing and plumbing to major commercial services such as banking and retailing. Because the types of service being provided are so diverse, the aims and objectives are also often very different. Examples are given in Table 3.

The profit motive

Businesses can be divided into those that have profit as a major aim and those that do not.

Profit making businesses Many, if not most, businesses have the

Table 3 *Aims and objectives in tertiary industry*

Type of service	Examples of aims and objectives
Supermarkets	As essentially all of the goods are the same, the aim becomes providing a service that is significantly different to that of competitors.
Premier League Football teams	Qualifying for European competitions.
Computer services help lines	Providing accurate and rapid solutions to customers' problems.
Advertising agencies	Ensuring each business's message and image is put across effectively.

primary aim of making profits. These are called profit-making businesses. They include most of the well known businesses such as BP, Virgin, Sainsbury, British Telecom and HSBC. There are, however, two other major sections of business where making profit is either not an aim or it is only a way of reaching a more important aim.

Non-profit making businesses These orgnaisations have little or no interest in making profits, so this is not one of their aims. Their only concern, as far as profits are involved, is that they may need to make enough money to cover costs. Examples of these types of businesses include:

- local sporting clubs;
- most schools and colleges;
- charities;
- interest groups, such as the Countryside Alliance.

With State funded businesses, such as schools, costs are paid by the State and nothing is being sold, so profit is irrelevant. Other businesses, such as local clubs, take in subscriptions to pay for providing the facilities and staff, but make no profits. This is done because they were set up for a more important reason. Local clubs are there to provide their members with leisure and recreation. Figure 1 shows an example of a non-profit making business organisation.

Not-for-profit businesses These are businesses that do make profits, but this is not for the benefit of the owners. Typical examples of this kind of business are charity shops, such as Oxfam, Scope and Age Concern.

Figure 1 *The Ramblers' Association objectives*

- Safeguarding Britain's unique network of public paths.
- Providing information to help you plan your walk and enjoy it in safety and comfort.
- Increasing access for walkers.
- Protecting the countryside and green spaces from unsightly and polluting developments.
- Educating the public about their rights and responsibilities and the health and environmental benefits of walking so that everyone can enjoy our wonderful heritage.

Source: adapted from www.ramblers.org.uk.

Public and private sectors

One method of classifying business by ownership is into private and public sectors. Businesses can be classified by how they are owned. This has important effects on how the businesses are run and on their aims and objectives.

The public sector

State owned businesses should have the primary objective of providing goods or services that benefit the public. Examples are shown in Table 4.

Because the businesses are owned by the state it is the state that decides how they will be run and how they will be financed.

Table 4 *Aims of state owned businesses*

State owned business	Major aims
The National Health Service	'The aim of the Department of Health (DH) is to improve the health and wellbeing of people in England.'
Department for Education and Skills	'Our aim is to give children an excellent start in education, enable young people to equip themselves with life and work skills, and encourage adults to achieve their full potential through learning.'
British Nuclear Fuels Limited (BNFL)	'To be trusted as a quality supplier to deliver safe, environmentally sound and profitable nuclear services and products.'
HM Treasury Aims and Objectives	'Aim: To raise the rate of sustainable growth and achieve rising prosperity and a better quality of life, with economic and employment opportunities for all.'
Copmanthorpe Parish Council	'Our aim: Your Parish Council is committed to retaining our traditional village life and representing the whole village in matters that affect us all.'

Figure 2 *Private and public sector ownership*

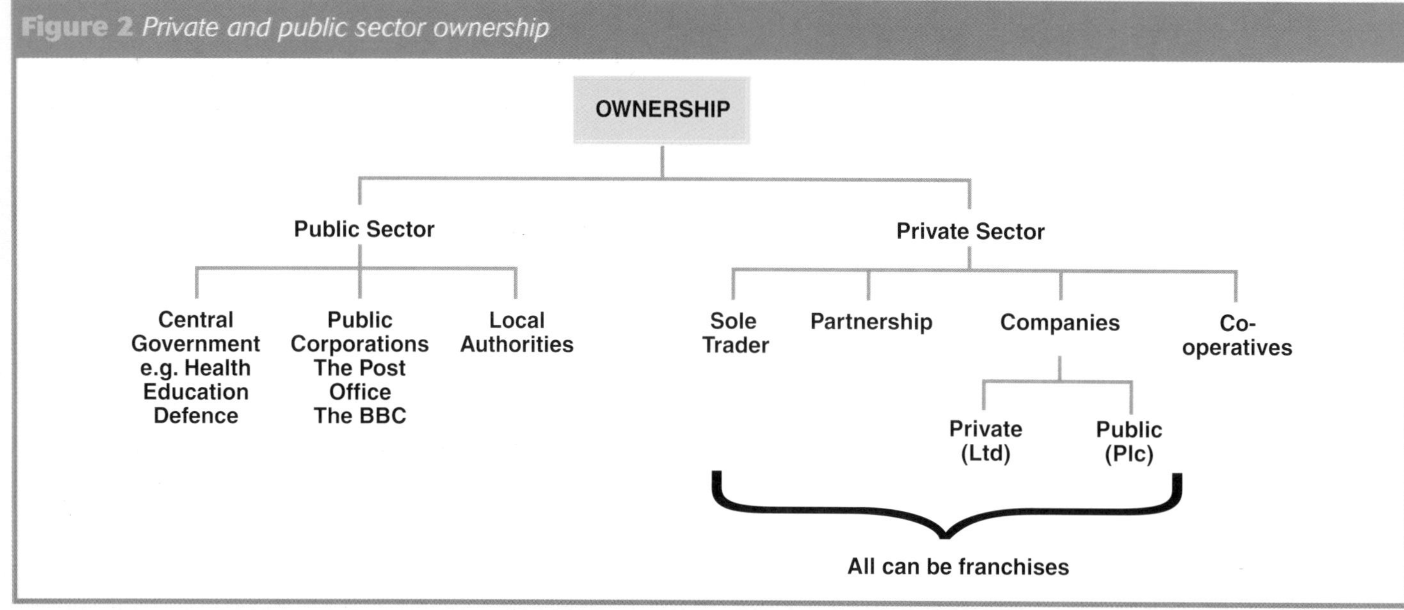

Most schools, for example, are financed by money that has come from central government and has been passed first to the Local education authorities and then to the schools and colleges themselves. How much an individual school will get is decided by government, as is the general way in which it can be spent.

Public private partnerships

In the past many major sections of UK industry were owned by the state including gas, electricity, coal, railways, telephones and steel. Today most of these are in the private sector. However, there are also many examples where the state still owns the business but produces in partnership with private companies. These can be found in education, the health service and in the transport system.

Where these partnerships exist there will be different aims for each of the partners. The public sector part is interested in providing services that benefit the general public and the private sector part will be interested in making profits. If the partnership works, both aims can be achieved through efficient production and the reduction of costs.

For example, in the 1990s London Underground was unable to cover all of its costs and important investments of up to £1.2 billion had not been made. In 1998 the government announced a Public Private Partnership (PPP) through which the track, signalling, bridges, tunnels, lifts, escalators, stations and trains would be transferred to three private companies. Contracts were signed in 2002 with Tube Lines and in 2003 with Metronet. Publicly owned London Underground Ltd has overall responsibility for the underground system and has, as its major aim, 'To perform to the highest possible standard, and to deliver a world-class Tube service for the three million customers who rely on us each and every day'.

The private sector

The aims and objectives of both public and private sector businesses will be determined by certain basic factors. These include how they are owned, how many owners there are, how they are financed and how much money is available, how easy it is to set them up, how they are controlled and what risks are involved in running the business and hence whether limited liability status is needed.

Sole traders These are businesses owned by one person. They tend to be, but do not have to be, small businesses. Typical sole traders are shown in Table 5.

Table 5 *Examples of sole traders*

• Window cleaners	• Writers
• Minicab drivers	• Farmers
• Mobile hairdressers	• Plumbers
• Stallholders	• Artists

The owner has complete control over the business so the aims and objectives tend to reflect his or her personal interests. These may be expansion, survival, or providing the best customer services. But they may also be simply working for oneself without unwanted pressures. As sole traders usually have limited financial backing some aims may be out of reach, such as becoming a multinational business, and some may only be possible in the long run.

Partnerships These are businesses where two or more people, usually to a maximum of twenty people, own the business together. They are not, however, companies. Typical partnerships are shown in Table 6.

Table 6 *Examples of partnerships*

• Doctors	• Dentists
• Architects	• Estate agents
• Solicitors	• Stockbrokers

With more and more risks involved in running business, many firms are now becoming companies in order to benefit from limited liability. Businesses that remain as partnerships tend to provide services, where they are not likely to run up heavy debts. They may not, therefore, need the protection of limited liability although some large accountancy firms may become limited liability partnerships. Aims are likely to include:

- providing customers with high quality services;
- ensuring that partners' funds in the business are safeguarded;
- expanding through efficiency and a good reputation.

Companies Companies can be **private limited companies (Ltd)** or **public limited companies (PLC)** but in both cases they are owned by private individuals, not the state. Both types of companies are set up through Companies House in London (http://www.companies-house.gov.uk/). Companies are treated by the law like individuals, which is why the companies and not the owners will have claims against them for debt. The owners have **limited liability**.

Companies frequently have owners who do not actually run the business, so a major aim is to protect the owners' investments and make them increase in value.

Control in companies is generally decided by how many shares a shareholder has, usually one vote per share. Major decisions, such as taking over other businesses, selling off parts of the business, or changing from a national to an international or even global business are usually put to all the shareholders for them to vote on. They will, therefore, be creating new aims together.

When registering with the Registrar of Companies these businesses have to complete Articles and Memorandum of Association documents. In the Memorandum the company must state, in the object clause, what type of business it will be involved in. This provides a basic aim for the business and it will not be allowed to do anything that is not listed in the object clause.

Private limited companies (Ltd) These are usually owned by one or a small number of shareholders. Shares can only be sold privately so the owners have control over what can happen to the business. Many small businesses which have high levels of raw materials or make products over a long period of time before they sell them may be private companies because of the danger of getting into debt and having to sell personal possessions in order to pay for them. Examples of private limited companies are shown in Table 7.

Many private companies are owned by just two people and frequently one of the owners has most of the shares. It is also possible to have single owners of companies. With these two types of company, the single, or main, owner will set the aims and objectives. With larger private companies the major shareholders will work together to set the objectives.

Table 7 *Examples of private limited companies*

- Builders
- Local grocery stores
- Local garages
- Garden centres
- Merchant banks
- Large farms

Public limited companies (PLC) These are called 'public' because any member of the general public can buy shares in the company. The general public can do this because the company's shares are available to buy on the Stock Exchange. There are some fairly small companies, in terms of capital value and turnover, on the Stock Exchange, but most PLCs are very large companies and generally ones that are very well known, as shown in Table 8.

Table 8 *Examples of public limited companies*

Company	Industry
Barclays	Banking
British Oxygen Company (BOC)	Chemicals
Dixons	General retailing
Tate & Lyle	Food processing
Weatherspoons	Leisure & hotels
Rio Tinto Zinc	Mining
Vodafone	Telecommunications
easyJet	Transport
Severn Trent Water	Utilities

For these very large companies the major shareholders can be other companies. These other companies include insurance businesses, investment businesses, such as unit trusts, and pension companies. The major reason why these companies buy shares on the Stock Exchange is to generate funds so that they can pay out insurance claims, give their customers the increase in value on their investments that they promised and pay pensioners what they were promised as they retire.

To achieve this they need profits because this provides an income for them. They also need capital gains because this means their shares will be worth more when they sell them. Where these **institutional investors** have a major part of the shares, the PLCs have to set, as major aims, high profit levels and an increase in the capital value of the business.

There is a significant number of PLCs which are so powerful that they can ignore their individual shareholders and set their own aims and objectives. Usually these businesses have aims that include:

- being the market leader;
- capturing market share;
- taking over other businesses in the same market or forcing them to close;
- moving from national to international to multinational;.
- cutting costs in order to increase profits;
- establishing a good public image.

Franchises A **franchise** is a contractual agreement between two businesses. It is not a separate form of ownership. All franchises are sole traders, or partnerships or companies. The **franchisor** is a business which has an idea to sell to other businesses. The **franchisee** is a business that wants to use this idea and is willing to pay the franchisor for the right to use their name and idea. Well known franchises are shown in Table 9.

Table 9 *Examples of franchises*

- McDonald's
- Subway
- Prontaprint
- Dyno-rod
- Cash Converters
- Thorntons

When a franchisee takes on a franchise, it agrees to run it in a particular way. This usually dictates what the main aims will be. For example, it could be to:

- promote the image of the franchise;
- maintain the quality expected by the franchisor;

- make sufficient profits to pay what is owed to the franchisor and what is a reasonable minimum for the franchisee;
- expand by taking on additional franchise units.

The franchisor will also have specific aims related to the nature of franchising, such as:

- providing advice and support, including financial support, for the franchisees;
- expanding through establishing new franchised outlets;
- maintaining and promoting the image of the franchise on a national and even international level.

Although Mothercare owns its own stores in the UK it has expanded internationally by selling franchises. The main aim is to 'work with its franchisees to build profitable retail businesses around the world'.

Co-operatives Co-operatives are businesses that are either owned by members who are workers or by members who are consumers. The first co-operative was the Fenwick Weaver Co-operative Society in 1769 although the Rochdale Pioneers Society in 1844 was the inspiration for many others. Now co-operatives can be found across the world. They follow certain basic principles.

- Membership is open and voluntary - all those who qualify for membership must be allowed to join.
- Equal control, by members only - one member one vote.
- Outside investors do not have control and receive only a limited return.
- Any profits distributed among members should be done so fairly.
- There are educational and social objectives, not just commercial ones.
- Co-operatives try to co-operate with each other.

These principles mean that co-operatives have very specific aims and objectives that make them different from other types of business. There are two main types of business co-operatives.

Worker or producer co-operatives These are companies that are owned and controlled by the people who work in them. They will still have profit as a major motive, but the profits will be shared by the workers rather than being given to outside shareholders who do not work in the business. Most of these co-operatives are private companies, but there are also partnerships.

Consumer or retail co-operatives These are businesses owned and controlled by members who are consumers. They were set up so that the people who were shopping would be charged a fair price for their goods. Prices were set at the same level as those of competitors, but any profits made were then given back to the members. Generally this was done on the basis of how much they had spent in the shop.

Figure 3 *Worker and retail co-operatives*

Sheffield Co-operative Development Group

South Yorkshire has a successful worker co-operative sector, employing nearly 200 people and a combined turnover of £4-5 million. Businesses include:

- Boat Builders and Chandlers;
- Computing Services;
- Contract Cleaning and Property Maintenance;
- General and Precision Engineering;
- Nursery Day Care;
- Pre-Cast Concrete;
- Printers and Typesetters;
- Theatre Groups and Actors' Agents;
- Wholefood Suppliers;
- Woodworkers.

The **Co-operative Group** is the largest retail co-operative in the UK, with all of the following retail outlets:

- over 1,700 food stores;
- over 380 branches of Travelcare arranging holidays.
- over 500 branches of Co-operative Funeralcare, the largest funeral business in the country;
- the Co-operative Bank, Co-operative Insurance Society (CIS) and 'Smile', the Internet bank;
- over 300 branches of Co-op Pharmacy.

Source: adapted from www.co-op.co.uk.

Examination practice • Dennis Publishing Ltd

Dennis Publishing Ltd is one of the world's leading independent publishers, publishing magazines with such well known titles as *Auto Express, Bizarre, Maxim, Viz, Computer Buyer* and *Computer Shopper*. The company is privately owned and aims to deliver what customers and advertisers want, as well as demonstrating independence, risk-taking and innovation in its choice of magazines and its editorial approach. The company has consistently identified, launched and developed new titles, creating fresh markets and opportunities for advertisers.

The business started in 1974 in the UK and then joined with an American publisher. Group turnover has increased dramatically in the last few years, mainly in the USA.

Source: adapted from www.dennis.co.uk.

Figure 4 *Turnover, Dennis Publishing*

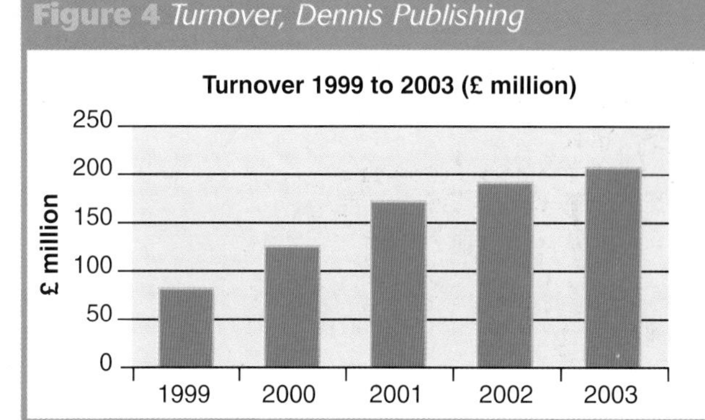

(a) Does Dennis Publishing operate in the primary, secondary or tertiary sector of industry? Justify your answer. (2 marks)

(b) Explain what aim Dennis Publishing was most likely trying to achieve when it formed an agreement with an American Publisher. (2 marks)

(c) Explain why being a private limited company can help Dennis Publishing to remain independent, risk-taking and innovative. (9 marks)

(d) Every year staff vote for the seven most deserving employees who then receive an all expenses paid trip to the island of Mustique. Explain how this is likely to help the business to meet its objective of delivering what customers and advertisers want. (5 marks)

Meeting the assessment criteria

Trident Water Garden Products Ltd of Coventry is the world's largest manufacturer of water garden products, such as pumps, pond liners and filters. The business exports to twenty three countries around the world.

The company's stated aim is to manufacture 'products of the highest quality using only first-class components and state of the art technology'. All products and services are supported by a dedicated after sales and technical support team.

Source: adapted from www.tridentwatergarden.com.

(a) Which major sector of industry does this business operate in? **(1 mark)**

Exemplar responses

- *Secondary.*
- *Manufacturing.*

Mark allocation

1 mark for identifying sector. **(1 mark)**

(b) This business is a private limited company. Considering what it produces, why would it be important for Trident to have limited liability? **(4 marks)**

Exemplar responses

- *Limited liability will limit the debts of the owners (term) – the company is manufacturing (what is produced) – it will make goods before it can sell them (situation) – it could, therefore, run up large debts and not sell anything (why needed).*
- *Making pumps and filters (product) costs a lot of money (situation) and the company is likely to spend money producing the pumps before it gets paid (situation) – it might therefore make a loss and need protection if it is sued (implied term).*

Mark allocation

1 mark for showing understanding of the term (may be implied).
1 mark for identifying what is being produced.
1 mark for why limited liability is needed because of the product/or business situation (maximum 2 marks). **(4 marks)**

(c) The stated aim of the company is to manufacture products of the highest quality using only first-class components and state of the art technology. List **TWO** objectives that would help to make sure that this overall aim was met. For each objective state why it would help to meet the overall aim. **(4 marks)**

Exemplar responses

- *Check all products to ensure there are no faults – faults will be identified and corrected so only highest quality products will be sold.*
- *Identify suppliers who produce high quality components – this should ensure that when used in pumps or filters they do not fail.*
- *Ensure continuous research into new production techniques – will help to improve quality as new technologies are developed.*

Mark allocation

1 mark for objective.
1 mark for how this helps aim.

(1 + 1) x 2
(4 marks)

3 Business functions

Functions and departments

Understanding the difference between the terms **functions** and **departments** is important, although sometimes people use the terms as though they were the same thing and often the major functions are the names given to the departments.

The **functions** of a business are what are carried out in order to make and sell products. Producing, financing and selling are all functions.

Departments are the names given to the different sections of a business, such as Production, Finance and Marketing. These departments are carrying out the function of the business.

Frequently a department is responsible for a particular function in a business, but this is not always the case. Some functions, such as administration, can be found in most departments. In small businesses more than one major function is often carried out by just one department.

There is a number of major functions that need to be carried out by nearly all successful businesses. These are shown in Figure 1.

Figure 1 *Business functions*

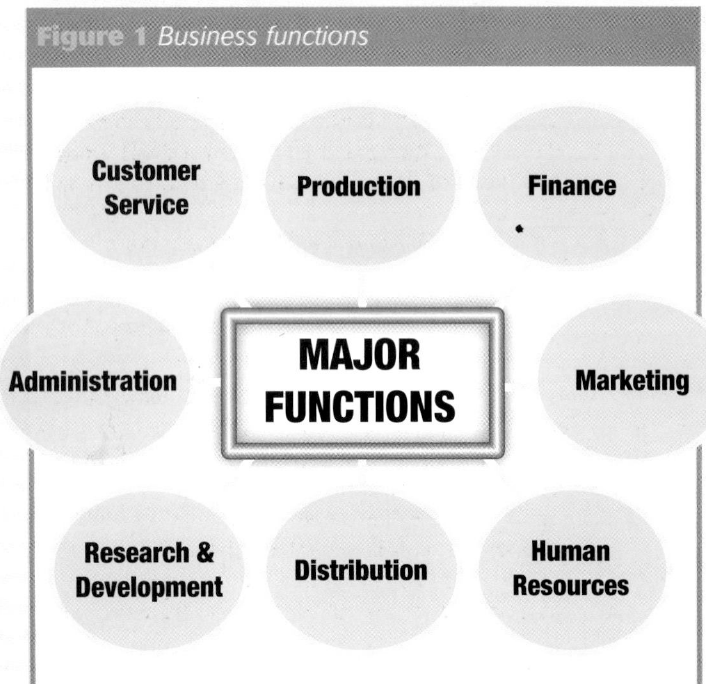

Production

Production is the process of combining factors (inputs) together so that a product is made (output). This product might be a good, such as a car, or a service, such as banking. This is shown in Figure 2.

The actual inputs will depend on what is being produced and this will vary significantly depending on whether goods or services are being produced and what sector of industry the business is in.

Examples are given below of different production processes from inputs to the final product. At each stage value is being added.

Figure 2 *Inputs and outputs*

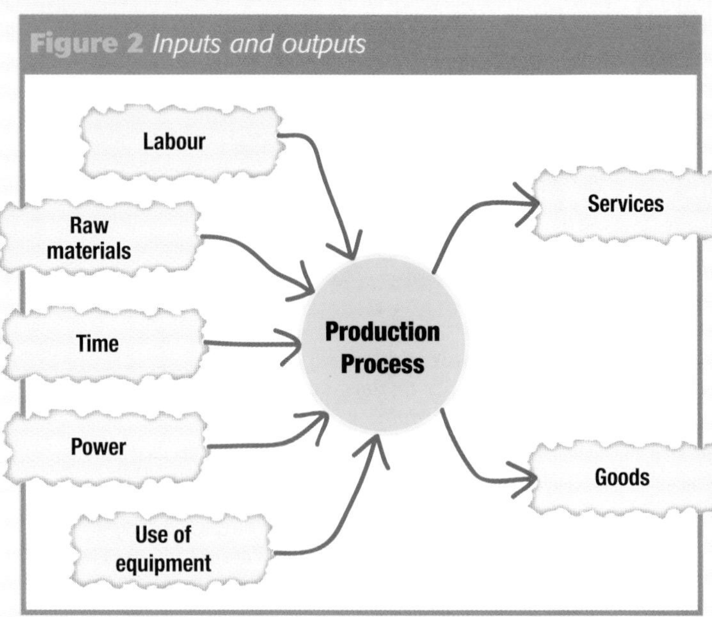

Dairy farmer Inputs (cattle feed, straw, tractors, farm labourers) ⇨ breeding cattle ⇨ milking the cows ⇨ storing milk in churns ready for collection by the dairy.

Pottery manufacturer Inputs (clay, labour, electricity) ⇨ making clay into pottery ⇨ painting and decorating pottery ⇨ firing the pottery in kilns ⇨ packing pottery ready for wholesalers and retailers.

House builder Inputs (wood, bricks, cement, cement mixers) ⇨ digging out and making the foundations ⇨ building the basic structure out of breeze blocks, bricks and wood ⇨ fitting the floors and ceilings ⇨ installing the plumbing and electrics ⇨ plastering, painting and decorating.

Clothes retailer Inputs (labour, stocks of clothes) ⇨ Placing clothes on display ⇨ Serving customers.

Banker Inputs (Labour, stationery, use of telephones, money transfer systems) ⇨ providing services for saving and borrowing money ⇨ allowing customers to pay in or take out money ⇨ transferring money from one account to another ⇨ advising customers on the bank balances ⇨ providing a range of other financial services.

Human Resources/Personnel

Human Resources (Personnel) management is the function of managing the employees of a business and will include:

- recruitment;
- training;
- retention;
- appraisal and monitoring performance;
- dismissal;
- ensuring the laws relating to employment are followed.

It is important that human resources are managed to meet needs. For example, in March 2005 *The Herald*, reported that

Sainsbury's improvement coincided with the recruitment of 3,000 extra staff in order to address customer complaints about poor product availability.

Marketing

It is the employees who produce the goods or services and they will feature in all of the functions. However, it is not just enough to produce the products. They must also be marketed.

Marketing is a very diverse function because it deals with all aspects of identifying who a product should be targeted at through market research, to how to promote and sell the product that has been produced. It also applies to all organisations, e.g. businesses and government.

In 2004, for example, a number of businesses ran successful marketing campaigns aimed at students. They included Endsleigh, NatWest, STA Travel, Red Bull, Malibu, *The Guardian*, Barclaycard and Orange.

Marketing will involve all the elements in Figure 3. Marketing is covered in detail in Unit 3 of this textbook which explains why marketing is so important for businesses.

Finance

In the past the finance function tended to relate to providing monies for running the business and recording all transactions. Today the planning side of the finance function has become far more important. Finance can be divided into the following specific functions.

Management accounting This deals with company budgets and strategic planning, such as:

- preparing business plans;
- monitoring performance against set targets;
- suggesting ways in which the financial performance of the business can be improved;
- giving advice on how decisions in other departments, e.g. production or marketing, will affect the business financially.

Financial accounting This deals with the keeping of the business's financial records, such as:

- keeping records of all financial transactions in the business;
- monitoring cash flow;
- ensuring that the accounts are managed correctly;
- checking that monies owed to and by the business are paid on time;
- checking customers' credit positions if customers are being offered credit.

Internal auditing This involves checking the finances of each department and how the departments are managing their finances.

Payments This includes:

- wages and salaries;
- calculation and payments of taxes;
- payments to suppliers.

Raising finance This includes:

- negotiating loans and overdrafts with the bank;
- dealing with government for grants and subsidies;
- establishing leasing agreements with other businesses;
- managing the profits of the business for re-investment;
- dealing with share issues.

Details of how many of these functions operate within a business are covered in unit 2.

Figure 3 *Elements of marketing*

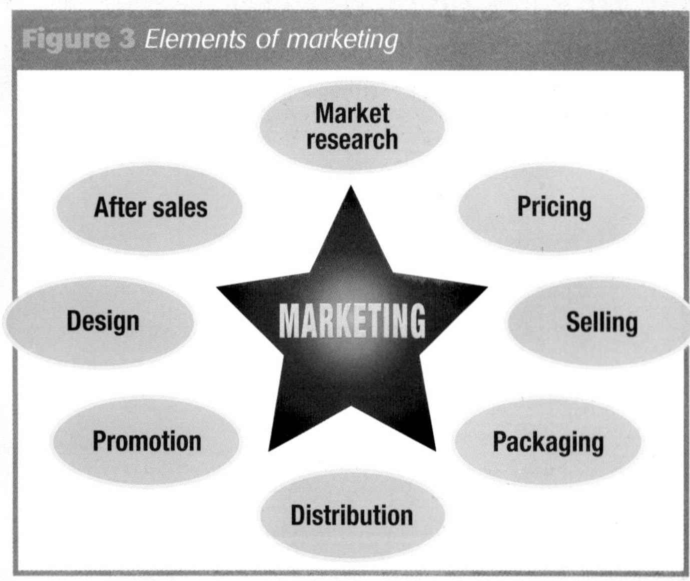

Research and Development

For many businesses the improvement of existing products or the creation of new products is vital for the expansion and even survival of the business. This is especially true of highly competitive markets where these innovations give a business a major competitive advantage.

The role of research and development is to look at actual products. The role of researching the market to find what customers want and where there may be new markets to sell into is a function of marketing. They are closely linked and marketing may be able to tell research and development what products will be worth developing.

For goods the research and development is likely to be technical, such as:

- making computers faster;
- manufacturing safer cars;
- building environmentally friendly houses;
- finding ways of growing vegetables that stay fresh longer;
- creating new media for recording music on.

For services the research and development is likely to be about how the service is delivered, such as:

- providing banking by phone or the Internet;
- offering air passengers no frills very cheap travel;
- supporting buyers of computers with a 24 hour helpline;
- providing gas, electricity and telephone services from a single supplier;
- offering customers an 'eat-all-you-can' option in a restaurant.

Some types of production, especially in the realm of new drugs, require very heavy investment in research and development as shown in Figure 4.

Administration

Administration is the management of services that help to support the smooth running of departments.

All departments will need administration and frequently this function will be carried out by the individual departments. In a larger business there is often a separate Administration Department. Either way, the following functions will be carried out somewhere in the business.

Figure 4 *Research and development spending (£ million)*

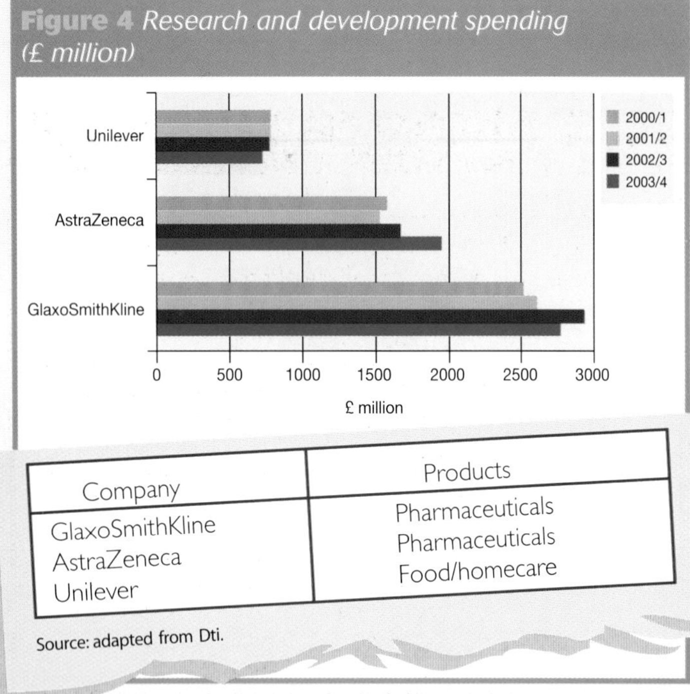

Company	Products
GlaxoSmithKline	Pharmaceuticals
AstraZeneca	Pharmaceuticals
Unilever	Food/homecare

Source: adapted from Dti.

- Reception - greeting people visiting the business, checking who they are and who they will be visiting, taking outside telephone calls and connecting people to the right departments.
- Receiving and distributing mail from outside.
- Security of the building, property and staff.
- Cleaning, maintenance and catering or arranging for outside contractors to carry out these jobs.
- Clerical work - making records and managing records, filing and photocopying.
- Organising meetings and keeping minutes.
- Internal communications, through post, intercoms, e-mails and memos.
- Monitoring staff - clocking staff in and checking pay against attendance.

Distribution and Logistics

For many businesses the efficient distribution of their products to their customers is so vital that it becomes a major aim and function. This function is now often referred to as 'logistics' and can be summarised as 'having the right thing, at the right place, at the right time'.

The Distribution Department will normally carry out all the following functions.

- Preparing packing lists of the goods to be moved.
- Packing the products into boxes, crates and then into lorries or vans.
- Working out delivery schedules, showing where and when goods are to be distributed.
- Delivering the goods if the business has its own vehicles or arranging for another firm to deliver them.
- Receiving any returned goods and dealing with replacements.

For example, it was reported in 2005 that New Look, the high street fashion retailer, would have its new, automated national distribution centre at Newcastle-Under-Lyme completed in the autumn. The centre would provide warehousing and transport and distribution to other 'outbases' located throughout the UK. The centre would respond to orders with automatic sorting and distribution to packing areas.

Customer services

All businesses need to ensure that their customers are being provided with good service. In many businesses this is considered so important that a separate Customer Services Department is set up. This is particularly important when the business is dealing with the general public.

Customer service is both internal and external.

Internal customer service This is about providing supportive services for the people who work in or own the business. Internal customers include:

- employees;
- managers;
- different departments;
- providers of internal services, such as catering;
- owners.

Each of these internal customers will require support which in many cases will come from existing departments as with appraisal and training for staff by the Human Resources Department, the setting up and running of meetings by Administration and the payment of profits to shareholders by the Finance Department.

External customer service This is about providing good service to people or organisations which are outside of the business. External customers include:

- individuals;
- families;
- other business customers;
- suppliers;
- the state and society.

The kinds of customer service that these external customers may expect include:

- a wide range of value for money products;
- good after sales care;
- prompt payments if they are suppliers;
- correct payments of taxes;
- production which does not harm the environment.

Other functions

In many businesses the functions described above are divided up and placed into their own departments. There will also be distinct and different functions that are needed because of the type of product being produced and the type of business involved.

For example, many businesses rely very heavily on **purchasing** large quantities of raw materials that are vital for their businesses and so they have created separate Purchasing Departments. Such businesses include:

- supermarkets;
- major chain stores;
- hospitals;
- the armed services.

Information and communication technology is now so common and important in business that setting up and running systems for the benefit of the business have become major functions in their own right. Many businesses also now have websites that need to be created and maintained.

How the business functions work together

For businesses to operate successfully all of the functions mentioned above need to work together and support each other. Typical links can be shown by tracing through how particular products are produced, as in Figure 5.

Figure 5 *Developing a new breakfast cereal*

- Market Research identified a gap in the market.
- R & D develops and trials the new product.
- Finance decides budgets for new product and provides funds.
- Marketing decides on a suitable price and where to sell the product.
- Sales representatives approach retailers with samples of the product.
- Human Resources arranges for training of staff to produce the new cereal.
- Production starts producing the new cereal.
- Marketing designs the packaging to appeal to customers.
- Distribution provides lorries for transporting products to retailers.
- Finance sends out invoices to retailers for payment.
- Marketing provides TV advertising to coincide with the launch.
- Customer Service contacts retailers to ensure they are happy with the product and the service.
- Finance and Marketing monitor the success of sales.

Table 1 shows other examples of when each function needs to work with another function. Details of the support from Administration have been given before.

Table 1 *Functions working together*

Function	Situation
Marketing & Production	Marketing will identify what Production needs to produce. Production will tell Marketing when the product will be ready for promotion campaigns.
Marketing & Finance	Marketing will inform Finance of likely level of sales. Finance will approve Marketing's promotional budget.
Finance & Production	Finance will pay for the raw materials and equipment. Production will monitor production costs and keep Finance informed.
Human Resources & Production	HR recruits employees for producing the goods or services. Production provides details of staff absences for HR.
Marketing & Human Resources	Marketing provides details on the likely size of new markets that will need staffing. HR provides training for new sales representatives.
Human Resources & Finance	HR provides Finance with details of all employees. Finance pays all employees.
R & D & Production	R & D provides Production with details of new products. Production runs trials on the new products.
Sales & Production & Distribution	Sales informs Production and Distribution when customers need products. Production informs Distribution when products are ready. Distribution delivers goods to customers.
Customer Services & other departments	Customer Services provides Marketing with customer feedback on in-store promotions, Production with details of complaints about products and HR with requests for training in handling difficult customers.
ICT & other departments	ICT provides web pages for Marketing, EDI facilities between branches so sales figures go direct to Finance, Staff databases for HR, CAD and CAM support and training for R & D and Production, and recording facilities so that Administration can check security.

Examination practice • Anthony Alan Foods Ltd

Anthony Alan Foods Ltd is the UK's leading supplier of low fat cakes and pastries, sold under the Weight Watchers brand. In 2005 it launched a brand new range of Weight Watchers savoury pastries, including Sausage Roll, Pork & Apple Roll, Cheese & Onion Slice and Chicken & Stuffing Slice. The new products were tested for satisfaction using consumer panels and then supported at their launch with extensive advertising. This successful launch was achieved with the full involvement of the company's highly trained and motivated staff at its Barnsley premises.

Source: adapted from www.aafoods.eu.com.

(a) From the data, describe how the marketing function would have been involved in the launch of the new Weight Watchers savoury range. (4 marks)

(b) Explain what contribution each of the following functions is likely to have made to the new savoury range of products.

(i) Research and development. (3 marks)

(ii) Finance. (3 marks)

(iii) Production. (3 marks)

(c) Explain how the fact that the staff at Anthony Alan Foods are highly trained and motivated will help the business to introduce this new range. (6 marks)

Meeting the assessment criteria

Ford's Halewood plant on Merseyside was totally modernised in the late 1990s, ready for production to switch from producing high-volume Escorts to the prestige Jaguars. More than £300 million was invested in the plant. Part of this modernisation was to prepare for the production and well publicised launch of the new V6 X-Type Jaguar. Workers also agreed to new working practices to help ensure that the plant was competitive.

In 2004 Jaguar took on 600 extra workers to help produce the X-Type. Of these 600 workers, some 200 were to be laid off in 2005, as they were only temporary workers. Half of these were offered re-deployment to the West Bromwich plant.

Source: adapted from various sources.

(a) Identify **THREE** major functions referred to in the data and say how each has helped to make the new Halewood plant a success. **(6 marks)**

Exemplar responses

- *Production – changing production from Escorts to Jaguars.*
- *Finance – providing £300 million for the modernisation.*
- *Marketing – publicising the launch of the X-Type Jaguar.*
- *Human Resources – recruiting 600 extra workers in 2004/negotiating new working practices with staff.*

Mark allocation

1 mark for each function.
1 mark for how that has helped the Halewood plant/production of Jaguar. **(1 + 1) x 3**
(6 marks)

(b) As part of the modernisation a rail terminal has been built nearby, which allows 90% of cars destined for export markets to leave the plant by rail rather than road. Explain how this will affect the Distribution Department. **(4 marks)**

Exemplar responses

- *Distribution will have to decide how cars get to customer – now 90% will go by train – less lorries will be needed – drivers may need to be laid off.*
- *Distribution needs to arrange transport – main method will now be by train – will need to buy/rent rail transporters – also need to keep some road transporters for the 10%.*
- *As most of the transport is now by rail – need to ensure that rail schedules are known – have cars ready to meet these schedules (understanding has been implied).*

Mark allocation

1 mark for showing understanding of the distribution function (may be implied).
1 mark for recognising changed situation.
1 mark for how Distribution will be affected (maximum 2 marks).
(4 marks)

(c) Explain how the fact that Jaguar cars are being exported will affect:

(i) the Finance Department?
(ii) the Marketing Department? **(4 marks)**

Exemplar responses

Finance

- *Dealing with different currencies – foreign buyers may wish to pay in their own currency.*
- *Should check what government support is available – exports receive specific help from the government/Export Credit Guarantees may be available.*

Marketing

- *Will need to work out appropriate prices – exports need to be priced in the other country's currency/prices need to be set in relation to the foreign country's income.*
- *Advert will need to be changed – export countries may have other languages/cultures/advertising laws.*

Mark allocation

1 mark for how affected.
1 mark for why that comes from exporting. **(1 + 1) x 2**
(4 marks)

4 Organisational structures & job roles

Organisational structures

This section examines the way in which businesses are structured and the major job roles in those structures. Section 3 explained that businesses have various functions that need to be carried out. These often become the responsibility of specific departments, with the different parts of the main function being divided up within that department. Specific roles and responsibilities are given to different sections and people within each department. As the business makes these divisions into departments, it is creating a structure through which the functions of the business operate.

These structures can be divided in various ways, as in Figure 1, although the main one is often division by function. The usual way of showing how the structure of a business is divided is through an **organisation chart**. This shows the structure in the form of a diagram.

Figure 1 *Organisational structures*

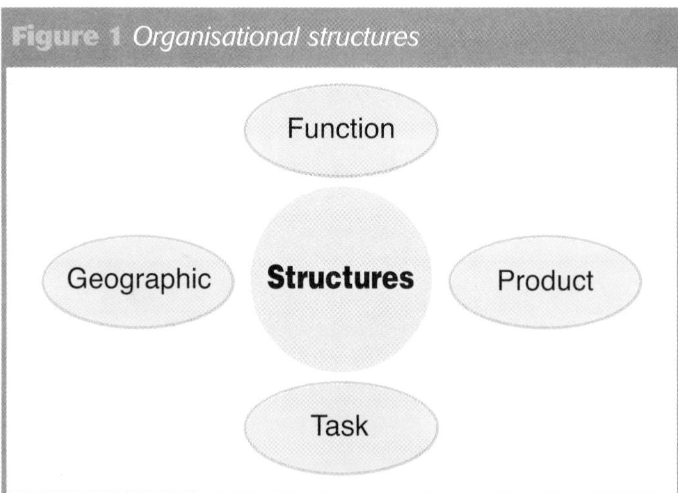

Figure 2 *Organisational structure of an energy company*

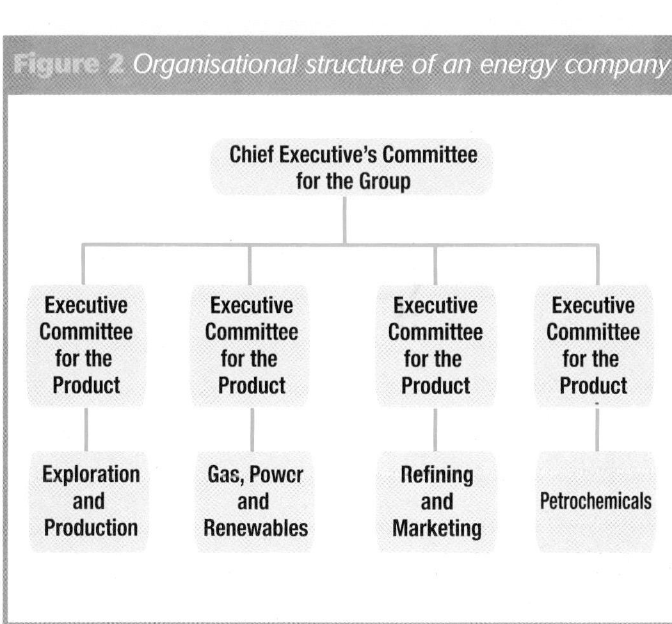

Division by product

Where businesses produce a range of very different products they are sometimes divided in terms of these products. The basic breakdown for an energy company by product is shown in Figure 2. Division by product allows the business as a whole to pass over the running of the individual sections to managers who are experts in those types of production.

Geographical division

Many businesses have production units in different parts of the country and even in different parts of the world. Often these businesses will divide their operations on a geographical basis. This allows the managers in the different regions to run the production in the areas where they are, rather than having it run by managers who are a long way away.

For example, Arts & Business (A&B) is a not-for-profit business set up to promote links between business and the arts. It runs, events, seminars and training throughout its 18 offices which are divided by region across the UK. Its structure is shown in Figure 3.

Figure 3 *Regional structure for Arts & Business*

Division by function

Even where there is a basic division by product or geographical area, it is still normal for the business's activities to be further divided by function. This also involves levels of authority, showing who is in charge of whom and who is responsible to whom.

Three basic structures are common in business – flat, tall or hierarchical and matrix.

Flat structures These are ones where there are very few levels in the way the business is structured, usually only two, but never more than three. A flat structure shows that the manager, in small businesses often the owner, is directly linked to the staff. Because of this there are certain characteristics that flat structures are likely to have.

- The business is likely to be fairly small, otherwise it would be difficult for the manager to deal with everyone at the lower level.
- Communications are likely to be good because the manager is in direct contact with the staff.
- The direct contact with management is likely to make control more friendly and less formal.
- The cost of management is likely to be fairly low because there is only one level of management.
- The burden of management falls on only one person.

Tall structures These tend to have a minimum of three levels and frequently have more. A tall structure separates the senior managers from the staff at the bottom of the structure and this also leads to certain characteristics.

- The business is likely to be fairly large, otherwise there is no point in creating many layers of management.
- Communications between one level and the next may be good because each person is likely to be dealing with only a few people below them. Communication from the top of the structure to the bottom can, however, be poor because of the number of stages involved.
- Control and decision making is likely to be very formal with each person having clearly set out responsibilities and authority. This can lead to a less friendly working environment.
- The cost of management as a whole may be high because there are so many levels.
- Each person in the organisation will have a distinct role and this will allow people to specialise in what they are best at.
- There is usually a clear route for promotion and this may act as an incentive to work hard.

Figure 4 *Flat and tall organisational structures*

Flat

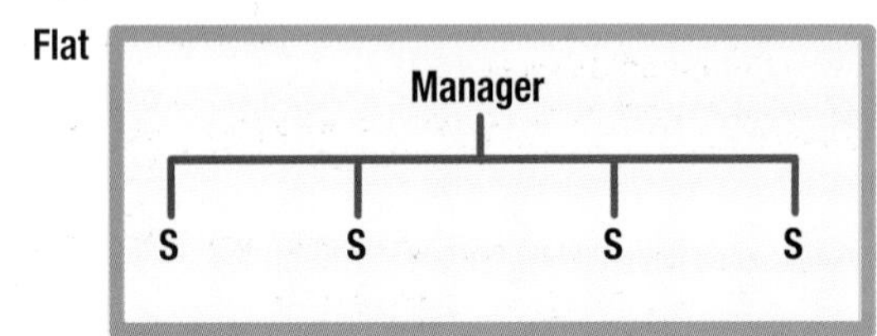

Tall

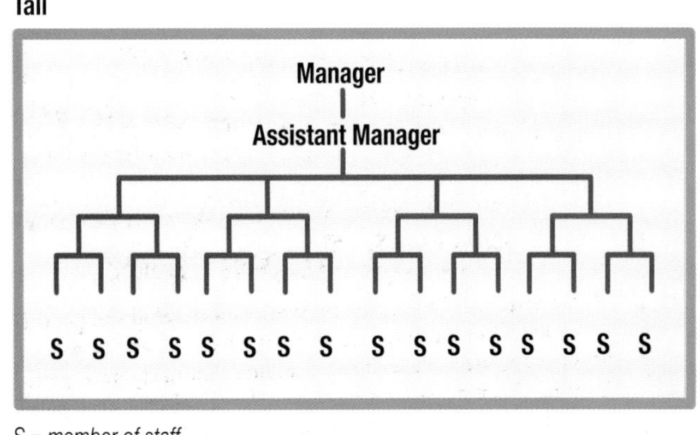

S = member of staff

These tall structures are usually **hierarchical** because they also place staff in different grades, with the major decisions being made at the top and lesser decisions being made at lower levels.

The span of control This refers to how many people someone in the structure is directly responsible for. It is estimated that a span of control of more than six people starts to become inefficient in terms of managing what they are doing. Typical narrow and wide structures would be as shown in Figure 6.

Figure 5 *Hierarchy in an organisational structure*

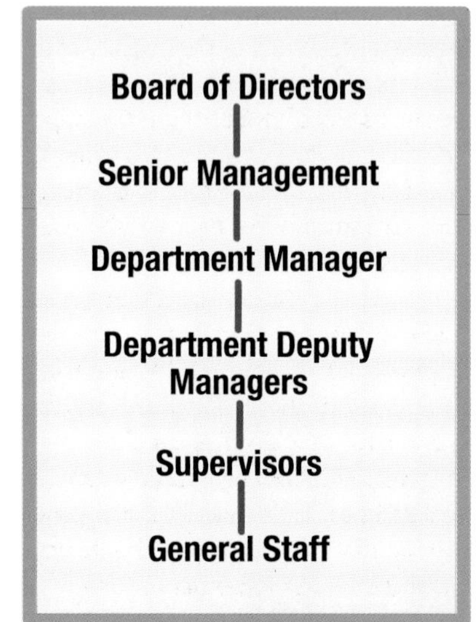

Figure 6 *Span of control*

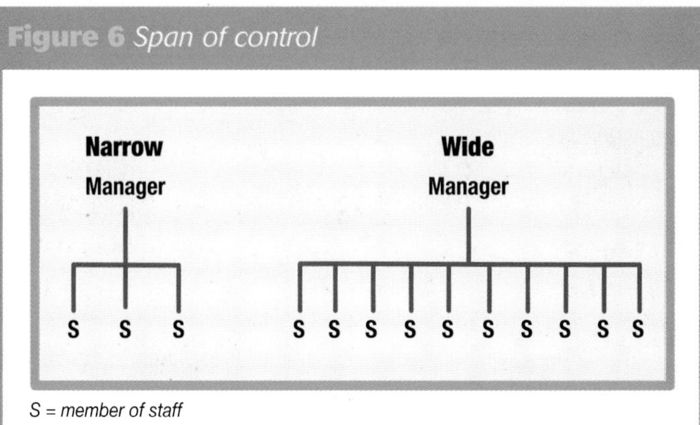

S = member of staff

Figure 7 *Matrix structures*

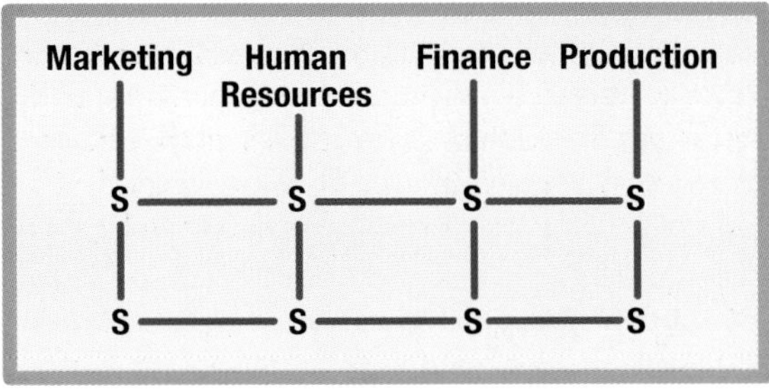

S = member of staff

Matrix structures A matrix structure is one that allows the business to operate across different levels of authority and across different functions. When decisions need to be made, a group of people work together to decide what is best for the business. It is called a matrix structure because everyone in the structure is linked to everyone else in the structure. This is shown for four main departments and two levels of staff in Figure 7.

Often these groups are formed to look after one particular product, project or section of the business. Such groups are known as **project groups** or **task groups** as in Figure 8. Where the aim of the group is to look at the quality of the product and try to find ways of improving it, they are known as a **quality circle**.

Matrix structures tend to have the following characteristics.

- Although the main control still rests with senior management many important decisions are made lower down the structure.
- Work is often carried out in teams with members jointly making decisions.
- Decisions may take longer to be reached.
- Because all staff are involved in the making of important decisions the staff may be more motivated and may work harder for the business.
- Communication takes place directly between all levels in the business.

Major job roles

This section will look at only the major job roles, some of which have been shown in the organisation charts above. It will not deal with specific job roles, which vary considerably from business to

Figure 8 *Task groups*

TASK

Finance Manager
Production Manager
Human Resources Manager
Production Staff
Finance Staff
R&D Staff
Marketing Staff
Marketing Manager
R&D Manager

Figure 9 *Advertisements for jobs roles*

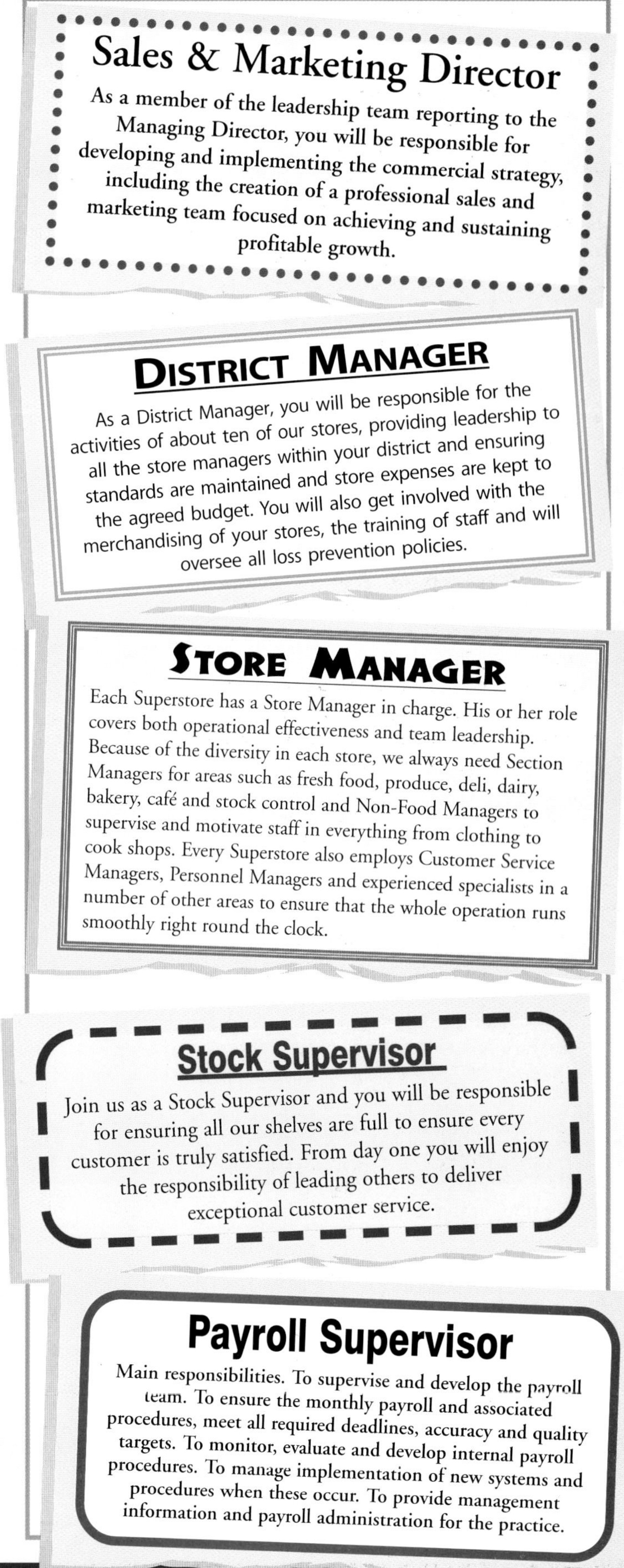

Sales & Marketing Director

As a member of the leadership team reporting to the Managing Director, you will be responsible for developing and implementing the commercial strategy, including the creation of a professional sales and marketing team focused on achieving and sustaining profitable growth.

District Manager

As a District Manager, you will be responsible for the activities of about ten of our stores, providing leadership to all the store managers within your district and ensuring standards are maintained and store expenses are kept to the agreed budget. You will also get involved with the merchandising of your stores, the training of staff and will oversee all loss prevention policies.

Store Manager

Each Superstore has a Store Manager in charge. His or her role covers both operational effectiveness and team leadership. Because of the diversity in each store, we always need Section Managers for areas such as fresh food, produce, deli, dairy, bakery, café and stock control and Non-Food Managers to supervise and motivate staff in everything from clothing to cook shops. Every Superstore also employs Customer Service Managers, Personnel Managers and experienced specialists in a number of other areas to ensure that the whole operation runs smoothly right round the clock.

Stock Supervisor

Join us as a Stock Supervisor and you will be responsible for ensuring all our shelves are full to ensure every customer is truly satisfied. From day one you will enjoy the responsibility of leading others to deliver exceptional customer service.

Payroll Supervisor

Main responsibilities. To supervise and develop the payroll team. To ensure the monthly payroll and associated procedures, meet all required deadlines, accuracy and quality targets. To monitor, evaluate and develop internal payroll procedures. To manage implementation of new systems and procedures when these occur. To provide management information and payroll administration for the practice.

business and nor will it look at the major job roles in terms of specific functions, i.e. it will look at the role of the manager rather than the role of, say, a Marketing Manager.

The following roles will be considered, with examples - directors, managers, supervisors, professional staff, operatives and general staff. Examples of advertisements for these job roles are shown in Figure 9.

Directors Directors are appointed by the shareholders of a business. Their primary function is to ensure that the business is being run for the benefit of shareholders - the owners. Where there are more than just one or two directors they will meet and make decisions about the business as the Board of Directors. Major decisions in the business, ones which have a major impact on the shareholders, will be decided by the Board, or put to the shareholders by the Board for them to vote on.

Some directors, called Executive Directors, will be involved in running the business, although the day-to-day running of a business is the responsibility of the managers. Others take very little part in running the business and are non-executive directors. Some of these are appointed simply so that the business can say that it has someone famous as part of the business.

Managers Managers are the people who run businesses and make most of the important decisions. Where directors make decisions about how the business should be run and instruct other people what to do, they are also acting as managers.

It can sometimes be difficult to identify exactly what management involves because it can, and does, operate at many different levels within a business. A major national business may well have all of the following managerial roles.

- Managing Director – who manages all of the other directors.
- Executive Director – who will manage one aspect of the business on behalf of the shareholders.
- District or Regional Manager – who will be responsible for all branches in a certain area.
- Branch or Store Manager – who will be responsible for the operation of a specific branch.
- Departmental Manager – in charge of a specific function or major department such as marketing or finanace.
- Department Manager – in charge of a section of the business within the branch, e.g. food, bakery, restaurant, clothes.

Managers will be in charge of staff and responsible for what they do. They will also generally be in charge of financial budgets and decide how these will be allocated and used. It will be managers who decide many of the policies and strategies of the business.

Supervisors Supervisors also have a management role, but at a lower level than the senior managers. They will be in charge of a particular department or unit and the staff that work in there. In some businesses these junior roles are described as supervisors and in others they are still referred to as managers.

Professional staff Professional staff are those staff who have been trained or have qualifications in a particular profession. In the past this applied to jobs in which academic skills were expected or ones which require a long period of apprenticeship. Examples of jobs are shown in Table 1. Today many more jobs require specific qualifications, skills or training, Examples of such jobs are also shown in Table 1.

Professional staff tend to be respected because of their qualifications and skills and they tend to be fairly well paid. Most professions also have a hierarchy through which staff rise because they have gaining additional qualifications, have greater experience, and sometimes simply by staying with the business long enough.

Operatives Operatives are skilled workers, especially in industry. Some of the skills require basic qualifications, others require experience, but many will be taught on-the-job. Examples include:

- Installation Operative – tasks could include unpacking and assembling the equipment in Hospitals, Health Centres, Clinics, Care Centres, Schools and Colleges and also at customers' homes.
- IT Helpdesk Operative – tasks could include taking and logging support calls, performing appropriate diagnostics on operating systems and referring complex issues where necessary.
- Production Operative (textiles) – tasks could include producing high quality cloth on rapier looms and replacing the cones for weft as required.
- Warehouse Operative – tasks could include dealing with goods in/out, picking, packing, and despatch as well as having a licence to drive both counter balance and reach forklifts.

General staff In many businesses there are also staff who have no specific skills or qualifications when they enter the business. With training they gain skills and are able to perform their duties effectively and gain promotion to more senior jobs, such as operatives, supervisors and managers.

Examples of general staff positions in retaling and in other industries are shown in Table 2.

Table 1 *Traditional and modern professionals*

Traditional professionals	
• Doctors	• Dentists
• Nurses	• Barristers
• Architects	• Teachers
• Solicitors	• Stockbrokers
• Accountants	• Printers
• Army Officers	• Pilots
Modern professionals	
• Broadcasters	• Chefs
• Landscape gardeners	• Plumbers
• Footballers or golfers	• Prison warders

Table 2 *General staff*

Retailing	
• Shelf stackers	• Waiters
• Checkout staff	• Cleaners
• Shop floor staff	• Receptionists
• Bar staff	• Paper delivery staff
Other industries	
• Farm labourers	• Road sweepers
• General building labourers	• Refuse collectors
• Leaflet deliverers	• Market research interviewers

Examination practice • Chesterham Golf Club

Table 3 shows a list of the staff working at Chesterham Golf Club.

Table 3 *Job roles at Chesterham Golf Club*

Housekeeper	Front House Supervisor	Housekeeper	Gardener
Barperson	Housekeeper	Operations Manager	Receptionist
Chef	PGA Golf Professional	Waiter	Head Chef
Trainee Manager	Front House Supervisor	Gardener	Business Director
Managing Director	Admin. Manager	Head Housekeeper	Function Supervisor
Waiter	Farm and Golf Director	Chef	Greenkeeper
Head Greenkeeper	Kitchen Domestic	Head Receptionist	Chef
Restaurant Manager	Chef	Marketing Director	

Source: adapted from author research.

(a) Choosing an appropriate structure, draw an organisation chart to include all of the listed staff. (8 marks)

(b) From Table 3 identify TWO different examples of each of the following job roles.
(i) Professional staff.
(ii) General staff. (4 marks)

(c) From Table 3 select ONE example of each of the following job roles.
- **Directors.**
- **Managers.**
- **Supervisors.**
- **Explain what each job role selected is likely to involve. (6 marks)**

(ii) Explain how the roles will differ because they are referred to as directors, managers, or supervisors. (4 marks)

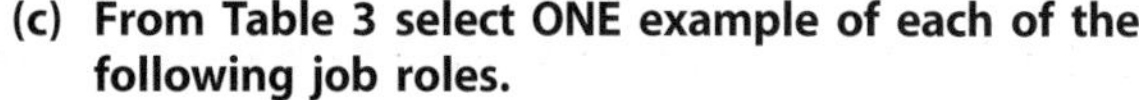

Meeting the assessment criteria

The organisation chart in Figure 10 is a fairly typical chart for a secondary school. Figure 10 shows part of the structure.

(a) (i) Explain why this organisation would be described as hierarchical. **(2 marks)**

Exemplar responses

- *Hierarchical structures have many levels – chart shows up to 8 levels.*
- *Hierarchy suggests levels of authority/status – here there are heads and deputies, etc.*

Mark allocation

1 mark for showing meaning of term.
1 mark for explanation related to the chart. **(2 marks)**

(ii) Using appropriate examples, explain how being hierarchical would affect the way in which the school was run. **(5 marks)**

Exemplar responses

- *What schools must teach is dictated by government (authority) shown by being at top of the structure (hierarchy) – examples include Maths, English and ICT (example).*
- *Head of Department in charge of a specific subject area (authority) – Departments have deputies and subject teachers (hierarchy) – Head of Department will decide who teaches which classes (example).*

Mark allocation

1 mark for recognising the authority element (may be implied).
1 mark for example (maximum 2 marks).
1 mark for how that shows the hierarchy (maximum 2 marks).
(1 + 2 + 2) 5 marks)

(b) Using appropriate examples, explain when staff on the curriculum side of the organisation would need to communicate with staff on the pastoral side. **(3 marks)**

Exemplar responses

- *When writing reports - subject staff will write reports - form tutors will collate them/discuss overall reports with students.*
- *When there has been a disciplinary incident in class - subject teacher will report to form tutor/head of year - form tutor/head of year will contact parents.*

Mark allocation

1 mark for situation.
1 mark for why each side would need to be involved (2 marks).
(3 marks)

(c) Which job role listed on the chart does not require professional staff? Justify your answer. **(2 marks)**

Exemplar responses

- *School Governor – No specific qualification is required/they are not staff in the school.*

Mark allocation

1 mark for role.
1 mark for justification. **(2 marks)**

(d) Give TWO examples of administrative tasks that would be carried out by the school office and explain how each of these could help teachers. **(4 marks)**

Exemplar responses

- *Photocopying – providing class copies of exercises.*
- *Manning telephones – teachers able to ring in and arrange cover if they are late.*
- *Collecting and banking money for trips – allows teachers to concentrate on planning the trips.*

Mark allocation

1 mark for each task.
1 mark for how that helps teachers. **(1 + 1) x 2**
(4 marks)

Figure 10 *Organisation chart of a secondary school*

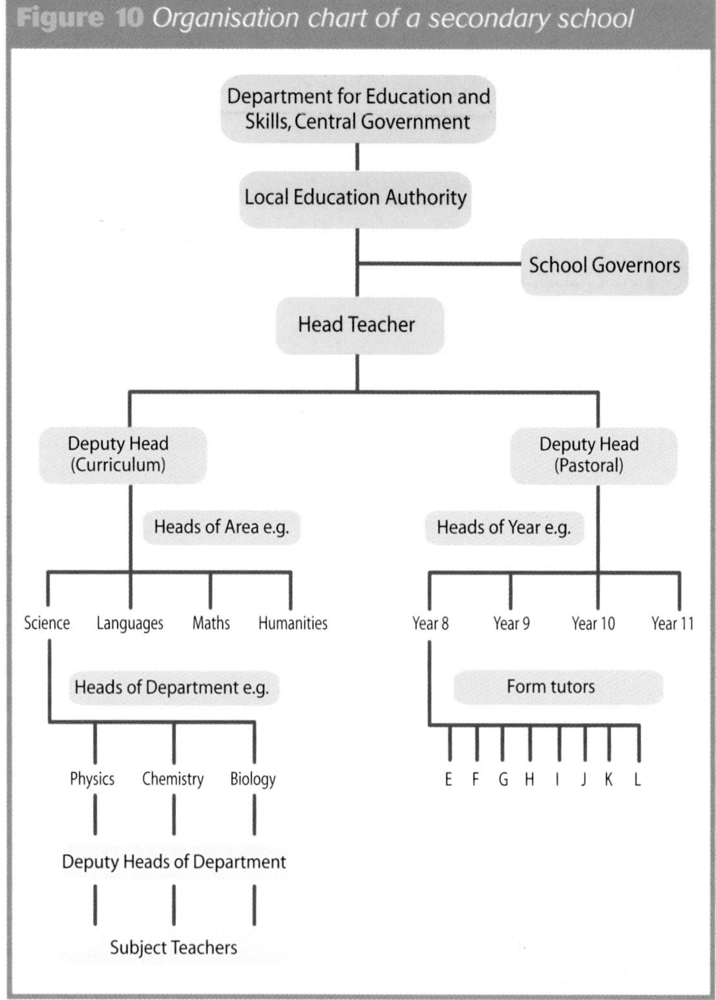

5 Reasons for recruitment

Who are employees?

All businesses require some form of labour so that they can operate. With very small businesses there may be only one person working, the owner. In the UK there are many people who do work for themselves and alone. They are **self-employed**.

This section deals with people who are employed by the business itself. As an **employee** a person is employed as a specific named person by the business, with a contract of employment. The business will decide what the person does and how much they will be paid. In this section the terms employee and staff will be used interchangeably.

In many businesses people may be paid to do specific jobs for the business, but they are not actually employees in terms of the law. They will have a contract to carry out a specific job but they will not have a 'contract of employment'. For example, many builders will have contracts with self-employed plumbers, carpenters and electricians to carry out specific parts of the building of a house. These people are sometimes referred to as workers and this category would also include agency workers, contractors, freelancers and volunteers.

Reasons for recruiting

There are many reasons why staff need to be recruited, but the basic reason is that there is a vacancy to be filled. Recruitment can be **internal**, i.e. from staff already in the business, or **external**, from people outside the business. Which of these is most appropriate will depend on why the vacancy has arisen and factors such as cost, time, and the importance of having experience of how the business operates.

The reasons why there may be a vacancy include the following.

- The business is starting up and needs staff.
- The business is expanding and needs more staff.
- Staff have been promoted internally and new staff are needed to take their place.
- Existing staff have left and need to be replaced.
- The job roles in the business have changed and staff with different skills are needed.
- Other reasons, for example getting a better ethnic balance in the workforce.

Starting up

New businesses will be recruiting staff for the first time. It will, therefore, be very important that they get the right kind of staff and ones that will help to rapidly establish the business in the market place. It may also be the case that the owners or managers recruiting employees have not done this before and, therefore, need to consider very carefully how to recruit effectively. For example:

- what job roles need to be filled?
- what structure will the business take? For example will managers or supervisors be needed?
- which jobs need to filled immediately and what recruitment will be needed in the future?
- where and when to place advertisements?
- how to select the right people for interview?
- how much training they will need to provide?

For example in 2004 a Barclays Bank survey stated that 453,000 new businesses were started in the UK of which 40,000 were in the construction industry. Other sectors of industry that had the most number of new businesses were leisure, transport and communications. The number of new catering businesses was around 20,000. Researchers concluded that this was because TV chefs have made dining out more trendy, with around a fifth of consumers now eating out more than once a week and experimenting with different dishes.

Expanding businesses

As businesses expand they will generally need additional staff. The main difference between these businesses recruiting staff and businesses setting up is that the management should know the type of staff they will need and they will already be experienced in the recruiting process.

There will, however, still be important decisions to be made because this is expansion and more staff in total are being employed. For example:

- should internal staff be promoted into the new jobs or would experienced staff from other businesses be more suitable?
- will the new staff be dynamic and ready to exploit new markets?

Recruitment decisions will also depend on how the expansion is taking place, as shown in Table 1. For example *The Belfast Telegraph* reported in April 2005 that the city could gain up to 750 new jobs as a leading UK operator opened a new call centre in West Belfast. LBM, one of the UK's largest privately owned direct marketing companies, was setting up a new contact centre that

Table 1 *Recruitment decisions*

Method of expansion	Examples of decisions
Internal growth on site	1. Are new levels of management needed? 2. How well will new staff fit in with existing staff?
Moving into new markets at home or abroad	1. Should national or international advertising be used? 2. Will foreign language speakers be needed?
Taking over business	1. Will it be necessary to replace another some of the staff in the other businesses with new staff loyal to this business?
Expansion through diversification	See the section on changed job roles below.

was expected to create 300 new jobs in the medium term and potentially as many as 750.

Promoting internal staff

When staff are promoted internally to fill spaces created by someone leaving or to fill newly created posts, this will leave vacancies for the more junior posts. The business will then have to answer the following kinds of questions in addition to the usual questions about where to advertise.

- Do we fill the post from our existing staff or do we recruit from outside the business?
- What experience did the person have in the business and how much training will be needed to replace the person?
- How quickly does the post need to be filled?

Figure 1 *Recruitment due to promotion*

Branch Manager

Due to promotion, the role of Branch Manager at Milton Keynes with Robert Half Ltd is available. Robert Half is a NYSE traded international staffing firm specialising in finance and accounts.

Source: adapted from roberthalf.co.uk.

Staff have left

The **turnover of staff** in a business refers to how many staff are leaving compared to how many staff are normally employed. When staff leave there may be a considerable cost involved in advertising for, selecting, interviewing and training new staff. It is therefore important for the business to establish why staff are leaving, as shown in Figure 2.

Retirement When staff retire, they are frequently older and more experience staff. They may also be in a more senior position than younger staff. The business will therefore need to consider the following specific questions.

- Is the post still required or would this be a good time to scrap it?
- Do we recruit internally or externally?
- Do we look for someone with the same level of experience or train someone?

Figure 2 *Reasons why staff leave*

- Do we look for a young person who will be in post for many years?

Promotion Internal promotion has been dealt with above. When promotion takes place because a person has left for a better job in another business, the business needs to consider the following questions before trying to recruit a replacement.

- Did the person leave because there were no internal promotion prospects and is that likely to happen again?
- Did the person leave for higher pay and should we, and can we afford to, raise our pay?

De-motivation Staff may be de-motivated for many reasons. The business needs to think about what the actual reason was and try to improve the situation before recruiting replacements. If the underlying causes are not dealt with, it is highly likely that the same problem will arise again. The factors that might lead to de-motivation and hence staff leaving are dealt with in sections 9-12.

Family commitments Family commitments are generally outside the control of the business and would include such factors as:

- illness and the need for staff to leave in order to take care of someone;
- a husband or wife moving out of the area because of his or her job and the partner is moving as well;
- the family is moving so that the children can attend a better school;
- staff are leaving to have children.

Although the business can often do little about the person leaving, it will need to consider the following sorts of questions.

- Is the vacancy temporary or permanent? The law states that staff on maternity leave must have their job kept open for them.
- Would higher rates of pay prevent this happening in the future?
- Would it help future retention of staff if part-time work, flexible hours or job sharing was offered?

Dismissed Staff may be dismissed because their jobs are no longer needed **(redundancy)**, in which case recruitment of new staff will not be an issue. However, they may have been dismissed because they have done something wrong. If that is the case, it is vital that the business works out why this has happened so that it can ensure that, when new staff are appointed, the same thing does not happen again. Legislation states the situations where dimissal might be legitimate and legal, without breaking employment legislation conditions on unfair dismissal. These are shown in Table 2.

Table 2 *Reasons for dismissal which do not break legislation*

- Where the employee's conduct has been unacceptable and even criminal.
- Where the employee has been unable to provide work of a satisfactory quality.
- If the employee is made redundant because there is not enough work to be done.
- Where it would be illegal for the employee to continue work, e.g. if a bus driver had lost his/her licence.
- Where a job had only been offered for a set period of time, e.g. until a member of staff returned from maternity leave.

Changed job roles in the business

In many cases, what businesses produce and sell and how this is done change over time. Most businesses now use computers somewhere in their business and this means that they will need staff who understand both the hardware and software involved. It may be possible to recruit staff internally if they have the basic skills, but if people within the business cannot be re-trained to deal with these changes then new staff will have to be recruited.

Job roles within a business can change for many reasons.

- The introduction of new technology, e.g. computers and marketing through web-sites.
- Changing what is produced, e.g. new ranges or totally new types of product as when Tesco started to sell petrol.
- Changing the structure of the business, e.g. introducing a new layer of District Managers.

As the job roles are new it will be a vital starting point for the business to very carefully consider what is involved in the role so that the right staff for the job can be recruited. An example of changing roles is shown in Figure 4.

Other reasons

Because businesses are so different in terms of how they are owned and run, what they produce, whether they are expanding or contracting and their size there are many other specific reasons why staff are recruited.

- Businesses that only operate or have increased production at certain times of the year, as with some fun fairs, summer schools and farmers harvesting their crops.
- Family businesses that want to pass the business on to their sons or daughters and recruit them so that they can learn how it should be run.
- Businesses that are trying to achieve a representative ethnic balance. For example, in December 2004 Warwickshire had just 32 ethnic minority officers in a force of more than 1,000. Warwickshire Police Force urged people from minority ethnic communities to attend a recruitment event in Coventry. The session was open to anyone interested in a career in the police service, but the force were keen to encourage more people from ethnic minorities to apply.

Figure 4 *How job roles changed in farming*

Farmers in England made almost £300 million from new ventures such as tourism, sports and recreation in 2004. Defra's Farm Business Survey shows that:

- 48 per cent of full-time farmers have diversified;
- average earnings were £5,000 per farm from diversification;
- turnover from diversification had risen to £550 million (£425 million in 2002-3);
- 2,200 farms had turnovers of more than £50,000 from diversified businesses;
- the amount of diversification varies across England. 68 per cent of farms in the South East have diversified, compared to 37 per cent in the North. Farmers in the South East earned most, more than £111 million, from new enterprises.

Source: adapted from Defra, January 2005.

Examination practice • Global Resources

Figure 3

Are you Ex Management, Redundant, Self Motivated, Ambitious, Ready for a Change? If you are then we need to talk!

We need people with the following experience:- Network Marketing, Senior Management, Trainers, HR Managers, Logistics and Supply Chain Professionals, Sales Executives, Business Development Managers, Marketing Managers, Team Builders, ex military, Teachers.

We are looking for motivated ambitious people to fill Trainee Manager, Manager, Senior Manager and Leadership Manager positions in several locations around the UK & in Europe. We have just started phase two of our UK growth and we expect our turnover to move from £30million last year to £100million within the next 3-4 years and then £200million five years after that. This has created massive opportunities at all income levels in several locations around the country.

Source: adapted from Global Resources (natural health products industry).

(a) Identify ONE job role that is being specifically advertised in Figure 3. (1 mark)

(b) Justify why 'expansion' is the main reason why Global Resources is recruiting in the UK. (4 marks)

(c) The advertisement suggests that some job applicants may have left other businesses or may still be with other businesses. Identify ONE example of each and explain why it shows this.
(i) Have left other businesses.
(ii) Still with other businesses. (4 marks)

(d) Some of the new jobs will be in Europe. Explain how this may affect the kind of people Global Resources would want to recruit. (4 marks)

Meeting the assessment criteria

Figure 4 shows the main reasons why staff left businesses in 2003 as a percentage of all staff leaving. The figures are taken from all businesses returning details.

(a) (i) The pie chart shows that by far the greatest number of staff left their jobs voluntarily. Give **TWO** different reasons why people, in this case 71%, may have left their jobs. **(2 marks)**

Exemplar responses

- *Seeking promotion outside the business.*
- *Looking for higher pay.*
- *Family commitments, e.g. husband/wife moving to new job in another area.*
- *Pregnancy.*
- *Looking for a more interesting job.*
- *(Do not accept 'retired'.)*

Mark allocation

1 mark for each clearly different reason. **(2 marks)**

(ii) For each of the reasons you have given in (i) above, explain how the business could successfully encourage staff to remain with the business and state why this might be difficult. **(6 marks)**

Exemplar responses

(Three examples are given below)

<u>Promotion</u> – provide better jobs within the business – staff may be leaving because of lack of opportunities – there may simply be no posts available.

<u>Higher pay</u> – increase pay – will now be paid as much as in other jobs – additional cost/other employees will want the same.

<u>Husband/Wife moving</u> – offer to pay travel costs – may be prepared to travel if no personal extra cost – if move is to, say, another country could be impossible in terms of time.

Mark allocation

1 mark for method.
1 mark for why that would encourage staff to stay.
1 mark for why it may be difficult. **(1 + 1 + 1) x 2 (6 marks)**

Figure 4 *Reasons for labour turnover by cause (UK & Ireland, 2003)*

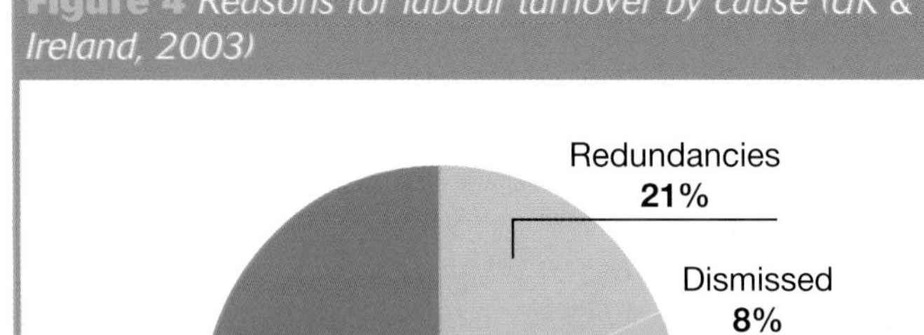

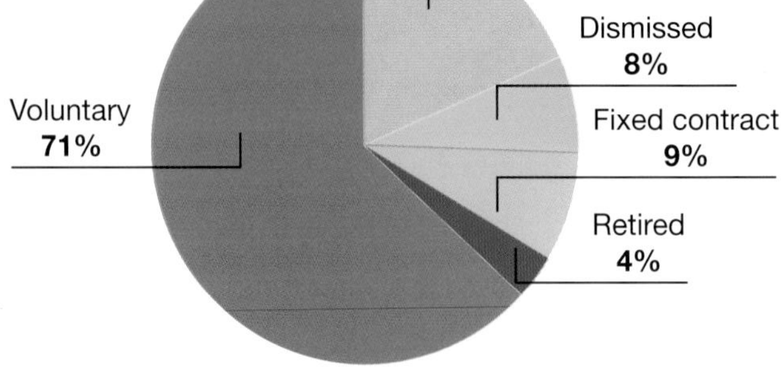

Source: adapted from Labour Force Survey.

(b) For each of the following reasons for staff leaving:

1. Redundancy
2. Dismissal
3. Fixed contract
4. Retirement

(i) state whether or not the business is likely to be seeking to recruit new staff;
(ii) explain why it will or will not be looking for new staff;
(iii) and if it is recruiting new staff state **ONE** way in which the reason for staff leaving is likely to affect the recruitment process. **(10 marks)**

Exemplar responses

<u>Redundancy</u> – will not – staff being made redundant because less staff are needed.

<u>Dismissed</u> – will – if staff dismissed for wrong doing/poor work the post will still exist – need to be more careful when selecting replacement.

<u>Fixed contract</u> – will not – staff were probably employed to get a specific job done and that is no longer needed.

<u>Retirement</u> – will – when people retire the job usually still needs to be done – may need to consider the level of experience needed to fill the post.

Mark allocation

1 mark for likelihood of recruitment.
1 mark why recruiting or not.
1 mark for how this will affect new recruitments. **(1 + 1 + 1/0) x 4 (10 marks)**

6 The recruitment process

The basic steps in recruitment

When businesses recruit staff they should consider carefully what post needs to be filled, the kind of person needed to fill it and how this can be successfully achieved. For some posts the process will be very short. For example, a newsagent employing a delivery worker could involve advertising in the window and having a short talk with the boy or girl to explain the job, starting work the next day. Others may be much longer, as with civil service jobs or senior management which may have many rounds of interviews and tests.

Figure 1 shows a typical list of steps a business might go through when recruiting and selecting the right person for a vacancy.

Identifying the vacancies to be filled

It could be suggested that it should be obvious to a business if there is a vacancy that needs filling. However, it really depends on why the vacancy has occurred and how any recruitment fits in with the overall strategy of the business.

Figure 1 *Typical stages in recruitment and selection*

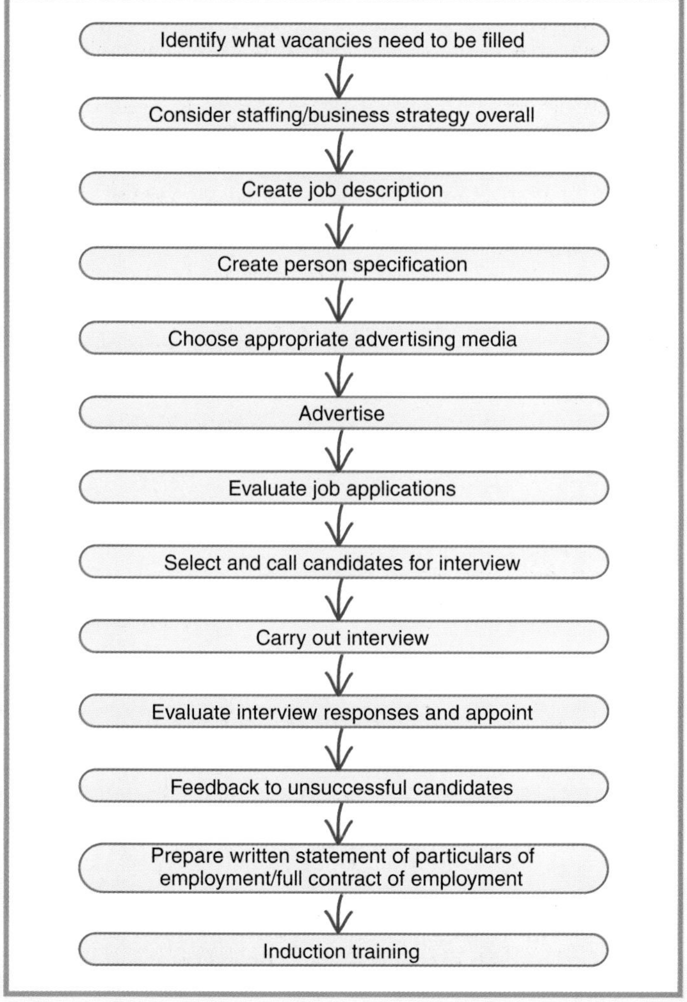

Identify what vacancies need to be filled
↓
Consider staffing/business strategy overall
↓
Create job description
↓
Create person specification
↓
Choose appropriate advertising media
↓
Advertise
↓
Evaluate job applications
↓
Select and call candidates for interview
↓
Carry out interview
↓
Evaluate interview responses and appoint
↓
Feedback to unsuccessful candidates
↓
Prepare written statement of particulars of employment/full contract of employment
↓
Induction training

As explained in section 5, the reason why a vacancy occurs may affect how the business should think about new vacancies. For example, when vacancies occur because the business is starting to produce a totally different product, the first step must be to think about the skills that will now be needed. On the other hand if a supervisor in a supermarket is promoted, the supermarket should know exactly what type of person is needed to fill the vacancy.

When deciding on which vacancies need to be filled the business must also look at the overall business strategy.

- Is the business expanding or contracting? If it is contracting perhaps the vacancy does not need to be filled.
- Is the businesses trying to reduce the number of levels of management (**delayering**)? If so, perhaps some management vacancies do not need to be filled.
- Is the business becoming an international or multi-national business? Will recuitment need to be made abroad? Will speakers of foreign languages be needed?

Planning ahead when filling vacancies is very important. Figure 2 shows on average how long it takes for vacancies to be filled in various industries.

Figure 2 *Number of weeks taken on average to fill different types of job roles (UK, 2003)*

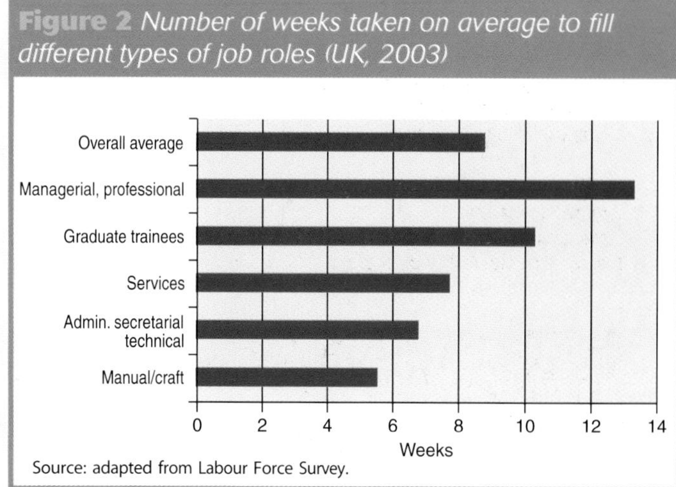

Source: adapted from Labour Force Survey.

Job descriptions and person specifications

When a business has decided which vacancies need to be filled, the next step is to create a job description for the post to be filled and a person specification to identify what sort of person would be best.

Job description A job description gives details of the duties and responsibilities associated with a particular job. Job descriptions do vary from job to job and from business to business, but they will tend to include the following categories:

- job title;

- who the employee is responsible to;
- where the job is located;
- a brief description of what the job entails;
- a list of duties and responsibilities;
- hours of work;
- the working conditions and pay.

Figure 3 shows a possible job description for the position as Team Leader at Little Chef.

Job descriptions are important because they:

- make the business think about what the job really involves;
- make it clear to the employee what is expected;
- provide a basis for measuring job performance;
- state clearly what duties must be carried out if there was a dispute.

Figure 3 *Job description for Little Chef post*

Job Title: Team Leader
Salary: £10,000 - £13,000
Location: Nationwide

Job Description

Job Purpose To effectively organise and control front of house activities and when required to open or to close the restaurant. To act as a key team member, consistently delivering the highest standards of customer service.

Principal Accountabilities

- To supervise Front of House activities ensuring that the highest levels of service are delivered in accordance with the required standard of hospitality and customer care.
- To adhere to legislation, company standards and procedures in a consistent manner.
- To demonstrate active selling skills, leading by example within the restaurant.
- To adhere to all cash handling procedures, ensuring the security of all company assets contained within the unit.
- To efficiently carry out all duties required of fully trained team members.
- To support the Manager and Assistant Manager/s in the achievement of company objectives.
- To undertake specified tasks/responsibilities when required and to support the Management Team by taking full shift responsibility to cover periods of absence.

Source: adapted from www.little-chef.co.uk.

Person specification A person specification gives details of the characteristics that would be expected of the successful applicant. It will be very closely related to the duties and responsibilities listed in the job description.

Person specifications usually set down requirements under the following headings:

- skills and experience;
- education, qualifications and training;
- personal qualities.

The personal qualities are likely to be very wide and will depend very heavily on the type of job.

- Farm labourers may need to be physically fit.
- Teachers in primary schools need to have a good rapport with young children.
- Army officers may need to be able to show authority.
- Part-time workers may need to be flexible about their hours.
- Employees in fast-food restaurants usually have to be happy to work in a team.

It is now common to split basic requirements into those which are 'essential' and those which are simply 'desirable'. Figure 4 shows an example of a person specification for the job of Police Driving Instructor for the Devon & Cornwall Constabulary.

Creating person specifications are important because they should:

- help to decide where and how to advertise the vacancy;
- give a set of standards against which the job applicants can be measured;
- tell the applicants, very clearly, what the minimum requirements are in terms of their own personal qualifications, experience and attitudes.

Figure 4 *Person specification for a police driving instructor*

Job Title: Police Driving Instructor
Main duty: Carrying out driving instruction and assessment to a Police Standard and Advanced level, including specialist courses, e.g. Stinger, TPAC, where necessary.

Person specification

Essential	**Desirable**
Qualified to Police Driving Instructor Class I Level or equivalent	PCV and LGV licence
Excellent communication skills	Experience of Skid Car training and other specialist driver training qualifications e.g. TPAC, Surveillance, VIPEG
Up-to-date knowledge of current legislation and Police procedures	ADI
Excellent inter-personal skills	IT skills
Prepared to undertake further training and development in order to achieve and maintain National Standards	Stinger Instructor
Knowledge of National Police Training working practices	Assessing/teaching qualifications, i.e. D32/33.
Experience of working unsupervised	

Application forms and letters of application

Many businesses produce their own job application form for job applicants to fill in. The benefit of doing this is that the form can be set out so that it asks applicants to provide details that will be particularly useful to that specific business.

Application forms can, however, be fairly general and ask for:

- name and address of the applicant;

- personal details such as age;
- the post applied for;
- education and qualifications;
- present post and previous employment;
- relevant skills, knowledge and experience;
- the names and addresses of referees.

This information would be required for the job in Figure 5.

Figure 5 *Job requirements of a sales ledger assistant*

SALES Ledger Assistant required immediately by small London publishing company. Must have experience of customer liaison (private and trade customers) and of computerised ledger system. Varied, demanding full-time permanent position.

Because application forms usually cover many different jobs in a business, job applicants are often asked to complete a **letter of application**. This is used by the applicant to explain why they want the specific job on offer and why they would be particularly suitable for the job.

Sometimes there is no application form and job applicants should then send a letter of application and a **curriculum vitae**. Curriculum vitae sum up most of the information that would be put on an application form, although not the references, but would also have a short section for main interests. Many potential employers expect this information to be put on no more than one side of A4 so that it is easy to read, although this would depend on what job is being applied for.

Advertising

Advertising available posts needs to be thought about carefully to ensure that the message reaches the right people. Internal recruitment might use notice boards, memos, company intranets, newsletters and even word of mouth.

External recruitment may be highly targeted if the business knows specific people who would be good for the job. This includes:

- **head hunting** – where specific individuals are invited to apply;
- **'The milk round'** – where businesses visit universities to try to persuade students to apply as they approach their final examinations.

Other advertisements and approaches will be more general, using newspapers, trade magazines, the Internet, recruitment agencies, radio and in-store leaflets and for smaller or more local firms, window displays, local newspapers or leaflet drops.

It is important to get the right information into the advertisement so that it will attract the right people, and stop unsuitable people from applying.

Selecting candidates for interview

When it has been decided that job applicants should be called for an interview, the business needs to ensure that the right candidates are invited. The following steps should then be followed.

- Decide how many candidates will be invited.
- Read through each of the job applications.
- Compare them to the job description and the person specification.
- Consider other criteria, such as the notice needed in the current job, where they live and potential costs of moving and ensure that there is no illegal discrimination taking place.

This process of selecting the people to be considered for interview is call **short listing**. With some jobs there will be a number of interviews or tests and at each stage a smaller and smaller short list will be created. Sometimes businesses create a long list and then reduce it to a short list

The Interview

Where a business calls candidates for interview and then decides which person to appoint on the basis of the interview, it needs to think very carefully about how the interview is going to be conducted.

There are legal issues that need to be understood, especially in terms of potential discrimination. These are considered in section 8. There are also very important practical issues which should be planned.

Providing details Each interviewee should be given full details about:

- where, when and how the interviews will be carried out;
- details of the costs that will be covered by the business, e.g. travel;
- copies of job descriptions, person specification and the business ethos if they have not already been provided;
- informing them of any tests they may be expected to take as part of the interview process.

The nature of the interview Deciding if the interview will be:

- one to one – the interviewer and the interviewee;
- a panel – a group of interviewers and one interviewee;
- a group interview – a group of interviewees with one or more interviewers.

Selecting the interview panel This should include:

- the person with authority to make the appointment;
- a senior member of the department in which the person will be working;
- other experienced interviewers who know how to get answers that will make the decision easy and correct.

Conducting interviews effectively is a skill. The interviewees needs to be put at their ease. But at the same time the interviewer needs to find out just how good the applicants are for the job, what their real feelings are about the job and whether they are answering questions truthfully. Asking the right questions in the right way is important for a successful interview. This often means that the interviewers need to give applicants space to develop their answers.

The interview stage in many businesses will include tests. The two most common tests that are used are as follows.

Aptitude tests. These are designed to find out if an applicant can actually do the job. They would include the following common examples:

- secretarial jobs – being asked to type or take shorthand to test the speed at which they can carry out the specific duty;
- teaching jobs – being asked to teach part of a lesson to assess how well it was planned and delivered;
- senior civil service or management jobs – where problem solving tasks are set.

Psychometric tests. These test the way the applicant thinks and feels about things and they can also test basic skills, as with intelligence tests. They would include tests to show the following.

- The way people think.
- How motivated they are.
- Their attitudes to other people.
- How they would approach problems.
- Intelligence.
- How open they are to new ways of doing things.

These tests may be very structured and formal like an examination. They may be filled out at, before or after the interview. Their purpose is the same, to get useful information from the applicants. It is equally important that the right questions are asked at the interview itself and in the right way.

Some questions will be asked to put the interviewee at their ease, such as 'How was your journey here?' Some questions will want specific answers and may be **closed questions** with set answers expected, such as 'Have you worked with Microsoft Word before?'

Other questions will be **open questions** which invite the person to develop answers in the way they want, such as 'What skills do you think you could bring to this job?' Each type of question is trying to find out information in a different way so that the right final choice can be made.

Figure 6 *Advice to interviewees*

'Interviews are never easy, but some can be much worse than others. Being scrutinised and assessed is rarely going to feel comfortable, but if you've never had a truly dreadful job interview, you haven't lived. If you have, don't let it dent your confidence. Thinking about what you can learn will help you to move on.'

Irene Krechowiecka

Source: http://www.ivillage.co.uk/workcareer/findjob/interviews/articles/0,,186_167095-1,00.html.

After the interview

In some cases the successful and unsuccessful applicants will be told immediately after the interview. With other jobs the applicants have to wait to be told later on.

Whichever way is used, the business will think carefully about what was said in the interview, check the results of any tests, possibly look at the application forms, letters of application and the CVs and then decide on the best candidate for the job. Usually applicants have been asked in advance whether they would take the job if it was offered to them, so informing the successful applicant creates the appointment.

Most businesses will also give some feedback to the unsuccessful applicants. This is the courteous thing to do, but it also makes business sense because these may be people that the business might like to work for it in the future.

All employees require, by law, a written statement of the particulars of their employment within two months of starting work. This needs to be drawn up. For more details see section 15 on legal issues. Most employees will have some kind of induction training to introduce them into the business. For more details see section 7 on training.

Examination practice • Job research

With reference to a specific job that you have studied answer the questions below. The job must be one in which an important interview stage took place.

(a) (i) Name of the business.
(ii) Name of the job.
(iii) Details of the main duties of the job. (4 marks)

(b) Identify which of the following documents were used for recruiting for this job and for each explain why they were, or were not, important for this specific job.
(i) Curriculum vitae.
(ii) Application form.
(iii) Letter of application. (6 marks)

(c) Describe the type of interview used (one-to-one, panel or group) and explain why that type of interview was used. (4 marks)

(d) Give TWO examples of an open question and TWO examples of a closed question used in this interview and explain why that type of question was used for the questions you have given.
(i) Closed.
(ii) Open. (8 marks)

Meeting the assessment criteria

Figure 7 *Job advertisement for Sales Administration Assistant*

SALES ADMIN ASSISTANT

We are looking for a hard working individual with good keyboard and telephone skills to assist our Sales Manager in a variety of duties at our Head Office in London.

- ***Excellent working environment***
- ***Interesting and varied role***
- ***Attractive package***

Write in the first instance to
Jason Freeland at Kapland Ltd
125 New Way, London, WC20 4RR

Figure 7 shows an advertisement placed in a London magazine. Before the advertisement was designed and created a job description and person specification would have been created.

(a) Explain the main purpose of each of the following in the recruitment process.
(i) A job description.
(ii) A person specification. **(4 marks)**

Exemplar responses

(i) Job description
- *Gives details about what the job involves – allows the business to match applicants' details against the job.*
- *Gives basic details of what the job involves – will tell the applicant if it is worth applying.*

(ii) Person specification
- *Gives details of the type of person required – allows the business to reject unsuitable applicants.*
- *Gives details of skills/personality needed to do the job – could form the basis of aptitude or psychometric tests.*

Mark allocation

1 mark for what it is/description.
1 mark for its basic purpose in the recruitment process.

(1 + 1) x 2
(4 marks)

(b) From the advertisement shown in Figure 7, identify TWO details that would come from the Job Description and TWO details that would come from the Person Specification. **(4 marks)**

Exemplar responses

(i) Job description
- *Job title/Sales Admin. Assistant.*
- *Location/London Head Office.*
- *Responsible to/Sales Manager.*

(ii) Person specification
- *Skills/good keyboard/telephone skills.*
- *Personal qualities/hard working.*

Mark allocation

1 mark for each detail. **(1 + 1) x 2**
(4 marks)

(c) Someone interested in the job should contact Jason Freeland. He may then ask them complete a document that he sends out to them and possibly send in two documents that they have created. What are these three documents and what are their basic functions? **(6 marks)**

Exemplar responses

- *Application form – a standard form which will list the main details that the business needs.*
- *Curriculum Vitae/CV – provides personal details of the applicant in terms of address, education and qualifications.*
- *Letter of application – gives details of why the applicant feels the job is specifically suited to them.*

Mark allocation

1 mark for each document.
1 mark for its basic function/main points it will include.

(1 + 1) x 3
(6 marks)

(d) If you were designing tests for an applicant for this job, what aptitude and psychometric test would you create? Justify your answers.
(i) Aptitude.
(ii) Psychometric. **(6 marks)**

Exemplar responses

(i) Aptitude
- *Will test specific skills – test how fast they can type – good keyboard skills are required.*
- *Will test if applicant can do job – ask them to work for fifteen minutes in the office taking telephone calls – good telephone skills required for the job.*

(ii) Psychometric
- *Will test personality – a test where applicants are faced with a wide range of tasks – test ability to deal with a varied role.*
- *Will test attitude to work – ask them to carry out demanding tasks – should identify hard working individual.*

Mark allocation

1 mark for showing understanding of the term (may be implied).
1 mark for identifying a specific suitable test.
1 mark for justifying why this is aptitude/psychometric or why it is valuable for this job.

(1 + 1 + 1) x 2
(6 marks)

7 Methods of training employees

Training

At some stage in employees' lives they will need training for the job they are doing or going to do. Some employees may have skills from their education or from previous jobs and therefore need little additional training. Others will need extensive training.

How much training and what kind of training is needed will depend on the type of job involved and the amount of training that has already been given through education and courses and the natural skills of the person employed. This section will be looking primarily at the type of training provided by businesses to their employees.

Reasons for training

Businesses train staff for a number of reasons, as shown in Figure 1. When asked by a client 'What if you train staff and they leave' a manager replied 'What if you don't train staff and they stay'. This suggests that businesses with untrained staff can have problems and the benefits of training staff outweigh the possible problems.

Figure 1 *Reasons for training staff*

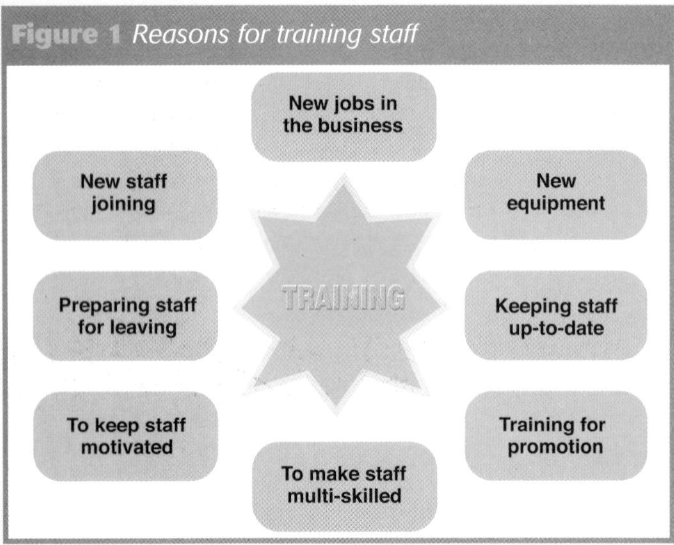

New staff joining There are very few jobs where absolutely no training is required when staff join a business. Even for a very basic job, such as washing up plates and dishes in a restaurant, the employee will need to be told where the washing up materials are kept, where to stock dried plates or where to put dish towels ready for the laundry.

In other jobs extensive training will be needed when new staff join. This would be for the following reasons.

- The type of job is new to the person.
- The equipment, e.g. a software package, is unique to the business.
- The business wants to recruit inexperienced people so that it can train them as it wants.
- The training is a continuous part of their education, as with junior doctors in a hospital.
- The work is very technically difficult, as with flying a fighter aircraft.

Most new staff will be given some kind of induction training (see below) when they join. For the more technical and professional training mentioned above this will be delivered through continuous training.

New jobs in the business Most businesses are developing all the time, introducing technology and developing and selling new products. When this happens, new jobs will be created in the business and often a business will decide that the easiest way to staff these jobs is to train people already in the business.

New equipment In many cases in business the job being done does not change very much but the equipment on which it is being done does change. Staff then need to be trained to use this new equipment effectively so that they can carry on doing their job. Examples of this would include:

- new photocopying machines in an office;
- new forklift trucks in a warehouse;
- new fast speed passenger trains on the railways;
- new cookers in a restaurant.

Keeping staff up-to-date Many jobs have frequent changes in their products or the way that jobs are expected to be carried out. This would include:

- learning how to use new software packages;
- training staff in new health and safety procedures;
- explaining new electrical products to sales staff so that they can advise customers.
- Providing teachers with training when examination syllabuses change.

Multi-skilling There are many definitions of multi-skilling. One is multi-skilling means you've been trained to cover a range of different jobs in your workplace.' The main benefit for the business is that staff can move from one job to another and that will help to cover unexpected absences, provide additional staff when demand for a particular activity is especially high or, move staff when someone leaves. This provides the business with added flexibility.

The main benefit for the staff is that they will now have additional skills which can improve promotion prospects and make it easier for them to move to new jobs in different businesses if they wish. Figure 2 shows an example.

To keep staff motivated Training can be an important motivator for staff. It makes them feel that someone is thinking about what they need. It can also lead to higher rates of pay, promotion prospects and greater job satisfaction, all of which will act as motivators.

Training for promotion In many businesses the way in which staff progress and move to higher pay scales is through promotion. Figure 3 shows a possible promotion route for staff in a supermarket.

Figure 2 *Training for promotion and retirement*

Barclays Bank implemented a multi-skilling strategy in its call centres, known as Barclays contact centres, as a direct response to employee demands for career progression and a more varied workload. The new training structure aimed to address a major problem affecting call centre staffing - high turnover rates.

Source: adapted from European Finance Director.

The Warwick Business School was commissioned by the FA Premier League, the Football League, the Football Association, and others, to provide a training programme to develop the management skills of footballers who wanted to move into club management positions.

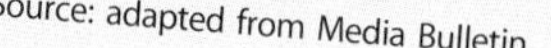
Source: adapted from Media Bulletin.

At each stage of the promotion process staff will need to learn new skills and techniques so that they can deal with the different duties and added responsibilities of the higher post. Most businesses will provide training to help staff make the move.

Preparing staff for leaving Some businesses will specifically train staff to help them when they leave. There are two main reasons why they do this.

- Because the staff are only employed for a fixed period of time and providing them with training for other jobs will help with initial recruitment and keep staff motivated. This is a common practice in the armed forces.
- Helping staff to cope with retirement. Most people who retire have a very significant fall in income and need to adjust to not going out to work. Some businesses help their staff to make this transition. An example is shown in Figure 2.

Figure 3 *A promotion route for staff in a supermarket*

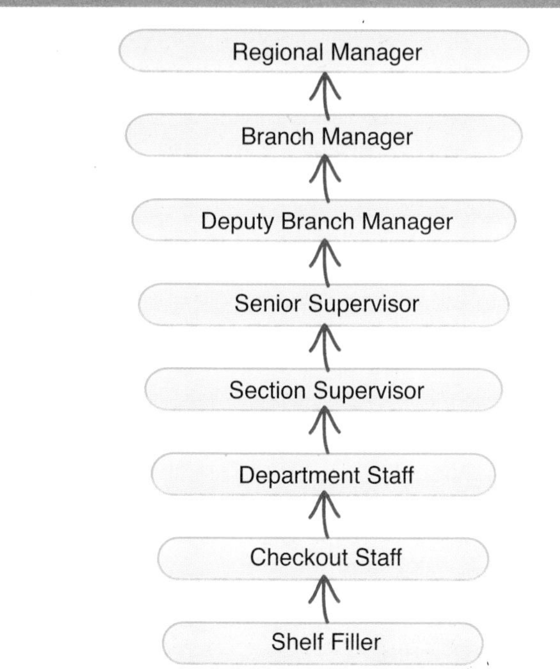

Types of training

The exact type of training given will depend on what the job is, the current level of skill and experience of staff and constraints such as cost and time.

Induction training Induction training takes place when new employees join a business. The main purpose of this is to ensure that they know what they are doing and to make them familiar with the business itself. The following are all typical elements in an induction training programme.

- Meeting senior staff.
- Conducted tour of the premises, including toilets, canteen, recreation facilities.
- Details of basic health and safety procedures.
- Use of internal and external communications systems.
- Main company aims and objectives.
- Company policies, e.g. on smoking.
- Dress code.
- Disciplinary procedures.
- Meeting people that the employee will work with.
- An introduction to the job itself.

On-the-job training On-the-job training takes place as someone is actually doing his or her job. Because the training takes place as someone is working, it has various benefits and drawbacks as shown in Table 1. Training for many job roles is done on-the-job, especially where the required skills are fairly limited, as with fast food restaurants, or where the employee is highly skilled and is simply learning new techniques, as with computer programmers.

Table 1 *Benefits and drawbacks of on-the-job training*

Benefits
- Work is being done so something is being produced.
- The trainees learn by actually doing the job.
- Practice should help to improve skills.
- Often easy to arrange.

Drawbacks
- If the trainee gets it wrong the product, or customer, may be lost.
- Difficult for the trainee to concentrate whilst working.
- Dangerous for others, e.g. surgeon, airline pilot.
- Trainers may have to stop their jobs to do the training.

Off-the-job-training Off-the-job training takes place when the person is not actually doing the job. This may or may not take place at the workplace. The benefits and drawbacks of off-the-job training tend to be the opposite of on-the-job training as shown in Table 2.

Table 2 *Benefits and drawbacks of off-the-job training*

Benefits
- If a trainee does something wrong an actual product will not be affected.
- Easier to concentrate.
- Does not put customers in danger.
- Can be done after the normal hours of work.

Drawbacks
- No work is being done so it costs more.
- Problems and how to deal with them may only appear when real work starts.
- It needs to be organised and may take time.
- Can disturb other employees if training involves watching them.

On-and off-site training On-site training means that the training is taking place where the person works. It may or may not be on-the-job. Off-site training means that the training is taking place away from where the person is working. It will, therefore, automatically be off-the-job.

The decision as to whether to train staff on or off site will usually depend on whether or not the business has the facilities to train on-site. The comparative advantages of the two methods of training are shown in Table 3.

Table 3 *On-site and off-site training*

On site
- Usually cheaper.
- Trainees can see the job they will actually be doing.
- There is no time lost in travelling or staying overnight.
- Likely to be less worrying for staff as it is in familiar surroundings.

Off site
- Special training facilities can be used.
- Staff may see the training as a special privilege.
- Unlikely to be distracted by daily work commitment.
- Can meet with other businesses. staff.

In-house training This is used to describe training that is provided by the business itself. It may be any of the four types of training mentioned above. Today, however, the term in-house is also used for training that is supplied by outside providers and is tailored for the specific needs of the business.

Apprenticeships Apprenticeships are jobs in which training forms a major part of the agreement between the employer and the employee. In these agreements the employees are trained on-the-job, actually doing the work, but they are also often trained both off-the-job and off-site in local colleges. This may be through day release, where the person spends, say, one day a week at college or through night school after work.

There were over 234,000 apprentices in UK businesses in 2005 and many major businesses and many companies used this method of training with younger staff. British Gas, which has over 7,000 engineers, planned to recruit at least 50% of these through apprenticeships by 2010.

Many apprenticeship schemes come from government initiatives. The main benefits to the apprentices are:
- they are trained;
- usually they gain additional qualifications.

The main benefits to the businesses are:
- they finish up with well trained staff;
- many of the schemes receive some kind of monetary support from the government.

On-going training The majority of training that takes place in a business is on-going training. This is training that continually supports the member of staff and helps him or her to progress. It also helps to ensure that the members of staff will be able to perform duties efficiently.

If on-going training is going to be effective it is vital that the business first of all assesses the need for training and how that fits with the needs of the individual member of staff and the main aims and objectives of the business, as shown in Figure 4.

Figure 4 *Aims and objectives of on-going training*

Meeting the business's objectives.
- Review aims and objectives.
- Establish staff training needs to meet these.
- Cost the training needed.
- Provide suitable training to increase staff's effectiveness.

Meeting employees' needs.
- Monitor employees' performance.
- Assess employees' needs through appraisal interviews, discussion and observation.
- Agree targets and establish training needs.
- Check training needs against business aims and objectives.
- Plan and implement training.
- Evaluate the success of the individual's training.

To ensure the best training for individuals it is important that line managers establish a close professional relationship with their staff. In some businesses a mentoring system will be established. In other businesses the approach taken is coaching.
- Mentoring means acting as a trusted advisor. In business this means that the mentor must understand what is best for the person they are mentoring and ensure that that person gains the best advice and training possible.
- Coaching means giving specific instructions and training to staff in order to achieve a specific outcome. In businesses that needs to be matched to the aims and objectives of the business or to the aspirations of the individual member of staff.

Government training schemes

The Department for Trade and Industry (Dti) states that:
A well-trained and professional workforce is better equipped to:
- work effectively with minimal supervision, helping to raise productivity;
- improve customer satisfaction by giving knowledgeable responses to enquiries;

- be flexible so staff can be employed on related jobs and cope with work-level fluctuations and absences;
- take a creative approach to business problems and develop new products and services;
- appreciate the value of developing their personal skills and be highly motivated.

The government believes that all businesses should provide regular and on-going training for their staff. It has, therefore set up various schemes to encourage and support businesses.

Investors in People 'Investors in People' (IiP) is the national standard that sets a level of good practice for the training and development of people. It was created by leading businesses and business organisations such as the CBI and TUC and the Employment Department.

The standard lays down a set of conditions that a business must meet in terms of its training provisions before it can be award the title of Investors in People. These standards relate to each of the ten indicators shown in Figure 5.

Figure 5 *Investors in People standards*

1. A strategy for improving the performance of the organisation is defined and understood.
2. Learning and development is planned to achieve the organisation's objectives.
3. Strategies for managing people are designed to promote equality of opportunity in the development of the organisation's people.
4. The capabilities managers need to lead, manage and develop people effectively are clearly defined and understood.
5. Managers are effective in leading, managing and developing people.
6. People's contribution to the organisation is recognised and valued.
7. People are encouraged to take ownership and responsibility by being involved in decision making.
8. People learn and develop effectively.
9. Investment in people improves the performance of the organisation.
10. Improvements are continually made to the way people are managed and developed.

Details can be found at http://www.investorsinpeople.co.uk.

Skills Strategy The government's first Skills Strategy was launched in July 2003. In March 2005 the government published a white paper, *Skills: Getting on in business, getting on at work*, to build on the original strategy. The White Paper emphasises two main aims:

- ensuring that employers have the right skills to support the success of their businesses;
- helping individuals to gain the skills they need to be employable and personally fulfilled.

The White Paper sets out proposals and reforms designed to:

- put employers' needs centre stage in the design and delivery of training. This will be met through a new National Employer Training Programme (NETP) and Skills Academies;
- support individuals in gaining the skills and qualifications they need to achieve the quality of life they want. This will include, from 2006/7, an entitlement to free tuition for a first Level 2 qualification;
- reform supply. This aims to improve the provision of training in schools and colleges and from other training providers.

Apprenticeships policy The Learning and Skills Council supports businesses in England who take on apprentices in a variety of ways. Apprenticeships are managed nationally through 47 local offices and a network of learning providers. Large businesses are supported by National Contracts Service which can put them in touch with a suitable learning provider and works with them to find suitable training programmes for their apprentices. Details can be found at http://www.apprenticeships.org.uk.

Changes to the existing Apprenticeship scheme were announced in May 2004. In summary, these:

- removed the upper 25-year age limit on Apprenticeship training;
- introduced a new Advanced Apprenticeship award at Level 3;
- created Young Apprenticeships to give school pupils at Key Stage 4 the opportunity to experience real work environments;
- brought in pre-Apprenticeship courses for young people who were not yet ready for the full-blown award.

Examination practice • Training in the UK

Figure 6 shows the percentage of all employees receiving job related training as collected by the Labour Force Survey. The total has then been divided to show the percentage of that total in each age group.

(a) Explain, using examples of on-site and off-site training, what job related training is. (5 marks)

(b) Explain why the 16 to 17 sector is so small when compared to the other sectors. (3 marks)

(c) Which sectors could the Learning and Skills Councils support through its Apprenticeship programmes? Justify your answer. (2 marks)

(d) Figure 6 shows that all groups of working age receive some job related training. Outline how this training is likely to benefit:
(i) the business;
(ii) the individual employee. (10 marks)

Figure 6 *Employees receiving job related training by age (Winter 2004/05)*

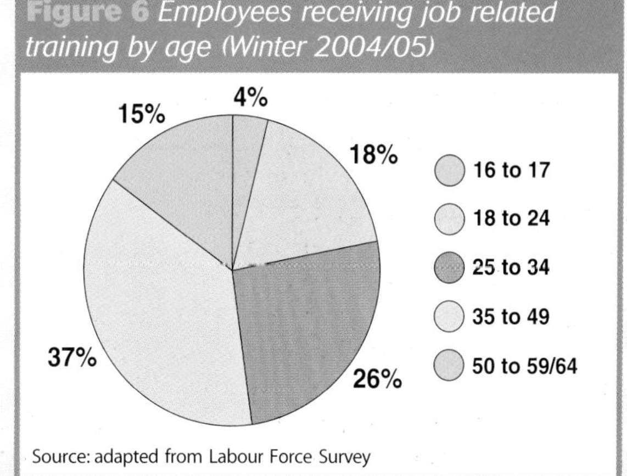

Source: adapted from Labour Force Survey

Meeting the assessment criteria

(a) Identify from Figure 7 which parts of the training programme were likely to have been conducted:
(i) on-the-job;
(ii) off-the-job.
For each, explain why they would have been on-the-job or off-the-job. **(6 marks)**

Exemplar responses

- *Classroom tutoring, off-the-job - it is taking place in a classroom not producing chemicals.*
- *Safety training could be either - may be shown how to handle chemicals on-the-job, may be shown fire exits off-the-job.*
- *Written assessments could be either - if a line manager is assessing, this could be done whilst watching staff work, if staff are writing the assessment they cannot do this whilst producing chemicals.*

Mark allocation
1 mark for identifying part and on or off.
1 mark for reason why on or off.

(1 + 1) x 3
(6 marks)

(b) Explain the meaning of the following terms and for each explain how they might help the business.
(i) Multi-skilled.
(ii) Self-directed teams. **(6 marks)**

Exemplar responses
Multi-skilled
Having more than one skill – provides staff flexibility – can move staff to other jobs as they have the additional skills.
Self-directed teams

- *Teams which plan and carry out their own work – more production – providing individuals with responsibility acts as a motivator.*
- *Team chooses how to work – encouraged additional investment – investors could see improved on-site culture.*

Mark allocation
1 mark for showing meaning of term.
1 mark for benefit to business.
1 mark for explaining how this comes from the initiative.

(1 + 1 + 1) x 2
(6 marks)

(c) Health and safety is likely to form a major part of the induction training for BASF plc. State why this is likely to be so important for BASF and explain the kind of training that could be included. **(8 marks)**

Exemplar responses
Meaning and basic reason

- *Training provided when employee joins the business – chemical firm so more potential health and safety issues.*

Figure 7 *BASF training*

BASF training programme saves £4m

One of the world's leading chemical companies, BASF plc, recognised the benefits of training through improved business performance.

At its Seal Sands site near Middlesborough, the implementation of a major training programme included classroom tutoring, safety training, and written assessments.

The benefits were numerous and included the development of 150 employees towards multi-skilled self-directed teams, secured savings of £4m for 2001 due to improved performance, increased staff morale, and an improved on-site culture that attracted investment and secured the company's future in the region.

Also, other companies now use BASF plc as a good practice benchmark for adopting new training processes.

Source: adapted from www.dti.gov.uk.

Likely elements of training

- *Fire drill procedure – tells staff what to do if fire breaks out/fire is a real possibility where there are chemicals.*
- *What protective clothing to wear – show staff how to prevent damage from chemical spills.*
- *How to handle/store dangerous chemicals – tries to ensure staff will not be injured whilst working.*
- *What to do if accidents do occur – help to limit the injuries that might be caused by this.*

Mark allocation
1 mark for showing understanding of the term (may be implied).
1 mark for why so important to BASF.
1 mark for each item likely to be included (maximum 3 marks).
1 mark for why this will be included (maximum 3 marks).

1 + 1 + [(1 + 1) x 3]
(8 marks)

8 Legal and ethical responsibilities - discrimination and equal opportunities

What is discrimination?

Businesses have many ethical and legal responsibilities towards their employees. A major responsibility is to prevent discrimination at work. Discrimination is about choice. In the work environment the term discrimination usually refers to the unethical or illegal choice of one person rather than another.

What if a business required an experienced sales assistant to work in an office in London? When making the selection the business:

- chose a male candidate rather than a female and argued that a male was required to work with customers, even though a female could do the job equally well;
- people from ethnic minority groups were rejected as the job was in London;
- a candidate in a wheelchair who was not able to drive was rejected even though driving was not required for the job.

In this case the business is unlikely to be meeting its legal and ethical responsibilities. It is likely to be discriminating against certain people.

What are equal opportunities?

Equal opportunities are when everyone has the same chance and everyone is treated the same. It is important for businesses to ensure that there are equal opportunities and equality of treatment when recruiting and selecting employees. If equal opportunities exist in a business then there is a greater chance that discrimination can be prevented. Figure 1 shows an example of equal opportunities at the Virgin company.

Figure 1 *Equal opportunities at Virgin*

We strive for equal opportunities for all present and potential employees

- There is a diverse workforce and an equal opportunities policy in place. We aim to employ people who reflect the diverse nature of society and we value people and their contribution irrespective of age, sex, disability, sexual orientation, race, colour, religion, marital status or ethnic origin.
- We do not discriminate against anyone for their membership or affiliation to any trade unions or political parties.
- We do not tolerate any sexual, physical or mental harassment of our employees.
- Procedures are in place to respond to accusations of workplace discrimination, harassment and victimisation.
- An effective employee grievance procedure is in operation, and the policy is properly communicated to our people.

Source: adapted from www.virgin.com.

Types of discrimination

Employers are ethically and legally bound to prevent discrimination in business. It is often suggested that certain types of discrimination must be prevented in business. These are shown in Figure 2.

Figure 2 *Types of discrimination*

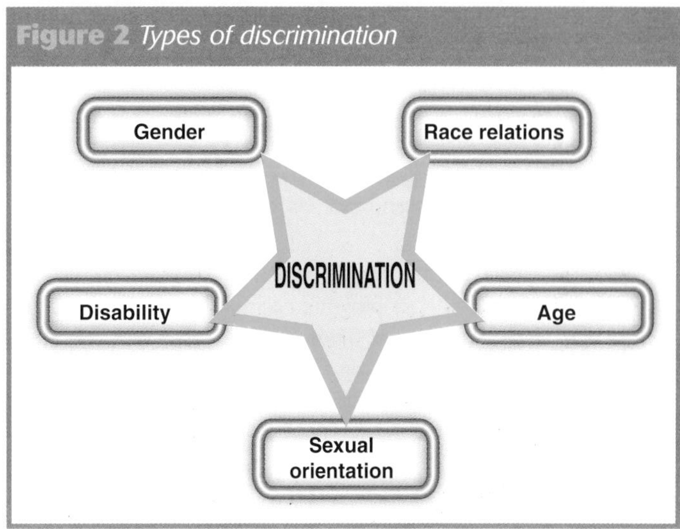

Gender or sex discrimination This is discrimination against one sex or another. An example might be employing a male director rather than a female director when the gender of the director has no influence on the job.

Racial discrimination This is discrimination against a person on the basis of their race. An example might be refusing to employ a bank assistant because he is from an Asian ethnic minority group.

Disability discrimination This is discrimination against disabled people. An example might be refusing to employ a person with hearing difficulties when this does not affect their performance in the job.

Age discrimination This is discrimination against people of a certain age, usually older people. An example might be refusing to employ a 61 year old just because of their age.

Sexual orientation discrimination This might include refusing to employ a person because of their sexual preference.

There is a variety of legislation that affects businesses. This legislation will affect the ways in which a business recruits and selects its employees.

Gender discrimination legislation

Gender discrimination legislation aims to prevent discrimination against one gender or another. It is usually used to prevent discrimination against women, but it can apply to men. Certain legislation in the UK and the EU promotes gender equality.

The EU Equal Treatment Directive, 1976 This states there must be equal treatment of men and women as regards access to employment, vocational training and promotion and working conditions. In 2002 it was amended to prevent sexual harassment.

Equal Pay Act, 1970 This states that employees are entitled to the same pay and conditions as others doing broadly similar work. It was amended in 1983 to relate to equal pay for work which makes the same demands.

The EU Equal Pay Directive, 1975 This states that men and women should receive equal pay for equal work. Equal work is work which is of equal value determined by job evaluation.

The Sex Discrimination Act, 1975 This makes it unlawful to discriminate on grounds of sex or marital status or for there to be sexual harassment at work. It makes it unlawful to discriminate:
- directly - treating someone less favourably than another person because of their gender;
- indirectly - where women have less chance of meeting employment conditions.

Employees who feel that they have been discriminated against can take their case to an employment tribunal, to court or to the European Court of Justice. These bodies rule whether discrimination has taken place and have the power to force business to comply with legislation. The Equal Opportunities Commission is a government body set up to advise and help employees who feel that they have faced discrimination. Table 1 shows how ethical and legal responsibilities regarding gender might affect businesses.

Race relations discrimination legislation

Race relations discrimination legislation aims to prevent discrimination on the grounds of:
- colour;
- race;
- nationality;
- ethnic, national or religious origin.

The **Race Relations Act, 1976** is the main legislation in the UK designed to promote racial equality. It states that it is unlawful to discriminate directly or indirectly on the grounds of colour, race, nationality or ethnic origin. In 2002 it was amended to include nearly all public functions such as the police force and health service. The **Race Relations (Amendment Act), 2000** includes a right to claim against ethnic harassment and the **Employment Equality (Religion and Belief) Regulations 2003** outlaw discrimination on religious grounds. Again, people who feel that they have faced discrimination can take their case to an employment tribunal. The Commission for Racial Equality is a non-government publicly funded body which helps to promote racial equality in the UK.

Disability discrimination legislation

Disability discrimination legislation aims to prevent

Table 1 *Gender - how ethical and legal responsibilities might affect businesses*

Situation	Possible effects
Clothing for administration employees	Do not prevent women from wearing trousers in the office if males do.
Advertising for a Refuse Collector	Use non-gender based terms in advertisements, for example Binman should not be used and replaced by Refuse Collector.
Designing person specifications for a machine operator	Carefully word the person specification, for example do not state only people over 6'4" as few women are this tall. This is a form of indirect discrimination.
Pay rises at a travel agent	Do not pay a male travel agent more than a female doing the same job.
Promotion of a manager	Can not chose a single male for promotion rather then a married woman because of the possibility of leave to have children.
Work situation	Training will be required to prevent sexual harassment and encourage equality of treatment.

Table 2 *Race relations - how ethical and legal responsibilities might affect businesses*

Situation	Possible effects
Clothing for employees	Do not prevent Sikhs from wearing turbans in the office.
Advertising a post	Cannot state generally that people of certain nationality, colour or ethnic origin may not apply.
Designing person specifications	Carefully word the person specification, for example cannot state generally that the post must be held by someone born in the UK.
Conditions at work	Take into account religious holidays of all ethnic groups.
Interviews	Do not discriminate against certain nationalities with language in written tests or questions.
Selection for training	Cannot refuse to select people from particular nationalities.
Work situation	Training will be required to prevent racial harassment and encourage equality of treatment.

Figure 3 *Possible changes that a business might make to comply with disability discrimination legislation*

- Modifying telephone handsets for people with gripping difficulties
- Adding a ramp to the building for wheelchair access
- Allowing absences for physiotherapy for people with mobility problems
- Creating wider workspace for workers in wheelchairs
- Modifying computer software or hardware for people with sight or hearing difficulties

discrimination against people with disabilities. The **Disability Discrimination Act, 1995** makes it illegal to discriminate against employees with disabilities unless there is a substantial, relevant and justified reason. For example:

- not selecting a candidate for a position in a call centre because they use a wheelchair might be discrimination as only minor changes to work conditions may be required;
- not selecting a candidate who uses a wheelchair for a job as a roofer might not be discrimination because there may be a justified concern for safety, the person may be unable to carry out the job and major changes may be needed to the conditions.

The Disability Rights Commission is an independent organisation set up by government to prevent disability discrimination. Part of its duties includes producing a code of practice for businesses to show how they can meet the requirements of legislation.

Age discrimination

Protection for older employees in the past was mainly in the form of conditions of service in their employment contracts. This is dealt with in sections 12 and 15. However, all EU countries must introduce laws to comply with the EU **Employment Framework Directive, 2000**. This aims to prevent all workplace discrimination. By 2006, the UK must introduce legislation that will make discrimination on the basis of age illegal. A business can not reject an applicant under 25 for not being mature enough or someone over 50 for being too slow to train. Possible examples of effects on businesses are shown in Table 3. There are a situations where differences in treatment related to age may be allowed. For example, a business may be able to set a seniority level before an employee can become a director.

Table 3 *Effects of complying with age discrimination legislation when recruiting and selecting*

Situation	Possible effects
Application forms	Cannot state that people over 50 can not apply in applications.
Interviews	Assumptions can not be made about candidates who look old or young, for example an older looking candidate will be less enthusiastic.
Experience	A business cannot be able to state how many years experience are needed as this might disadvantage younger candidates.
Work situation	Training will be required to prevent harassment on the basis of age and to encourage equality of treatment.

Sexual orientation discrimination

The **Employment Equality (Sexual Orientation) Regulations 2003** makes discrimination on grounds of sexual orientation illegal. Both direct and indirect discrimination and harassment are unlawful.

Reasons to prevent discrimination

There are reasons why a business may want to prevent discrimination at work.

The well-being of employees Good employers are concerned about the well-being of their employees. They want them to be as happy and motivated as possible in work and are concerned about their welfare. Preventing discrimination is a way of helping employees feel that the business takes their interests into account.

Motivation Increasingly, businesses are recognising that people are an important asset. Well-motivated employees are likely to be productive at work. This will help the business to be profitable. So it could be argued that preventing discrimination will help a business to be profitable. Staff are also likely to stay with a business that takes their interests into account. This can reduce staff turnover, which is a cost. It also helps the business to retain important personnel and their skills.

Other methods used to motivate employees and protect their well-being are dealt with in section 12.

Public image Ensuring that discrimination does not take place will improve the image and reputation of a business in the eyes of customers. They may buy more products as a result. It may also help to attract the best candidates for a post. They may be attracted by statements such as 'We are an equal opportunities employer'.

Financial issues Businesses that break laws regarding discrimination may face fines or compensation, or a court may impose conditions on them, which are costly. Preventing discrimination cases will help to reduce these costs.

Examination practice • Sidell Construction

Sidell Construction is a construction company which builds roads and other infrastructure. It has recently won a government contract for work in the Midlands area. It has decided to advertise for a new project manager to handle one of the construction teams working on road clearance.

The main role of the project manager will be to monitor progress of the work and ensure that deadlines are met. A number of important characteristics that the business wanted from the job holder were identified in the person specification. The business decided to place an advertisement in national newspapers and trade journals. It was keen to stress in the advertisement that it was an equal opportunities employer.

The business interviewed three applicants for the post. At the interview they were asked about their previous experience and given problem solving activities which the business felt would help to make a decision about the most suitable candidate.

(a) What should the business mean when it says that it is an equal opportunities employer? (2 marks)

(b) Suggest TWO reasons why a business might want to state that it is an equal opportunities employer. (4 marks)

(c) Explain how the:
(i) Equal Pay Act;
(ii) Race Relations Act;
would affect the advertisement for the post. (4 marks)

(d) Advise the business on TWO ways in which it might avoid discrimination when recruiting and selecting the candidate. (6 marks)

Meeting the assessment criteria

Sara responded to an advertisement for a job as a clerical assistant in a London firm of solicitors. She was invited for an interview which she felt went well. When she got home she received a call from the firm to ask her whether or not she was Jewish. She said that she was. She was then asked whether she intended to take all the Jewish holidays, but explained that she planned to take only one, as part of her leave.

Sara waited to hear whether she had been successful. After four days with no response she rang the company who said that she had not been offered the job. She was told that the successful candidate 'had different circumstances'. Sara decided to take her case to an employment tribunal.

Source: adapted from Commission for Racial Equality, www.cre.gov.uk.

(a) Suggest TWO pieces of legislation, other than the Race Relations Act, that might affect the advertisement of a post for a clerical assistant at a firm of solicitors and for each Act suggest how the wording of an advertisement might have broken the Act. **(4 marks)**

Exemplar responses

- *The Sex Discrimination Act, 1975 – if the advertisement had said only women should apply.*
- *Disability Discrimination Act, 1995 – if the advertisement had said no facilities for wheelchairs, when there were facilities.*

Mark allocation

1 mark for naming a relevant Act.
1 mark for examples of how the wording would contravene the Act.

(1 + 1) x 2
(4 marks)

(b) Discuss whether or not the London firm of solicitors is likely to have broken the Race Relations Act in its dealings with Sara. **(5 marks)**

Exemplar responses

Reasons why and counter point

- *She was asked if she was Jewish – but all candidates may have been asked this as part of checking ethnic origins.*
- *She was asked if she was taking all the Jewish Holidays – may have been asked this to help with staff planning.*
- *Successful candidate had different circumstances which might mean they were not taking Jewish holidays – the exact difference was not stated.*

Conclusion

- *Taken together the references to the particular position of Jewish people sounds like discrimination, so Act broken.*
- *There could have been a valid explanation for all the apparent discrimination, so Act not broken.*

Mark allocation

1 mark for reason why the Act may have been broken (maximum 2 marks).
1 mark for argument of why Act not broken (maximum 2 marks).
1 mark for reasoned conclusion

(2 + 2 + 1)
(5 marks)

(c) If Sara had been employed, the Employment Rights Act, 1996 would have required that she was given:
(i) a written statement of particulars of employment within two months of starting work.
(ii) a written itemised pay statement every time she was paid.
Explain what each of these requirements means and how each protects Sara. **(6 marks)**

Exemplar responses

- *(i) Details of the terms on which Sara will work must be written out for her – for example when employment begins/how much the pay will be/the expected hours of work – Sara will have written details in case there is any dispute.*
- *(ii) Details of how Sara's pay has been worked out – rates of pay per hour and hours worked/details of deduction such as income tax, NIC – will allow her to check that she has been paid correctly.*

Mark allocation

1 mark for showing understanding of requirement.
1 mark for likely details in requirement.
1 mark for how that protects Sara.

(1 + 1 + 1) x 2
(6 marks)

9 The importance of motivation and de-motivation

Why motivate?

It is sometimes argued that staff motivation is the most important factor for the success of a business. For some, the key role of motivation is expressed in the following formula:

Performance = ability x motivation.

Frequently the ability that one member of staff has is the same as other members, but the levels of motivation are different. The effect is usually very clear. Motivated staff, generally, work harder than de-motivated staff and, therefore, tend to produce more, provide better quality products and encourage staff around them to work harder.

In 2004 the Learning and Research Council, which is responsible for post-16 education and training outside universities, surveyed 72,100 employers in England. The results showed that 2.4 million workers were classed by their employers as not being proficient in their current jobs. Lack of skills was the main cause, but 33% of the employers also stated lack of motivation as a cause.

This section looks at what happens if staff are de-motivated. If staff are well motivated these negative effects will be reversed.

Effects of poorly motivated staff

Five important effects of poorly motivated staff are examined below, although there are many more. For each negative effect, the opposite will be the case with well motivated staff.

Figure 1 *Effects of poorly motivated staff*

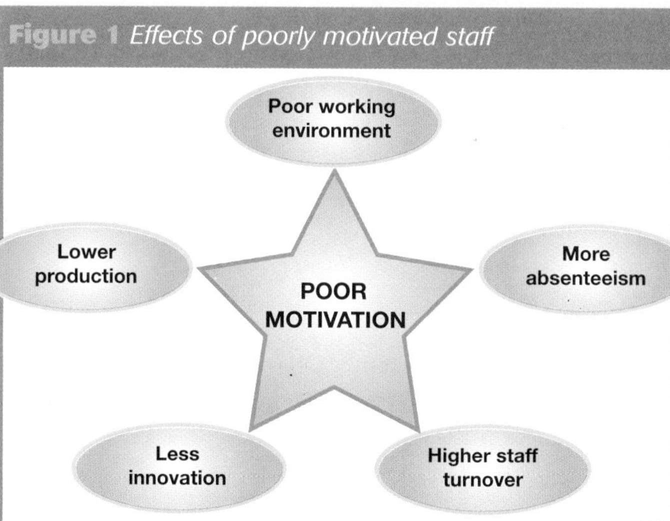

'It's often difficult for managers in a production area, like mail or shipping, to keep their employees motivated. There are several factors that lead to this, including relatively low pay, working in what is often considered a low-status department, and the high turnover of personnel. You're now faced with another phenomenon that works against you - the rapid rate of change in the technologies used to do your job. To counter these obstacles, you must motivate your employees by instilling pride in their jobs.'

Source: adapted from The Berkshire Company.

Lower production

When trying to identify poorly motivated staff the following definition has been used.

'They are people who often don't try to do their best and who are rarely willing to spend extra time and effort to get the job done.'

De-motivated staff tend to feel that their jobs are not important and management does not respect them. They, therefore, see little point in working hard. The result is that they produce less than they could and respond negatively to what management is asking them to do.

Poor working environment

De-motivated staff may suffer in silence. But normally they are only too willing to voice their dissatisfaction to other staff, their family and friends and even to the customers.

This can create a negative impression of the business to those outside. It can cause loss of sales and a reluctance in people to look for jobs in the business. It can also affect other people in the business. Negative effects could include:

- other staff becoming de-motivated and working less efficiently;
- pressure put on managers who may react negatively and either blame themselves and become de-motivated or openly blame the staff and create a confrontational atmosphere in the business;
- creating a general atmosphere of negativity, where getting anything done is difficult and, in extreme cases, pointless.

Figure 2 *Motivation and the work environment*

Tackling bullying and harassment at work is the topic for the latest guide for trade unionists from the Labour Research Department (LRD). Bullying and harassment remain widespread in UK workplaces, despite improved legal protection for the victims. One-in-five workers reports being bullied in the last five years and more than one-in-ten in the last six months. Often it is linked to poor management and high workloads, and men and women are just as likely to be bullied and to be bullies.

Source: adapted from Unison, Feb 2005.

Greater absenteeism

When staff are de-motivated they do not generally think that there is very much point in going to work, except that they will be paid.

In many cases staff can take days off, claiming to be sick and still get paid for them. De-motivated staff, therefore, have relatively high levels of absenteeism. Some of these are genuine and some are not. If staff are not motivated:

- they may become depressed and need absences to cope with this;
- they may prefer to be at home and simply take days off when they feel like it;
- they may feel that any minor illness becomes a good reason for not going to work.
- staff can feel that the business is exploiting them and therefore taking days off is a justified way of getting a fair level of payment for the work done.

According to Susan Rhodes, Associate Professor emeritus of human resource management at Syracuse University, employees miss work for two reasons:

- either they can't come to work;
- they don't want to come to work.

Those who can't come to work usually have legitimate reasons such as illness, transportation problems or childcare/eldercare responsibilities. However, those who lack the motivation to come to work pose the greatest challenge.

Higher staff turnover

Many staff who are de-motivated will simply leave the business. When this happens staff turnover will rise. The level of staff turnover is often a good indication of the level of motivation in the business.

High staff turnover can also lead to additional motivation problems.

- De-motivated leavers usually make the reasons for leaving clear to other colleagues.
- Remaining staff may feel that they should also get out and feel demoralised if they cannot.
- New staff are likely to ask why people left and may pick up on the feeling of negativity.

Less innovation

Many businesses operate in highly competitive markets and finding new products, new promotions, new customer service or provisions is what makes the business stand out. In order to achieve this, however, businesses generally rely upon the inspiration and innovation that comes from their staff.

When staff are de-motivated this inventive flair is one of the first things to go. Staff reactions to a new challenge go from 'This sound interesting, let's see what I can do with it' to 'Who cares'. Firms which have poorly motivated staff often have uninspiring and out-of-date products.

The Employers Council argues that 'Suggestion boxes are making a comeback. More and more companies are taking their boxes into cyberspace - creating suggestion boxes that can be accessed with computers. Suggestion boxes can strengthen your employee's communications and retention efforts. Suggestions - the ones that don't get ignored by management - can improve employee morale and foster a sense of cooperation between employees and management and reduce the level of employee discontent.'

Figure 3 *Turnover of nursing staff*

In 2004 about 50,000 UK trained nurses left the profession. 15,000 of these retired but the rest left for a number of reasons including violence of patients, rigid working hours and dissatisfaction with the pension scheme. These reasons for leaving reflected a worrying level of de-motivation in the profession. With only 20,588 UK trained nurses entering the profession in 2004, that left a huge shortfall.

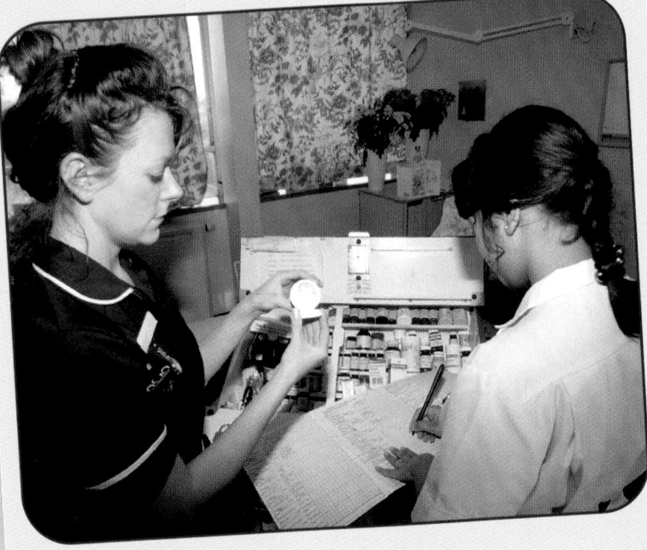

Source: adapted from RCN Reports.

Positive effects of motivation

Generally, the positive benefits of well motivated staff are that the problems listed above should not happen.

- Motivated staff will be happy to work for the objectives of the firm and production and output per employee should be high.
- The working environment will be positive and workers will support each other and want to improve performance.
- Staff will look forward to coming to work and so absenteeism will be low.
- Staff will be committed to the business, feel part of it and want to stay. Staff turnover will, therefore, be low.
- Staff who are motivated and feel valued by their businesses want to be involved with its development. They, therefore, contribute to the innovation process.

Examination practice • Sainsbury's 'us and them' bonuses

J Sainsbury's new boss was to get share options worth around £1.5m, just as staff have learned they are to lose a long running Christmas cash bonus. The firm confirmed that for the first time in 25 years, full-time staff would not be getting their festive bonus in 2004, worth around £100. Instead the supermarket chain's staff would have to make do with a 5% extension in their store discount. The decision to end the Christmas bonus would affect 100,000 full-time Sainsbury's staff.

Staff reaction

'I work for Sainsbury's and am disgusted that hard-working staff like me are to lose our Christmas bonuses.'

'I work for Sainsbury's at the moment and worked there previously for eight years. It is amazing how much staff moral has gone down in the last eight years – they simply don't care about the general staff, only the fat cats in their suits.'

Source: adapted from BBC News, 21.5. 2004.

(a) Identify TWO decisions by Sainsbury that are likely to de-motivate staff. Explain why each could de-motivate. (4 marks)

(b) Explain the likely effects that these decisions might have on general staff at the business in terms of:
(i) production;
(ii) the working environment;
(iii) absenteeism;
(iv) staff turnover.
For each of these, justify why it might have that effect. (12 marks)

(c) Examine whether these decisions might cost the business more than it will save. (9 marks)

Meeting the assessment criteria

In 2004 the Royal Mail introduced an incentive system for its workers, specifically designed to reduce the level of absenteeism. This included rewards for not taking days off for sick leave. Rewards included new cars (37 workers), £2,000 holiday vouchers (70 workers) and other £150 vouchers (90,000 workers). The Royal Mail recorded a fall in sickness absences from 6.7% to 5.7%.

Source: adapted from various sources.

(a) State TWO likely reasons, other than sickness, for absenteeism at the Royal Mail. **(2 marks)**

Exemplar responses
- *Dissatisfaction with the job/de-motivation.*
- *Staff extending their weekends.*
- *Family issues, e.g. a child is sick.*
- *Hangovers after a heavy weekend.*
- *Person experiencing stress.*

(The reasons should reflect the fact that absenteeism can be both habitual and occasional).

Mark allocation
1 mark for each reason. **(2 marks)**

(b) Explain why it may be difficult for the Royal Mail to tell the difference between sick leave and other forms of absenteeism. **(3 marks)**

Exemplar responses
- *Staff may lie about why they are absent – with sickness they will be paid, for other reasons they may not be paid – may show they are sick when they are not.*
- *Some causes of absences are difficult to categorise – feeling stressed/de-motivated may or may not be sickness – the figures may, or may not, be recorded as sickness.*

Mark allocation
1 mark for basic reason.
1 mark for how this relates to sickness or example or development of reason.
1 mark for why it is therefore difficult to tell the difference. **(3 marks)**

(c) With reference to the data about the Royal Mail, explain why the incentive system was so important for the business and why it was successful. **(5 marks)**

Exemplar responses
- *Absenteeism was very high/6.7% – this would cost the business in terms of lost production/sickness payment – incentives offered looked very generous/new car – rewards only offered if no sick days were taken off – staff saw incentives as sufficient to actually go to work every day.*

Mark allocation
1 mark for why it was needed (maximum 2 marks).
1 mark for example of an incentive scheme from the data.
1 mark for explaining how the incentive schemes achieved this effect (maximum 2 marks). **(5 marks)**

10 Motivation theories

Motivation theories and practice

Section 11 deals with the ways in which businesses actually motivate their staff. In many cases the businesses are putting into practice some of the best know motivational theories dealt with in this section. The theories have developed slowly over time and are continuing to develop. This section will look at the theories of:

- Taylor – Scientific Management;
- Mayo – Behavioural Management;
- McGregor – Theory X, Theory Y;
- Maslow – Hierarchy of Needs;
- Herzberg – Motivation-Hygiene Theory.

F.W. Taylor (1856 - 1915)

Fredrick Taylor believed that the main factor that motivated workers was money. He argued that providing workers with the opportunity to earn more money by producing more efficiently would be beneficial to both the workers and the business.

Taylor, working in the steel industry, noticed that many workers were producing well below what they were capable of. He noted three reasons for this.

- The belief amongst the workers that if they produced more individually some would lose their jobs.
- Pay systems that did not motivate them to work harder.
- Producing products in an inefficient way.

He then set about trying to find the most efficient way of producing products. He used a stop-watch to time each part of the production process and to check how quickly it could be done. This became known as time and motion study. When he had worked out the most efficient way to produce, he then changed the work practices at the business. This involved the following changes.

- Using specialist equipment.
- Breaking jobs down into very simple tasks.
- Devising a set procedure for workers which they had to stick to.
- Training workers in these specific jobs.
- Using piece rates to encourage people to produce more.

This approach essentially treated the workplace and the workers as though they were part of a scientific experiment which is why Taylor's approach is known as **Scientific Management**.

The main drawback of Taylor's approach was that it treated workers as just a basic factor of production with no choice as to how they would do their work. The manager was autocratic and decided exactly how the worker would work. It also ignored the fact that workers are not just motivated by pay.

An example of this scientific approach is shown in the calculation of the minimum wage for piece workers in Figure 1.

Figure 1 *Piece rate rewards*

Whilst the National Minimum Wage (NMW) ensures that all workers receive a basic rate per hour £5.05/hour from October 2005, it is more difficult to protect workers who are paid for 'rated output work' (piece rate). The law now requires that workers on piece-rate will be paid as follows.

The employer must work out how many pieces can be made by the average worker in one hour and then set the rate of pay so that the average worker will get at least 120% of the minimum wage (i.e. £6.06). Faster workers will get paid more but really slow workers could get paid well below the NMW.

Source: adapted from DTI, *Guidance on new system for 'fair' piece rates.*

Elton Mayo (1880 - 1949)

Elton Mayo's studies of how people worked started with experiments on changing physical conditions in the workplace, for example giving workers longer breaks. At the Hawthorne Works of the General Electric Company in Chicago he expanded this work to find out what effect fatigue and monotony had on job productivity and how to control them through varying rest breaks, work hours, temperature and humidity.

Part of this research involved interviewing all 10,000 employees to find out why some worked better than others even when the rest periods were reduced. What he discovered was that what really determined how well people worked was not so much their physical environment as how well motivated they were and their social interaction with other workers.

He came to certain conclusions.

- Work is a group activity.
- The need for recognition, security and a sense of belonging is more important in determining workers' motivation and productivity than the physical conditions under which they work.
- Informal groups within the workplace have a major effect on work habits and attitudes of the individual worker.

To ensure that workers work efficiently, it becomes necessary to manage the way they behave, including managing the environment so that they will be motivated and want to work. This is why his approach is referred to as **behavioural management**.

Douglas McGregor (1906 - 1964)

Taylor had put forward the theory that workers are motivated solely by money and need to be told what to do. Mayo showed that other factors affected how people work, especially the social environment and whether or not they felt valued.

Douglas McGregor essentially summed up these two theories when he described two opposing ways of managing workers. McGregor saw two extreme styles of management which he called **Theory X** and **Theory Y**. The style of management chosen depended on what the managers felt was the attitude of their workers to work. The characteristics of the two management styles are shown in Table 1.

Table 1 *Theory X and Theory Y management styles*

Theory X	Theory Y
1. The average worker dislikes work and avoids it whenever possible.	1. Workers see work as a natural activity which can be enjoyable.
2. Most people have to be persuaded, controlled, directed and even threatened with punishment to achieve goals.	2. Working conditions will affect how workers feel about their work so the right conditions need to be provided.
3. Security of environment is important.	3. Workers can be committed and this should be recognised and rewarded.
4. The average worker dislikes responsibility and needs supervision.	4. Motivated workers will seek additional responsibility and need less directing.

- Theory X Managers. They use close supervision and dictate how workers should carry out their jobs, monitoring them carefully to make sure they do the work set.
- Theory Y Managers. They will give workers more responsibility and praise and will ensure that they have a positive working environment.

Abraham Maslow (1908 - 1970)

Abraham Maslow was a psychologist who originally studied the way in which monkeys behaved and then applied these studies to an examination of how humans behaved and what motivated them. He saw a hierarchy of needs, where it was generally necessary to meet one set of needs before the next and higher set of needs could be met. Typically these needs are shown in the form of a pyramid as in Figure 2.

For employers and managers, recognising these needs and providing for them was the way to motivate workers and increase productivity and efficiency and improve the working environment. Some examples are shown in Table 2. In one way or another, Maslow's theories and approach can have an impact on all businesses.

Figure 2 *Maslow's hierarchy of needs*

Table 2 *Meeting Maslow's hierarchy of needs in business*

Need	Employer provides
Physiological The basic needs of hunger, thirst and warmth.	Pay and sometimes food and accommodation.
Security The need to be protected from danger and feel secure.	Job security and a safe and healthy working environment.
Belongingness The need to feel part of something and be accepted.	Opportunities to be part of a team, in a friendly working environment.
Esteem The need to be recognised and praised for achievements.	Opportunities to make decisions, and rewards for and acknowledgement of success.
Self-actualisation The need to find self-fulfilment and to achieve one's potential.	Challenges for employees and the freedom to carry out employees' own ideas.

Frederick Herzberg (1923 - 2000)

Maslow's studies were generally not in the workplace. Frederick Herzberg, like Taylor and Mayo, researched actual workers. He interviewed employees in a number of different jobs about what they felt about their work.

Herzberg concluded from his studies that there were two elements needed for people to succeed in their work. Motivation was vital. However, before that was possibly certain basic needs, which he called hygiene factors, had to be met. If not, motivation would be negatively affected. These are shown in Table 3.

In his interviews with employees he asked them what pleased and displeased them about their jobs. He found that what pleased people were the **motivators**, and what displeased them were negative aspects of the **hygiene factors**.

The importance for employers and managers is that, if they want their employees to be motivated, they must first of all provide an acceptable level of basic hygiene factors. Then they must provide the motivators. An example is shown in Figure 3.

Table 3 *Motivators and hygiene factors*

Hygiene factors	Motivators
• Salary • Security • Working conditions • Position in the business • Company policy • Supervision • Interpersonal relationships	• Achievement • Recognition of achievement • Interesting work • Responsibility • The chance of advancement

Figure 3 *How hygiene factors are important*

A survey carried out in small and medium sized enterprises (SMEs) found that a third of employees felt that they were unable to improve their own performance because of lack of effective training. As many as 80% wanted the training to provide them with more flexibility in terms of their jobs. They also wanted the training to involve more face-to-face contact as part of the training.

Source: adapted from Bizhel p24, April 2005.

Examination practice • new leadership style in local authorites

Traditionally local authorities are managed from the top down. In the 1990s there was an attempt to change, to a fairer and more democratic approach, where motivation of staff was considered equally important. Unfortunately, in the end, these leaders ultimately regarded themselves as the font of power and knowledge.

The Rosen Group in the USA, studying a similar situation, compared one team led by an Interactive Leader and other teams in the same organisation led by traditional leaders. It found that the only team able to be consistently successful in the long-run was the interactive team, where employees were 'customer-focused, agreed a shared purpose and consulted other employees on their ideas'. They were ecouraged to take risks, strive for the best solutions and received praise for their efforts. They out-performed all other teams in the company.

Source: adapted from Employers' Organisation for Local Government '21st Century Leadership'.

(a) Explain, giving an appropriate example from local government, what is meant by:
(i) 'managed from the top down';
(ii) 'Interactive Leader'. (4 marks)

(b) Identify which parts of the Rosen Group's study match different needs identified by Malsow. Justify your choices. (8 marks)

(c) Evaluate whether the management style in UK local authorities is closer to McGregor's Theory X or to his Theory Y. (8 marks)

Meeting the assessment criteria

When label manufacturer, MTM Products Ltd, was made Joint UK Small Employer of the Year it summed up its approach to employee/manager relations. 'We work on the basis of mutual trust between managers and employees and are now benefiting from the extra commitment and innovative ideas generated by many of our employees.'

The business also employs a work-life balance policy, ensures involvement of all staff in policy decisions and actively practices equality of opportunity. The result has been excellent staff retention, lower absenteeism, higher motivation and increased profitability.

Source: adapted from www.workingfamilies.co.uk.

(a) Identify which elements of the work at MTM Products Ltd. fit the following sections from Maslow's hierarchy of needs.
- (i) Security and safety.
- (ii) Belonging.
- (iii) Esteem.
- (iv) Self-actualisation. **(4 marks)**

Exemplar responses

(i) Practices of equality of opportunity.
(ii) Trust between managers and employers.
(iii) Involvement in all policy decisions.
(iv) Innovative ideas from employees are encouraged/work-life balance policy.

Mark allocation

1 mark for each element. **(4 marks)**

(b) Using Mayo's approach to human resource management, and information in the article, explain why there was increased profitability at MTM Products Ltd. **(7 marks)**

Exemplar responses

Basic reason
- *Increased motivation.*

Explanation with reference to Mayo
- *Group activity – staff involved in all policy decisions – helps to encourage innovation – new ideas could be profitable.*
- *Sense of belonging – mutual trust between managers and employees – employees will feel part of the business – employees will work to make it a success and increase profitability.*
- *Receive recognition – involved in policy decisions – feel their ideas are being listened to and become more committed/work harder.*

Mark allocation

1 mark for basic reason without reference to Mayo.
1 mark for Mayo approach (maximum 2 marks).
1 mark for identifying appropriate feature at MTM (maximum 2 marks).
1 mark for how this would lead to increased productivity (maximum 2 marks). **(7 marks)**

(c) As part of its overall employee policy MTM allows employees to change working hours during school holidays and it also offers, part-time and home working. Staff repay this caring approach by offering to work when additional staff are needed urgently. Explain why this approach does **not** match Fredrick Taylor's view of what motivates workers. **(6 marks)**

Exemplar responses

- *Workers primarily motivated by pay according to Taylor – but staff have other concerns such as their children – MTM caters for these other needs.*
- *Staff should be told exactly what to do according to Taylor – staff are allowed to innovate – staff involved in policy making.*
- *Decisions are made by management according to Taylor – staff negotiate some of their working condition – flexibility is offered by both sides/holiday arrangements & willing to work extra when needed urgently.*

Mark allocation

1 mark for Taylor's view (maximum 3 marks).
1 mark for why each view is not the approach in MTM (maximum 3 marks). **(6 marks)**

11 How businesses motivate

Motivation in practice

Many students reading this book have part-time jobs and for them there may be two main motivators:

- pay;
- job satisfaction.

In contrast, for businesses the two most likely reasons for their choice of the way in which they will motivate employees could be:

- which way will gain most profits for the business;
- which way will keep employees motivated and producing efficiently.

This section will be looking at the real factors that motivate staff and real incentives that businesses use. Many of these factors will show that the theorists in section 10 got it right. Other factors will show that in the real world simple explanations of why people work, e.g. pay, pressure, family commitments, are more significant.

Real motivators

Research carried out in 2004 found that what actually motivates staff to go to work is very different to what motivates them when they are at work. 1,500 staff were questioned. The results are shown in Figures 1 and 2.

This survey shows that pay is the primary drive, which is not surprising and matches the first level of Maslow's hierarchy of needs. Pay also provides security, the second level, and in many cases the level of pay also shows recognition.

Whilst at work and actually doing the job, pay is less important because that has already been sorted out, which was the main reason why the person took the job in the first place. Now Maslow's higher levels come into effect, with esteem needs being met by responsibility and recognition.

The list of what the staff felt motivated them at work also matches many of the motivators identified by Herzberg.

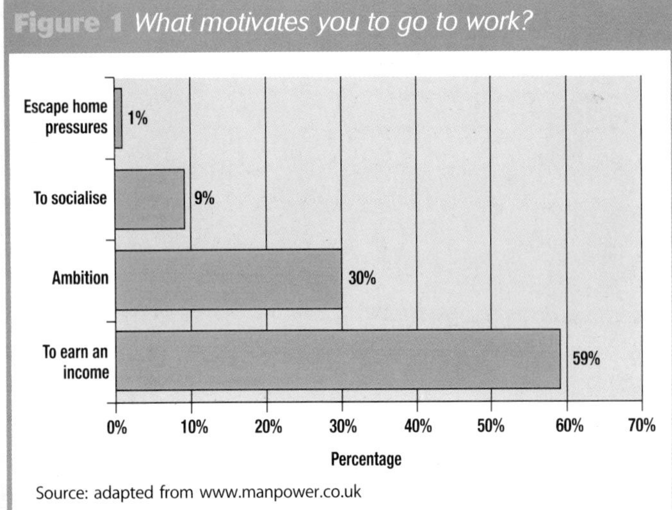

Figure 1 *What motivates you to go to work?*

Source: adapted from www.manpower.co.uk

Figure 2 *When you are at work, what motivates you?*

	Percentage
Recognition from colleagues	10%
Financial incentive	17%
Career advancement	30%
A sense of responsibility	41%

Source: adapted from www.manpower.co.uk

What motivates individuals either to go to work or in their work depends on the nature of the job and individual circumstances.

The nature of the job

Most people need to take a job so that they are paid and can afford to buy the necessities and sometimes the luxuries of life. But there are many different types of job, ranging from charity work to dealing in the financial markets in London and these frequently show that people are motivated by very different factors. Table 1 shows some general examples.

Table 1 *Examples of jobs and their motivations*

Charity work, e.g. Oxfam	The main motivation here is to help to make other people better off. In Oxfam shops some staff are even unpaid.
Vocational jobs, e.g. teaching and nursing	Here the motivation is generally the belief that the job is worth doing and that there are positive results in terms of examination grades or patients getting better is a major motivator.
Inspirational jobs, e.g. performing music.	Creating something worthwhile and being recognised for that are likely to be major motivators.
Jobs in highly competitive businesses	Here success is vital and people are likely to be motivated by succeeding, receiving recognition, gaining higher pay and achieving promotion.

Individual circumstances

In reality every individual is likely to have their own set of factors that motivate them and therefore it is difficult to pin down exactly what motivates people at work unless each person was given a lengthy individual interview.

It is, however, possible to suggest some general motivators which typically fit with people in different circumstances, as shown in Table 2.

Table 2 *General motivators*

Students	They frequently have a relatively low income and pay will be a major motivator.
People over the age of retirement	Again, they may be relatively poorly off and need the money to supplement their pensions. For the better off keeping active and being with other people is often a major motivator.
Mothers with young children	Flexible working and fitting round school hours will be important as will be, for many people, continuing to progress in a career.
People taking out mortgages for the first time	They will need a reasonable level of pay, but also job security and hopefully promotion prospects so that they can comfortably pay off their mortgage.

What businesses offer

When most businesses provide jobs they do recognise that motivating staff is vital. This is needed in order to keep staff productive and to ensure that they stay with the firm. Businesses therefore offer a range of incentives and benefits. An example is shown in Figure 3.

Figure 3 *Benefits for a Business Development Manager*

Business Development Manager
(Oxford): Kitchens
THE PACKAGE:
Basic Salary : £25-30,000
Commission/Bonus : £7,000 Commission
Company Car : Peugeot 407
Benefits : Mobile, Laptop, BUPA, Pension, Lunch Allowance

Benefits and incentives

In many cases the basic motivations are clear to the business and it provides these as a matter of course. They may include the following.

- A good rate of pay.
- Promotion prospects.
- Generous holiday provisions.
- A company pension scheme.
- On-site facilities, such as a staff canteen.

Many more specific benefits are related to the type of business involved. Examples of these are shown in Table 3.

Although these kinds of benefits do not usually make people choose to work for that business, they can help to motivate staff who are already there.

Table 3 *Motivators for particular occupations*

Banks	Cheap loans and mortgages.
Airline companies	Cheap or free flights for staff and for their immediate families.
Car salesroom	Use of demonstration models to get to and from work.
Fast food restaurants	Free meals and drinks.
Public schools	Reduced fees for children of staff.
Clothes retailers	Discounts on clothes.

Providing the right working conditions

Many businesses will provide staff with good working conditions in terms of a pleasant working environment, practical furniture, the right equipment and canteens or at least access to facilities to make hot drinks. They will also provide a safe working environment because that is a legal requirement.

Other businesses will think more about how people work and how to provide motivation. This may involve providing the following kinds of environment.

- The possibility of working in teams.
- Open access to senior management so that staff can discuss problems and ideas.
- Regular appraisal sessions.
- Flexible working arrangements.
- Planned career development.

An example is shown in Figure 4.

Figure 4 *Motivation at Lyreco UK*

Relationships throughout the company are good. When the managing director eats lunch in the low-cost canteen, employees 'plonk' themselves next to him for a chat. He must be a good talker, as 82% think he is full of positive energy.

Source: adapted from www.business.timesonline.

Negative motivators

Generally motivators are thought of as being positive incentives that make staff want to work harder because they will be better off because of this. There are, however, also negative motivators which are threats rather than rewards that make staff work harder. These negative motivators may include:

- the threat of being sacked if staff do not work harder;
- insisting on unpaid overtime if jobs are not completed on schedule;
- possibly bullying.

In some cases what looks like a motivator, such as performance-related pay, may simply be a clever way of the employers getting more out of their employees with little thought about their welfare. Performance-related pay can often lead to additional pressure, stress and even illness.

These two approaches are sometimes referred to as the carrot and stick approach. The carrot motivates workers positively (an incentive or reward) and the stick motivates workers negatively (a punishment or threat).

Examination practice • Motivation at First Direct

First Direct, the telephone and Internet bank, owned by HSBC has a majority of female staff, about 70%. 53% of staff are under 35 years old and staff turnover is 12%. To support working mothers there is an on-site crèche and facilities for children of school age during the holidays. Staff are also offered flexible shift patterns, overtime if additional money is needed and at least 25 days holiday a year.

HSBC has decided that the 4,000 call centre jobs will be transferred to India, China and Malaysia by the end of 2006 and this has greatly reduced the confidence staff have in their senior management.

Source: adapted from *The Sunday Times,* 100 Best Companies to Work For.

(a) Considering the type of staff that work for First Direct, assess how appropriate the support is that the business provides. (6 marks)

(b) By the end of 2006 all call centre jobs will be transferred abroad.
(i) Explain how this is likely to affect motivation during 2006. (4 marks)
(ii) Explain what measures First Direct could introduce to ensure that during 2006 motivation in the business is kept at a high level. (6 marks)

Meeting the assessment criteria

Pinnacle has a strong team spirit. 81% of staff say they have a laugh with colleagues and 83% believe they make a valuable contribution to the company's success. A 'take it to the top' initiative allows staff direct access to the chief executive at pre-advertised monthly visits. They can raise any issue they like and 82% describe him as 'full of positive energy'.

Staff are given the choice of a wide variety of working options, including job sharing, part-time working, flexible working hours, occasional and permanent home working and team-based self-rostering. Holidays are set at 25 days for everyone, but staff can sell or buy five days. Life insurance is offered at four times salary and employer contributions to the pension scheme are 7% for staff and 10% for directors, with an employee contribution of 2.5%.

The company offers performance-related pay. Other awards include employee of the month and best suggestion of the year where the employee is rewarded with a week's holiday in the executive chairman's villa in Italy.

Source: adapted from The *Sunday Times,* 100 Best Companies to Work For.

For each of the following benefits for staff explain why they would motivate staff and outline ONE problem that providing staff with that benefit might create for the business.

(i) A 'take it to the top' initiative.
(ii) Team-based self-rostering.
(iii) Life insurance at four times salary.
(iv) Employee of the month awards. **(12 marks)**

Exemplar responses

- *Allows staff to approach senior management on a regular basis – staff will feel their views are valued by senior management – may tie up valuable time for senior managers.*
- *Teams can choose between themselves when they will work – allows staff more flexibility – may not match when management wants staff to be working.*
- *Life insurance cover provided at four times current salary – will give staff a sense of security for their family – premiums will have to be paid by business.*
- *One employee will be selected each month as the best employee – will satisfy the esteem need/achievement will be recognised – staff who never get the award may feel de-motivated and work less.*

Mark allocation

1 mark for showing understanding of the benefit.
1 mark for why it would motivate.
1 mark for why it would cause a problem for the business.

(1 + 1 + 1) x 4
(12 marks)

12 Legislation and employees' well-being and motivation

Protecting employees

Section 8 explained that businesses have legal and ethical considerations to take into account when recruiting and selecting employees. These affect the equality of treatment of employees. Once staff have been employed, businesses then need to ensure that staff are happy in work and well motivated. Well motivated employees are likely to work hard for the business and help towards its success.

Contracts of employment

When employees are first appointed to a post they are given a contract of employment. This is either a verbal or written agreement by the organisation to employ the worker.

Figure 1 *Written statement of terms and conditions of a CNC machine operator*

You
Darren Hayles
began employment with
Peabody Engineering
on
1 April 2005
Your previous employment with
Jones Ltd
does count as part of your period of continuous employment which therefore began on
25 August 2002
You are employed as
A machine operator responsible for operating CNC machinery
Your place of work is
Peabody Engineering, Unit 135 Ainscough Trading Estate, Newcastle
And the address of your employer is
As above
Your pay will be
£18,000 annually
You will be paid
On 24th of each month for work in the previous month
Your hours of work are
9am – 5pm each day
Your holiday entitlement is
25 days plus statutory holidays
Particulars of any terms and conditions relating to incapacity to work due to sickness or injury, including any provision for sick pay, can be found in
The company handbook
Particulars of terms and conditions relating to pensions and pension schemes, can be found in
The company handbook
Particulars of the amount of notice of termination of your employment you are entitled to receive and are required to give are given in
The company handbook
Your employment is permanent - subject to above and to general rights of termination under the law
You are not expected to work outside the UK (for more than one month)
The disciplinary rules which apply to you can be found in
The company handbook
If you are dissatisfied with any disciplinary (or, from 1 October 2004, dismissal) decision which affects you, you should apply in the first instance to
Your line manager, Mrs J Sheering

Source: adapted from www.dti.gov.uk.

- The **Employment Rights Act, 1996** states that employers must then provide a written statement of employment within two months, stating the terms and conditions of employment. An example of a written statement is shown in Figure 1.
- The **Wages Act, 1986** sets out conditions for payments to workers and any deductions, such as National Insurance contributions, income tax or pension or trade union membership payments.

The terms and conditions of employees shown in their contract of employment will affect their well-being and motivation. There is a variety of legislation in the UK and the EU that exists to protect employees in a number of areas. Employees are given certain rights at work by these laws. Areas where they may be affected are shown in Figure 2.

Time spent working

The amount of time that employees spend at work is influenced by legislation. Workers must be protected from working for too long, so maximum amounts of continuous time that employees can be made to work are often set out in legislation. This could be:

- the number of hours worked at one time;
- the number of hours worked in a week;
- the number of days worked in a year.

The **Working Time Regulations, 1998** limit the maximum amount of continuous time that employees can be made to work in a week to 48 hours. There are some exceptions, however. These include executives and junior doctors. Employees must also be given a 20 minute rest break after every 6 hours worked. Workers who work at night may be particularly affected. Their work time is limited to 8 hours in any 24 hour period.

Figure 2 *Legislation protecting the well-being of employees*

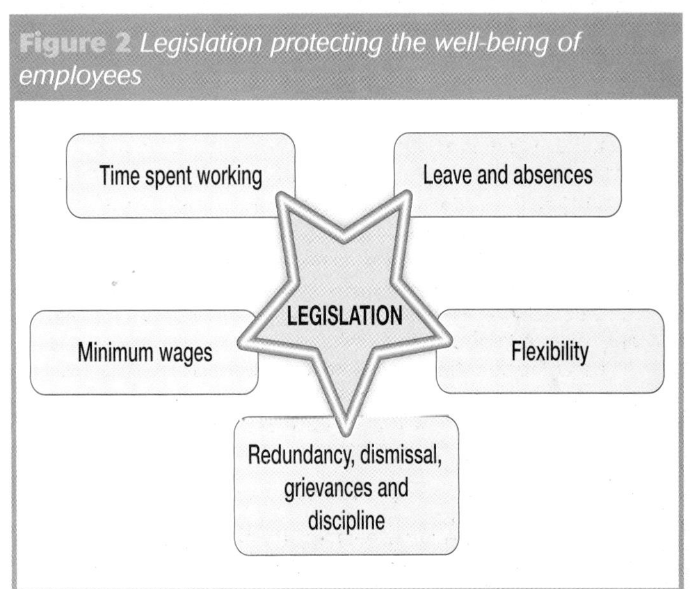

Figure 3 *Problems in working too long*

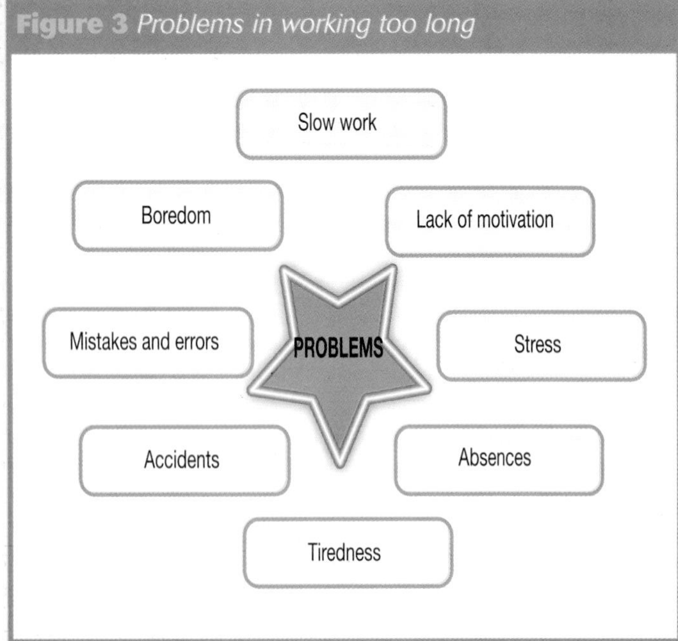

If employees work too long they may experience certain problems, as shown in Figure 3. This can be a problem for both employees and businesses.

Employees Employees who work too long may become tired, bored and stressed. This may result in slow work or errors. Workers may have accidents or be off work with stress, losing earnings.

Businesses Errors and slow work can be costly for the business. Output may fall, errors may be costly to replace and their reputation may be affected.

Leave

Employees are entitled by law to regular leave. This is often in the form of a number of days each year. The **Working Time Regulations, 1998** state that employees are entitled to 4 weeks' annual paid leave a year. They are also entitled to statutory holidays as well, such as Christmas Day, Boxing Day and bank holidays. Employees who work too long are likely to face the problems in Figure 3.

Employees are also entitled to leave to have children. The **Employment Act, 2002** states that employers must give:

- maternity leave to mothers having children;
- paternity leave to fathers whose partners or wives are having children.

The Act states that parents and adoptive parents are entitled to a period of leave when children are born and sets rates of pay. Mothers are also given the right to return to work as long as this is within one year.

Minimum wages

The **Minimum Wage Act, 1998** states that employees must be guaranteed a minimum wage. This is the minimum amount that they must be paid each hour. It is unlawful for businesses to pay employees less than the minimum wage. Table 1 shows how the rate has changed over a number of years.

It is argued that employees will benefit from a minimum wage because:

- they will be guaranteed a minimum level of payment which could prevent poverty and perhaps sickness and absences;
- they will be more motivated knowing that they are earning a fair wage;
- it helps to reduce wage differences by erasing the pay of lower paid workers;
- it may encourage people to take jobs that they might not have otherwise taken due to low pay.

Minimum wages do increase the costs of businesses. But a better paid and more motivated workforce could be more productive for the business and offset these costs.

Table 1 *Changes in the minimum wage rate, per hour*

	2000	01	02	03	04	05*	06*
18-22 year olds	3.20	3.50	3.60	3.80	4.10	4.25	4.45
22 year olds +	3.70	4.10	4.20	4.50	4.85	5.05	5.35

* Future rates in April 2005.
Source: adapted from www.dti.gov.uk.

Flexibility

Employees may have a number of opportunities to work flexibly. Certain legislation protects employees in this area.

- People job share. This is usually where two employees do one job. One employee might do the job in the morning and the other in the afternoon. An example could be a rail tickets sales person, where one person sells tickets in the morning and the other in the afternoon.

Figure 4 *Minimum wage rates*

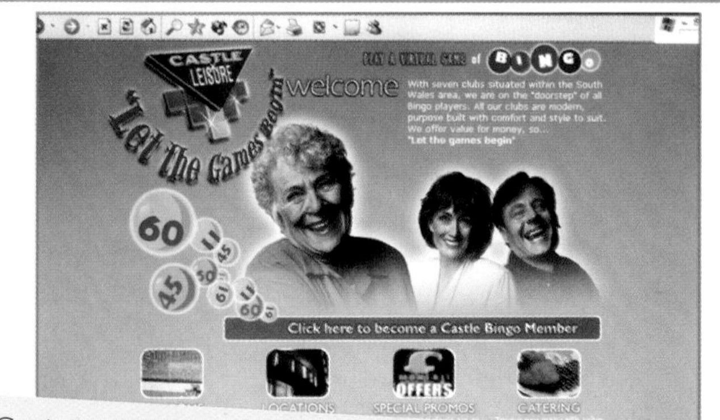

Castle Leisure, the Bingo Hall operator, aims to maintain a 25 to 30 pence differential between its rates and the national minimum wage. In 2004 its lowest starting rate was £4.75 an hour rising to £5.25 an hour.

In 2004 HSBC amalgamated its lowest clerical grades, increasing the minimum rate by 22% from £10,000 a year to £12,500.

Source: adapted from www.unison.org.uk and Low Pay Commission.

- Shift work. In some businesses, such as car manufacturing, employees work different shifts. There might be three shifts (early morning start, afternoon start, night shift).
- Annualised hours. This is where an employee's contract states they will work a certain number of hours a year. But they may be able to vary the number of hours they work each day, week or month.
- Part time work. This is where employees only work part of the day or week. The **Part-Time Workers (Prevention of Less Favourable Treatment) Regulations, 2000** and the **Employment Relations Act, 1999** prevent part-time workers from being treated less favourably than full-time employees over pay, conditions, leave, pensions and holidays.
- Flexible hours. The **Employment Act, 2002** gives certain employees, such as parents with children under 6 or disabled children under 18, the right to request flexibility in their terms of employment, such as working flexible hours. This must be granted by employers unless there are valid business reasons.

Employees and businesses may benefit from working flexibly. Example are shown in Table 2.

Table 2 *Effects of flexibility*

Employees	Employers
Better work/home life balance	Motivated employees
Work when they want	Work takes place at times that suit conditions
Can change work to suit conditions	May reduce costs
Reduced stress	Less stress and absences

Redundancy, dismissal, grievances and discipline

Laws exist to protect employees in the areas of redundancy, dismissal, grievances and discipline.

Redundancy Employees can be 'made redundant' by a business. But a business cannot simply tell a person that they no longer 'have a job'. Employees have certain rights under the **Employment Rights Act, 1996**.

- Redundancy can only take place if there is no job or insufficient work. Employees can not be made redundant one day and another person employed to do the same job the next.
- Employees who have worked for a certain period are entitled to redundancy or severance pay.
- A period of notice must be given by the business.

Table 3 *Legal and unfair dismissal – possible examples*

Legal dismissal

- Incapable of doing the job.
- Unqualified for the job.
- Deliberately providing false information during the selection procedure.
- Serious misconduct such as theft.

Unlawful dismissal

- Joining a trade union.
- Pregnancy, although able to do the job.
- Following incorrect procedures.
- Breaking legislation regarding gender, race or age. This is dealt with in section 8.

Grievances Employees sometimes have complaints or grievances at work. If these are not dealt with the employee may become demotivated, take days off or look for another job. Examples of grievances might be:

- being overlooked for promotion when qualified and the best candidate;
- being singled out for unfair criticism;
- being continually selected for difficult tasks or those which are not part of the job.

The **Employment Act, 2002** introduced minimum grievance procedures that businesses must have.

Dismissal Employees can not just simply be 'dismissed' and told that they have no job. Legislation protects the right of employees in this area. The **Employment Act, 2002** sets out conditions in which employees may be dismissed. Employees must have worked for one year to qualify. Dismissal may be legal or it may be unfair dismissal. Examples are given in Table 3. Before dismissal takes place, employees must be given verbal and written warnings. Employees who feel that they have been unfairly dismissed can take their case to an employment tribunal. It has the power to reinstate employees and pay compensation.

Discipline Employees must comply with the terms and conditions of their contract. If they break these they may be liable for disciplinary procedures. The **Employment Rights Act, 1996** sets out the conditions and rules of these procedures. Employees must be:

- informed of these procedures;
- the consequences of breaking them;
- investigations of complaints;
- rights of appeal.

Examination practice • Whitbread plc

Whitbread PLC is a leading UK hospitality company. It manages a number of hotels, restaurants and health and fitness clubs. These include:

- Premier Travel Inn;
- Brewers Fayre;
- Beefeater;
- Costa;
- T.G.I. Friday's;
- David Lloyd Leisure.

It also has a strategic investment in Pizza Hut (UK).

Whitbread has around 67,000 employees. The leisure industry accounts for one in every ten jobs. It will account for one in every five new jobs created. So recruitment is a big issue. In order to attract and retain the best staff Whitbread's commitment to caring for and developing its people is one of the company's most important concerns.

Whitbread recognises that commitment to its employees also has a direct impact on the business. In short, content and satisfied people equate to satisfied customers, which equals happy shareholders. Whitbread treats its people according to three basic principles.

- It cares for them.
- It makes clear what is required from them.
- It treats people as individuals.

There are, of course, a number of things that Whitbread has to do for its people. Most of them legal requirements, such as the Minimum Wage and the Working Time Directive. David Lloyd Leisure, for example has a commitment to pay more than the minimum wage.

Source: adapted from www.whitbread.co.uk and www.unison.org.uk.

(a) State FOUR pieces of information that should be contained in the contract of employment of an employee at Whitbread. (4 marks)

(b) Examine THREE ways in which employees at the business might be affected by its approach. (6 marks)

(c) Considering the service offered by the business, identify THREE pieces of legislation that would particularly affect it in terms of its employees. Explain why the legislation is so important. (9 marks)

Meeting the assessment criteria

Connahs Quay Antiques is a business that restores and then re-sells old prices of ceramics and furniture. It scours the markets around the UK or attic clearances looking for unusual pieces that may be a little damaged but sell for a cheap price. The business has three shops in the North Wales area. Repairs are carried out at its repair centre in Flint. It employs three specialist repair workers. The oldest is aged 40 and has spent many years working in the trade. The other two are 21 and 18, with little experience, but are important to help share the workload. One works part-time. The other has a child under 6.

In the summer of 2005 the business bought a number of 'job lots' from attic sales. This has meant working hard in a very short period to repair the pieces. The business has spent a lot of money buying these 'lots' and needs to sell the products as quickly as possible. It was concerned about the impact of holidays that the two younger employees might take, although it wanted to be flexible. Working long hours also meant that the two younger repair workers did not always have enough time when they needed it. They asked whether they could work less at other times or they may consider looking for other jobs.

Source: adapted from company information.

(a) From the data identify THREE pieces of legislation that might affect the business and say why the legislation would apply. **(6 marks)**

Exemplar responses

- *Minimum Wage Act, 1998 - states the minimum wages to be paid to different age groups.*
- *Working Time Regulations, 1998 - state the number of hours in a week and rest breaks that must be taken.*
- *Employment Relations Act, 1999 - prevents part-time workers from being treated less favourably than full-time employees.*
- *Employment Act, 2002 - gives employees the right to request flexible working time in the case of children under 6.*

Mark allocation

1 mark for Act.
1 mark for why.

(1 + 1) x 3
(6 marks)

(b) State and explain THREE benefits for Connahs Quay Antiques in having staff that are motivated. **(6 marks)**

Exemplar responses

- *Share the workload - the senior repair worker can not do all the work.*
- *Staff turnover - may leave the business and take skills elsewhere, perhaps to competitors.*
- *Cash flow reasons - the business must make the repairs quickly and sell products to recover expenditure.*
- *Prevent errors - can be costly and time consuming to put right.*

Mark allocation

1 mark for benefit.
1 mark for applied explanation.

(1 + 1) x 3
(6 marks)

13 Environmental issues

What are environmental issues?

The environment is the surroundings in which people live and in which businesses operate. As businesses manufacture goods or provide services they make use of the environment. Consider the manufacture of a piece of furniture as shown in Figure 1. It will move through a number of stages in production. At each stage the environment is likely to be affected by the activities of businesses involved in the production process.

Figure 1 *The production process for a piece of furniture*

Stages	Issues
Grow the trees ↓	*What damage will be done to the woodland?*
Cut down the trees ↓	*Will they be replaced?*
Transport the trees to a factory ↓	*How much fuel will be used? What exhaust fumes will there be?*
Cut the wood ↓	*What will happen to waste?*
Use other processes to make the furniture ↓	*How many other resources will be used? Will the factory be an eyesore? Will fumes emit from the factory? What noise will there be?*
Transport the product to the retailer ↓	*Will traffic congestion be caused?*
Sell the product	*Will out of town retailers be located on greenfield sites?*

The example in Figure 1 helps to illustrate some of the major environmental issues facing businesses. When businesses make goods or provide services they:

- use up resources;
- create waste;
- create pollution;
- affect the surrounding area in which they operate;
- create other problems such as warming of the atmosphere;
- create transport difficulties and congestion.

Society is becoming increasingly concerned with the impact of businesses on the environment. These environmental issues will affect businesses and their employees in different ways.

In some cases government legislation exists which constrains business activities. Some pressure groups, as explained in section 14, are set up to promote the protection of the environment. In some cases businesses self-regulate their own activities as a result of their own business aims and environmental policies. Figure 2 shows some of the main environmental issues facing businesses.

Figure 2 *Environmental issues*

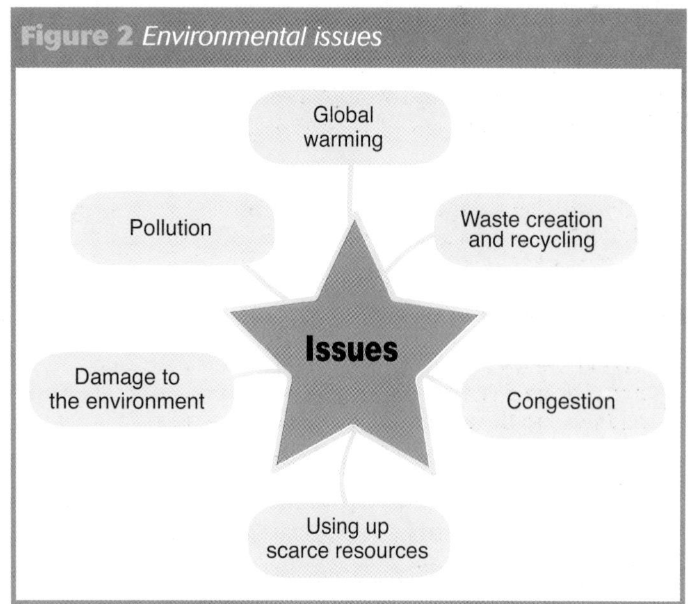

Pollution

Pollution issues are about the contamination of the world's resources. Businesses may cause pollution by their activities in a number of ways.

Air pollution This is where business activities cause gases to be emitted into the atmosphere from machines, factories and vehicles. Examples of air pollution may be:

- a foundry producing smoke which is released into the air;
- the release of carbon dioxide into the air from the exhausts of lorries delivering materials;
- the release of nuclear energy due to safety failure in nuclear plants.

Water pollution This is the pollution of rivers, lakes and the sea as a result of business activity. Examples might be:

- pesticides used in agriculture passed into rivers or lakes;
- dumping of waste by factories near rivers, such as breweries;
- oil from cargo ships leaking into the sea, polluting water and fish and also damaging wildlife and the coast.

Noise pollution This is the creation of excessive noise levels in business activity which disturb society. Examples include:

- bars staying open late into the night with noisy customers;
- noise created by vehicles;
- noise from outside machinery used in road repair or building;
- late night flights.

A variety of pressure groups exist which attempt to put pressure on businesses to control pollution or on government to pass laws to limit or cut pollution levels. Examples in the UK include Friends of the Earth UK, Greenpeace UK and the National Society for Clean Air (NSCA).

Legislation to limit pollution in the UK includes:

- the **Environment Act, 1995** set up The Environment Agency to monitor pollution and set in place regulations on pollution issues such as air quality;
- EU **Air Quality Limit Regulations, 2003** set targets for EU countries to reduce ozone in the air.

Businesses that break legislation regarding pollution may be forced to pay compensation to those affected.

Some examples of how different businesses and their employees might react to limit or cut pollution are shown in Table 1.

Table 1 *How businesses and employees might be affected by pollution control*

Business	Supermarkets
Pollution	Air
Activity	Ensure refrigerators are checked and replaced with non-CFC units
Business	Delivery business
Pollution	Air
Activity	Change vehicles regularly, use diesel or lead free petrol
Business	Clubs
Pollution	Noise
Activity	Site away from residential areas
Business	Farming
Pollution	Water
Activity	Use natural pesticides
Business	Chemical factory
Pollution	Air
Activity	Use more efficient production methods, replace and maintain machines regularly.

Waste creation and recycling

Businesses create waste in the manufacture of goods and the provision of services. Waste is what is left over which is not required for production or not required by consumers who use the end product. Examples might include:

- waste metal left over when making car body parts;
- waste created in services such as hairdressing;
- equipment such as oil rigs or CNC machinery which are no longer able to be used in production because they are worn out;
- packaging which is only needed to support or protect products, such as toy packaging or pizza delivery boxes.

Legislation exists in the UK to control the illegal dumping of waste. The **Environment Act, 1995**, for example, has regulations controlling the amount of waste businesses create. Businesses breaking legislation can be forced to pay compensation. The **Landfill Tax** is a tax on dumping of waste at waste disposal sites. The charge is designed to encourage businesses to reduce the waste they create. Pressure groups such as Waste Watch attempt to influence businesses to cut waste.

The recycling of waste is becoming increasingly popular by businesses. They may be able to reuse waste materials to create other products, which may cut cost or increase sales.

Some businesses have set up especially to make products from recycled materials. Some examples of products that may be created by recycling are shown in Figure 3. Other examples of how different businesses might react to reduce waste or make use of it are shown in Table 2.

Figure 3 *Products made from recycled materials*

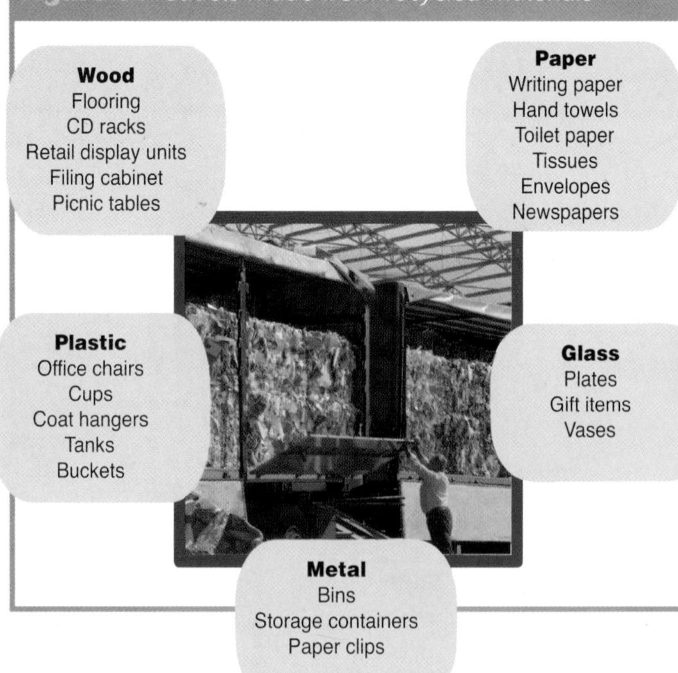

Table 2 *Methods to control waste*

Re-use e.g. toner cartridges for printers after being refilled.

Change production methods e.g. use more accurate measuring techniques and selection methods to reduce waste for example in food production.

Change designs and materials e.g. make smaller products which do the same job but do not require as many materials.

Disposable or reusable packaging e.g. reusable heated pizza bags.

Implications for businesses providing recycling services may include:

- training for employees;
- finding suitable supplies and suppliers;
- using suitable production techniques;
- finding appropriate customers who want to buy recycle products.

Implications for businesses wanting to recycle more may include:

- changing production methods;
- changing work practices, eg regular collections of materials to recycle, providing recycling collections or bins;
- buying materials that can be recycled for office use.

Global warming and the ozone layer

Global warming is a major environmental issue facing society. It is argued that the emission of 'greenhouse gases' into the atmosphere are causing a 'greenhouse effect' where the planet's atmosphere is warming up. The result could be the melting of polar ice caps and drastic changes in climate conditions.

A further problem is that the ozone layer around the earth which filters harmful radiation passing into the atmosphere and prevents it affecting us is being depleted by CFCs and other ozone depleting substances (ODS). This 'hole' in the ozone layer could result in harmful sun's rays passing unfiltered to the earth.

Many countries meet to agree targets to limit pollution which cause these effects. For example, the Kyoto Protocol limits greenhouse gas emissions by various countries, although not all countries sign up to the agreements. The Montreal Protocol limits ODS.

Steps that businesses and their employees may take to limit these effects by controlling the emission of gases into the atmosphere include using:

- efficient machinery which limits emissions;
- switching to pollution limiting production techniques;
- using smaller cars or train travel;
- changing product designs to reduce emissions.

Damage to the countryside

Business activity can cause damage to the surrounding area. Examples might be:

- open cast mining which often scars the land and leaves waste areas after mining ends;
- new factories or offices which can often not 'fit in' with the look of the landscape or the area in which they are built;
- road building to new premises which reduces green areas and the countryside ;
- airports which take up large areas of land and surrounding areas for access.

Businesses that take into account their effects on the landscape may consider a number of methods to limit any damage. They may fill in waste areas which are no longer required. They may ensure that designs are complementary to the surrounding buildings. They may also redesign landscapes so that they are aesthetically pleasing perhaps by adding grass or park areas.

Using scarce resources

Society is increasingly aware of the speed with which resources are being used up in production. Fuel sources such as coal and oil are becoming harder to find. Materials used in production leave fewer resources in the ground. Future generations may suffer as a result.

Businesses can follow a number of strategies to take these into account.

- Make use of alternative power sources, such as solar, wind power or hydro-electric to generate electricity.
- Find ways of conserving fuel, such as better insulation.
- Make use of renewable resources. For example, timber businesses may plant two new trees for every one cut down.
- Redesign products so that fewer resources are used.

Congestion

Road and traffic congestion is an issue facing society, particularly in a relatively small country such as the UK which has limited land space. Traffic congestion might be caused in a number of ways. Businesses might consider alternatives to solve these problems as shown in Table 3.

In the UK government has also introduced various schemes to reduce traffic on roads and in city centre areas. These include congestion charges for cars using inner London and Durham.

Effects on employees

Dealing with environmental issues can affect employees within a business in many ways. This will include managers making decisions and the job roles and operations of other employees.

Pollution Businesses concerned with pollution may:

- introduce no-smoking policies or have smoking areas and staff who want to smoke will have to take this into account in their work breaks;
- encourage high levels of testing of machinery by maintenance staff to prevent fumes;
- encourage staff to turn off mobile phones to stop noise pollution;
- ensure staff wear protective clothing;

Table 3 *Congestion*

Causes	Possible reactions by business
Lorries delivering materials or components to factories.	Use rail if possible. Deliver early in the morning or late at night or at weekends.
Vans delivering supplies to supermarkets.	Deliver early in the morning or late at night or at weekends. Deliver more stock but less often.
Sales representatives using cars to visit city centres.	Use email or conference calling for meetings if possible. Send samples by post.

- encourage managers to carry out regular audits to check waste disposal into water and the use of landfill sites.

Waste resources Businesses concerned with wasting resources may:

- introduce recycling policies where office staff are asked to save waste paper and place it in recycling bins;
- encourage managers to buy supplies from fuel-efficient suppliers or those which replace resources;
- train workers in recycling techniques;
- have targets for managers and employees to meet for recycling or reducing waste, with penalties or incentives if they are or are not met;
- ask staff to turn all power and lights off when not in use.

Congestion Businesses concerned about the impact on the environment of cars may:

- encourage train travel by their sales teams;
- have limited parking spaces;
- encourage shared rides to work with incentives.

Examination practice • EU pollution

In October 2004 The European Commission warned that a number of British businesses could face penalties for discharges into air and water. The European Pollutant Emission Register, based on data from members, highlighted pollution in EU countries. GlaxoSmithKline, for instance, was said to be responsible for 64.6% of the dichloromethane discharged directly into water in the EU via operations in Middlesex. The British arm of Huntsman Petrochemicals, the US group, was said to account for 19% of the benzene, toluene, ethylbenzene and xylenes pumped into water. BP Chemicals was said to be responsible for a further 11.6%.

American-owned Solutia in Newport and Runcorn was said to account for 29.2% of phenols discharged into water. Magnesium Elektron, based in Swinton was said to account for half the sulphurhexafluoride discharged into the air, while Ineos Chlor, the chemicals company in Runcorn was said to account for 23% of dichlorethane discharged into the atmosphere.

An EU spokesperson warned that firms could fall foul of a 1996 EU directive. 'They might want to evaluate their potential for improving their environmental performance' she said.

Source: adapted from *The Guardian*, 9.10.2004.

(a) Identify and explain TWO environmental issues facing the businesses in the article. (4 marks)

(b) Examine TWO reasons why the businesses may face problems as a result of these environmental issues. (4 marks)

(c) Explain THREE ways in which managers at the businesses should react to deal with these issues. (6 marks)

Meeting the assessment criteria

The CK Group of companies are one of the fastest growing plastic recycling and waste management companies in the UK today. The business can call upon over 30 years of experience in plastic recycling, polymer compounding, film blowing, plastic trading, paper processing and waste management.

- CK Polymers plastics division buy and sell plastic waste, reground, recycled compounds and off-spec polymers. We also provide a range of plastic recycling and waste management services.
- The paper processing division SGS Paper Ltd are specialist converters and slitters of high quality (photographic grade) paper for a range of applications.
- CK Waste Solutions Ltd offer a fully outsourced recycling and waste management solution saving you time and money by giving you a single point of contact.

Source: adapted from www.ckpolymers.co.uk.

(a) Explain why this business is likely to take into account environmental issues. **(2 marks)**

Exemplar responses

- *It is recycling materials – it is taking into account that materials can be recycled into different forms and reused rather than disposing of them and creating waste and wasting resources.*
- *Has been in the business for 30 years – earns its income from recycling and waste.*

Mark allocation

1 mark for identifying recycling/waste management.
1 mark for why it is doing this. **(2 marks)**

(b) Identify and explain THREE ways in which the business's approach to the environment might affect its employees. **(6 marks)**

Exemplar responses

- *Training – employees will need to be trained on how to use recycling equipment and other processes involved in recycling.*
- *Finding suitable resources for recycling – staff will need to identify businesses that can provide materials/pick ups may be necessary.*
- *Need to wear protective clothing – materials may contain harmful chemicals.*

Mark allocation

1 mark for way.
1 mark for explaining the effect on employees. **(1 + 1) x 3**
(6 marks)

(c) Identify TWO possible environmental issues that this business may create as it carries out its work and explain how it can effectively minimise any problems caused. **(6 marks)**

Exemplar responses

- *Air pollution as it processes waste – maintain machinery, replace worn out machinery – less likelihood of escaping fumes, etc.*
- *Pick up at slower times of day for traffic – don't make lots of journeys / effective loads of waste – will not have lorries on the road at times of heavy traffic use / less journeys will mean less congestion.*

Mark allocation

1 mark for identifying issue.
1 mark for appropriate method of minimising issue.
1 mark for why this method will be effective.

(1 + 1 + 1) x 2
(6 marks)

14 Social and ethical issues

Social responsibilities and ethics

Businesses do not operate in isolation. They are affected by the societies in which they work and sell products. Their decisions can affect people in society and the decisions of people can affect them.

It is often argued that businesses have social responsibilities. Businesses obviously have to make a profit for their owners or they would go out of business. But they also need to take into account wider issues which society feels are important.

Ethics is about the 'right' or 'wrong' of any decision. Businesses often have to take into account what is morally or ethically right or wrong when making decisions. Some of these decisions are dictated by law, in which case the government has decided what is right or wrong and the law states what a business can or cannot do their own. In many other situations businesses have to make ethical decisions.

This section examines how taking into account the needs of society and making ethical decisions affect a business and the decisions of its managers and employees.

Business ethics

Ethics are about doing, morally, the right or wrong thing. Business ethics are therefore about making moral decisions in manufacturing and selling goods and providing services. There is likely to be some debate about ethically what is the right thing to do. People have different opinions and in some situations all people in business may not agree. Some ethical issues which affect businesses are shown in Figure 1.

Although there may be a debate about what might be the right or wrong decision, there is often a number of areas where people agree about the right thing to do. For example, most people in the UK might agree that a company should not use its employees' pension funds to stay in business or that widespread bribery should not take place to win road building contracts from government. Businesses that act ethically are often said to make these decisions. They take into account the needs of society and their social responsibility when making decisions.

Legislation can control and constrain businesses to act ethically. For example:

- the **Minimum Wage Act, 1998** ensures that employees cannot be paid lower than a certain wage per hour;
- the **Food Safety Act, 1990** makes it illegal to provide food which is unfit for human consumption;
- the **Environment Act, 1995** regulates air quality and waste.

Acting ethically might affect businesses, managers and employees in business in a number of ways. Table 1 shows how the decisions of people in a food business which has an ethical policy might be affected.

Codes of practice

Codes of practice are regulations drawn up which will affect how decisions are made by businesses. They tend to be voluntary agreements which businesses agree to conform to. The regulations will usually include factors designed to increase the social responsibilities of business and promote ethical practices.

Figure 1 *Ethical issues*

Employee rights Examples of decisions which might be questioned in this area.
- Should a business pay very low wages to cut costs?
- Should a business use its employees' pension funds for its own means?
- Should all businesses have a workplace creche?

Animal rights Examples of decisions which might be questioned in this area.
- Should animals be experimented on to produce products which may benefit society's health?
- Should businesses make real fur coats?
- Should animals be forced fed to produce certain types of food?

The nature of products Examples of decisions which might be questioned in this area.
- Should a business sell toy guns to children?
- Should a business include lots of fat or salt in products to be tasty, but which might lead to obesity or health problems?

Trading policies Examples of decisions which might be questioned in this area.
- Should a business trade with a supplier from a country which abuses human rights?
- Should a business trade with a supplier which pays very low wages to workers in low income countries?
- Should a business sell arms to a country with a history of military action?
- Should a business use any means to compete, for example stealing classified information from other businesses?
- Should a bribe be offered to win an order?

The environment Examples of decisions which might be questioned in this area.
- Should a business pollute the environment to cut costs?
- Should a business dump waste in water?

This is dealt with in section 13.

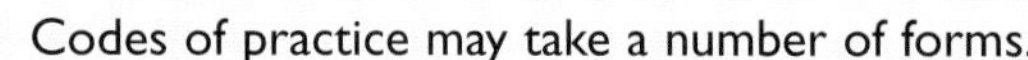

Table 1 *How ethical policies might affect a food manufacturing business and its employees*

- Employees might be more motivated to work for the business rather than another which has poorer conditions of service and benefits.
- Managers might switch suppliers if they are found to be exploiting workers by paying them low wages.
- Employees might need to undergo training on how to ensure the highest quality standards.
- Managers might face higher costs by rejecting low price ingredients which do not conform to standards.

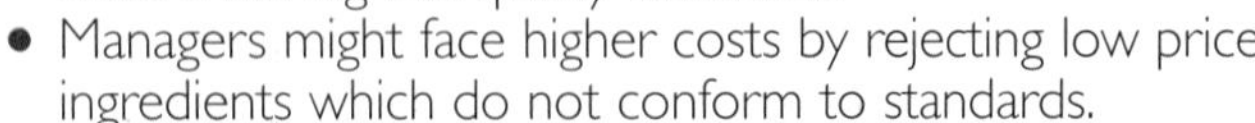

- Employees in product design departments might develop low fat alternatives to products.
- Employees must be careful when designing marketing campaigns so that customer sensibilities are not offended.
- Managers might not invest employees' pension funds in businesses which deal in arms.
- Managers and employees might face more work if customers respond positively to the image by buying more products. Profits might increase and so might rewards to employees.

Figure 2 *Ethical policies at the Co-operative Bank*

'To ensure that the bank's Ethical Policy is implemented effectively, Ethical Policy compliance systems are integrated into our everyday bank procedures. On applying for banking services with The Co-operative Bank, all business customers are required to complete an Ethical Policy questionnaire. These questionnaires are passed through to a Business Relationship Manager, and/or a member of the bank's New Business Centre, who undertakes an assessment of the proposal, against our Ethical Policy.'

'Only where no conflict with the policy is identified is a business offered banking facilities. This means that the bank will decline investment opportunities, regardless of any potential financial gain - the bottom line is ensuring that customers' expectations, as expressed through the Ethical Policy, are upheld. In line with this, in 2002, the bank declined 29% of businesses referred to its Ethical Policy Unit.'

Source: adapted from www.co-operativebank.co.uk.

Codes of practice may take a number of forms.

- They many be general codes of practice which can be tailored to individual needs. For example, the Institute of Business Ethics helps individual businesses devise codes.
- They maybe internal codes of practice produced by a business itself. Businesses such as Balfour Beatty, the buildings, rail and engineering group and Scottish Power, the provider of gas and electricity have codes of practice.
- Businesses in the industry might develop a code of practice. For example, the Association of the British Pharmaceutical Industry (ABPI) is the trade association for about a hundred companies in the UK producing prescription medicines. It produces a code of practice for all members.

Figure 3 shows how a leisure centre belonging to the Fitness Industry association might be affected by its code of practice.

Figure 3 *How FIA code of practice might affect a leisure centre*

FIA Code of Practice

Are you thinking of joining a health club or leisure centre?

Click here for the ten essential questions you should ask before joining a fitness facility!

For further information on FIA member clubs, please contact info@fia.org.uk.

- Ensure staff training takes place for work tasks, e.g. spotting hazards, supervision of spa/pool hygiene, carrying out emergency procedures.
- Ensure documents that show emergency procedures, such as a fire evacuation, are in place.
- Ensure equipment is kept in a safe condition and inspected periodically.
- Carry out risk assessment.

Source: adapted from www.fia.org.uk.

Stakeholders

Businesses have a variety of stakeholders. These are groups with an interest in the decisions and activities of a business. Taking into account the needs of different stakeholders can affect the business itself and people who work in the business in many ways.

Owners The owners of the business will be different depending on the type of business organisation. Some businesses are owned by just one person, a sole trader. Some are owned by a few people in partnership and companies are owned by shareholders. All owners of the business are likely to expect the business to make a profit, so that it can continue trading and the owners will earn an income. In order to make a profit businesses must ensure that revenue from sales is maximised and costs are minimised. It will be one of the roles of employees and managers in the business to organise the business so that this is achieved.

Employees Businesses must also take into account the needs of their employees. These may include:

- being motivated;
- feeling valued at work;
- feeling safe;
- having equal and fair opportunities;
- being well and fairly rewarded.

How businesses do this and the effects on businesses and their employees is dealt with in sections 8, 12 and 15.

Customers and consumers Customers are people or organisations who buy the products of businesses and consumers are users of the end product. They have a wide variety of needs including:

- having a choice of products;
- buying safe products;
- buying products which are highly valued or are value for money;
- not being deceived regarding the nature of the product.

Legislation in the UK protects consumers. The effects on businesses and their employees is dealt with in section 15.

Suppliers Suppliers are other businesses that provide businesses with products, components or materials. Meeting the needs of suppliers will affect different businesses in different ways. Some examples are given in Table 2.

Table 2 *Meeting suppliers' needs*

Supplier	Possible effect on business
Supplier of parts from the US.	To allow time for delivery. To make payment in dollars.
Small supplier of food ingredients.	To make prompt payment to prevent cash flow problems.
Large supplier of food products to supermarkets.	Have storage and shelf space available. Make large regular orders.

Figure 4 *Tesco computers for schools*

Tesco computers for schools is a company initiative designed to reward customer loyalty and strengthen community relationships. The programme involves an annual voucher redemption promotion to help local schools obtain free computers and other information and communication technology (ICT) equipment. During a promotional period, customers were given 1 voucher for a certain amount spent in a store. Schools could then collect these tokens and redeem them for computers and ICT related equipment from a catalogue of equipment.

Source: adapted from www.bitc.org.uk and www.computersforschools.co.uk.

Figure 5 *Pressure groups and their possible effects on businesses*

Name Action on Smoking and Health (ASH).
Aim To reduce and eliminate health problems caused by tobacco.
Possible effect on business Reduced cigarette sales and advertising, changes in packaging to include warnings.

Name Society for the Protection of Ancient Buildings.
Aim To save old buildings from decay, demolition and damage.
Possible effect on business Employment and training for traditional skills, change projects from demolition to renovation for construction businesses.

Name The Vegetarian Society.
Aim The promotion of vegetarian lifestyles.
Possible effect on business Changing ingredients for food manufacturers to non-meat alternatives.

Name Noise Abatement Society.
Aim To promote the control of noise levels.
Possible effect on business Reduce noise levels in the design of aircraft or car engines, location of 'noisy' premises such as clubs away from residential areas.

Name London Cycling Campaign.
Aim To make London a world class cycling city and promote cycling.
Possible effect on business Increased demand for cycles and cycle accessories.

Name Greenpeace.
Aim To combat threats to the world's biodiversity and environment.
Possible effect on business These are dealt with in section 13.

Government The government earns money from businesses that sell products and make profits. Businesses pay Value Added Tax (VAT) on the sale of some goods. They pay National Insurance contributions on their employees. Companies pay Corporation Tax on profits. Government spends this money on a variety of activities including defence, social services and education. To satisfy government needs employers need to have effective systems for recording, collecting and paying revenue to government.

Financiers These are organisations such as banks, which provide businesses with funds. They require businesses to make regular repayments on time and keep records of payments.

Community Section 13 explained how businesses have a social responsibility. They affect and are affected by the communities in which they operate. Businesses that take into account the needs of communities provide services such as:
- training or play schools for children;
- road building and landscaping of the environment;
- support for education or social services.

An example is shown in Figure 4.

Pressure groups

Pressure groups are groups of people with similar interests that try to influence the decisions of government and businesses. Interests that people may have vary from the protection of animal rights or the environment, to the promotion of interests that they think should be highlighted like nuclear energy, to the support of particular products, industries and occupations. They use various methods to attract attention to their causes such as:
- rallies and marches;
- advertising on posters, in magazines on the Internet or radio and television;
- gaining support from government ministers.

Some pressure groups are large and well organised and have funds to spend. Others are set up from 'one-off' causes and action, such as the diversion of a road around a village.

Examples of pressure groups in the UK and some possible effects on businesses and their employees are shown in Figure 5.

Meeting the assessment criteria

In 2005 Nike's corporate responsibility report acknowledged that the business had some of its products manufactured in foreign factories which made use of 'sweatshop labour'. The business had bowed to international pressure from a variety of sources. Previously the company had refused to disclose details of its 700+ factories. It also admitted that some factories had harassed workers and that many had been made to work overtime. Over half of the factories had working hours of over 60 hours a week. Almost one in ten workers outside the USA were below the 'Nike Standard' of 16 years of age for making equipment and 18 years of age for trainers. A number of the factories also had restricted access to toilets and water.

A spokesperson said that the company wanted to show that it realised there were problems and was trying to put them right.

Source: adapted from *The Daily Star*, 15.4.2005.

(a) Explain ONE way in which the business might not have been following its own code of conduct. **(2 marks)**

Exemplar responses
- *The Nike Standard, is to employ workers over 16 years old for making equipment and 18 years old for trainers – 10% of workers outside the USA were younger.*

Mark allocation
1 mark for code of conduct.
1 mark for explaining why it has not been followed. **(2 marks)**

(b) Identify THREE other ways in which employees at the business might have experienced problems. **(3 marks)**

Expected answers
- *Working week of over 60 hours causes tiredness and fatigue.*
- *Harassment might reduce motivation.*
- *Restrictions to water and toilets might delay production and lead to demotivation and affect productivity.*

Mark allocation
1 mark for each way. **(3 marks)**

(c) Suggest TWO ways in which the business might react and how this might affect:
(i) employees;
(ii) the business. **(6 marks)**

Exemplar responses
- *Reduce working week – more productive workers (employees), more employees – perhaps increased labour costs (business).*
- *Employ older workers – workers more suited to employment and paid higher wages (employees) – different recruitment policies (business).*
- *Improve conditions – motivation improved (employees) – increased costs (business).*
- *Reduce harassment – improve motivation (employees) – introduce rules on conduct (business).*

Mark allocation
1 mark for way it might react.
1 mark for effect on employee.
1 mark for effect on business. **(1 + 1 +1) x 2**
(6 marks)

Examination practice • Cadbury Schweppes

Cadbury Schweppes is an international confectionery and beverages company. It has a strong portfolio of brands sold in almost every country in the world. It has nearly 54,000 employees and products which fall into two main categories:

- confectionery;
- beverages;

Brands include Schweppes, Dr Pepper, Orangina, Trebor, Bournvita and Cadbury itself.

The core purpose of Cadbury Schweppes is 'working together to create brands people love'. It aims to be judged as a company that is among the very best in the business world - successful, significant and admired. The company has set five goals to achieve this. One relates to Corporate Social Responsibility. It aims to be 'admired as a great company to work for and one that is socially responsible to its communities and consumers across the globe'. This goal clearly states Cadbury Schweppes' responsibilities and recognises that what it does as a business impacts on communities and the lives of consumers.

Cadbury Schweppes takes its corporate social responsibility agenda seriously. It is a member of organisations like Business in the Community, International Business Leaders Forum and the Institute of Business Ethics. These organisations seek to improve the impact companies have on society.

A key part of the Cadbury Schweppes approach to business lies in its ethical behaviour and close relationship with its stakeholder groups. It believes that 'Respecting human rights and trading ethically is fundamental to the way we work, not just within our owned and operated businesses but also in how we interact with our wider value chain.'

The original Cadbury company was influenced by the Quaker values of the Cadbury family who started the chocolate business. They promoted justice, equality and social reform. The business argues that it continues to follow these principles today. It has always treated employees with respect and cared for their welfare. The company's site at Bournville, near Birmingham, is more than a factory with extensive amenities such as housing, sports facilities and parks all being part of the original complex.

Source: adapted from www.thetimes100.co.uk.

Figure 6 *Cadbury Schweppes stakeholders*

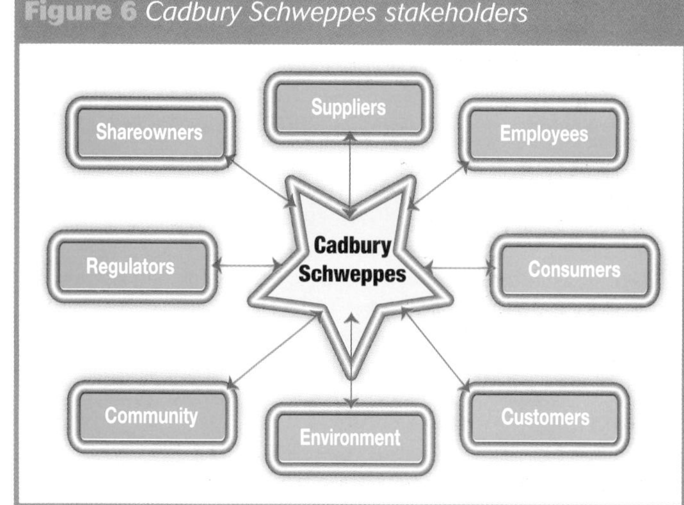

(a) Identify FIVE ways in which Cadbury Schweppes responds to the needs of its stakeholders. **(5 marks)**

(b) Identify and explain THREE ways in which the business and its employees might react to a pressure group aiming to improve the nation's health. **(6 marks)**

(c) Evaluate to what extent the business is an ethical company. **(5 marks)**

15 Legal and self regulatory constraints and issues

Constraints

Constraints on businesses are the restrictions placed on their activities. Restrictions on a business will limit how employees who work for the organisation operate.

Sections 8 and 12 explained how employees' well-being and motivation can be affected by their conditions of work and their equality of treatment. These are internal issues which affect employees and managers. This section examines external issues which limit and constrain how businesses act and affect people who work in them.

Legislation Some of these constraints are legal constraints imposed on the business. If businesses break legislation and are taken to court they can face fines under criminal law or a consumer might sue the business under civil law.

Self regulation Not all constraints are imposed. Some are self regulatory constraints. These are decisions by a business to limit its activities for its own reasons, perhaps due to the nature of the industry in which the business competes.

Competition law

Businesses are in competition with each other for the custom of people who buy goods or services. Businesses use a variety of strategies and tactics to compete with each other. Many of these are within the law. However, the government has decided that some practices must be restricted.

Legislation often takes place when government decides that one or more businesses have an extremely unfair advantage compared to others and this advantage is often gained by unfair means. Competition law will affect both employees and managers within a business.

Competition may be constrained for two reasons.

- There is a monopoly. This is where one business controls a market. In practice this is very rare today, so it usually means that a business has over 25% of a market. Monopolies are often created by mergers, the joining together of two or more businesses.
- There is collusion between businesses. This where a few businesses work together to benefit at the expense of other businesses. They often use restrictive practices to restrict trade.

Legislation can take a number of forms.

The Competition Commission (CC) This is an independent organisation that investigates mergers. The **Enterprise Act, 2002** gave the CC the power to investigate mergers and anti-competitive practices. The CC can stop mergers or anti-competitive practices.

Office of Fair Trading (OFT) The OFT:

- enforces legislation such as the **Competition Act, 1998** which prevents businesses from taking part in activities that prevent competition and businesses abusing a dominant position. It can refer businesses to the CC;
- enforces consumer legislation, for example taking action against unfair traders;
- investigates markets and may recommend stronger legislation.

The European Commission (EC) The EC can investigate anti-competitive practices in EU countries, for example the setting of prices across all EU countries.

Regulatory watchdogs These are organisations set up to constrain the activities mainly of former government owned monopolies such as water and gas as shown in Figure 1. They have the power to;

- set prices;
- help introduce competition.

Figure 2 shows how the actions of Ofwat might have affected employees and managers at a business.

Figure 1 *Regulatory bodies*

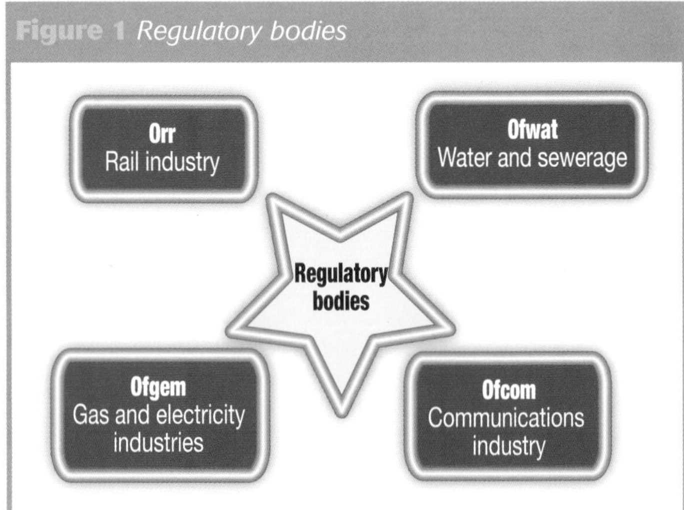

Figure 2 *Effects of Ofwat on Pennon*

In 2004 Pennon, the water and waste recycling group, said that it would not contest Ofwat's decision to cap its price increase for South West Water customers at 25% above the rate of inflation for the next five years.

It announced that about 100 jobs would have to go as part of its drive to meet the demands placed on it by the industry regulator's review.

Ofwat's price review meant that South West Water customers would pay an average of £444 a year by 2009-10 for water and sewerage, the highest in Britain.

Source: adapted from *The Guardian*, 10.12.2004.

Consumer protection

Consumers are the users of the end product. They might be a person:
- eating a tin of baked beans;
- using a washing machine at home;
- travelling by airline;
- buying insurance;
- having their hair cut.

It is sometimes argued that consumers must be protected from the activities of business. Without constraints from legislation businesses would exploit consumers to gain greatest profit. The phrase *caveat emptor*, meaning 'let the buyer beware' is often used when referring to how businesses might operate without legal constraints.

A wide variety of legislation exists to protect the consumer. Different pieces of legislation affect employees within businesses in different ways. Some of these are shown in Table 1.

Table 1 *Examples of consumer legislation and how it affects managers and employees*

Act Weights and Measures Acts 1951, 1963, 1985. **Constraint** Prevent underweight products. **Possible effects** Managers must design quantity checks and employees must constantly check quantities.
Act Trade Descriptions Act, 1968. **Constraint** Prevent misleading descriptions. **Possible effects** Employees must be careful when writing product descriptions.
Act Unsolicited Goods and Services Act, 1971 **Constraint** Prevents sale of goods which have not been ordered. **Possible effects** Managers must update consumer lists. Employees must deliver and supply to correct consumers.
Act Consumer Credit Act, 1974. **Constraint** Protects consumers buying goods on credit. **Possible effects** Employees must ensure payments are taken correctly.
Act Consumer Safety Act, 1978. **Constraint** Prevents the sale of harmful goods. **Possible effects** Ensure toys are designed with safety in mind.
Act Consumer Protection Act, 1987. **Constraint** Makes firms liable for any damage that goods might cause. **Possible effects** Ensure goods are tested widely before sale.
Act Food Safety Act, 1990. **Constraint** Ensures food is safe. **Possible effects** Managers must provide clean and safe conditions for work. Employees must prepare and cook food in a clean and safe way.
Act Financial Services and Markets Act, 2000. **Constraint** Prevents crime and protects consumers in financial markets. **Possible effects** Managers and employees must ensure consumer confidentiality.

Employment protection

Employment protection refers to legislation and self-regulation that looks after the interests of employees. Many of the laws affecting business and employees were covered in sections 8, 12 and 15, which give details of how legislation affects the motivation and well-being of employees. Legislation can affect employees in a business in a variety of ways.

Equal opportunities Equal opportunities legislation protects employees against unlawful and unfair discrimination at work in a number of areas.
- Pay. It is unlawful to pay two people different wages for doing the same job or work that is valued the same.
- Sex discrimination. It is unlawful to reject one person for a job rather than another simply because they are male or female.
- Race relations. It is unlawful to reject one person for a job rather than another simply because of their colour, race, nationality or ethnic background.
- Disability. It can be unlawful to reject one person for a job simply because they are in a wheelchair unless substantial changes are required.
- Age. After 2006 in the UK it may be unlawful to refuse to employ a person because they are over a certain age.
- Sexual preference. It can be unlawful to reject one person for a job simply because of their sexual preference.

Appointment, terms and conditions When employees are first appointed they are given a contract of employment. This states the terms and conditions under which they will work. Legislation protects these terms and conditions in a number of areas.
- Hours of work. There is a limit on the amount of time employees can work in a week and continuously work without a break.
- Leave. Employees are entitled to leave and absences for sickness with pay.
- Minimum wages. Employees of certain ages must be guaranteed a minimum wage.
- Flexibility. Employees are entitled in certain circumstances to work flexibly.

Redundancy, dismissal, grievances and discipline Legislation affects business in a variety of situations, including situations where employees:
- are made redundant and must be paid;
- are dismissed for breaking their terms and conditions;
- have a complaint against a business;
- must be given warnings regarding their behaviour.

Figure 3 *Benefits of flexible practices*

P&O Ferries

'We have 60 staff members, including officers, working part-time in the fleet who would probably have left if we had been inflexible. There is a lot of expertise to lose and we have incurred considerable costs in recruiting and retraining replacements.'

Source: adapted from www.dti.gov.uk.

Table 2 *How legislation and self-regulation can affect managers and employees in a business*

Organising work time	Managers might need to build leave into human resources plans. Employees can take time to look after family members.
Recruitment	Advertisements must be carefully worded by managers. Disabled employees can expect adjustments to help them work.
Selection	Managers must use tests that do not discriminate. Employees are given equal chances of promotion.
Costs	Managers can not simply sack staff to reduce costs. Younger employees have to be paid a minimum wage.

Self regulation also takes place in some businesses. For example, banks such as Barclays and HSBC pay more than the minimum wage. Figure 3 shows an example of flexible practices and their effects. Legislation and self-regulation can affect managers and employees in a business in a number of ways as shown in Table 2.

Health and safety

The health and safety of employees at work is protected by a wide variety of legislation. The main Act in the UK which affects businesses is the **Health and Safety at Work Act, 1974**. Under this Act, government can set regulations in place which affect how businesses operate and the activities of managers and employees.

The Act states that businesses have a duty to ensure the health and safety of staff so far as is reasonably practical. Managers and employees might be affected in a number of ways.

- There must be a written policy on health and safety on public display to all workers.
- Managers and employees must comply with this policy.
- Managers must give employees training, information and supervision on health and safety issues.
- Safety representatives must be appointed.
- Safety equipment and clothing must be provided free.

Different businesses are likely to have different risks. Some of these are shown in Figure 4. Businesses must have checklists of risks that must be prevented. It is vital that businesses assess risks regularly and take steps to prevent accidents.

The Health and Safety Executive and Health and Safety Commission are responsible for ensuring that the Act is carried out. Inspectors have the power to visit businesses and investigate. Businesses that do not comply with the law can be taken to court and fined.

Preventing accidents at work can benefit employees and managers. It can:

- improve motivation;
- reduce accidents;
- reduce absences or loss of work due to injury;
- reduce insurance claims and claims against the business;
- prevent errors.

Figure 4 *Risks and checklists in different businesses*

Construction company
Equipment is safe
Materials can be carried safely
Hard hats are worn
First aid training given
Scaffolding provided
Regular breaks
Number known for emergencies

Call centre
Regular breaks given
Correct posture training given
Not too close to screen
Screen glare prevented
Regular eye check ups
Phones and computers are safe

Trade union work

Trade unions are organisations set up to protect and promote the interests of employees who are their members. They have a variety of objectives as shown in Figure 5. If they are successful in achieving these objectives then managers in business and employees will be affected, as shown in Figure 5.

Wage negotiations Trade unions negotiate with business owners over the pay and conditions of employees. Negotiating on behalf of all workers is known as collective bargaining. If unions are successful in improving the wages and other benefits of their members, then:

- the terms and conditions of employees will improve;
- higher wages are likely to increase the costs of employees to businesses. Managers may be asked to cut costs in other ways to pay for these higher wages. They may have to find cheaper supplies, find more efficient ways to work or make some workers redundant.

Trade unions may take industrial action to strengthen their position in wage negotiations. This is dealt with later.

Figure 5 *Trade union objectives*

TU objectives
- Higher wages and other benefits, such as pensions and sickness benefits
- Guarantee safe working conditions
- Prevent the loss of jobs
- Provide services such as insurance, education and mortgages
- Other representation
- Support causes

Guaranteed safe working conditions Trade unions negotiate to improve the working conditions and safety of members. Improved safety conditions may lead to increased costs for managers as explained above. Employees who feel safe are likely to be more motivated and fewer accidents may mean less sickness leave.

Prevent the loss of jobs Trade unions often take action to prevent job losses or improve their position in wage negotiations. Action taken may involve:

- working to rule – so employees only carry out tasks in their job description;
- a go slow – where employees do their job but as slowly as possible;
- an overtime ban – a refusal to work any extra time;
- a strike – which can be all out strikes by all members for a long period, one day strikes or selective strikes in certain areas.

Owners and managers may react to strikes by:

- locking out employees;
- threatening to withdraw benefits which are not part of the contract of employment;
- threatening to make workers redundant.

Industrial action by trade unions can have a number of effects on employees and managers as shown in Table 3.

If disputes are not resolved, the Advisory, Conciliation and Arbitration Service (ACAS) may be asked to help with conciliation (help both sides find a solution) or arbitration (suggest a solution which both sides accept).

Providing services Trade unions often provide services for their members on other areas. These may include:

- providing insurance schemes or mortgages;
- setting up and running courses;
- discounts on travel;
- financial and legal advice;
- credit cards.

Support causes Trade unions support causes. These may include supporting a political party, a cause such as the campaign for nuclear disarmament or improvement in public sector transport. If successful, employees may benefit indirectly.

Working with business Trade unions are also increasingly becoming involved in business union partnerships and representing employees' views on European Works Councils.

Table 3 *Effects of industrial action*

- May improve conditions of employees if successful but raise costs for the business.
- Employees could face reduced earnings during action.
- The business' s image may be harmed, leading to loss of sales and possible job losses in future.
- Bad feeling may develop during the action, which continues afterwards and working relationships may suffer.
- It may clear the air so that each side appreciates the others' concerns.
- Managers may need to reorganise work, use temporary employees or refuse to take on work during the action.

Legislation A variety of legislation exists which controls the actions of employees and employers in industrial disputes and in other areas. Examples include:

- the **Employment Act, 1990** which made secondary picketing illegal. This is picketing outside premises by workers who are not employed at those premises.
- the **Trade Union Reform and Employment Rights Act, 1993** which states that strike action can only take place after a ballot and a majority vote for action.
- the **Employment Relations Act, 1999** which allows employees to vote for union recognition in certain cases.

Voluntary codes of practice

Some businesses have voluntary codes of practice which constrain their activities. They are regulations or conditions drawn up by businesses in a particular industry or by an organisation for business. They are not legal, but guide the activities of businesses. Examples are:

- Defra which has a Voluntary Code of Practice for the fast food industry to reduce the amount of fast food-related litter;
- the Advertising Standards Authority (ASA) which has a code of practice for advertising;
- a code of practice for commercial leases of property in England and Wales prepared by businesses in the property industry.

Examination practice • BT's services

BT allows other telecom businesses to make use of its telephone lines and other infrastructure. This is the wholesale part of BT's business. In February 2005 BT put forward proposals to re-organise its wholesale business in response to Ofcom's call for changes to increase competition for the UK's telecoms network infrastructure. The company voluntarily suggested creating a new access services division to provide clear and equal access to BT's local network for rival telecom providers.

Ofcom had warned that it could:

- deregulate the industry;
- impose regulations to create equal access;
- or force BT to split its business to offer access to other operators at a similar price to those supplied to BT's retail business (which provides telephone services to customers).

BT also aimed to cut a range of its wholesale broadband prices and pledged to introduce faster services and reaffirm its commitment to fair network access and a greater uptake of broadband.

Source: adapted from www.itweek.co.uk.

(a) Using examples from the telecom market, explain the difference between:
(i) self regulation;
(ii) regulation by Ofcom. (4 marks)

(b) Suggest TWO ways in which increasing competition might affect:
(i) BT managers;
(ii) BT employees. (4 marks)

(c) Examine TWO ways in which offering greater broadband access might affect employees at BT. (4 marks)

(d) Explain TWO ways in which the advertising of BT's broadband services might be affected by consumer legislation. (4 marks)

Meeting the assessment criteria

Dock workers in the UK were voting on industrial action in August 2004. It would be the first national strike since 1989.

Dockers, drivers and other workers at 20 ABP enterprises had rejected a 2.9 per cent pay offer and were voting on strike action. According to the company, only 300 of its 3,000 employees are covered by collective bargaining.

The Transport and General Workers' Union (T & G) was demanding a minimum wage of £7.50 an hour for all employees, a 5% rise for all rates over £7.50 and £10 an hour for drivers. It also wanted an hour off the 39-hour working week and other improvements to holidays, sick leave and parental leave. TGWU official Graham Stevenson argued 'If it takes a full national strike ballot to make progress so be it.'

Source: adapted from mua.org.au, 10.8.2004.

(a) Identify THREE objectives of the T & G. **(3 marks)**

Exemplar responses

- *Improved pay.*
- *Minimum wage.*
- *Shorter hours.*
- *Longer holidays.*
- *Sick pay.*
- *Parental leave.*

Mark allocation

1 mark for each objective. **(3 marks)**

(b) State FOUR features of a health and safety checklist for a dock worker. **(4 marks)**

Exemplar responses

- *Safe equipment in working order and maintained.*
- *Adequate training in the use of equipment.*
- *Provided with safety clothing.*
- *First aid equipment available.*
- *Safety office nominated.*
- *Adequate safety equipment and barriers.*

Mark allocation

1 mark for each answer feature. **(4 marks)**

(c) Explain TWO ways in which a strike might affect:
(i) employees;
(ii) managers;
at the business. **(4 marks)**

Exemplar responses

Employees

- *Reduced income - will not be working.*
- *Improved conditions if successful - strike is for lower hours.*
- *Conflict with employers could lead to poorer working relationships - strike is a major challenge.*

Managers

- *Many need to reorganise work - less staff available.*
- *May need to delay work - staff away, hopefully temporarily.*

Mark allocation

1 mark for each effect.
1 mark for why it comes from a strike.

(1 + 1) x 2
(4 marks)

(d) Evaluate the possible success of the strike action to benefit employees at the business. **(5 marks)**

Exemplar responses

For the action

- *Has a lot of support.*
- *Backed by a large trade union (T & G).*
- *legal if approved by a majority vote.*
- *Could gain in many areas.*

Against

- *Not a history of successful action for many years.*
- *Even if improvements agreed, few covered by collective agreement.*

Conclusion

- *Even if strike leads to some improvement in conditions and wages, not everyone will benefit.*

Mark allocation

1 mark for arguments for improvement (maximum 2 marks).
1 mark for arguments against (maximum 2 marks).
1 mark for conclusion.

(2 + 2 + 1)
(5 marks)

16 Setting up a business

Enterprise

People who set up businesses are called entreprenuers. They are the owners and without these types of people businesses would not exist in the private sector. The roles played by an entrepreneur in setting up and running a business are summarised in Figure 1.

Figure 1 *Entrepreneurial roles*

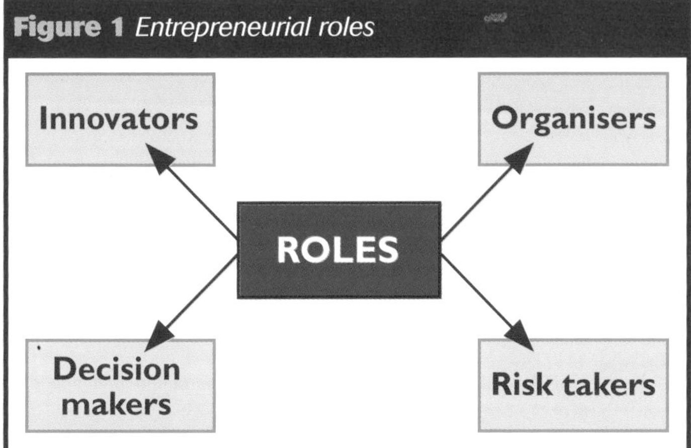

- Entrepreneurs are innovators. This means that they provide the business idea. Innovation is discussed below.
- Organising involves buying or hiring resources, such as materials, labour and equipment. These are used to make a product or provide a service. Organising also involves giving instructions, making arrangements and setting up systems.
- Entrepreneurs have to make lots of business decisions. These might relate to product design, method of production, business location, price charged, who to recruit or what wages to pay.
- Entrepreneurs take risks. They have to pay money in advance for materials, labour and other resources. Some of this money is likely to be their own and if the business fails they could lose some or all of it. But if the business does get established it may make a profit. This belongs to the entrepreneur.

Who are entrepreneurs?

Not everyone has what it takes to become an entrepreneur. A wide range of skills is required to be successful. There is no strict list of characteristics but entrepreneurs do tend to be:

- hard working;
- ambitious;
- independent;
- highly motivated;
- creative;
- prepared to take a risk.

People set up businesses for a variety of reasons. They may:

- lose their job;
- be unhappy at work;
- not like working for someone else;
- develop an interest into a business;
- think they can make a lot of money;
- have a really new and innovative business idea.

Innovation

Innovation is to do with developing an idea into a product that is commercially viable. Entrepreneurs are innovators because they try to make money out of selling goods or services based on their business idea. Where do business ideas come from?

Exploiting a skill or interest A person may be very good at golf so they could start a business giving golf lessons.

Copying or adapting an existing idea Many businesses are set up by copying what another business does. A person may open an Italian restaurant in a different part of town to other restaurants. There may be slight differences in price, service and menu choice.

Spotting a gap in the market An entrepreneur might feel that a particular customer need is not being met in the market. For example, there might be a gap in the market for an express bus service between Cardiff and Liverpool.

New inventions Occasionally a business will emerge because a new product is invented. For example, Betfair, the UK betting exchange, was set up by Andrew Black when he introduced some revolutionary new computer software. Set up in 2000, Betfair had a turnover of £50m and won the Queens Award for Enterprise in 2004.

Market research Some business ideas come from analysing market research information. It may be simple research such as a questionnaire asking football supporters what sort of new magazines they would like to see. For example, according to Figure 2, there may be demand for a magazine based on European football.

Types of ownership

There are different legal forms which a business can take.

Sole trader Most businesses start out as sole traders. This is

Figure 2 *Market research results*

200 football supporters were asked 'which of the following leagues need more magazine coverage?'

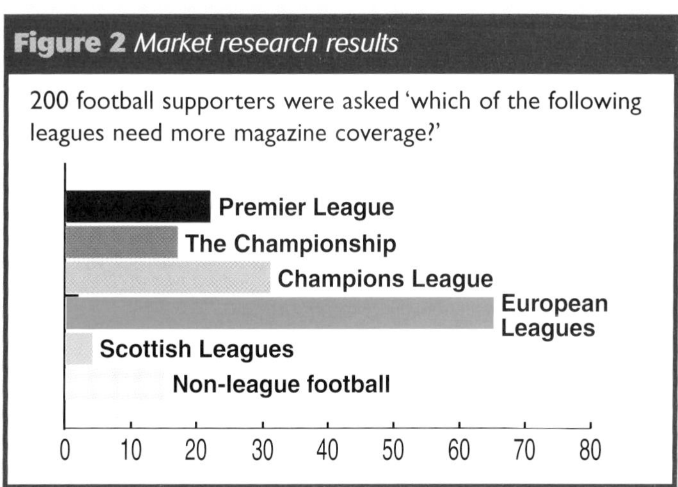

where the business is owned by a single person. That person is responsible for making all the decisions, organising all the resources and raising enough money to set the business up. If the business makes a profit, it all belongs to the sole trader. The advantages of this type of ownership is that there are no legal restrictions when setting up and it is the simplest and most common form of business. But owners have unlimited liability. Their personal assets can be taken to pay for business debts.

Partnership Some businesses are owned by two or a small group of people. This arrangement is called a partnership and the responsibility of running the business, generating the start-up capital and making decisions is shared between the partners. The profit or loss will also be shared. Unless a Deed of Partnership states otherwise, profits and losses are likely to be shared equally. The Deed of Partnership is a document which outlines the rights of partners. It is legally binding but does not have to be drawn up by law.

Private limited company Some businesses are set up by selling shares to a small group of people, perhaps a family. The money from the shares is used to set up the business and each shareholder is involved in decision making. The more shares a person has, the more control over decision making they enjoy. A lengthy legal process must be followed when forming a private limited company. Legal documents have to be drawn up and sent to the Registrar of Companies. There are also company laws which have to be followed. Shareholders have limited liability. They are only liable for the debts of the business. So they can only lose the money invested in the business, not their personal savings or possessions if there are debts.

Public limited company Some firms 'go public'. This means their shares are made available on the stock market where anyone can buy them. A lot more money can be raised this way but the company comes under closer legal scrutiny. Public limited companies have to follow the rules and regulations of the stock market in addition to the company laws mentioned above. It is expensive to become a public limited company and the process of 'going public' also takes a long time. Shareholders have limited liability.

Franchising Franchising is where the owner of a business idea (the franchisor) sells the rights to other businesses (franchisees) to sell its products or use its ideas. The franchisor may provide facilities and help, such as marketing, for a charge. It allows businesses to make use of a well known brand name, such as McDonald's.

Stakeholders

When setting up and running a business the owner will have to take into account the needs of other stakeholders. A stakeholder is someone who has an interest in a business. This means they might be affected by its activities in some way. Different stakeholders are likely to have different needs.

- Owners or shareholders have a financial stake in the business. They risked some of their money when it was set up. They are likely to want to make a profit and to see the company grow.
- Employees are hired to help make products or deliver services. They want fair wages, good working conditions, strong leadership and to be valued.
- Managers are employed by the owners when a business grows. They are responsible for organising and making decisions. They have similar needs to other employees. But since they can influence the success of the business they tend to want more.
- Customers want businesses to provide good quality products at fair prices. They do not expect to be exploited and prefer businesses that offer good customer service, such as friendly and well trained staff.
- Suppliers want regular contracts with businesses, prompt payment and fair prices for their goods and services.
- The government wants businesses to prosper because they pay tax and provide employment. They enforce laws which are designed to protect other stakeholders from exploitation by businesses.
- Local communities rely on local businesses for training and employment. They may also provide local people with goods and services. Communities also want businesses to respect the local environment, keeping congestion down for example.
- Financial institutions and other financiers provide funds to allow businesses to set up or expand. They need businesses to be successful so funds can be repaid.

Legal implications

Owners have to be aware of certain laws and legal obligations when running their businesses.

Tax Sole traders and partners have to pay income tax on business profit. Limited companies have to pay corporation tax. Once turnover reaches a certain level businesses have to add VAT on to customer bills. Employers must also deduct income tax from their employees' wages.

National Insurance contributions Employers have to pay National Insurance contributions to the government. They also have to deduct these from employees' wages.

Licences Some types of business activity require a licence to operate. For example, a licence is needed to sell alcohol, fireworks and certain medicines. Licences are also needed to operate a bus or taxi service or to slaughter animals for meat processing. It is against the law to operate without such licences.

Consumer legislation There are many laws designed to protect

Figure 3 *Business stakeholders*

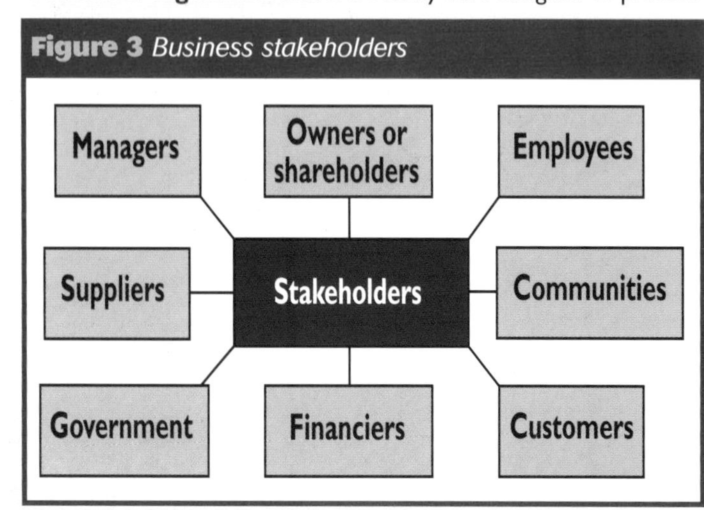

consumers from exploitation by businesses. For example, the **Trade Descriptions Act, 1968** prohibits businesses from making misleading or false statements about their products.

Employment legislation This is designed to protect employees from exploitation. For example, the **Employment Act, 2002** gives mothers and fathers of children under 6 the right to request flexible working hours.

Health and safety legislation This is also designed to protect employees. For example, the **Health and Safety at Work Act, 1974** requires firms to give health and safety training at work.

Environmental legislation This is designed to protect the environment. For example, the **Clean Air Act, 1993** limits emissions by businesses into the atmosphere.

Keeping records Businesses have to keep records of all their transactions. They are used to produce accounts which help show how the business is performing and may be required by the Inland Revenue to calculate tax.

Documents When trading businesses use documents. They provide evidence of transactions. Examples include, invoices, receipts, credit notes and delivery notes.

Insurance Businesses insure against theft, fire, damages and accidents to employees and the public.

Business advice

When setting up a business it is a good idea to get advice. For most entrepreneurs it will be the first time they have ever run a business. Good advice might improve the prospects of the business and help owners to avoid costly mistakes. Specialist advice is available from many different sources.

Individuals These include:
- friends and relatives who are already running businesses;
- accountants;
- solicitors.

Business Links These provide support, guidance and advice to firms that are about to start up. A number of areas are covered such as:
- business planning;
- raising finance;
- tax issues;
- legislation affecting business;
- business management.

Government agencies The Small Business Service runs a number of initiatives to help business start-ups and small businesses.
- Enterprise agencies help small and growing businesses. They offer free advice on business start-ups and training courses.
- Business Bridge organises forums where owners and managers can meet to exchange information and discuss problems.
- The Small Business Research Initiative encourages small firms to get involved in government research.
- Young Enterprise runs business education programmes for young people.
- Tendering for government contracts is a document which shows businesses how to bid for public sector work.
- Local Business Partnerships are used to help businesses and local authorities to streamline regulations together.
- The Ethnic Minority Business Forum advises ministers on helping ethnic minorities in business.

Banks Most commercial banks are happy to provide advice to entrepreneurs. They offer free consultations and provide information packs on setting up and running businesses. They are particularly good at helping with business plans, raising finance and other financial matters.

Others A wide range of other organisations can also offer help. These include the local Chambers of Commerce, Trade Associations, The Prince's Trust, Shell Live Wire, Business Clubs and the Federation of Small Businesses. Most of these have websites on the Internet or distribute free information using leaflets and documents.

Portfolio practice · Stonehaven

Stonehaven is a guest house run by Brenda and Ronnie Pimlott. They are equal partners in the business and share all of the responsibilities and work. They had always wanted to run a business together and decided to buy Stonehaven when Ronnie was made redundant from his sales job. Before they set up they got advice from their bank, a friend of Brenda's who is an accountant and the local tourist board in Devon. They also joined a local business club. Before opening they had to spend a lot of their own money refurbishing the rooms. They also had to get a fire certificate to comply with health and safety regulations. They now employ two part-time staff who help out at meal times and undertake various housekeeping duties. Most of their guests come at weekends. However, since Stonehaven was listed in a county accommodation guide, it has been getting busier during the week.

Source: adapted from author research.

(a) (i) Identify FOUR stakeholders in Stonehaven.
(ii) What is the legal form of the business? Explain your answer.
(b) (i) Describe the needs of any two stakeholders.
(ii) Describe the advice that Ronnie and Brenda might have received before setting up.
(c) Analyse the legal implications of setting up the business.

Visit the websites of some of the organisations that offer business advice OR obtain a business start-up pack from a bank.

- What types of advice do they give?
- What information is given about the types of skills and qualities that are needed to run a business?
- What information is given about the type of business you could set up?
- What financial information is given?
- What legal information is given?

Research task

Meeting the assessment criteria

For your chosen business you need to consider the factors that are important when setting up the business. You must investigate the motives for setting up, the type of ownership, the stakeholders, the legal implications and the advice the owner received.

Business example - Websters Tanning Salon

Websters is a tanning salon in Leeds. The main features of the business are:

- it is a sole trader owned by Angie Webster;
- £3,000 has been invested by Angie;
- there are two part-time staff employed;
- Angie got advice from her bank and her solicitor when setting up.

Source: adapted from company information.

Mark Band 1 *Provide basic knowledge and understanding of the key factors associated with starting a business, such as its legal form and stakeholders.*

Angie Webster set up a tanning salon in a Leeds suburb. She used £3,000 of her own money. The nearest one to where she lives is 12 miles away. She is going to operate as a sole trader which means she keeps all the profit. She is going to employ two students to help out at weekends. These staff are stakeholders. Angie is also a stakeholder and so are the customers and the local community. When setting up she got some legal advice from a solicitor about the use of sunbeds and the possible danger to customers. She also spoke to her bank.

Mark Band 2 *Provide sound knowledge and understanding of the key factors associated with starting a business, such as its legal form and stakeholders.*

Angie Webster is risking £3,000 of her own money to set up a tanning salon in a Leeds suburb. She thought it would do well because there was not another for 12 miles. She is going to operate as a sole trader which means she is the sole owner, makes all the decisions and keeps all the profit. She is going to employ two students to help out at weekends. These staff are stakeholders and Angie understands that she has to meet their needs. She pays them £1 above the national minimum wage and lets them have a break every two hours. She also paid for them to go on a customer services training day. Angie is also a stakeholder and so are the customers and the local community. When setting up she got some legal advice from a solicitor about the use of sunbeds and the possible danger to customers. She was advised to take out some insurance in case anyone made a claim against her. She also spoke to her bank. They gave her information on keeping a record of transactions and what documents would be necessary when trading.

Mark Band 3 *Provide comprehensive knowledge and understanding of the key factors associated with starting a business, such as its legal form and stakeholders.*

Angie Webster operates as a sole trader. She opened a tanning salon in Leeds using £3,000 of her own money. She spotted a gap in the local market for this service. The nearest salon was 12 miles away. As a sole trader she will be in complete control of the business. Angie will make all the decisions, organise other resources and keep the profit if the salon is successful. However, she is taking a risk. If the salon fails to attract enough customers the business could fail and Angie could lose her £3,000. Angie is a stakeholder because she has a financial stake in the business. Her customers will also be stakeholders and will want a good service with fair prices. In particular, they will want to be sure that the tanning machines are safe to use. Angie employs two part-time staff. These are also stakeholders and will want fair pay and good working conditions. Before opening the salon Angie took some advice. She spoke to her solicitor about what to do if a customer took out a claim against her for skin damage caused by a tanning machine. She was advised to take out some insurance. Angie also visited the bank manager to find out about VAT, keeping business records and the use of business documents. As a result she had some receipts printed.

17 Business planning

Why is planning important?

If an important event is going to be successful it has to be planned carefully. For example, how many people would go on holiday, move house, get married or throw a big party without planning it first? Without planning things might go wrong and the consequences can be very unpleasant. Setting up any business can be complex and time consuming. However, with careful planning the process is easier, less stressful and costly mistakes might be avoided.

Planning and resources

Business activity often uses lots of resources. For example, a small retailer selling gifts and souvenirs may have to:

- obtain a bank loan;
- find suitable premises;
- refurbish and fit the premises;
- arrange for utilities such as water, electricity, telephone and gas to be connected;
- buy in stocks of gifts and souvenirs;
- obtain a till and some printed till rolls;
- print some posters to promote the business;
- get some stationery and trading documents, such as receipts, printed;
- recruit some staff to help out.

In each of the above cases, gathering the resources takes time, organisation and planning. For example, when refurbishing the premises it may be necessary to draw up plans, get planning permission, get quotations from builders and decorators, choose fixtures, fittings, floorings and colour schemes, place orders and employ contractors, supervise the whole operation and deal with unexpected problems, such as builders failing to turn up. If an entrepreneur tries to set up a business without proper planning, many things can go wrong. The most common problems are that the opening of the business can be delayed and the start-up costs can be higher than anticipated.

Planning and monitoring performance

Once a business is set up the owners will want to monitor its progress and performance. Without proper planning it is difficult to do this. Unless specific plans are made it is difficult to know whether a business is living up to its expectations. Businesses might identify a number of key performance indicators. For example, Crown Cork & Seal, part of the US corporation Crown Holdings, makes a range of cans for food and drinks. It collects data to monitor its key performance indicators. These are summarised in Figure 1.

The company plans to reach a specified standard in each of these indicators. If the standard is not met an investigation is carried out to find out why. If a business does not plan to reach performance targets it is more difficult to judge whether the firm is doing well or not.

Figure 1 *Key performance indicators at Crown Cork & Seal*

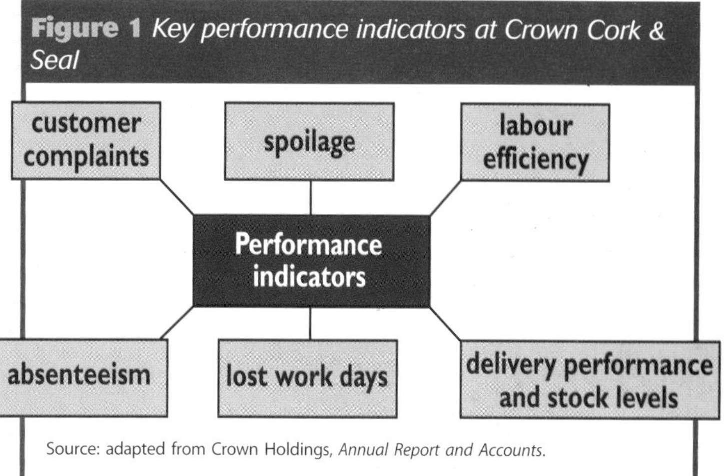

Source: adapted from Crown Holdings, *Annual Report and Accounts*.

Planning, aims and objectives

The whole planning process is driven by the firm's aims and objectives as explained in section 1. When setting up a business it is much easier to make plans if the business has something specific to aim for. In the early stages of running a business the aims and objectives might be quite modest. For example, survival is likely to be a priority. A business might want to ensure that it is still trading in twelve months' time. Planning will also be easier if the objectives are SMART. Figure 2 outlines what this means.

Other examples of aims and objectives that a business might have when first setting up include:

- breaking even in the first year;
- reaching a specific sales target;
- achieving a specific market share;
- reaching a specific production target;
- making a specific amount of profit.

The particular aims and objectives a business chooses will influence the plans. For example, Sally Leibowitz set up a business selling luxury food hampers. She wanted to break even in the first year and worked out that she would have to sell 100 hampers to achieve this aim. Sally would have to make plans to ensure that she has all the resources to do this. If the business wanted to sell 150 hampers, however the plans would have been different. Sally would have needed to acquire more resources. She may have needed more money to set up, for example.

Once a business becomes established the aims and objectives might change. For example, a business may consider growth, profit maximisation, increasing shareholder value or social responsibility. Achieving these will need some strategic planning. This may involve introducing company-wide policies. For example, Tesco has developed its Tesco Express stores and has diversified into non-food products to achieve growth.

Figure 2 *SMART objectives*

Specific- stating exactly what should be achieved;

Measurable- able to be measured to decide if they have been achieved;

Agreed- everyone in the business understands and approves the aims;

Realistic- able to be achieved after taking into account resources, competition and market;

Time specific- state a time by which they should be achieved.

Key elements in business planning

There are certain key elements in business planning.

The market Once a business idea has been developed and objectives set, the next step is to look at the market. It would be very risky indeed to go ahead and set up a business without first analysing the market. This might involve:

- finding out the size of the market and whether or not it is growing;
- researching the main strengths and weaknesses of competitors. By doing this it may be possible to gain some advantage;
- constructing a customer profile. This involves identifying the characteristics of the people who are likely to buy the product. Customer profiles help businesses to target their products and marketing materials more accurately;
- deciding which marketing methods are appropriate and what prices to charge;
- organising a launch. For example, a new restaurant might invite potential customers, media and local dignitaries to a free evening on the first night. This will help to raise the profile of the business.

Although market research is expensive, it might help a new business avoid making some serious mistakes. Market research should also be ongoing. Consumer tastes can change quickly and it is important to keep in touch with market trends. Market research is explained in detail in sections 34 and 35.

Finance One of the most important tasks when setting up a business is raising finance. The objectives set at the beginning of the planning process will help determine how much is needed. It is normal for the owner to provide some of the finance needed but rarely is this enough. There is a number of different sources of finance, although many small businesses rely on bank loans. Other sources include the sale of shares for limited companies, venture capitalists, business angels, government grants and loans, bank overdrafts, hire purchase and leasing. Once a business is established it can use retained profit as a source of finance. These different sources of finance are discussed in detail in section 18. When providing finance for business start-ups money lenders need to be convinced that the business is capable of repaying the loan. The chances of obtaining finance will be improved if business owners:

- provide a clear and realistic business plan;
- risk their own money;
- provide some collateral (some property or other assets to secure the loan);
- communicate their ideas effectively;
- produce some evidence of market research;
- demonstrate that they have the skills and commitment to make the business a success.

Production This aspect of planning is about choosing the methods of production and deciding which resources to use. However, most business ideas today involve providing a service, therefore, owners need to plan how the service will be delivered. Examples of tasks that might have to be planned include:

- finding a suitable location;
- determining what production methods will be used;
- deciding which resources will be needed;
- working the costs of the resources needed.

Personnel Human resource planning is an important activity in a large business. It involves forecasting the type and number of staff that will be required to meet the firm's objectives. When setting up a small business it is unlikely that large numbers of staff will be needed. However, assuming that some people will be employed, the owner will have to decide how many, what type, how they will be trained, how much they will be paid and what their roles will be in the organisation. Unit 1 looks at the importance of people at work in detail.

Cash flow One of the most important aspects of business planning is financial planning. It is common for business owners to overlook or misunderstand the importance of financial planning. This can lead to the business having financial difficulties. Owners must plan ahead so that they do not run out of cash. Without cash a business cannot trade. Constructing a cash flow forecast will help a business in the planning stages. This shows the expected monthly:

- cash inflows;
- cash outflows;
- net cash flow (cash inflow - cash outflow);
- closing cash balance (opening cash balance + net cash flow);

over a future time period.

Once the planned closing balances have been calculated, owners can see, for example, whether or not they will need more cash in the future. Figure 3 shows the closing cash balances for Robert Henshaw's van delivery business in the first six months of trading. The graph, which is based on figures in his cash flow forecast, shows that the business will need some more cash in July.

The cash flow forecast can also be used to monitor the performance of the business. The planned cash balances can be compared with the actual cash balances. Cash flow forecasting is

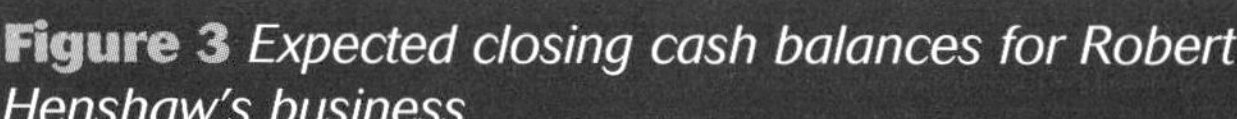

Figure 3 *Expected closing cash balances for Robert Henshaw's business*

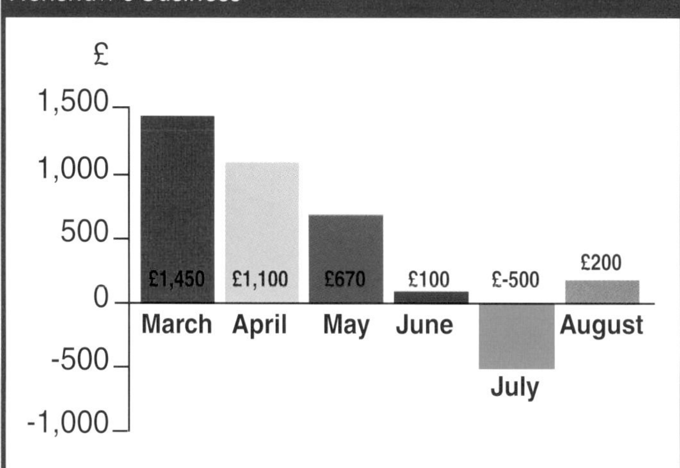

discussed in detail in section 22.

Profit Most businesses aim to make a profit at some stage. Expected profit can be calculated by subtracting the expected costs from the estimated revenue. At the end of the year a business will produce some financial statements which show how much profit has been made. These can be used to assess the performance of the business and help see whether objectives have been met. Profit is discussed in more detail in section 20.

Planning It is recommended that entrepreneurs should produce a comprehensive document outlining their plans in detail. This is called a business plan. Moneylenders or other investors will want to see this before providing funds.

Portfolio practice · The New Ale Co.

The New Ale Co is being set up in Birmingham by Ali Grant. After visiting Marble Beers, Manchester's only organic and vegan brewery, she decided that she could do the same in her home city. Ali was a vegan and knew that vegans could not drink real ale. This is because it contains a material called finings, a clearing agent made from fish bones. Yet real ale is a natural product and one that vegans might want to buy if there were no finings. Ali did some more market research. She used a vegan friend's website to post a questionnaire. Some of the results are shown in Figure 4. During the planning stage Ali spent a lot of time working out the costs of setting up. It would not be cheap, however, she planned to fund most of the set-up with £35,000 of her own money. She produced a cash flow forecast and wrote a comprehensive business plan. She needed to borrow a further £10,000 from a bank and wanted to breakeven in the first year.

Source: adapted from company information

(a) (i) Describe FOUR resources that Ali will need when setting up her small brewery.
(ii) What is likely to be Ali's aim when starting the New Ale Co?

(b) (i) Does Ali face much competition with her new product? Explain your answer.
(ii) What does the market research data say about Ali's business idea?

(c) Outline FOUR factors that Ali might include in her business plan.

Figure 4 *Extracts from vegan questionnaire (1,300 responses from vegans)*

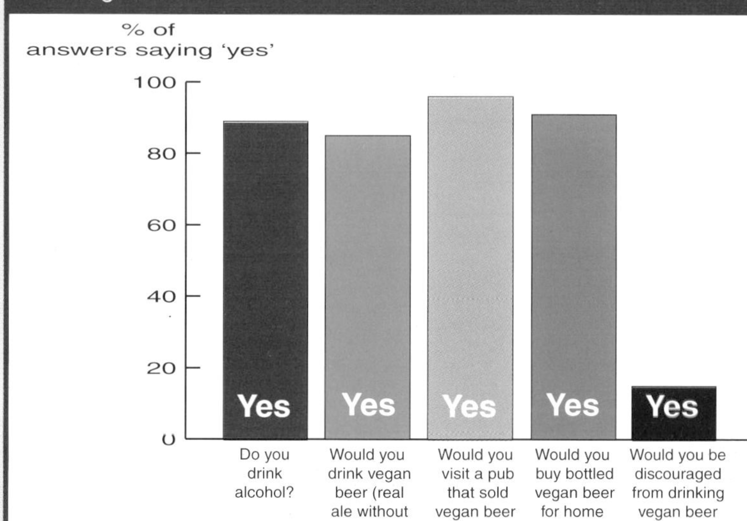

Obtain a copy of the *Yellow Pages* for your area.

- Find the restaurants section and record how many Italian, French, Indian, Thai, Chinese and Mexican restaurants there are in your area.
- Produce a graph or pie chart to show the data gathered above.
- If you were opening a restaurant, which would you choose? Give your reasons why.
- What other market information might you gather before opening a restaurant?

Research task

Meeting the assessment criteria

In your investigation you need to consider the factors that are important when setting up the business. You will be investigating the aims of the business, the importance of planning and the key elements in business planning. You will pay particular attention to market analysis.

Business example - Bean-there.com

Bean-there.com is an Internet café in Derry, Northern Ireland. It was set up by Aisling Collins who won the 2001 Entrepreneur of the Year Award. The main features of the business are:

- the idea came from a working holiday in Australia;
- it sells good quality Italian coffee, gourmet sandwiches, cakes and cookies;
- it is ideally located near to a major bus stop, tourist hostels, offices and shopping centre;
- it has modern décor – spiral staircase and bright colours;
- it charges £2.50 for half an hour or £4.50 per hour for Internet access.

Source: adapted from www.startups.co.uk.

Mark Band 1 *Provide basic knowledge and understanding of the key factors associated with starting a business such as planning and market analysis.*

Aisling Collins launched Bean-there.com in July 2000. Located in the diamond area of Derry city, this Internet café provides high speed Internet access for tourists, shoppers and local small businesses. During the planning stage she realised how important a good location was going to be. She managed to find a prime site that was currently empty. It was near to a bus stop, tourist hostels, offices and a shopping centre. During the planning stage Aisling also looked at the market. She noticed that the food provided by other cafés in the area was basic such as egg butties and watery tea. She decided that her café would sell more high quality food and drink.

Mark Band 2 *Provide sound knowledge and understanding of the key factors associated with starting a business such as planning and market analysis.*

Bean-there.com, located in the diamond area of Derry city, is an Internet café that provides high speed Internet access for tourists, shoppers and local small businesses. It was set up by Aisling Collins who won the Entrepreneur of the Year Award in 2001. Aisling understood the importance of thorough planning and spent quite a lot of time looking for the perfect site. She managed to find a prime location that was currently empty, although it took a while to track down the owner. It was near to a large bus stop, tourist hostels, offices and a shopping centre. The Derry tour bus drops off passengers right opposite the café. During the planning stage Aisling also looked at the market. She discovered that there was not a single Internet café in the city. She also came to the conclusion that the food provided by other cafes was basic, lacking in choice and poor in quality, such as egg butties and watery tea. She decided that her café would sell more high quality food and drink.

Mark Band 3 *Provide comprehensive knowledge and understanding of the key factors associated with starting a business such as planning and market analysis, including a consideration of the pricing policy.*

After travelling around the world and working in San Francisco, where she learnt everything she needed to know about the Internet, Aisling Collins set up an Internet café. Bean-there.com, located in Derry City, provides high speed Internet access for tourists, shoppers and local small businesses. Aisling noticed the increasing numbers of tourists in the city since the Good Friday Peace Agreement, and set about creating a business that meets the new visitors' needs. Aisling linked up with local tour guides and proposed the café as a stop along the city's historical walking tour route. Tourists can now have a break, contact home, gather information on the area and even book visits to other attractions. The location of the café was a serious consideration in the planning stage. Aisling spent a long time searching for the prime location. She eventually found an empty site in the diamond district, but had to spend a further amount of time tracking down the owner.

Aisling also gave a lot of thought to the café menu. During the planning stage she undertook some market research. The was no other Internet café in Derry but plenty of conventional cafes. She visited them to see what they were offering. Generally, their menus were poor, offering things like fried egg butties and watery tea.

Bean-there.com has a modern design with seating capacity for 40 people. There is a spiral staircase and the café is decorated with bright colours. It boasts an extensive gourmet sandwich menu, including a wide range of speciality breads and wraps. Bean-there.com also supplies breakfast and lunch platters to local businesses.

During the planning stage, like many other start-up businesses, Aisling found it difficult to raise money. Banks would not take her seriously. Finally, since there was no other Internet café in Derry, she was able to charge premium prices for Internet access. She charged £4.50 per hour or £2.50 for half an hour.

18

Business resources

Managing business activities

Once a business plan has been finalised, the next stage in setting up is to gather the resources needed to run the business. Most owners will begin the process by organising the funding of the business. Until the business has finance it cannot acquire the other resources it needs. Business start-ups are usually funded by the owners. However, additional financial resources may be needed to meet the full cost of setting up and to help pay for the initial stages in trading. Once money has been raised the physical resources can be obtained. These include:

- premises;
- machinery;
- equipment;
- materials and stocks.

The types of physical resources needed will depend on the nature of the business. Before the business begins trading it may be necessary to recruit some staff to help out. Some very small businesses may need limited human resources to start with. However, if they are successful and start growing, it is likely that additional workers will be required. Once the business is up and running it will be important to monitor its progress and performance. This will help to ensure that the objectives are met.

Financial resources

Most businesses will have to obtain financial resources at some stage. There is a wide variety of different sources. But many small businesses can struggle to persuade lenders and investors to provide funding. Small businesses are often considered too risky by those providing funds.

Long term sources of finance

Figure 1 shows the different sources of long term funding available to businesses. Long term funding refers to money that is borrowed for and paid back over longer periods, such as five years or more. It is used to pay for resources that are likely to be used by the business for long periods of time. For example, a business might take out a 25 year loan to pay for its premises.

Share capital Limited companies can raise money by selling shares. Share capital is usually permanent capital. This means that share capital stays in the business for as long as it trades. Shareholders are entitled to dividends - a share of the profit made by the business. They may also be involved in decision making because shareholders are part-owners of a company. However, in public limited companies shareholders are only entitled to vote on who runs the company. An advantage of raising money by issuing shares is that large amounts can be raised because there are so many contributors. However, there are many administrative costs and the profit made by the business has to be spread more thinly.

Mortgage This is a long term loan that is secured on property.

Figure 1 *Long term sources of finance*

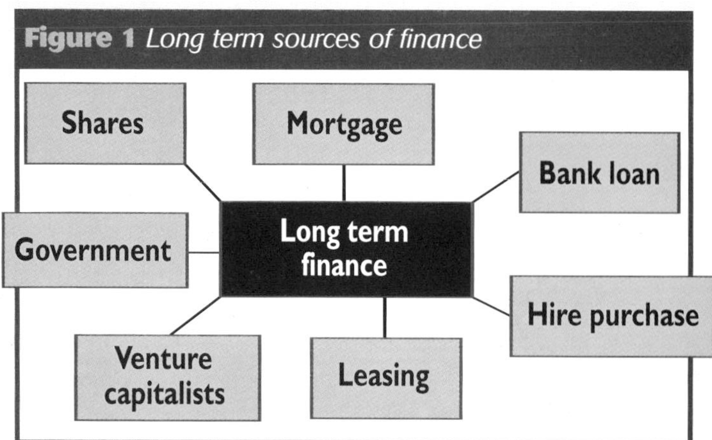

This means that if a business cannot keep up the loan and interest repayments, the lender is entitled to take ownership of the property. The interest rates paid on mortgages are relatively low and money can be borrowed for long periods such as 25 years.

Long term loans Financial institutions such as banks may provide loans. Most loans are **secured**. If a business does not repay the loan or make interest payments the bank can repossess assets, such as stock, machinery or money owed as debts. **Unsecured loans** are rare, as banks lose out. Interest rates on these loans tend to be higher to compensate for the risk.

Hire purchase (HP) Businesses can obtain machinery and equipment using hire purchase. Money is borrowed from a specialist called a finance house. For example, a business may buy a delivery van on HP. The finance house pays the supplier of the van and the business pays the finance house monthly instalments until the full cost plus interest has been met. The van will not belong to the business until the last instalment has been made. Until then the van legally belongs to the finance house. HP can be expensive because interest rates are high. However, it is relatively easy to get HP.

Leasing Leasing is the same as renting. Businesses can lease property, vehicles, machinery or equipment if they cannot afford to buy outright. It is a good way of acquiring such resources if they are only needed for a short period of time. The leasing company also meets the cost of repairs and maintenance. However, if resources are leased for a long period of time it may be an expensive form of finance.

Venture capitalists Many small businesses raise money from venture capitalists. These are businesses that specialise in providing 'risk capital' for young or fast growing companies. Some examples include Apax Partners, 3i and ECI. They raise their money from financial institutions and private investors. They may provide loans but are more likely to want a stake in the business. They often invest for between three and seven years. Some venture capitalists are individuals. They are called Business Angels and look to invest amounts ranging from £10,000 to around £100,000. They often have business experience and are prepared to take a risk.

Government Government funding is attractive because it is often cheap. For example, the Small Firms Loan Guarantee Scheme guarantees loans from financial institutions for small firms that have viable business proposals but which have tried and failed to get a conventional loan because of lack of security. Loans are available for periods of between two and ten years on sums from £5,000 to £100,000. There is a variety of other grants and loans available. But to qualify for financial help firms often have to set up in areas where unemployment is relatively high, for example.

Short term sources of finance

Short term finance is money that must be repaid within twelve months. Figure 2 shows the different short term sources available to businesses.

Figure 2 *Short term sources of finance*

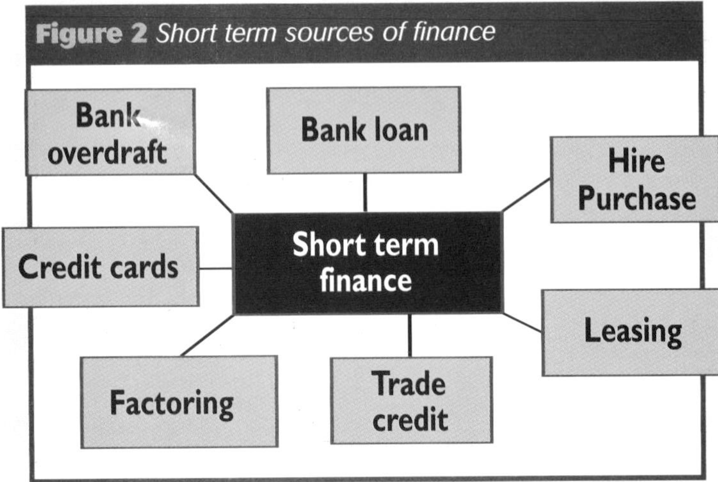

Bank overdraft This is a common type of short term business finance. It involves a business spending more money than it has in its account. Businesses can use the bank's money to go overdrawn up to an agreed limit. Bank overdrafts are flexible and interest is only charged when the business is overdrawn. Interest rates are competitive but if a business exceeds its overdraft limit the rates can be very high.

Bank loan A business may take out a short term loan with a bank, for example. The amount, plus interest, must be repaid in regular monthly instalments, usually within a short period such as a year. This can be inflexible and the interest charged might be quite high.

Hire purchase (HP) HP can be used as a short term source of finance if a business buys some equipment, for example, and pays for it over a year in monthly instalments.

Leasing Leasing is also a short term source of finance if a resource is rented for twelve months or less. For example, a small construction business might lease a crane for two weeks.

Trade credit Sometimes a business can obtain goods and not have to pay for them straight away. Payment might be after 30, 60 or 90 days, for example. This is trade credit. It might appear to be a cheap way to borrow money. However, by delaying payment to suppliers businesses might be losing out on cash discounts if they had settled their bill immediately.

Factoring Factors are financial specialists that are often owned by financial institutions such as banks. They provide businesses with cash if they are owed money by their customers. Factors may take responsibility for the collection of debts. They may give a business between 80-90% of the value of an invoice when it is issued and then pass on the rest when the customer pays the bill. The factor charges a fee for this service.

Credit cards Credit cards can be used to obtain materials, services and fuel, for example. There is no exchange of cash when a credit card is used. Credit card users receive a statement at the end of the month listing all the transactions and showing the total amount owed. If users settle the bill within about 25 days there is no interest charge. However, if the bill is only paid in part, the interest charged on the outstanding amount is very high.

Retained profit

When a business makes a profit it is likely that some of it will be returned to the owners. However, the remainder will be retained and used to fund business activity. It might be used to boost working capital or it might be invested in a new venture, for example. The main advantage of using retained profit as a source of finance is that no interest has to be paid. It is also convenient because the money will already be in the bank account and there are no administration charges.

Physical resources

Businesses need a variety of physical resources to operate. When setting up some businesses will prefer to lease or rent resources. For example, retailers might lease shops and manufacturers might lease their factory units. It is also possible to lease plant, machinery and equipment. Leasing resources can help the cash flow of a business in its initial stages.

Premises One of the major resources of a business may be its premises. The type of premises needed will depend on the nature of the business. For example, a business that plans to sell clothes will need a shop in an appropriate location such as a shopping centreor high street. A manufacturer may look for an old disused factory or a new factory unit on an industrial estate. A solicitor setting up a new law practice will need an office. Estate agents will be able to provide information on the cost and availability of business premises.

Plant, machinery tools and equipment Nearly all new businesses will need to acquire a range of tools, equipment and machinery. Again, the type of resources needed will depend on the type of equipment. Some businesses need specialist equipment. For example, a dentist setting up a practice will need specialist dental tools and equipment that no other type of business would use. On the other hand, some equipment like vehicles, office furniture and computers, can be bought by a range of different businesses.

Materials and other physical resources Manufacturers need to buy raw materials and components. For example, a dressmaker will have to buy fabric, lace, ribbon, cotton, sequins, buttons and other materials. Office based businesses will have to buy stationery, toner for the photocopier and ink cartridges. Retailers will have to buy stock to resell. It will also be necessary to arrange for premises to be connected to water, gas, electricity and telephone. Other services, such as insurance, advertising and cleaning, will have to be organised. When buying resources like these there is often a choice of suppliers. Business owners must decide which suppliers to use. Their decision will be based on cost, quality, continuity of supply and reliability.

Human resources

Human resources are the people who work for the business. Various factors will affect the human resources of a business.

Staff quality Business will need to recruit staff. When first setting up staff may be limited. But as a business grows it will require a variety of employees with many skills. Business owners will want to recruit high quality staff. Generally, businesses will want to employ people who are:

- honest and trustworthy;
- reliable and punctual;
- flexible and cooperative;
- well motivated and willing to learn.

In some cases staff with particular skills, qualifications and experiences will be needed. For example, a small IT company might need to recruit staff with a degree in IT and some programming experience. Because a lot of new business activity involves providing services, it is often important to recruit staff with good people and communication skills. It may also be important to select staff who are good team workers because a lot of businesses organise their workforce into teams.

To help make sure that the best quality staff are appointed, businesses use references from previous employers to judge whether or not they are suitable. It might also be possible to test people before they are appointed. To improve the quality of the workforce a business might train their staff. If staff are well trained they will be able to do their job more effectively. They might also feel valued because the business has invested money in them, in which case they might be better motivated.

Cost and availability Businesses will want to recruit staff as cheaply as possible. However, if a business pays its staff poorly it might affect their motivation and productivity. Business owners have to pay staff at least the minimum legal wage. Generally, higher wages will attract better quality staff. In addition to wages businesses have to pay National Insurance contributions to the government. There is also the cost of training. Training is expensive and staff might leave soon after completing their training. This means that the money is wasted.

If a business needs to employ some specialist staff there may be availability problems. For example, if a local newspaper needs to recruit some reporters, there may not be any available in the town. This might mean that reporters have to be attracted from another area which could be expensive. When unemployment is low in the economy it becomes harder for businesses to attract and retain staff. The availability of workers might vary around the UK. Figure 3 shows that staff might be harder to recruit in the South because these regions are where unemployment is relatively low.

Figure 3 *Regional unemployment, Spring 2003*

SCOTLAND 5.7%
NORTHERN IRELAND 5.4%
NORTH EAST 6.6%
YORKSHIRE AND THE HUMBER 5.5%
NORTH WEST 5.1%
EAST MIDLANDS 4.3%
WEST MIDLANDS 5.9%
WALES 4.6%
EAST 4.2%
LONDON 7.1%
SOUTH EAST 3.9%
SOUTH WEST 3.9%
UK - 5.1%

Source: adapted from *Regional Trends*, Office for National Statistics.

A retailer requires some premises to lease for a clothes shop.

- Visit some local estate agents and compile a list of six suitable premises. The agent will possibly give you some written details.
- Draw up a table showing the location, size, rent, features and other details for each property.
- Write a recommendation suggesting which property would be the best.

Research task

Meeting the assessment criteria

In your investigation you need to identify the resources needed by the business. You will need to consider why particular resources are being used and how the business manages them to produce quality output.

Business example – Bennett's Fencing

Mike and Liam Bennett recently set up a small fencing business in Tamworth. They make a range of wooden fencing panels and supply local residents and two garden centres in the area. The business:

- leases a factory converted from a barn in a rural location about 8 miles from the centre of Tamworth;
- buys wood from suppliers in Scotland on 60 days trade credit;
- employs two full-time staff and four temporary staff. The temporary staff are laid off during the winter;
- leases most of its machinery, but purchased tools for £1,000;
- was set up using a £12,000 ten year bank loan and £18,000 of the owners' capital. A £5,000 bank overdraft was also agreed.

Source: adapted from company information.

Mark Band 1 *You need to provide a basic knowledge and understanding of managing resources in a business.*

Bennett's Fencing is located in a rural area. The isolated location was important so that people were not disturbed by the noisy electric saws used in production. The business was financed by a ten year £12,000 bank loan and a £5,000 overdraft. The owners also put some capital in and the main raw material is bought on trade credit. A lot of the start-up capital was used converting the barn into a factory. This meant that expensive machinery had to be leased. However, the leased machinery was very 'state-of-the-art' and efficient. The Bennetts employed two full time staff who are well paid. However, the temporary staff are unskilled and only get the minimum wage. Temporary staff were a problem because they keep leaving.

Mark Band 2 *You need to provide a sound knowledge and understanding of managing resources in a business.*

Once the funding for the new business was put in place, the Bennetts spent time finding suitable premises. It was important to locate the business away from residential areas because of the noise made by the electrical saws during production. The rural location was perfect. They also had a lot of space for storage, loading and unloading. The finance for the business was provided by a bank which allowed the brothers to borrow £12,000 over ten years. The bank also gave them a £5,000 overdraft. Another £18,000 was put in by the owners. Unfortunately most of the initial capital was used converting the barn and meeting health and safety regulations. This meant that the machinery had to be leased. However, leasing proved to be advantageous because the machines were new and their maintenance was the responsibility of the leasing company. The business did have one problem though. The Bennetts decided to rely quite heavily on temporary staff. This was because their demand was seasonal. However, the temporary staff proved to be unreliable and poorly motivated, probably because they were only being paid the minimum wage and were laid off in October.

Mark Band 3 *You need to provide a comprehensive knowledge and understanding of managing resources in a business and give reasons for their choice.*

Bennett's Fencing was funded from a variety of different sources. £18,000 capital was provided by the owners and a £12,000 ten year, long term bank loan was taken out. This was considered a suitable funding arrangement for this type of business because a lot of the start-up capital was spent on capital expenditure - converting the barn into a factory. One of the strengths of the business was its location. There was lots of open space and the noise from the factory did not disturb anyone in its rural location. Short term sources of funds included leasing, a bank overdraft and trade credit. The 60 day trade credit period for wood supplies was particularly helpful when the business first started trading. The Bennetts decided to lease their machinery. They wanted the best but could not afford to purchase it outright. Leasing gave them access to the best technology available. Leasing improved the cash flow of the business and the cost of repairs and maintenance was the responsibility of the leasing company. Human resources in the business were a bit of a problem. There were no real difficulties with full time staff. However, the decision to employ cheap, temporary staff during the busy summer months may have been a mistake. Staff turnover amongst the temporary workers was very high, probably because wages were set at the legal minimum. This resulted in production being disrupted, with customers receiving late deliveries. This was a problem that the Bennetts would have to address eventually.

Portfolio practice · Ma-Doner

Jo Dalton wanted to open a kebab shop in Ventnor on the Isle of Wight. She drew up her business plan and received £5,000 from The Prince's Trust to set up the business. However, she discovered that the money was not going to be enough to buy all the equipment she needed. Instead, she decided to use hire purchase. Jo priced up all the equipment she needed, including a fridge, cooker, chargrill, chiller cabinet, kebab burner and a carbon filter extraction fan.

Jo had problems finding a finance deal for the equipment, but persevered and found a local firm that sold catering equipment. They found a leasing deal to suit her and Ma-Doner is now paying for the equipment monthly. 'If I had had to pay upfront I probably wouldn't be here today' Jo said.

Buying the equipment on hire purchase has worked well for Ma-Doner. Jo managed to buy new equipment with guarantees, at only a slightly higher price than the reconditioned equipment that she had budgeted for. 'I have got peace of mind knowing that it is new and won't break down' she said.

Source: adapted from www.startups.co.uk.

(a) State FOUR physical resources used by Ma-Doner.

(b) (i) How was the start-up funded?

(ii) Discuss the advantages and disadvantages of using hire purchase to obtain equipment.

(c) (i) What human resources might Jo Dalton need if the business becomes a success?

(ii) Discuss how the quality of staff might be improved by Jo.

19 Monitoring quality and performance

Quality

Quality is vital for a business. Quality is a degree of 'excellence' achieved in business operations. A successful business must provide high quality products. These are products which meet standards and also the requirements of customers. For example, Figure 1 shows the features that may be considered important by a teenager when buying a computer. A business can sometimes gain quality standards for these features, such as:

- a Kite Mark for the quality of products such as crash helmets;
- a Wool Mark for the quality of woollen products;
- a Lion Mark for the quality of toys.

The quality of production processes is also vital. This might be the quality of manufacturing processes, such as the production of steel, textiles, printing or electronic components. It might also be the quality of a service such as transport, hotel hospitality, pest control or theme park entertainment.

The importance of monitoring quality

Businesses that achieve quality in production are likely to benefit. They might be able to:

- attract customers and increase sales;
- ensure waste is minimized and control costs;
- increase profits.

Business must ensure that quality is maintained at all times to achieve these benefits. This involves the use of various methods to ensure quality, including quality control, quality assurance and Total Quality Management (TQM).

The role of quality control

Traditionally the role of quality control was to inspect goods before they were dispatched to customers. However, although this prevented poor quality goods from reaching customers it did not prevent them from being made. Modern quality control attempts to prevent defective goods from being made. This is better because:

- customers never get to see a defective product;
- resources are not wasted in the production of a defective product that must be scrapped or reworked.

Modern quality control requires a commitment from every employee in an organisation to take responsibility for the quality of their own work. Businesses use a preventative approach to quality control where mistakes, errors and defects are prevented from happening in the first place.

Quality assurance

The aim of quality assurance is to develop an approach where quality is maintained throughout every stage in all processes used in the business. A business might identify certain quality standards at each stage in a process. These standards will satisfy or exceed customer expectations and staff will be committed to achieving them. If they are achieved, all of the time, then quality can be guaranteed or assured.

Some businesses try to achieve quality standards. These show that processes have been carried out to a high standard and to a stated specification. Once a business has been assessed and shown that it can reach and maintain these high standards, it will be accredited. For example, the International Standardisation Organisation (ISO) has standards which are recognized internationally. Many are highly specific and contain technical specifications or other criteria which must be met. A generic standard that can be gained by all businesses no matter what their product is the ISO 9000 accreditation. This shows standards that businesses achieve in managing their processes. It will help a business to:

- satisfy customers' quality requirements;
- comply with regulations;
- meet environmental objectives.

ISO 9000 accreditation is awarded by bodies such as the British

Figure 1 *Important features of a computer for a teenager*

Operation – does it have enough memory and speed?

Physical appearance – does it have a suitable style or design?

Reliability and durability – will it last?

Suitability – is it compact enough to fit in a small bedroom?

Guarantees – does the PC come with a guarantee that meets the cost of all parts and labour in the event of a breakdown?

After sales service – can it be delivered by the end of the week?

Image – is the brand name recognised?

Reputation – what do peers think of the business or product?

Standards Institution (BSI). Once a business has achieved accreditation, its processes are checked regularly to ensure that standards are being maintained. This approach to quality assurance will give customers confidence when buying products. Figure 2 shows the quality management principles for businesses wanting ISO 9000 accreditation.

Total quality management

Total Quality Management (TQM) adopts the modern approach to quality control. It is a philosophy which relies on a commitment to quality which is built into the system. It is a cultural approach and aims at preventing errors rather than identifying them.

Design TQM begins in the design stages of a product. For example, quality might be improved if certain materials are recommended or if a product can be made in such a way that errors do not occur.

Quality chains Every person working in a business is a link in a chain. They are both a customer and a supplier. For example, the work done by one employee at the start of a production line will affect those further down. The quality chain will break if poor work affects the next person down the line.

Total commitment TQM requires every single person in the business to be committed to high quality. This includes office staff, production workers, management and directors. Staff must take pride in their work and the people at the top of the organisation should lead by example.

Monitoring TQM relies heavily on monitoring a wide range of performance indicators to ensure that standards are being met. This involves gathering numerical information throughout the whole production process. The data must be analysed and if performance indicators do not reach specified standards there must be an investigation to find out why. This is called statistical process control.

Teamwork TQM requires the workforce to be organised into teams. This is the best way of solving problems because a team will have a greater range of skills, knowledge and experience than an individual. Teamwork also improves motivation because staff will support each other and communication will be better.

Customer focus TQM is customer driven. Businesses using TQM must focus on customers and be responsive to their needs and wants. Customers can help to set quality standards. For example, customer complaints can be analysed and used as a basis for product improvement.

Some benefits of TQM include:

- improved customer satisfaction;
- better quality right across the business;
- less waste and lower costs;
- improved communications;
- a foundation for further improvements.

However, TQM is expensive to implement because of high training costs. It also requires a lot of paper work and will only be successful if everyone is committed.

Figure 2 *ISO 9000 features*

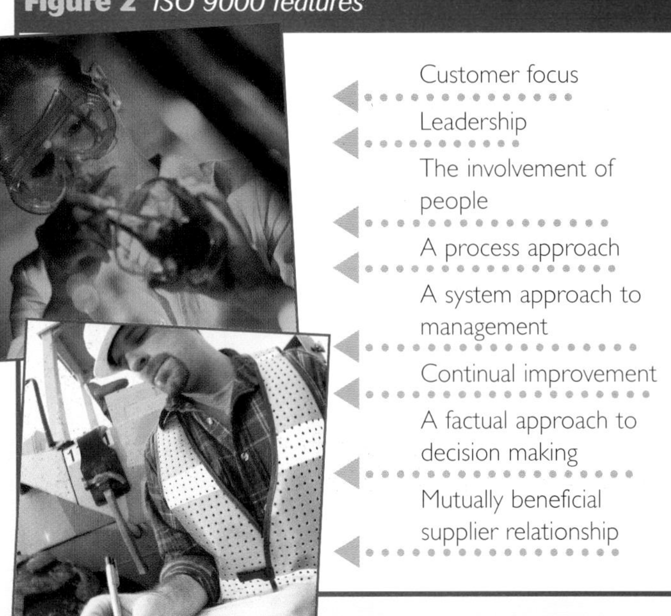

- Customer focus
- Leadership
- The involvement of people
- A process approach
- A system approach to management
- Continual improvement
- A factual approach to decision making
- Mutually beneficial supplier relationship

The importance of monitoring performance

Business owners have to monitor the performance of the business. This helps to:

- ensure that the objectives are met. Targets are usually set and unless checks are made there will be no way of knowing whether the business has met them;
- avoid trading difficulties. For example, by checking the cash position of a business regularly, it is less likely to run out of cash;
- identify times to take corrective action if the performance is not meeting objectives.

Solvency

One of the main aims of a business when it is first set up is to remain solvent. If a business becomes insolvent it has to cease trading. Insolvency occurs when a firm's liabilities (the amount it owes) are greater than the firm's assets (the value of resources owned). To remain solvent a business must avoid taking on too much debt and make sure it has sufficient cash to pay its immediate bills. One way of monitoring cash flow is to compare the planned cash position at the end of each month with the actual cash position. Figure 3 shows two bar charts for a new business. One is the planned cash position and the other is the actual cash position. The graphs show clearly that the actual cash position was worse than that planned after March. If this business had been monitoring its cash position on a regular basis, it may have avoided running out of cash in June.

A firm must also monitor its debt. It should compare regularly the amount it owes with the value of assets that are held. A business needs to ensure that the value of assets are greater than the value of liabilities. If the difference between the two is narrowing, this suggests that the business is losing money. It is also worth noting that a business can have cash but still be insolvent. For example, a business could borrow more cash to pay some bills but this would plunge the company further into debt.

Measuring profits

Owners will be particularly interested in the profit made by the

Figure 3 *Planned and actual cash position*

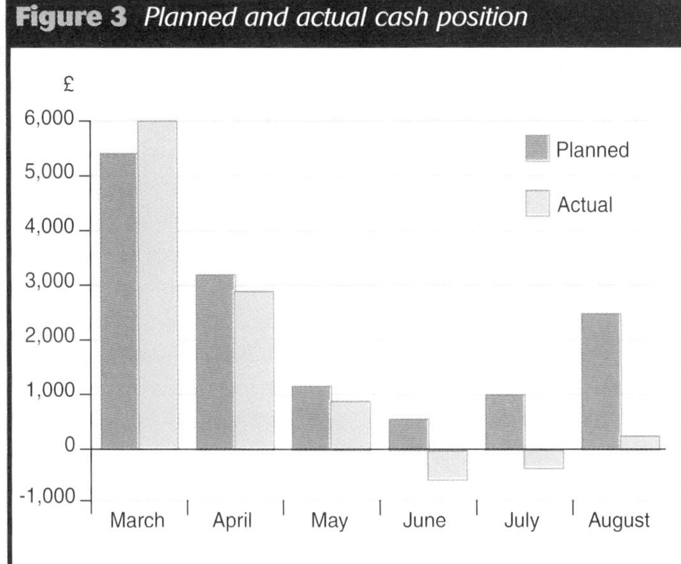

business. They will be interested in both profit levels and profit margins.

Profit levels Profit is the amount of money left over from sales revenue after all business costs have been met. A new business may not expect to make very much profit, if any, to start with. However, it must still monitor profit levels even if losses are made. A business might calculate the profit made each month and compare it with the planned profit figures. If the actual profit is below the planned profit, there may be a need for corrective action. For example, some more advertising might be needed to boost sales.

Profit margins Owners might also be interested in the profit margin. This is the amount of profit expressed as a percentage of sales revenue. For example, if a furniture manufacturer makes a table for £30 and sells if for £50, the profit made is £20. The profit margin is 40% (£20/£50 x 100). The higher the profit margin the better. Some owners may plan to achieve a target profit margin. Regular checks can be made to see if they are being achieved. Profit margins can be increased by raising prices or lowering costs. Profit margin calcualtions are dealt with in section 20.

Complying with laws

Businesses have to operate within the law. A number of laws have been passed which are aimed at businesses. These include:

- employment legislation;
- health and safety legislation;
- consumer legislation;
- environmental legislation;
- company laws.

If a business fails to comply with the law the consequences could be damaging and far reaching. For example, if a manufacturer infringes health and safety regulations at work, it may face problems. Failing to comply with legislation can incur legal costs and fines. It might also suffer a blow to its reputation. As a result it may lose sales and potential employees may be discouraged from applying for posts.

Depending on the type of business activity, a firm will have to use systems to ensure that they comply with the law. For example, if a business discharges gases into the atmosphere as a result of a burning process, it will have to make regular checks to ensure that the discharges meet with environmental standards. Businesses that employ people must for example, provide contracts of employment, adequate working conditions, health and safety training and at least a minimum legal wage. It is the responsibility of any business to ensure that it complies with the law. It may be necessary to get legal advice if a business is unsure about its legal position. This is dealt with in sections 8, 12 and 15.

Identifying areas for improvement

Most businesses will want to improve performance even if their objectives have been met. This is because business is an ongoing activity and will be subject to external influences such as competition. To maintain or grow market share businesses have to be innovative and ever-improving. Areas for improvement can be identified by:

- monitoring and analysing quality data and financial information gathered during the normal course of trading;
- listening to customers, for example monitoring complaints or doing market research;
- listening to staff, for example at team meetings or through staff suggestion boxes;
- listening to advisors or specialists that might be employed.

Performance can be improved by:

- training staff to higher levels and in more tasks;
- modifying or launching new products to meet ever-changing customer needs;
- raising productivity, for example by introducing new technology or new working practices;
- raising quality, for example by using better materials or improved production techniques;
- enhancing customer services for example by acting on customer complaints.

Obtain a complaints form from a local business. Travel agents, train and bus companies or large retailers might have them.

- What questions do they ask?
- Who deals with complaints?
- How do you think the information is used by the organisation?

Research task

Portfolio practice · McGregor & Son

McGregor & Son set up a salmon farm in Scotland. Salmon production is carried out in two phases. The first is a fresh water stage where the ova are hatched and the young (smolts) reared in tanks or in cages in fresh water lochs. This takes around 10 - 15 months (although new technology enables fish to be put into the sea from 6-7 months now). The second phase involves growing the smolts in cages in sea water until they reach market size, which may take around 12 – 18 months. Most of their output is sold to processors or smokers in Scotland.

The business required a range of resources such as an on-shore base to service cages, store feed and other materials and an area for net washing and repairs. Unpolluted and sheltered water was needed to hold the salmon cages. Equipment such as vehicles, boats, moorings, cages, nets, feeders and accessories, net washer, harvest boxes, ice machine and a jetty crane were also required.

McGregor had to obtain a 15 year lease from Crown Estate Commission (CEC) for use of the sea bed. He also had to go on a training course to familiarise himself with the 10 different statutory bodies and more than 50 pieces of legislation that address salmon farming. The business had to register with the Scottish Office Agriculture Environment and Fisheries Department (SOAEFD) as required by the Diseases of Fish Act 1983. The farm is visited regularly by the SOAEFD.

Source: adapted from SAC Farm Diversification web site.

(a) McGregor & Son are not likely to make a profit in their first two years of trading. Explain why.

(b) (i) What might McGregor & Sons customers want in terms of quality?

(ii) What role might the SOAEFD play in quality control?

(c) How might McGregor & Son monitor the performance of the fish farm?

Meeting the assessment criteria

In your investigation you need to explain how a business manages its resources to provide quality output.

Business example – Friends Abroad Ltd

Friends Abroad Ltd was set up to provide holidays for single people. It organises special interest holidays for single people. The business:

- takes special care to ensure that each client is sold exactly the right sort of holiday by asking clients to complete detailed questionnaires;
- is customer focused and interviews all clients over the telephone after their holiday for valuable feedback;
- provides a wide range of special interest holidays, such as skiing, walking, camping, snorkelling and diving, sailing, golfing, and visiting historic sites;
- records and monitors all complaints;
- is a member of ABTA, an organisation which protects consumer rights and listens to complaints.

Source: adapted from company information.

Mark Band 1 *You need to provide a basic knowledge and understanding of business resources and quality issues.*

Friends Abroad understands the importance of satisfying customers and providing a quality service. It gathers lots of information about clients to make sure that they are sold the right sort of holiday. It monitors performance by interviewing clients over the telephone when they return. This will provide the business with feedback which can be used to improve the service in the future. The company is also a member of ABTA which gives consumers protection.

Mark Band 2 *You need to provide a sound knowledge and understanding of business resources and describe relevant quality issues.*

Friends Abroad Ltd is customer focused. This means that its activities are driven by customers. For example, it gathers a lot of information from clients before a particular holiday is sold. It matches the interests and needs of clients with specific holidays. This helps to guarantee quality. Friends Abroad attempts to improve the quality of its service by interviewing clients when they return. The information it gathers can be used to improve holidays in the future. The company also has a complaints procedure to help monitor quality and performance. The owner of the company deals with complaints in person. Sometimes clients are offered a free holiday if she thinks the case is a deserving one. Friends Abroad is a member of ABTA. This organisation protects consumer rights and listens to complaints.

Mark Band 3 *You need to provide a comprehensive knowledge and understanding of business resources and analyse the firm's approach to quality.*

Friends Abroad provides holidays for single people. This is a specialist area and the business needs to gather as much information as possible to ensure that customer needs are met. It does this by asking clients to complete detailed questionnaires. This information is used to make sure that clients are sold the most appropriate holiday. If their needs are perfectly matched by the holiday sold the consumer will be satisfied. Friends Abroad monitors quality and product performance in two ways. It records all customer complaints and deals with each case thoroughly. The owner takes responsibility for all complaints and deals with them personally. The company also telephones clients when they return. It has gathered a lot of useful information when doing this. It has been able to improve the quality of the service and products based on some of the telephone conversations. Finally, Friends Abroad is a member of ABTA. This organisation helps protect consumers. For example, they safeguard client's money when a holiday company collapses.

20 The profit and loss account

What are accounts?

Businesses must keep a record of their transactions with customers and suppliers. These are needed to produce financial statements, which can be used to help monitor the financial 'health' of the business. These financial statements are called accounts. Two key statements are produced.

- **The profit and loss account.** This contains information about the revenue, costs and profit that a business records during the year.
- **The balance sheet.** This contains information about the debts, capital and resources owned by the business.

Accounts are useful for different stakeholders in the business. Owners, customers, employees, the Inland Revenue, other competitors and banks that may provide loans can see how well the business is performing.

The importance of profitability and liquidity

In the long term businesses have to make a profit. This is because the owners want a financial return on the money they invested in the business. Although businesses might have other aims and objectives, it is still necessary for them to make a profit. Profit is the reward to entrepreneurs for taking risk. If they do not receive an adequate financial return they will withdraw their interest. This is likely to result in the business closing down.

The profit made by a business is usually an indication of how well it is doing. If profit increases over time this suggests that the business is improving. Figure 1 shows the profit made by Tesco over five years. During this time profit increased from £1,054m to £1,962m. This is a significant improvement and the shareholders are likely to be pleased with this performance. The increase suggests that Tesco is doing well.

In the short term, however, a business may be able survive without making a profit. For example, when a business first sets up many owners do not expect to make a profit for the first few months or even years. But a business cannot survive without cash. It is therefore important to make sure the business has enough liquid resources. Liquid resources include cash and those, such as stocks, that can be converted into cash within 12 months. Without cash, a business cannot trade. Cash is needed to pay immediate bills such as wages, telephone, electricity and raw materials. If these bills are not paid the services are likely to be withdrawn and the business could not operate. Monitoring the firm's cash position is a crucial management activity. The management of cash flow is discussed in more detail in section 20.

Assets, liabilities, expenses and revenue

The transactions recorded by a business are sorted by bookkeepers and placed into various categories.

- **Assets** are the resources that a business owns and uses. Examples include plant, machinery, equipment, vehicles, stocks and cash. Details of these are shown in the balance sheet and

Figure 1 *Tesco gross profit before tax 2001-2005*

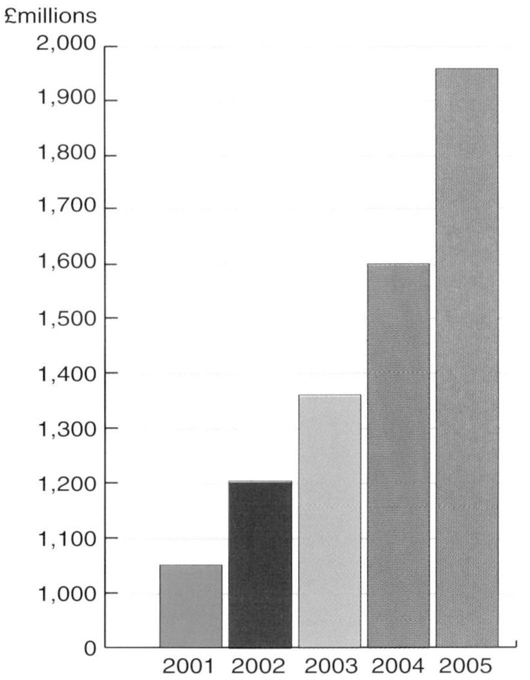

Source: adapted from Tesco, *Annual Report and Accounts.*

are explained in section 19.

- **Liabilities** are the debts of the business. The money owed to suppliers, bankers and other businesses for example. Details of these are also shown in the balance sheet and are explained in section 19.
- **Expenses** are the overheads of the business, such as rent, electricity and rates. Details of expenses are summarised in the profit and loss account.
- **Revenue** is the money that a business receives from selling its output. This is also shown in the profit and loss account.

Businesses will incur costs before they start trading, for example registering a company or converting premises. These may be called **start-up costs**. Once a business begins trading there will also be **running costs**, such as wages and heating.

The profit and loss account – sole traders

The amount of profit made by a business is calculated in the profit and loss account. The profit and loss account shows the income the business has received during a trading period. It also shows the expenditure on resources that have already been used and those that will be used within 12 months. Table 1 shows a profit and loss account for Manish Popat, a sole trader who set up an ice-cream parlour in Brighton in 2003. He has been trading for one year. What details does this profit and loss account show?

Turnover This is the revenue generated by Manish Popat's ice-cream parlour. In 2004 the business generated £67,500. This figure does not include VAT. This is because VAT does not belong to the business. It is sent to the government.

Cost of sales This is the cost associated with production. In this case it is likely to be the cost of buying in ice-cream and other stocks which are resold. For a manufacturer it could include the direct costs of labour, materials and other costs such as machinery maintenance.

Table 1 *Profit and loss account for Manish Popat*

Manish Popat
Profit and loss account y/e 31.7.04

	£	£
Turnover		67,500
Cost of sales		32,300
Gross profit		35,200
Less Expenses		
Wages	8,700	
Rent	10,200	
Heat & light	1,100	
Motor expenses	3,400	
Insurance	700	
Bank charges	550	
Other overheads	2,100	
		26,750
Net profit		8,450

Figure 2 *Cost of sales adjusted for stock*

	£
Opening stock	0
Add Purchases	34,400
	34,400
Less Closing stock	2,100
Cost of sales	32,300

The cost of sales has to be adjusted for stock. This is to take into account the stock the business had at the start of the year and how much was left over at the end of the year. Figure 2 shows the adjustments for Manish Popat's business.

In this case the opening stock is 0 because the business has just been set up. During the year Manish bought £34,400 of stock. Therefore the value of purchases for the year is £34,400 (£34,400 + 0). At the end of the year there was £2,100 left over. This is the closing stock and should be subtracted from the total above. The cost of sales is therefore £32,300.

Gross profit The gross profit for the business is found by subtracting cost of sales from the turnover. Gross profit is the profit made by the business before expenses have been subtracted. Manish Popat's business made a gross profit of £35,200. The top part of the account, where the gross profit is calculated, is known as the trading account.

Expenses These are sometimes called overheads. They are costs not associated with production. For example, Manish had motor expenses of £3,400. In total, the expenses for the year amounted to £26,750.

Net profit The amount of profit left over for the owner is called net profit. This is found by subtracting expenses from gross profit. Manish Popat's business made £8,450 in its first year of trading. Manish might decide to keep this or retain it in the business to provide extra funding.

Profit and loss account – limited companies

The accounts of limited companies are subject to some legal requirements and have slightly different features to those of sole traders. The profit and loss account for Moreton Ltd, a car maintenance and repair business, is shown in Table 2.

Limited companies have to publish their accounts by law. This means that anyone can see the accounts. It is usual for accounts to show two years' figures. This allows readers to make comparisons. The profit and loss account can be divided into three parts.

Table 2 *Profit and loss account for Moreton Ltd*

Moreton Ltd Profit and loss account y/e 31.12.04	2004 £000	2003 £000
Turnover	2,455	2,110
Cost of sales	1,430	1,270
Gross profit	1,025	840
Administrative expenses	820	710
Operating profit	205	130
Net interest payable	50	50
Profit on ordinary activities before tax	155	80
Taxation	40	20
Profit on ordinary activities after tax	115	60
Dividends	25	20
Retained profit	90	40

Trading account This is calculated by subtracting cost of sales from turnover, like a sole trader. It gives a figure for gross profit. Moreton Ltd made a gross profit of £1,025,000 in 2004.

The profit and loss account This is made up of a number of parts.

- Expenses are costs not linked to production, such as administration and distribution costs. They are totalled and entered as one figure to avoid cluttering up the account with detail. Moreton's expenses rose from £710,000 to £820,000 over the two years.
- Administrative expenses are subtracted from gross profit to show operating profit. This is net profit before tax and interest have been subtracted. Moreton's operating profit rose in 2004 from £130,000 to £205,000.
- Any interest paid or received has to be shown in the accounts of limited companies. Sometimes they are shown separately. However, in this case the net figure is shown (interest received – interest payable). In the Moreton account the net interest payable was £50,000 in both years.
- Interest is subtracted from operating profit to get the profit on ordinary activities before tax. For Moreton, net profit before tax has increased from £80,000 to £155,000.
- Limited companies have to pay corporation tax. This is subtracted to get net profit on ordinary activities after tax. Moreton's after tax profit rose from £60,000 to £115,000.

Appropriation account This shows what happens to profit which is earned. Some may be returned to shareholders as dividends, for example. This is subtracted from net profit to get retained profit. The dividend paid by Moreton rose by 25% to £25,000 in 2004. The retained profit will be used to buy new tools and equipment, for example.

Profit margins

Although the amount of profit made by a business helps to show how well a business is performing, a better indicator is the profit margin. This is the amount of profit a business makes in relation to its turnover.

Gross profit margin This is the gross profit expressed as a percentage of turnover. Figure 3 shows the formula to calculate the gross profit margin. Using this formula, the gross profit margin for Moreton Ltd in 2003 and 2004 were 39.8% and 41.8%. For example, in 2004 gross profit was £1,025,000 and turnover was £2,455,000, so the gross profit was £1,025,000 ÷ £2,455,000 x 100. The margins show a slight improvement. Whether a particular gross margin is good or not depends on the industry. Moreton would have to compare the 41.8% in 2004 with another car maintenance company.

Net profit margin The net profit margin helps to measure how well a business controls its overheads. If the difference between gross profit and net profit is small, this suggests that overheads are low. This is because net profit equals gross profit less overheads. The net profit margin is also expressed as percentage of the turnover and can be calculated using the formula in Figure 4. The net profit used in the formula is the profit before tax and interest, i.e. the operating profit. Moreton's net margins for 2003 and 2004 were 6.2% and 8.4%. For example, in 2004 net profit was calculated as £205,000 ÷ £2,455,000 x 100. Net profit margins have improved over the two years. Moreton would have to compare these with another company in the industry to judge whether the performance was good or not.

Figure 3 *Gross profit margin*

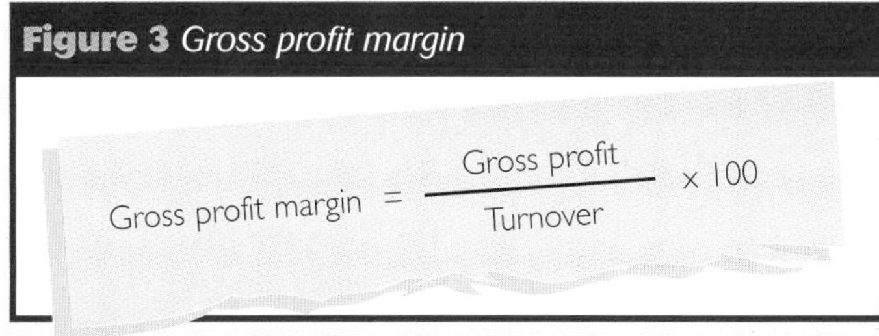

Figure 4 *Net Profit margin*

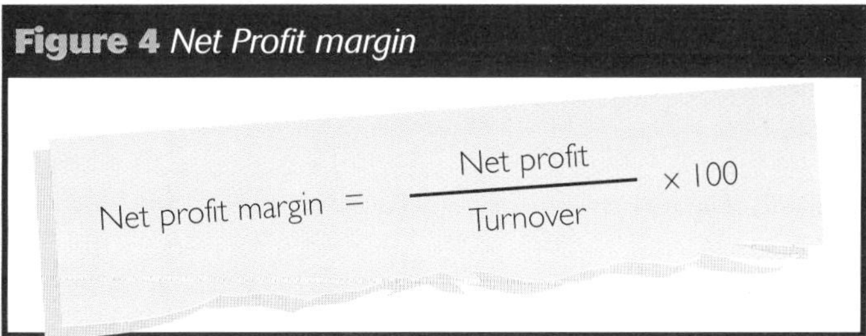

- Choose three companies that trade in the same industry.
- Obtain annual reports from these companies. Alternatively visit their websites where profit and loss accounts can usually be accessed.
- Find the profit and loss accounts for these companies.
- Calculate the gross and net profit margins for each one.
- Explain which is the best performing company.

Research task

Portfolio practice · J Sainsbury plc

Table 3 *Profit and loss account for Sainsbury*

	2004 £m	2003 £m
Turnover	17,141	17,079
Cost of sales	15,658	15,688
Gross profit	1,483	1,391
Administrative expenses	827	717
Operating profit	656	674
Other income *	14	53
Profit on ordinary activities before interest	670	727
Net interest payable	60	60
Profit on ordinary activities before tax	610	667
Taxation	206	206
Profit on ordinary activities after tax	404	461
Dividends	309	305
Retained profit	95	156

* Includes profits on disposal of assets, profits from joint ventures and profit from the sale of property.

Source: adapted from J Sainsbury, *Annual Report and Accounts.*

J Sainsbury, the supermarket chain, is a public limited company. It has experienced strong competition in recent years due to the growth of Tesco, Asda and Morrisons. Table 3 shows the profit and loss account for Sainsbury in 2004.

(a) Describe the running costs that Sainsbury incurs.
(b) (i) Explain how gross profit and net profit are calculated for Sainsbury.
(ii) How might Sainsbury use the retained profit?
(c) (i) Evaluate the performance of Sainsbury during 2004 and (ii) discuss whether the shareholders should be concerned.

Meeting the assessment criteria

For your chosen business you must identify and explain the start-up and running costs. You must also explain how the profit and loss account can be used to monitor the performance of the business.

Business example – Rejuvenations

Kelly Morrison practices aromatherapy, reflexology and stress management. Treatments range from a head and neck massage to a complete holistic consultation. Kelly spent £15,000 when setting up Rejuvenations. Most of the money was used to convert a shop into a treatment centre. The rest was spent furnishing the centre and buying essential equipment such as a treatment couch, computer, and treatment packs. In the first year of trading Kelly hoped to break even but exceeded her expectations. The profit and loss account is shown in Table 4.

Table 4 *Profit and loss account for Rejuvenations*

Rejuvenations
Profit and loss account y/e 30.6.04

	2004 £m	**2003 £m**
Turnover		71,600
Cost of sales		23,200
Gross profit		48,400
Less Expenses		
Wages	18,300	
Rent	12,000	
Heat & light	1,400	
Motor expenses	1,200	
Insurance	1,600	
Advertising	3,700	
Other overheads	5,200	
		43,400
Net profit		5,000

Source: adapted from company information.

Mark Band 1 *Provide a basic understanding of financial management by identifying some start-up and running costs and commenting generally on profit as a method of monitoring performance.*
Kelly Morrison started up by spending £15,000 converting a shop into a treatment centre and buying equipment such as a treatment couch. The money spent on decorating the premises and creating the right ambience was important for the type of business. Running costs can be seen in the profit and loss account. Examples include £18,300 paid in wages, £12,000 rent and £3,700 paid to advertise the company. In the first year of trading Kelly did well. She made a profit of exactly £5,000. This was better than she had planned.

Mark Band 2 *Provide a sound understanding of financial management by identifying some start-up and running costs and commenting generally on profit as a method of monitoring performance.*
When a business is first set up a lot of start-up costs are incurred. In this case, £15,000 was spent converting the premises into a suitable environment for a treatment centre. Money was used to decorate and furnish the centre to make sure that the ambience was appropriate for aromatherapy, reflexology, and stress management. Once a business starts to trade it incurs running costs. These are shown in the profit and loss account of Rejuvenations. Examples include cost of sales, such as oils and treatment materials, wages, rent, motor expenses and advertising. In the first year of trading Kelly hoped to break-even. However, according to the profit and loss account Rejuvenations made a £5,000 profit. This suggests that the business has performed well.

Mark Band 3 *Provide a comprehensive understanding of financial management by explaining the start-up costs and running costs and evaluating profit as a method of monitoring performance.*
Rejuvenations was set up by Kelly Morrison to provide treatment courses in reflexology aromatherapy and stress management. Treatments range from a head and neck massage to a complete holistic consultation. The start-up costs were about £15,000. Some of the money was used to convert a shop into a treatment centre. There were also decorating and furnishing costs. A number of assets were purchased such as a treatment couch, a computer and other equipment. Once the business started trading it had to meet a variety of running costs. The largest of these was the cost of sales. This is expenditure on materials such as oils and treatment packs. Other expenses which had to be met were wages, rent, heating, motor expenses and advertising. Despite these costs Kelly's business made a profit in the first year. She had hoped to break even but in fact Rejuvenations made £5,000. She planned to reinvest this in business. Finally, Kelly calculated the net profit margin. It was about 7%. She planned to increase this to 10% next year.

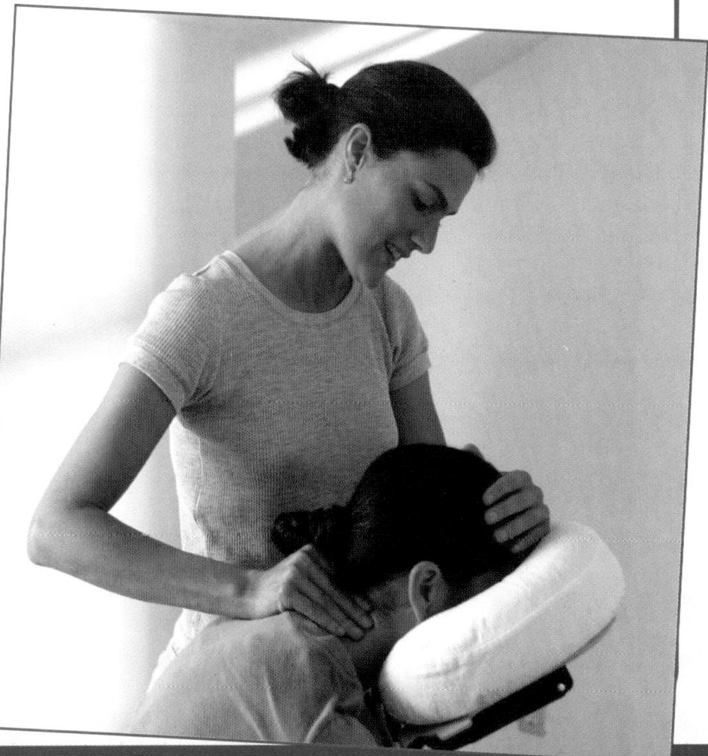

The balance sheet

What does a balance sheet show?

The balance sheet shows the financial position of a business at a particular point in time. It provides information about the firm's assets, liabilities and capital.

Assets These are the resources that a business owns and uses. In the balance sheet they are divided into **current assets** and **fixed assets**. Fixed assets are those which the business buys to use over and over again for a long period of time. Examples include premises, plant, machinery, equipment and vehicles. Current assets are those that are used up in production such as stocks of raw materials and components and cash. Debtors, the money owed by customers, is also a current asset.

Liabilities These are the debts of the business. In the balance sheet liabilities are divided into **current liabilities** and **long term liabilities**. Current liabilities include money owed that must be repaid within twelve months. Examples would be money owed to suppliers and a bank overdraft. Any money owed for more than one year is a long term liability. Examples might include a mortgage or a five year bank loan.

Capital This is the money put into the business by the owners. For example, a limited company raises capital by selling shares. This is listed as share capital in the balance sheet. Capital is often used to fund the setting up of the business.

The accounting equation

The accounting equation shows a very important relationship that exists between the assets, capital and liabilities of a business. It states that the value of all the resources owned by a business, i.e. its assets, must equal the value of all the money introduced into and owed by the business, i.e. the capital and liabilities. This is shown in Figure 1.

The two sides of the equation must always be equal to each other. This is because the value of all the money raised by the business from owners and other creditors, must be the same as the value of all the resources bought using that money. For example, Sheila Timms used £6,000 of her own money and a £3,000 bank loan to set up a PC repair business. She bought a new computer for £2,000 and a vehicle for £4,500. She put the rest of the money in a business bank account. After these transactions the financial position of Sheila's business can be shown using the accounting equation in Figure 1.

Figure 1 *The accounting equation*

Assets	=	capital	+	liabilities

£2,000 + £4,500 + £2,500 = £6,000 + £3,000

£9,000 = £9,000

Sheila's business owns three assets, a computer (£2,000), a vehicle (£4,500) and cash in the bank (£2,500). The total value of these assets is £9,000. The value of capital put into the business by Sheila is £6,000 and the amount owed to creditors is £3,000. Therefore the value of capital and liabilities added together is £9,000 (£6,000 + £3,000). This means that the value of assets and the value of capital and liabilities added together are both the same at £9,000. This will always be the case for any business at any time.

Rearranging the accounting equation, as in Figure 2, can be useful to understand the structure of the balance sheet.

Figure 2 *Re-arranging the accounting equation*

Assets – liabilities = capital

The structure of the balance sheet

The financial information shown in a balance sheet is set out in a particular way. It is based on the rearranged accounting equation shown above. Table 1 shows the balance sheet for Brigitte Dauche's business, a patisserie.

Table 1 *Balance sheet for Brigitte Dauche's business*

Brigitte Dauche
Balance sheet as at 31.12.04

	£	£
Fixed assets		
Ovens		4,700
Equipment		4,000
Vehicle		3,000
		11,700
Current assets		
Stock	1,200	
Cash at bank	2,950	
Cash in hand	550	
	4,700	
Current liabilities		
Trade creditors	3,450	
Net current assets		1,250
Long term liabilities		
Bank loan		(4,000)
NET ASSETS		**8,950**
FINANCED BY:		
Capital		
Opening capital		7,500
Add Net profit		12,300
		19,800
Less Drawings		10,850
Closing capital		**8,950**

What does the balance sheet show? The top part represents the left-hand side of the accounting equation, assets–liabilities.

Fixed assets These are assets which are intended for repeated use. The business has three fixed assets, ovens, equipment and a vehicle. According to the balance sheet these are valued at £11,700.

Current assets These are assets which are likely to be changed into cash within one year. The current assets are stocks of raw materials, cash at bank and cash in hand. The total value of current assets is £4,700.

Current liabilities Current liabilities are monies owed which have to be repaid within one year. The patisserie has just one current liability. This is trade creditors. £3,450 is owed to suppliers.

Net current assets This is current assets - current liabilities. Net current assets shows the working capital of the business. This is the amount of liquid resources a business has to fund daily trading. In this case working capital is £1,250 (£4,700 - £3,450).

Long term liabilities These are monies owed which are not due to be repaid for at least a year. The patisserie owes £4,000 to a bank. It is shown in brackets because it is a minus figure.

Net assets This is the total in the top part of the balance sheet. Net assets is total assets less total liabilities. It is calculated in the balance sheet by adding net current assets to fixed assets and subtracting long term liabilities. The net assets for Brigitte's business is £8,950 (£11,700 + £1,250 - £4,000).

The bottom half of the balance sheet shows the capital of the business. It deals with the interests of the owner and represents the right-hand side of the accounting equation.

Opening capital This is the amount of money owed to the owner by the business at the beginning of the trading year. It is the same as the closing capital balance at the end of the previous year. The opening capital for the patisserie is £7,500.

The opening capital is added to the net profit for the year. This comes from the profit and loss account. Brigitte's patisserie made £12,300 net profit during the year. The balance of opening capital and profit is £19,800.

Drawings Drawings are money taken by the owner for personal use. Drawings are subtracted from opening capital and net profit to get the closing capital balance. Drawings is the money taken out of the business by Brigitte during the year for personal use. The closing capital for the patisserie is £8,950 (£19,800 - £10,850). This will be the opening capital balance for next year's balance sheet.

Closing capital The closing capital balance of £8,950 is exactly the same as net assets. This shows that the balance sheet balances and that assets - liabilities = capital.

Limited company balance sheets

The balance sheet shown in Table 1 is for a sole trader. Limited company balance sheets have slightly different features. Table 2 shows the balance sheet for Prince Ltd, a manufacturer of leather garments and goods.

The structure of a limited company balance sheet is the same as that of a sole trader. The top section shows assets - liabilities and the bottom section shows capital. However, there are some differences.

Table 2 *Balance sheet for Prince Ltd*

Prince Ltd
Balance sheet as at 31.12.04

	£000	£000
Fixed assets		
Tangible assets	2,100	1,950
Current assets		
Stocks	122	109
Debtors	255	208
Cash at bank and in hand	90	120
	467	437
Creditors: amounts falling due within one year	210	188
Net current assets	257	249
Creditors: amounts falling due after one year	(290)	(312)
Net assets	2,067	1,887
Capital and reserves		
Called up share capital	1,000	1,000
Other reserves	340	421
Profit and loss account	727	466
Shareholders funds	2,067	1,887

- Fixed assets include a total for tangible assets of £2,100,000 in 2004. Tangible assets are physical assets such as plant and machinery, vehicles, tools and equipment.
- Many businesses also have intangible assets (non-physical). These are not usually shown on the balance sheet unless they have been bought. One example is goodwill. This is the difference between the value of net assets and what might be paid for firm if it was sold. The amount paid is likely to be higher because the business has an established customer base.
- Current assets are listed in the same way as in a sole trader balance sheet. However, current liabilities are called creditors: amounts falling due within one year. The two terms mean exactly the same. Net current assets are calculated in the same way as in a sole trader balance sheet.
- Long term liabilities are called creditors: amounts falling due after one year in a limited company balance sheet. The two terms mean exactly the same and the amount is subtracted from the fixed assets and net current assets.
- The bottom half of the balance sheet shows the capital and reserves of the business. In a limited company account this is the money owed to the shareholders. Called up share capital of £1,000,000 is the money put into the business by shareholders.
- Reserves are shareholders' funds that have built up over the life of the company. One of the main ones is retained profit. This is listed as profit and loss account in the Prince Ltd balance sheet.
- The total amount owed to shareholders is £2,067,000 in 2004. This is exactly the same as net assets.

How might the balance sheet be used?

- It provides a summary of all assets, liabilities and capital.
- It shows the value of working capital. This is important because it is the amount of liquid resources a firm has to pay its bills. It is often said that if current assets are between one and a half and two times the size of current liabilities, the business has enough working capital, although it depends on the business. Supermarkets, for example, run on very low levels of working capital because they are paid mainly in cash.
- It shows the asset structure of the business. This is how the business has used all of the money raised. Prince Ltd has invested about 80% of its money in tangible assets. This means that the business owns a lot of plant, machinery and equipment.
- It shows the capital structure of the business. This shows the different sources of funds used by business.
- The net assets in the balance sheet provides a rough guide to the value of the business. Prince Ltd is worth roughly £2,067,000. Also, if net assets increase over time, this suggests the company is growing.

Limitations of the balance sheet

- The balance sheet does not list all of the assets. Unless intangible assets have been purchased they do not normally appear on the balance sheet. This means that the value of the company could be understated.
- The values of some assets may be inaccurate. For example, fixed assets are valued at cost less depreciation. Depreciation, which allows for the falling in value of fixed assets, as they are 'used up', has to be estimated by accountants. Therefore if the estimations are inaccurate the fixed asset values will also be inaccurate.
- The balance sheet reflects the financial position of the business for one day only. The values of assets, liabilities and capital are likely to change the next day when trading continues.

- Obtain two company balance sheets from annual reports or from the Internet. Choose two companies in the same industry.
- Compare the financial positions of the two businesses. Look at working capital, net assets, the amount of debt the business has, the asset structure, the capital structure and the cash position.
- Suggest which company is in the best financial position.

Research task

Portfolio practice · Pass & Go

Pass & Go, a driving school, was set up 12 months ago by Nathan Sharpe. He used £12,000 of his own savings and borrowed £6,000 from a bank. Nathan bought a dual control car and a computer and operated from his home in Devon. At the end of the year he felt that things had not gone too well. Some of the costs were a lot higher than he anticipated. A balance sheet is shown in Table 3.

(a) (i) How much did Nathan take out of the business for his own personal use during the year?
(ii) What will be the value of opening capital in next year's balance sheet?

(b) (i) Explain TWO reasons why the business made a loss during the year.
(ii) Explain TWO limitations of a balance sheet as a means of financial management.

(c) Discuss the evidence in the balance sheet which might suggest that Pass & Go performed poorly in the first year.

Table 3 *Balance sheet for Pass & Go*

Pass & Go
Balance sheet as at 30.6.04

	£	£
Fixed assets		
Car		12,600
Computer		1,000
		13,600
Current assets		
Debtors	500	
Cash	100	
	600	
Current liabilities		
Trade creditors	2,100	
Bank overdraft	1,900	
	4,000	
Net current assets		(3,400)
Long term liabilities		
Bank loan		(6,000)
NET ASSETS		**4,200**
FINANCED BY:		
Capital		
Opening capital		12,000
Less net loss		2,800
		9,200
Less Drawings		5,000
Closing capital		**4,200**

Meeting the assessment criteria

In your investigation you need to consider how a business will monitor its performance. You might explain how the balance sheet can be used to do this.

Business example – J & C Herbs

J & C Herbs, set up three years ago, produces culinary and medicinal herbs in the south of Scotland. The business rents twelve acres of land and a building (used for storage, processing and packaging). It was set up with a bank loan and £15,000 of owner's capital. This was used to buy irrigation and protection equipment, harvesting and drying equipment, seeds, fertilisers and sprays and packaging materials. The 2004 balance sheet for the business is shown in Table 4.

Mark Band 1 *Provide basic knowledge and understanding of financial management. Perhaps use a balance sheet to describe briefly the financial position of the business.*

J & C Herbs looks to be in a good financial position. It has quite a lot of working capital. This is because its current assets are much larger than its current liabilities. The business is also very solvent. It has over £12,000 of cash. During the year the owner took out £26,250. Since the profit for the year was £27,300, not very much was retained by the business.

Mark Band 2 *Provide sound knowledge and understanding of financial management. Perhaps use a balance sheet to analyse the financial position of the business.*

The balance sheet can be used to help monitor the performance of the business. In this case the balance sheet for J & C Herbs shows the business to be financially stable. Current assets are three times the size of current liabilities. This means the business has a good amount of working capital. The cash flow of the business appears to be good. The business has £12,200 of cash. This represents more than two thirds of the total for current assets and could easily pay off the current liabilities of £5,300. The balance sheet also shows that the business made £27,300 profit last year. Most of this was withdrawn from the business by the owner. This means that not much profit was retained by the business. This may not matter because J & C Herbs has a lot of cash in the bank.

Mark Band 3 *Provide comprehensive knowledge and understanding of financial management. Perhaps use a balance sheet to evaluate the financial position of the business.*

The balance sheet can be used in the financial management of a business. It provides some important information. For example, it shows how much working capital the business has. J & C Herbs has more than adequate working capital. Its current assets are three times the size of current liabilities. The business also has a good cash position. There is £12,200 in the business's bank account. This represents about two thirds of the firm's current assets. This will reassure the owner and perhaps encourage some investment in the future. J & C Herbs has also grown slightly over the two years. The value of closing capital is slightly higher than the opening capital. The firm also made a profit of £27,300 in 2004. Most of this was withdrawn by the owner. Finally, although the balance sheet is useful it has some limitations. For example, it does not include intangible assets. This means the value of the business might be understated. It is also a static document. This means that it will be out of date when trading continues the next day.

Table 4 *Balance sheet for J & C Herbs*

J & C Herbs
Balance sheet as at 31.10.04

	£	£
Fixed assets		
Equipment		6,700
Tools		2,300
		9,000
Current assets		
Stocks	3,500	
Debtors	2,100	
Cash	12,200	
	17,800	
Current liabilities		
Trade creditors	5,300	
Working capital		12,500
Long term liabilities		
Bank loan		(5,000)
Net assets		**16,500**
Capital		
Opening capital	15,450	
Add Profit	27,300	
	42,750	
Less Drawings	26,250	
Closing capital		**16,500**

Source: based on industry information - SAC Farm Diversification web site.

22 Cash flow forecasting

The purpose of cash flow forecasting

An important part of the planning process when setting up a business is cash flow forecasting. This involves:

- estimating the cash coming into the business each month;
- estimating the cash going out of the business each month;
- calculating the expected monthly cash balance.

Businesses produce **cash flow forecasts** to help control their cash flow. It is important to monitor cash flow because without cash a business cannot trade. It needs cash to pay bills such as wages and raw materials.

Cash flow forecasts are useful for businesses in a number of ways.

Planning They are part of the planning process when setting up and running a business. When constructing a cash flow forecast business owners and managers are forced to think about the future. This is because they have to estimate future costs and revenues. The forecast will show how much cash the business is likely to have at the end of each period, such as a month, in the future. This will help to show whether a business has enough cash to survive and meet other spending needs.

Loan applications When a business is setting up it may have to borrow money. Bank managers, for example, will need evidence to show that the business can repay a loan or overdraft. A cash flow forecast could be used to provide some of this evidence. The forecast will help show whether a business can afford the repayments in the future. It also shows that owners or managers have taken business planning seriously.

Monitoring cash flow During the year and at the end businesses can compare the cash balances in the forecast with those on their bank statement. The figures on the bank statement show the actual flows of cash and monthly balances. By doing this they can find out where problems have occurred. For example, why in a particular month was too much money spent? Constant monitoring in this way should improve cash control.

Constructing a cash flow forecast

A cash flow forecast is a financial document and is usually produced using a spreadsheet. It shows how cash is expected to flow into and out of a business during a future time period. The forecast shown in Table 1 is for Jenkins Ltd, a supplier of cakes and pies to shops in Cornwall. When constructing a cash flow forecast the figures are placed in columns which represent a particular period, in this case a month.

Receipts Receipts are the expected inflows of cash. In this case most of the cash is from sales of pies and cakes. However, in June, £1,500 is expected to be received from another source, a tax refund perhaps.

Payments Payments are the expected costs that the business will have to meet. These figures represent cash outflows. For example, in May Jenkins Ltd expects to pay £2,000 in wages, £800 for raw materials, £1,200 in rent and £3,400 in other expenses. The expected total payments or cash outflows in May is £7,400.

Table 1 *Cash flow forecast for Jenkins Ltd (£)*

	May	June	July
Receipts			
Sales	10,500	11,000	10,000
Other receipts	0	1,500	
Total receipts	10,500	12,500	10,000
Payments			
Wages	2,000	2,000	2,000
Raw materials	800	900	1,000
Rent	1,200	1,200	1,200
Other expenses	3,400	3,800	7,600
Total payments	7,400	7,900	11,800
Net cash flow	3,100	4,600	(1,800)
Opening balance	2,100	5,200	9,800
Closing balance	5,200	9,800	8,000

Brackets show negative amounts.

Net cash flow Net cash flow is the difference between receipts and payments. If receipts are greater than payments net cash flow will be positive. If they are lower, net cash flow will be negative. The net cash flow for Jenkins Ltd is expected to be positive in May and June. For example, it is £4,600 (£12,500 - £7,900) in June. In July, however, it is negative at minus £1,800 (£10,000 - £11,800).

Opening balances The opening balance is how much cash the business is expected to have at the beginning of each month. For example, in July Jenkins Ltd expects to have £9,800.

Closing balances The closing balance shows how much cash is expected to be left after a month's trading. The closing balance is calculated by adding the net cash flow to the opening balance. For example, in May for Jenkins Ltd the opening balance is £2,100. The net cash flow is expected to be £3,100. Therefore, the closing balance is £5,200 (£3,100 + £2,100). In July the net cash flow is expected to be minus £1,800. This means that the closing balance will be lower at £8,000 (£9,800 - £1,800). The closing balance in each period becomes the opening balance in the next period.

Interpreting cash flow forecasts

Owners or managers have to interpret information shown in cash flow forecasts. A cash flow forecast is shown in Table 2 for Gurrinder Singh's photography studio which she plans to set up in April. What does it show?

- After a slow start sales are expected to rise steadily. They are expected to be relatively high near to Christmas.
- Gurrinder starts the business with £4,000 of her own money.
- Rent and advertising costs are expected to be stable each month

Table 2 *Cash flow forecast for Gurrinder Singh's business (£)*

	Apr	May	Jun	Jul	Aug	Sep	Oct	Nov	Dec
Receipts									
Sales	500	1,000	1,500	2,000	2,500	3,000	3,000	4,500	6,000
Own capital	4,000								
Total receipts	4,500	1,000	1,500	2,000	2,500	3,000	3,000	4,500	6,000
Payments									
Rent	1,200	1,200	1,200	1,200	1,200	1,200	1,200	1,200	1,200
Equipment	3,500				2,000				
Advertising	500	500	500	500	500	500	500	500	500
Other expenses	300	300	600	300	300	1,000	300	300	1,000
Total payments	5,500	2,000	2,300	2,000	4,000	2,700	2,000	2,000	2,700
Net cash flow	(1,000)	(1,000)	(800)	0	(1,500)	300	1,000	2,500	3,300
Opening balance	0	(1,000)	(2,000)	(2,800)	(2,800)	(4,300)	(4,000)	(3,000)	(500)
Closing balance	(1,000)	(2,000)	(2,800)	(2,800)	(4,300)	(4,000)	(3,000)	(500)	2,800

Brackets show negative amounts.

- Large amounts are expected to be spent in April and August on equipment.
- Other expenses are expected to be higher than normal in June, September and December.
- Net cash flow is not expected to become positive until September. This is common for a new business.
- The closing balance starts as negative and get worse until August. The cash position improves at the end of the year and becomes positive in December. The business is going to be short of cash between April and November. This might be because insufficient funds were provided in the first place. Since the forecast shows that Gurrinder's business is going to be short of cash, she would have to take some action, as explained below.

Suggesting appropriate action

After analysing a cash flow statement it may be necessary for a business to take some action. If the forecast shows that a business has liquidity problems (i.e. is running out of cash, shown by negative closing and opening balances) the following action might be appropriate.

- Borrow some money.
- Postpone all unnecessary spending.
- Sell stock cheaply for cash.
- Collect debts more aggressively.
- Extend credit with suppliers.
- Sell some unwanted assets.
- Sell assets and lease them back.
- Reduce drawings.

In the case of Gurrinder's business, some action will have been necessary because the closing balance was expected to be negative for eight of the nine months, probably because she did not have enough start-up capital. Start-up capital would have helped to pay for the equipment and keep the business afloat while it became established. By December the business expected to have a positive closing balance. If the business finds that its closing balance is getting bigger and bigger, cash could be taken out by the owners or used for investment.

Benefits of cash flow forecasts

Cash flow forecasts have certain benefits for a business.

- They can show whether a business will have enough cash in the future. They also warn owners about possible cash shortages in the future.
- They force owners and managers to plan ahead. This should help to run the business more effectively.
- They can be used to provide evidence about the financial performance of the business when making applications for loans.
- When produced on a spreadsheet it is possible to show the effect of changes in payments and receipts on the closing balance instantly.

Limitations of cash flow statements

Cash flow forecasts also have some limitations.

- Much of the financial information in the forecast is estimated. If the estimates are inaccurate the closing balances will also be

Use the Internet or financial sections of newspapers to find a business that is experiencing cash flow problems.

Explain:

- why the business has cash flow problems;
- what measures have been taken to resolve the cash flow problems;
- whether you think the business will survive in the future.

inaccurate. This could result in owners drawing wrong conclusions and taking inappropriate action.

- Some owners might manipulate forecasts. They might overestimate cash inflows to make the expected cash position look better than it really is.
- External forces such as competition or economic factors could affect the actual cash flows. This will make the forecast less useful. One way to allow for unforeseen events is to build contingency funds into the forecast by making a monthly allowance for unforeseen spending.

Meeting the assessment criteria

In your investigation you need to consider how a business will monitor its performance. You can explain how cash flow forecasting can play a role in this task.

Business example - Alan Frank Sandwiches

Alan Frank sells sandwiches and other cold snacks from a kiosk he rents in Brighton town centre. He prepares a cash flow forecast every six months to help plan the running of the business and to monitor its performance. For example, he uses it to see whether he will have enough cash in the future. At the end of the six months he compares the estimated closing cash balances with the business bank statements to see how accurate his forecast was.

Mark Band 1 *Provide basic knowledge and understanding of financial management. Use cash flow forecasts to describe briefly the performance of the business.*

Alan understands the importance of firm financial management when running his business. He produces regular cash flow forecasts to aid planning and help monitor the performance. For example, he uses it to see whether he will have enough cash in the future. The forecast in Table 3 shows that sales are expected to rise as summer approaches. This is probably because the town is busier in the summer months. The cash position of the business is expected to be healthy and improve throughout the year. The closing cash balance is expected to rise every month. Over the period the closing cash balance is expected to rise from £1,100 to £4,800. At the end of the six months Alan will compare the estimated closing cash balances with the business bank statements. This will show him how accurate his cash forecasts were.

Mark Band 2 *Provide sound knowledge and understanding of financial management. Use cash flow forecasts to analyse the performance of the business.*

It is important for business owners to monitor the performance of their businesses. One way in which Alan Frank manages his finances is to construct cash flow forecasts. Businesses produce cash flow forecasts to help control their cash flow. It is important to predict cash flow because without cash a business cannot trade. It needs cash to pay bills such as wages and raw materials. Alan's forecast in Table 3 shows clearly that the cash position of the business is expected to improve throughout the period. The closing cash balance is expected to rise from £1,100 in April to £4,800 in September. One reason for this is because sales are expected to increase during the summer months. The largest net cash flow is in April. This is because some new capital is expected to be introduced to boost the cash position. Without this fresh capital the closing balance would be just £100 in April. Raw materials costs are expected to rise throughout the year, but this is to be expected because sales also rise. Generally the business is expected to perform well over the future time period shown. Alan could take some cash out of the business later in the year when the balance is expected to rise above £3,000. However, this could depend on how much sales fall in the winter months.

Mark Band 3 *Provide sound knowledge and understanding of financial management. Use cash flow forecasts to evaluate the performance of the business. An intergrated approach might also be used by using break-even analysis for example.*

One way in which Alan Frank monitors the performance of his business is to construct cash flow forecasts. It is important to forecast the cash position carefully because without cash a business is not able to trade. Some cash is always needed to pay immediate bills. The forecast shows Alan what his expected closing cash balances will be for a six month period. He will also take the trouble to compare these closing balances with the balances on the bank statements each month. This will show how accurate his forecasts are.

The forecast in Table 3 shows that the business is expected to do well. The closing balances of the business are all

Table 3 *Cash flow forecast for Alan Frank's business (£)*

	Apr	May	Jun	Jul	Aug	Sep
Receipts						
Sales	2,000	2,500	3,000	2,900	3,000	2,100
Fresh capital	1,000					
Total receipts	3,000	2,500	3,000	2,900	3,000	2,100
Payments						
Rent	400	400	400	400	600	600
Raw materials	400	500	600	600	700	600
Other expenses	400	500	500	500	500	400
Drawings	400	400	400	400	400	400
Total payments	1,600	1,800	1,900	1,900	2,200	2,000
Net cash flow	1,400	700	1,100	1,000	800	100
Opening balance	(300)	1,100	1,800	2,900	3,900	4,700
Closing balance	1,100	1,800	2,900	3,900	4,700	4,800

expected to be positive and increase throughout the six month period. This is because sales are expected to rise and overheads are forecast to be be kept under control. The amount spent on raw materials is estimated to rise but this is to be expected if sales grew. By the end of the period the closing cash balance is predicted to rise from £1,100 to £4,800. Alan might decide to withdraw some of the cash for himself or invest it to improve the business.

Although cash flow forecasts are useful other methods of financial management might be helpful. For example, Alan might use break-even analysis to see if his business breaks even during the six months. To do this he would have to calculate costs and revenue for the period. If total costs are exactly equal to total revenue the business will break even. Finally, Alan would need to understand that cash flow forecasting has certain limitations. For example, much of the financial information in the forecast is estimated. If the estimates are inaccurate, the closing balances will also be inaccurate. This could result in Alan drawing incorrect conclusions and taking inappropriate action for the future period.

Portfolio practice · Shelly's Flower Shop

Shelly Simms plans to open a small flower shop in her home town of Worcester in March. She has found some premises which she can rent for just £400 a month. Shelly will put £1,000 of her own money into the business and borrow a further £1,000 from a bank in March. £900 of this money will be spent buying equipment and getting the shop ready for trading. Shelly expects running costs to be £100 a month except in August when she will have to pay an extra £1,000 for business rates. She plans not to take any money out of the business for personal use for three months. However, from June onwards she will pay herself £400 a month. She has estimated sales and stock purchases for a six month period. These are shown in Table 4.

(a) Using examples from the case study distinguish between start-up costs and running costs.
(b) Construct a six month cash flow forecast for Shelly's flower shop.
(c) Analyse the closing cash balances.
(d) Evaluate the options available to Shelly to deal with the cash position at the end of August.

Table 4 *Cash flow forecast, March-August, (£)*

	Mar	Apr	May	Jun	Jul	Aug
Sales	500	1,000	1,200	1,400	1,700	1,700
Stock (flowers & plants)	700	500	600	700	700	800

23 Budgeting

Budgets

A budget is a financial plan. It is often presented in a table or spreadsheet and shows how much money a business plans to spend or receive in a future time period. Budgets are usually produced for six or twelve monthly periods. Table 1 shows a cost budget for Intercafe, an Internet café. Each column represents monthly expenditure plans. For example, in January Intercafe plans to spend a total of £4,700. Some examples of planned spending in January include £1,000 for rent, £800 on wages, £500 on computer leasing and £500 on advertising. Over the six month period shown, Intercafe plans to spend between £4,450 and £5,090 per month. The pattern of planned spending is fairly steady. There are no sharp fluctuations.

Table 1 *Cost budget for Intercafe (£)*

	JAN	FEB	MAR	APR	MAY	JUN	Total
Rent	1,000	1,000	1,000	1,000	1,000	1,000	6,000
Wages	800	800	900	1,000	1,000	1,000	5,500
Computer leasing	500	500	500	500	500	500	3,000
Food purchases	700	800	900	900	1,000	1,100	5,400
Heating & lighting	900	900	800	700	400	400	4,100
Advertising	500	0	500	0	200	0	1,200
Other costs	300	450	490	500	600	600	2,940
Total	4,700	4,450	5,090	4,600	4,700	4,600	28,140

Types of budget

Businesses make use of different types of budgets.

Sales budgets The most important budget is probably the sales budget. This is because it affects all other budgets produced by a business. For example, if a business plans to increase sales during the year it will also have to produce more. This means that the production cost budget, the cash budget and the materials budget will all be affected. Sales budgets can show either the sales revenue planned by a business or the number of units it plans to sell. Table 2 shows the sales revenue budget for Aarzoo Kumar's business. Aarzoo supplies Indian foods to restaurants and other caterers in the West Midlands. The budget shows that sales revenue is planned to increase over the time period. It also shows that sales are expected to be significantly higher in June than all other months. This is because Aarzoo has some contracts to supply food for a number of weddings in June.

Table 2 *Sales revenue budget for Aarzoo Kumar's business (£)*

	APR	MAY	JUN	JUL	AUG	SEP	Total
Meat samosas	1,200	1,200	2,400	1,500	1,600	1,700	9,600
Veg. samosas	700	700	1,600	900	900	900	5,700
Shami kebabs	2,000	2,400	3,900	2,500	2,800	2,800	16,400
Sheek kebabs	1,000	900	2,100	900	1,000	1,100	7,000
Total	4,900	5,200	10,000	5,800	6,300	6,500	38,700

Production budgets Production budgets are used to plan production levels. They are influenced by sales budgets and stock levels. Production budgets can show the number of units a business plans to produce or the costs of planned production. Table 3 shows the production budget for Aarzoo Kumar's business. Aarzoo does not keep any stocks since her products are perishable. The production budget shows how many units of each product must be made to generate the revenue plans shown in the sales budget. For example, in April, 6,000 meat samosas (which sell for 20p each) must be produced to generate the £1,200 sales revenue planned. Vegetable samosas sell for 10p, shami kebabs for 50p and sheek kebabs for 50p.

Table 3 *Production budget for Aarzoo Kumar's business*

	APR	MAY	JUN	JUL	AUG	SEP	Total
Meat samosas	6,000	6,000	12,000	7,500	8,000	8,500	48,000
Veg. samosas	7,000	7,000	16,000	9,000	9,000	9,000	57,000
Shami kebabs	4,000	4,800	7,900	5,000	5,600	5,600	32,900
Sheek kebabs	2,000	1,800	4,200	1,800	2,000	2,000	13,800

Purchases budgets These show the planned purchases of materials and other resources that a business needs. The purchases budget will have an important impact on cost budgets.

Labour budgets These can show the amount of money a business plans to spend on labour in a future period. Alternatively they could show the different types of labour a business plans to use, the number of workers needed or the number of labour hours planned.

Capital expenditure budgets These show the amount of money a business plans to spend on tools, machinery, plant and equipment.

Cash budgets These show how much cash a business plans to spend and receive. They are similar to cash flow forecasts explained in section 22.

Profit and loss budgets These show the amount of profit or loss a business plans to make. It will list all the costs and expenses that a business plans and the revenues it expects to generate.

Marketing budgets These show the amount a business plans to spend on promoting its products. It can include expenditure on advertising or other forms of promotion such as public relations.

Purpose of budgets

Budgets are used to help the financial control of businesses. For example, budgets can help a business avoid overspending. Managers use budgets for a number of reasons.

Controlling Budgets can be used by managers to control the level of spending in a business. Since budgets are plans they provide financial targets which staff are expected to meet. If the targets are met then spending will have been contained.

Reducing fraud Budgets can help to reduce fraud in a business. All spending has to be authorised by budget holders. This means that money cannot be spent unless the budget holder has granted permission. This stops staff from spending money on things for their own personal use.

Planning Budgets force a business to plan ahead. This means that managers are more likely to foresee problems before they occur. For example, they may avoid running out of cash by spreading expenditure on new machinery. If budgets were not used managers could be tempted to run businesses on a day-to-day basis. This could result in future problems being overlooked until too late.

Motivation Budgets can be used to motivate staff. If they meet the targets set by budgets they could be rewarded. For example, sales staff might be given bonuses for reaching sales revenue targets.

Budgetary control

Budgetary control is an ongoing process that involves making plans by setting financial targets, measuring the firm's performance and taking corrective action if targets are not met. The different stages in budgetary control are shown in Figure 1.

- Preparing budgets. The first step is to prepare the budgets. This involves the setting of financial targets. They are represented by the spending or revenue plans in the firm's budgets. Budgets themselves are influenced by the firm's business aims and objectives.
- Calculating variances. At the end of the budget period the performance is measured by calculating variances. A variance is the difference between a budgeted value and an actual value. Variances can be adverse or favourable. **Favourable variances** occur when the actual figures are 'better' than the budgeted figures. **Adverse variances** occur when budgeted figures are 'worse' than the actual figures. Table 4 shows some examples. For example, if total costs were planned to be £200,000 and actual costs were only £187,000, there would be a favourable variance of £13,000 (£200,000 - £187,000) because costs were lower than planned. If budgeted total revenue was £350,000 and actual revenue was only £310,000, there would be an adverse variance of £40,000 (£350,000 - £310,000) because revenue was lower then planned.
- Analysing variances. Variance analysis involves looking at the variances and trying to determine why they have occurred. For example, an adverse labour cost variance may have occurred because staff were working too slowly.
- Taking action. Once the reasons for particular variances have been established, managers must take action. This will help to improve future financial performance. In the above example, workers might need some extra incentive to ensure that they work more quickly. Even if variances are favourable, managers can take action. They can act positively if they discover reasons why actual figures are better than the budgeted figures.

Table 4 *Favourable and adverse variances*

Budgeted costs	Actual costs	Difference	Favourable or adverse
£200,000	£187,000	-£13,000	Favourable (as lower)
£200,000	£210,000	+£10,000	Adverse (as higher)
Budgeted revenue	**Actual revenue**	**Difference**	**Favourable or adverse**
£300,000	£330,000	+£30,000	Favourable (as higher)
£300,000	£280,000	-£20,000	Adverse (as lower)

Types of variance

Sales variance A sales variance is the difference between the budgeted sales revenue and the actual sales revenue. Sales variances will occur if either the volume of actual sales is different from the budgeted volume or if the budgeted price is different from the actual price. Sales variances might arise if:

- discounts are offered to customers;
- new competitors enter the market and drive the price down;
- there are shortages in the market and higher prices can be charged;
- there is a fall in demand due to a recession;
- there are changes in the quality of the product;
- changes in marketing activities affect demand.

Figure 1 *Stages in budgetary control*

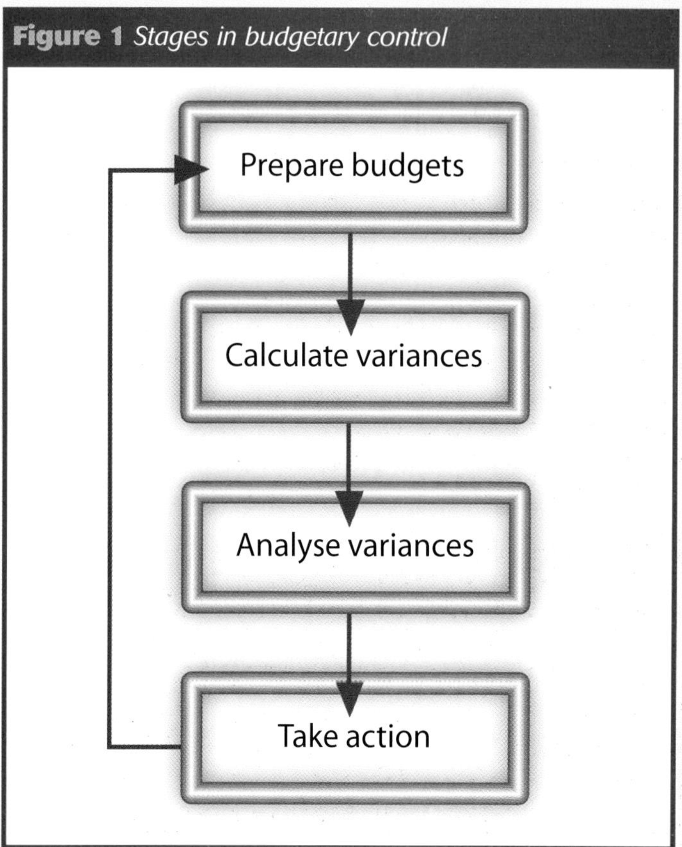

Materials variance A materials variance is the difference between the budgeted materials cost and the actual materials cost. Materials variances will occur if either the volume of actual materials is different from the budgeted volume or if the budgeted cost is different from the actual cost. Materials variances may arise if:

- materials are wasted in production;
- materials are bought from new suppliers at different prices;
- inflation causes the cost of materials to rise from suppliers;
- better quality or inferior materials are bought.

Labour variance A labour variance is the difference between the budgeted labour cost and the actual labour cost. Labour variances will occur if either the amount of actual labour is different from the budgeted amount or if the budgeted cost of labour is different from the actual cost. Labour variances may arise if:

- the productivity of labour changes;
- working practices change;
- workers are given better training or improved tools and machinery;
- wage rates change;
- the type of worker employed is changed.

Fixed overhead variance This is the difference between the budgeted fixed overhead and the actual fixed overhead. Fixed overhead variances might arise if:

- there are changes in overhead costs, such as rent, rates or insurance;
- efficiency is improved so that less factory space is needed for example.

Every year the government gives details of 'The Budget'. The Budget shows how much money the government plan to spend in the next financial year and where it is going to come from. Find out the following using either a publication such as the *Financial Times* from the library or placing 'The Budget' into a search engine on the Internet.

- How much does the government plan to spend in total?
- What are the main areas of government spending?
- Which is the highest item of government expenditure?
- How much is going to be spent on education?
- What are the different sources of government revenue?
- Which is the largest source of revenue?

Research task

Portfolio practice - Get Floored

Kerry Lau is a franchisee. She runs the Swallowfield branch of Get Floored which sells parquet blocks (herring bone and other patterns), plank and strip boards, skirting boards, architraves, stairs, boarders and matwells. The business also renovates and maintains existing wooden beams and staircases. She uses budgetary control to monitor the performance of the business. Table 5 shows budgeted overheads and actual overheads for the most recent six month trading period. During the year Kerry was ill for 6 weeks and was not able to work. Her assistant kept the shop open but was not able to carry out restoration work.

(a) Using this case as an example, explain what is meant by budgetary control.
(b) Complete Table 5 by calculating the overheads variances.
(c) Explain the difference between a favourable and an adverse variance using examples from the case.
(d) Analyse the variances calculated in (b).

Table 5 *Actual and budgeted overheads for a six month trading period for Get Floored*

	Budgeted	Actual	Variances
Rent	£9,000	£9,000	
Wages	£21,000	£27,000	
Heat & Light	£2,100	£2,300	
Insurance	£1,000	£1,000	
Motor expenses	£4,300	£3,800	
Other O'heads	£3,400	£3,600	
Total	£40,800	£46,700	

Meeting the assessment criteria

In your investigation you need to consider how a business will monitor its performance. You might explain how budgetary control can play a role in this task.

Business example - Liam's Gifts

Liam Johnson runs a small gift shop in Blackpool. After making a loss in the first year, his bank manager advised him to pay more attention to financial control. In 2004 he decided to set targets and use budgets. Table 6 shows the sales budget for Liam's business for the last six months of 2004. At the end of the year he calculated the monthly sales variances. These are also shown in Table 6.

Table 6 *Sales budget, actual sales figures and sales variances for Llam's gift shop, 2004 (£)*

	JUL	AUG	SEP	OCT	NOV	DEC	Total
Budgeted sales	13,000	15,000	14,000	10,000	8,000	5,000	65,000
Actual sales	15,000	18,500	14,000	9,500	7,000	4,000	68,000
Sales variance	2,000(F)	3,500(F)	0	500(A)	1,000(A)	1,000(A)	3,000(F)

Favourable variance (F)
Adverse variance (A)

Mark Band 1 *Provide basic knowledge and understanding of financial management. Perhaps use budgetary control to describe briefly the financial position of the business.*

After making a loss in the first year Liam followed the advice of his bank manager and paid more attention to financial control and monitoring. He decided to use budgetary control. This involves setting budgets, calculating variances by comparing budgeted figures with actual figures, analysing the variances and then taking corrective action. Liam decided to focus on sales revenue. In the last six months of 2004 actual sales were greater than budgeted sales. There was a favourable sales variance of £3,000 (£68,000 - £65,000). This means that sales for the budget period exceeded the target set by Liam. However, some months were better than others. Liam noticed that sales were better than planned in July and August but worse in October, November and December.

Mark Band 2 *Provide sound knowledge and understanding of financial management. Perhaps use budgetary control to analyse the financial position of the business.*

Liam wanted to improve the financial performance of his business and decided to follow the advice of his bank manager. Liam thought that if he set sales targets and monitored the monthly sales progress he would know what was going on and be able to respond to the information that he gathered. By setting targets for sales in budgets and analysing sales variances he might be able to improve sales levels in the future. In the last six months of 2004 there was a favourable sales variance of £3,000. However, some months were better than others. Liam thought that sales in July and August were higher than expected because the weather was generally good in those two months and there were more tourists in Blackpool. However, as winter approached sales figures did not meet targets. For example, in December there was an adverse sales variance of £1,000. Liam thought that one of the reasons for this was that the shop was only open at weekends in December.

Mark Band 3 *Provide comprehensive knowledge and understanding of financial management. Perhaps use budgetary control to evaluate the financial position of the business.*

Budgetary control can be used by businesses to improve financial performance. It encourages business owners to set targets and monitor performance indicators such as sales and costs. Liam adopted this approach and produced a six month sales budget for his small gift shop. At the end of the budget period he calculated monthly variances and attempted to analyse them. The sales variance for the whole budget period was favourable. Actual sales exceeded budgeted sales by £3,000. However, the pattern of monthly sales variances threw up some interesting observations. The sales variances in July and August were both favourable. Liam thought that this was due to extra tourists in Blackpool attracted by the good weather. He also felt that sales could be higher if he extended opening hours in the summer, until 9.00pm instead of 6.00pm. However, in October, November and December sales variances were adverse. This was due to a lack of tourist customers in these months. It may also have partly been because he lost a bit of interest in the business and often shut the shop. For example, in December he only opened at weekends. Next year Liam decided to open all week. He also decided to raise prices a little. Liam felt that tourists would not really notice a 5% increase in the prices of gifts. This would help to raise sales revenue and in next year's sales budget he planned to raise total monthly sales revenue by around 10%.

24 Break-even

Breaking even

Business owners often want to know how much they have to sell to break-even. The formula used to calculate break-even is shown in Figure 1.

Figure 1 *Calculating break-even*

A business will break-even where

total revenue = total costs

The **break-even point** of a business is where total revenue from sales is exactly the same as the total costs of producing a good or providing a service. The level of output where total costs and total revenue are the same is called the **break-even output**.

A business will need information about its costs and price to calculate the break-even output. For example, say that a business has total costs of £15,000 and charges £30 for its product. It will break-even at an output of 500 goods because £30 x 500 = £15,000. At this level of output the business neither makes a loss nor a profit. It simply breaks even.

The break-even point can be used to help monitor the performance of the business. For example, when setting up a new business an owner might aim to break-even in the first year of trading. If, by the end of the year, the business makes a small profit then the target has been exceeded. The break-even point is often crucial for owners. This is because they know that after the break-even point is reached, the sale of further units generates a profit. It can be an important 'milestone' for business owners.

Calculating break-even using contribution

One method used to calculate the break-even point is to use **contribution**. Contribution is the amount of money left over after variable cost is subtracted from the selling price of each unit of output.

Consider the example of Jack Bevan who plans to publish a lifestyle magazine called 'Highlife'. The magazine's fixed costs (FC) are £20,000 per month and its variable costs (VC) are £1 per copy. Jack plans to sell the magazine for £3.00. The contribution made by Highlife is calculated in Figure 2.

Figure 2 *Calculating contribution*

Contribution = selling price – variable cost

Contribution = £3 - £1 = £2

To calculate the number of copies needed to break-even a formula can be used. This is shown in Figure 3, which also calculates the number of copies Jack needs to produce and sell of the magazine to break-even.

Figure 3 *Calculating break-even using contribution*

$$\text{Break-even point} = \frac{\text{Fixed costs}}{\text{Contribution}} = \frac{£20,000}{£2} = 10,000 \text{ copies}$$

Jack Bevan's new magazine, Highlife, will break-even if 10,000 copies are sold. Total revenue will be £30,000 (£3 x 10,000) and total costs will also be £30,000 (£20,000 + [£1 x 10,000]).

Calculating the break-even point using costs and revenues

Another way of calculating the break-even point is to use total costs and total revenues. Jack Bevan's magazine will break-even if total cost is equal to total revenue. For Highlife fixed costs are £20,000 a month. Fixed costs are costs which do not vary with output. They might include the cost of a piece of machinery or buying a factory, for example. Variable costs increase as output increases, such as the costs of raw materials used in production.

Figure 4 *Calculating break-even using total costs and total revenues*

Total cost = fixed cost + variable cost x quantity sold

TC = £20,000 + £1Q

Total revenue = price x quantity sold

TR = £3Q

Break even is where:

TC = TR

£20,000 + £1Q = £3Q

To find Q:

20,000 = 3Q - 1Q

20,000 = 2Q

$$\frac{20,000}{2} = Q$$

10,000 = Q

Figure 5 *Break-even chart for Highlife*

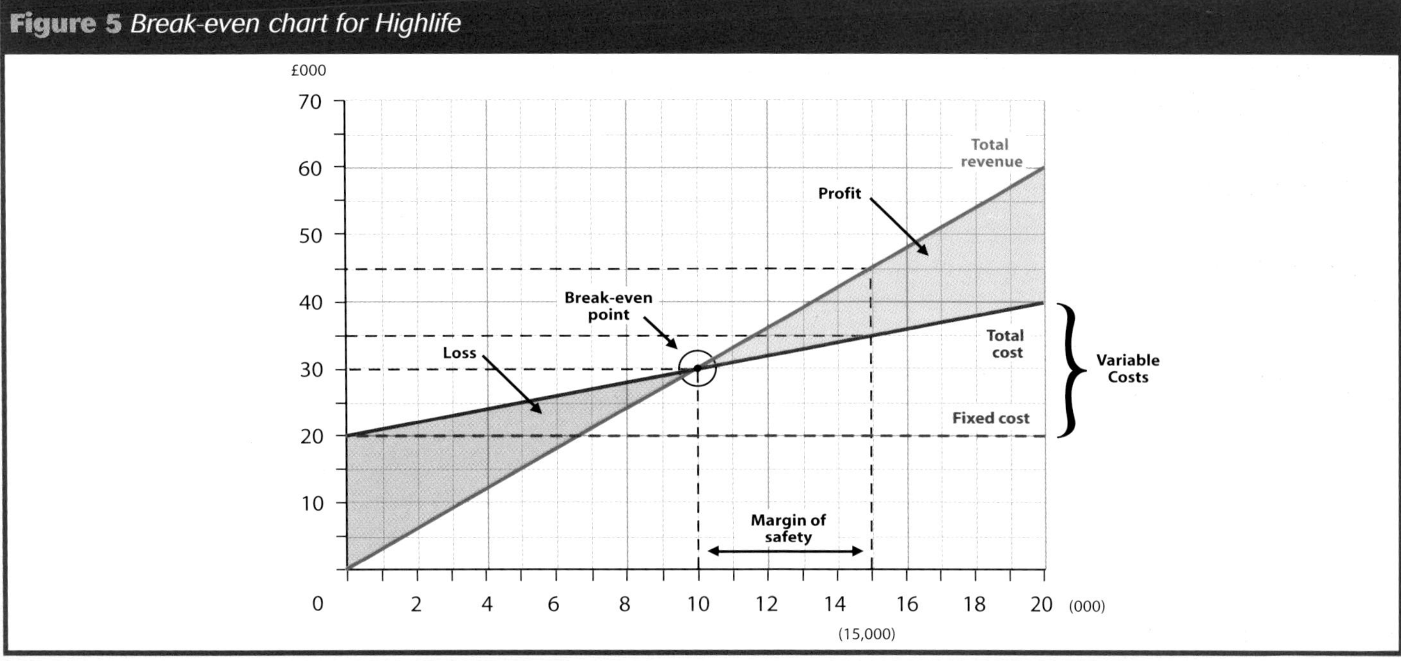

Variable costs are £1 per copy. The selling price is £3.00.

Figure 4 shows how the break-even output can be calculated. Note that this is the same output which was found using the contribution method of calculation.

Break-even charts

The break-even output for a business can be shown on a graph called a break-even chart. The break-even chart for Highlife is shown in Figure 5. The chart shows the total costs (TC), total revenue (TR) and fixed costs (FC) functions for the magazine. Output is measured on the horizontal axis and costs and revenue are shown on the vertical axis. What does the break-even chart show?

- The total revenue function shows the total revenue generated by different sales levels. For example, if 15,000 copies were sold, total revenue would be £45,000.
- The fixed cost function shows the level of fixed costs over a range of different production levels. Fixed costs do not change as output changes. In this case fixed costs are £20,000 at all production levels. It is not necessary to include the fixed cost function to show the break-even point.
- The total cost function shows the total cost of producing Highlife over a range of different production levels. For example, the total cost of producing 15,000 copies is £35,000. This is made up of fixed costs of £20,000 plus variable costs of £1 per magazine x 15,000 = £15,000.
- The **break-even point** is where total revenue equals total costs. In this case the **break-even level of output** is 10,000 copies of Highlife. Here both total revenue and total costs are £30,000.
- At levels of production above the break-even point **profits** are made. So, for example, if 15,000 magazines are produced and sold the business makes a profit of £10,000 (revenue of £45,000 - total costs of £35,000). The profit increases as more magazines are produced and sold.
- At levels of production below the break-even point **losses** are made. This is because total costs are greater than total revenues.
- The **margin of safety** shows the amount by which production can fall before the business breaks-even. So if 15,000 magazines are produced and sold the margin of safety is 5,000 (output of 15,000 - the break-even output of 10,000).

Constructing a break-even chart

The break-even chart for Highlife was constructed using the following steps

Calculate the break-even level of output This is shown above and is 10,000 copies.

Calculate points on the total revenue and total cost functions Both functions are straight lines so they can be drawn by joining two points that lie on each function. To plot the TR function we need to choose two levels of output and calculate the TR at each level. Any two levels of output could be chosen. However, construction will be simpler if 0 is chosen as one. It is also helpful to choose a second value which is twice the size of the break-even level of output. This would be 20,000 (2 x 10,000) in this case. Such a choice will ensure that the break-even point is in the centre of the chart. This will improve presentation. The value of TR at each output level is shown in Table 1.

Table 1 *Values of TR and TC at two levels of output for Highlife*

Q	Total revenue (TR)	Total cost (TC)
0	0 (0 x £3)	£20,000
20,000	£60,000 (20,000 x £3)	£40,000 (£20,000 + £1 x 20,000)

Plotting the TR function The TR function can now be plotted on a graph. The output axis should run from 0 to 20,000 copies and the vertical axis from 0 to £60,000. Using the information in Table 1, the two points, or coordinates, on the TR function are (0,0) and (20,000, £60,000). If these are plotted on the graph and joined up the TR function will appear as shown in Figure 5.

Plotting the TC function To plot the TC function we need to identify the total cost at two different levels of output. It is helpful to use the same values as those used for the TR function, i.e. 0 and 20,000. The total costs at each of these levels of output are shown in Table 1. The TC function can now be plotted on the graph. The two points which lie on the TC function are (0, £20,000) and (20,000, £40,000). If these are joined the TC function will appear as shown in Figure 5. Note that the TC function does not start at the origin like the TR function. This is because when output is zero fixed costs of £20,000 are still incurred.

The effect on break-even of changes in costs and price

The break-even chart can be used to show the effect on the break-even point of changes in fixed cost, variable cost and price.

Changes in fixed costs If fixed costs increase, a business will have to produce more to break-even. This is shown in Figure 6. When fixed costs rise both the fixed cost function and the total cost function shifts up. This means that the business will have to increase output from 20,000 to 30,000 to break-even. On the other hand, if fixed costs were to fall the business will break-even at a lower level of output

Figure 6 *The effect of an increase in fixed cost on the break-even point*

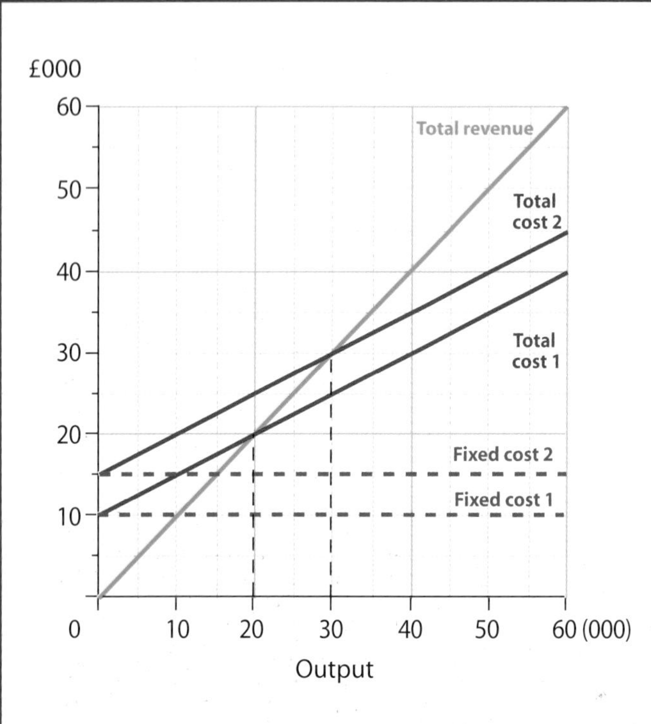

Find out whether any of the small business owners in your local area are familiar with break-even.

- Design a short questionnaire which could be used to ask them questions about break-even. Prepare about half a dozen questions but do not expect owners to discuss the financial details of their business.
- Visit about four or five small businesses.
- Write a short report discussing the importance of break-even to small businesses.

Research task

Changes in variable costs If variable costs increase, the total cost function will be steeper because total costs will rise at every level of output. This means that the business will have to produce more to break-even. On the other hand, if variable costs fall the business will break-even at a lower level of output.

Changes in price If price increases the total revenue function will be steeper because revenue will be higher at every level of output. This means the business will break-even at a lower level of output. However, if the price is decreased the total revenue function becomes flatter and more will have to be produced to break-even.

Limitations of break-even analysis

Break-even analysis is sometimes thought to be a little simplistic. Some of its assumptions are also unrealistic.

- Break-even analysis assumes that all output is sold by the business. However, many firms are not able to sell everything they produce. Also, some firms deliberately hold stocks of finished goods to help cope with fluctuations in demand.
- The break-even chart is drawn for a given set of business conditions. It cannot deal with sudden changes in business variables, such as a sudden increase in rent and prices or changes in technology.
- The model relies heavily on the accuracy of cost and price data. If this financial information is inaccurate or out of date, the conclusions drawn on the basis of the data are flawed. For example, if the actual price charged is lower than that shown on the break-even chart, the business will not break-even at the level of output shown on the chart. It will be at a higher level.
- The break-even charts used here have linear (straight line) functions. In reality the shape of the total cost and total revenue functions are not likely to be linear.

Break-even analysis is not very helpful when businesses produce a wide range of different products. It is likely that each product will have different prices and different costs. One particular problem is dividing the fixed costs of the business between all the different products. There are methods, but each has its faults. Therefore, if the fixed cost incurred by each product is unknown or uncertain, break-even analysis is less useful.

Meeting the assessment criteria

In your investigation you need to consider how a business will monitor its performance. You might explain how break-even analysis can play a role in this task. You will also need to understand the limitations of break-even analysis.

Business example - Webstart.com

Webstart.com, owned by Iqbal Khan, provides affordable website design without any need for technical know-how. You just point and click, and drag and drop, and the changes you make to your website are immediately live. Iqbal charges £15 for his online business service. Before starting, he did some research and checked out all the comparable products on the Internet. He found that most of them were American, too technical and too expensive. He paid £1,800 for a new laptop computer, so that he could be in touch with the business where-ever he was and spent a further £2,200 setting up the business. The variable costs were difficult to estimate, but he estimated that they were about £5 per customer. In the first year of trading Iqbal Khan hoped that he would get enough customers to break-even.

Source: adapted from company information.

Mark Band 1 *Provide basic knowledge and understanding of financial management. Perhaps use break-even analysis to describe briefly the financial position of the business.*
Iqbal Khan hoped to break-even in his first year of business. He wanted to recover the cost of his computer and other start-up costs. He had no experience of running a business and decided to carry on with his full-time job at a bank for the foreseeable future. His job would provide income to live off in the first year. If the business broke even he would not lose any money, but he would not make any profit either. Iqbal calculated that once his fixed costs had been covered, in the future, the contribution to profit would be £10 per customer.

Mark Band 2 *Provide sound knowledge and understanding of financial management. Perhaps analyse the financial position of the business using break-even.*
Iqbal Khan aimed to break-even in his first year of trading. He decided to use the information on costs and price to work out how many customers he would need to attract to break-even. He calculated the contribution each customer would make. It is:

$$\begin{aligned}\text{Contribution} &= \text{selling price - variable cost}\\ &= £15 - £5\\ &= £10\end{aligned}$$

This means that every sale made to a customer would contribute £10 to fixed costs or profit. The number of customers needed to break-even is:

$$\text{Break-even} = \frac{\text{Fixed costs}}{\text{Contribution}} = \frac{£4{,}000}{£10} = 400$$

Iqbal Khan now knows that if he attracts more than 400 customers in his first year of trading he will make a profit.

Figure 7 *Break-even chart for Iqbal Khan's business*

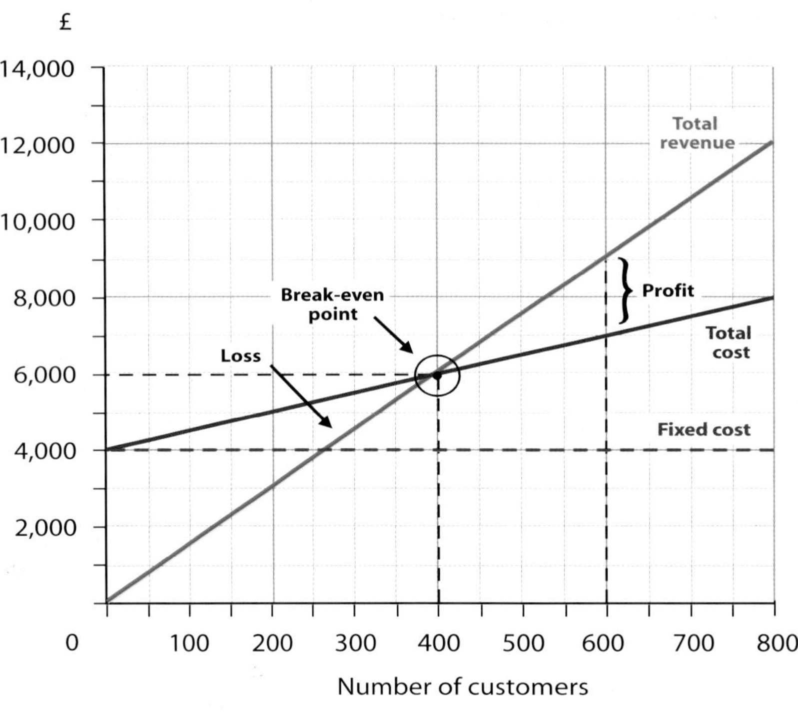

Mark Band 3 *Provide comprehensive knowledge and understanding of financial management. Perhaps evaluate the financial position of the business using break-even.*

After Iqbal Khan had decided to charge £15 for his websites he spent some time researching into the costs. He divided them into fixed costs and variable costs. Fixed costs were mainly the setting up costs, such as buying a new laptop computer. The variable costs, which were mainly administrative, were more difficult to establish. He estimated them to be £5 per customer. With this information he constructed the break-even chart shown in Figure 7. This shows that the business will break-even if he attracts 400 customers.

The chart helped Iqbal to analyse the financial position of the business. He can see how much profit or loss will be made depending on how many customers he attracts. For example, if he were to sell 600 websites he would make a profit of £2,000 (£9,000 - £7,000). However, he knew that break-even analysis had some limitations. If the variable costs were estimated incorrectly the break-even point would be different. For example, if he had underestimated the variable costs he would need to sell more websites to break-even. Iqbal Khan also knew that the break-even chart is drawn for a given set of business conditions and that it cannot deal with sudden changes in business variables, such as changes in costs and prices or changes in technology.

Portfolio practice • Mordue Records

Mordue Records is a small record company set up by Andrew Morgan providing an outlet for bands in the north east and Scotland. The label focuses on unusual and innovative styles of music and currently has about 12 bands signed up. It recently signed up a group called Abject Disorder and their first album, Distraction, was released as a CD two months ago. 2000 CDs were produced at a cost of £9,600. Mordue Records will sell the album to retailers and other outlets for £7 each. Variable costs are estimated to be £1 per album.

Source: adapted from company information.

(a) Calculate the contribution made by each CD.

(b) Calculate the number of CDs that Mordue must sell to break-even.

(c) Construct a break-even chart to show the break-even point and the amount of profit made if all 2,000 CDs are sold.

(d) Evaluate the usefulness of break-even analysis to a company like Mordue Records.

25 Spreadsheets, word processing and databases

The role of ICT in business

Most businesses today rely on Information and Communications Technology (ICT) to be efficient. ICT involves recording, storing, retrieving, manipulating and communicating information electronically. Computers are used to process information and transmit it to interested parties, both internally and externally. ICT has a wide range of applications in business, as explained in this section and section 26.

Administration Many routine tasks that involve 'paper work' can be carried out very quickly by computers. Examples might include the generation and posting of invoices and bills to customers, producing standard letters or memos, generating forms and other documents and storing huge amounts of information about customers, suppliers and staff. Computers can sort, store, manipulate, retrieve and transmit both written, numerical and visual information instantly.

Finance A lot of businesses use software to record their business transactions. Many of the systems used are integrated. For example, when a credit sale is made to a customer, the transaction is typed into the system once and is automatically entered into all the appropriate business accounts. The transaction will appear in the customer's own account, the firm's total sales list and the debtors list. Spreadsheets are also used a great deal in finance. They are very useful for presenting tables of financial information, such as budgets, cash flow forecasts and profit and loss accounts. Spreadsheets can perform calculations on tables of figures and produce graphs and charts.

Communications Developments in ICT means that information can be collected, sorted and sent electronically in a fraction of a second. Complex communications networks exist that are linked by computer and can be used to send instructions and information to people, departments and business sites all over the world. Mobile telephones, laptop computers, faxes and e-mail mean that people can work from a variety of locations. They can communicate with colleagues and access company information. The Internet provides wide ranging communication opportunities, including promotion, online selling and e-mailing.

Other applications ICT is used in production to feed information into computer numerically controlled (CNC) machines, to assist in stock control and to record and present production information, such as costs and performance indicators. It may be used in research and development (R & D) to carry out design work, tests and simulations. ICT is also used in personnel, security, marketing and many other areas of business.

Spreadsheets

Some types of information are best handled by spreadsheets. A spreadsheet allows a user to enter, store and present information in a grid on a computer screen. Most spreadsheets are used to manipulate numerical data. Table 1 shows that a grid is made up of a number of 'cells'. These cells are arranged in rows (information across the spreadsheet) and columns (information down the spreadsheet). Each cell is able to hold information which will fall into one of three categories.

- Numerical data. These are numbers which will be manipulated by the computer programme.
- Text. This refers to the words used in a spreadsheet, often headings.
- Formulae. These are the instructions given by the user which tell the computer how to manipulate the numerical data, for example add up a column of entries to give a total.

A spreadsheet is shown in Table 1. It is a sales revenue budget for Swaffham Motors. It contains information about the planned sales levels for each department over a six month period in 2005. Each column B to G shows the planned sales levels for each department each month. Each row shows the sales from a particular department over the entire six months. For example, row 3 shows the planned revenue from MOTs over the six months. Row 6 shows the total planned revenues for each month and Column H shows the planned total revenue from each department. Cell H6 shows the planned sales revenue for the whole period, i.e. £21,042,000. Totals can be calculated automatically in a spreadsheet. For example, the formula for cell B6 would be B2 + B3 + B4 + B5 or =SUM(B2:B5). If Swaffham Motors were to change any of the entries in the spreadsheet the totals will change automatically because of the formula.

Table 1 *A spreadsheet showing a six months sales budget for Swaffham Motors, 2005, (£000)*

	A	B	C	D	E	F	G	H
1	Department	JAN	FEB	MAR	APR	MAY	JUN	TOTAL
2	Repairs and maintenance	458	456	786	876	776	765	4,117
3	MOTs	110	98	97	89	103	130	627
4	Motor car sales	1,445	1,256	1,329	1,876	2,228	2,667	10,801
5	Parts and accessories sales	786	978	678	834	1,021	1,200	5,497
6	Total	2,799	2,788	2,890	3,675	4,128	4,762	21,042

Some spreadsheets are much larger than the computer screen with many columns and rows. The screen can only show part of the spreadsheet. However, scrolling enables the user to scan over the entire spreadsheet until the section required is shown on the screen.

Advantages of spreadsheets

There is a number of advantages of using spreadsheets.

- Numerical data is recorded and shown in a clear and ordered way.
- Editing allows numbers, text and formulae to be changed easily to correct mistakes or make changes to the data.
- It is easy to copy an entry or an entire series of entries from one part of the spreadsheet to another, or from one spreadsheet to another. This is particularly useful when one number has to be entered at the same point in every column.
- Numbers can be added, subtracted multiplied and divided anywhere on the spreadsheet.
- Spreadsheets calculate the effect of entry changes automatically. This is sometimes referred to as the 'what if' facility. For example, what would happen to cell X (total costs) if the entry in cell D (labour costs) increased by 10%? The answer can be calculated instantly.
- Many spreadsheets allow users to generate graphs and charts from the data.

Spreadsheets are used a lot to store and present financial information. They are used by management to aid decision making. One well known spreadsheet programme is Microsoft Excel. The budget in Table 1 was produced using Excel. Cash flow forecasts can also be produced using Excel. One of the problems when preparing cash flow forecasts is that if one of the entries needs to be changed, a lot of other numbers in the forecast, such as the closing balances, have to be changed as well. However, when an entry is changed in a spreadsheet any other cells linked by a formula will be changed automatically. This saves a lot of time and may prevent calculation errors providing entries are correct.

Table 2 *Break-even information in a spreadsheet*

	A	B	C	D	E	F
1	Quantity	Fixed cost	Variable cost	Total cost	Price	Total revenue
2	0	5,000	0	5,000	400	0
3	10	5,000	3,000	8,000	400	4,000
4	20	5,000	6,000	11,000	400	8,000
5	30	5,000	9,000	14,000	400	12,000
6	40	5,000	12,000	17,000	400	16,000
7	50	5,000	15,000	20,000	400	20,000
8	60	5,000	18,000	23,000	400	24,000
9	70	5,000	21,000	26,000	400	28,000
10	80	5,000	24,000	29,000	400	32,000
11	90	5,000	27,000	32,000	400	36,000
12	100	5,000	30,000	35,000	400	40,000

Break-even information can also be presented on a spreadsheet. Table 2 shows some break-even information. The fixed cost, variable cost, total cost, price and total revenue values are shown for a range of output 0 – 100 units. According to the table 50 units of output have to be sold to break-even. Both total cost and total revenue are £20,000 at this level of output. Again, the main advantage of using spreadsheets to present such information is the speed with which changes can be made to the figures if one entry has been amended.

Word processing

Word processing software, such as Microsoft Word, is likely to be used in all business departments. Documents such as letters, reports, forms and memos are likely to be used by a wide range of personnel. They can be produced, amended, updated and stored efficiently without generating huge amounts of paper that would have to be stored in a filing cabinet, for example. Using a computer for word processing has a number of advantages.

- Presentation can be of a high quality. All text is typed and users can choose from different font styles and sizes. Colour can be used and there is a choice of different presentation styles.
- Text documents can be drafted and 'polished' efficiently, by cutting and pasting and using a spell-checker. Word processing software applications can check grammar and punctuation to improve quality.
- Templates giving standard formats can be used for letters and forms. This saves time because much of the document will already be written. It might also help to build up a corporate image if standard documents contain the company logo, for example.
- Graphs, tables and clip art can be easily incorporated into text documents from spreadsheets and databases. It is also possible to merge documents.
- Documents can be sent to people as attachments using e-mail. This may avoid the need to print them out and save money on stationery and postage. This is particularly efficient if the same document has to be sent to a large number of recipients.

Databases

A database is really an electronic filing system. It allows huge quantities of data to be stored cheaply and efficiently. Every business which uses computers will compile and use databases. The information is stored so that it can be updated and recalled when needed. Table 3 shows part of a database for a furniture retailer. It gives details about the stock held by the business. The collection of common data is called a file. A file consists of a set of related records. In the database in Table 3 all the information on the Bathroom rails, for example, is a record. The information on each record is listed under headings known as fields, e.g. stock number, supplier, date delivered quantity and cost. A good database will have the following facilities.

- 'User-definable' record format, allowing the user to enter any chosen field on the record.
- File searching facility for finding specified information from a file, eg identifying all items of stock that were purchased before 31.5.04 in the file shown in Table 3. It is usually possible to search on more than one criterion, e.g. all stock purchased

Table 3 *An extract from a stock database*

Description	Stock no.	Supplier	Delivered	Quantity	Cost	Valuation
Bathroom rails	21-9911	A.G Fall	23.7.04	7	£32	£224
Bookcase	34-0011	Penrose	21.5.04	4	£56	£224
Dining table	13-3390	Simpsons Ltd	12.4.04	4	£200	£800
Dining chairs	13-3779	Simpsons Ltd	21.5.04	32	£20	£640
Hat stand	22-9871	IKEA	11.7.04	6	£7	£42
Settee (bed)	31-6620	Framping plc	4.7.04	7	£230	£1,610

before 31.5.04 that cost less than £150.

- File sorting facility for rearranging data in another order, e.g. arranging the file in Table 3 in order of age with the oldest stock at the top of the list.
- Calculations on fields within records for inclusion in reports. In this case the stock valuation is calculated by multiplying quantity and cost.

An example of a business using a database is shown in Figure 1.

How does computer software improve business efficiency?

Different computer software applications will aid businesses in different ways. For example, spreadsheets will help to speed up the construction of financial statements and word processing software will help produce standardised documents. However, business efficiency is improved due to some general features.

Speed Information can be processed much more quickly in computerised systems than manual systems. Therefore tasks can be completed more quickly, which will save time and money. Also, management can be supplied with up-to-date, accurate information more quickly, which will aid decision making.

Capacity Some businesses have huge numbers of customers and employees and conduct thousands or millions of transactions. They have to process vast quantities of information. Manual systems would require huge quantities of resources such as administration staff and storage space to store and process this information.

Data handling Computers allow information to be input and accessed from different locations around the country or even the world. For example, a customer database containing two hundred thousand entries could be accessed by any authorised employee anywhere in the organisation.

User friendly The design of most business software means that staff do not need any detailed knowledge of ICT to input and retrieve data. Consequently training costs could be lower and non-specialist staff might be employed in the business which will help keep labour costs down.

Accuracy Computerised systems are much more accurate than manual systems when processing data. Partly, this is because computers do not become distracted or tired when performing large numbers of routine operations. Also, managers will benefit from having more accurate information when making decisions. However, computers can only work with the information they are given. If data is entered incorrectly then the calculations from the computer are also likely to be incorrect.

Figure 1 *Boots' database*

The Boots Advantage Card was released in September 1997. When customers buy goods they are rewarded with points which can be exchanged for other goods. With the Advantage Card, Boots was able to gain information about customers.

- **Recency/Frequency/Value** - ultra frequent, very frequent, frequent, majority, occasional (own brand), occasional (proprietary), deal seekers, and large basket buyers.
- **Lifestyle/Lifestage** – customers were divided into two segments from age 16 to 65+/ Kids and No Kids.
- **Product Repertoire.**
- **Interests.**
- **Attitude/Needs.**
- **Shopping Mode.**
- **Demographics.**

This information is stored on a database and has been used in a number of ways, such as:

- customers were sent coupons based on their prior spending habits and encouraged to increase their average spending to earn the extra Advantage points;
- to introduce new products and services that data had indicated customers would welcome, such as the Mother and Baby at Home section.

Source: adapted from www.loyalty.vg.

Visit a local supermarket to find out about the ways in which ICT is used. You will be able see for yourself in the store how ICT is being used. However, with permission, you could use a short questionnaire to gather information from staff about how ICT makes their job easier. Use your findings to comment on how ICT helps:

- the business;
- employees;
- customers.

Portfolio practice · Felham Industries

Felham Industries makes hand crafted wooden products. Budgets are used to help the financial control of the business. Table 4 shows an incomplete production cost budget for the first six months of 2005. Fixed costs are £10,000, components are £20 per unit, labour costs are £50 per unit and other variable costs are £15 per unit. Felham Industries uses spreadsheets to produce nearly all of its financial statements. It also uses databases to store records such as customers, employees, suppliers, stock and fixed assets. All of Felham's employees undergo an ICT training course when they are inducted.

(a) Use a spreadsheet to complete the production cost budget for Felham Industries.
(b) Make the necessary adjustments to the budget if fixed costs fall to £9,000 and labour costs rise to £60 per unit.
(c) Explain the advantages to Felham Industries of using spreadsheets to produce budgets.
(d) Evaluate the affect that ICT will have on the efficiency of Felham Industries.

Table 4 *Production cost budget for Felham Industries (incomplete)*

	JAN	FEB	MAR	APR	MAY	JUN
Output (units)	100	150	150	200	300	350
Fixed costs						
Components						
Labour						
Other variable costs						
Total costs						

Meeting the assessment criteria

In your investigation you need to explain how software can support a business and help it operate more efficiently, make reference to the types of software used and how it is relevant to your chosen business.

Business example – Renita's Costumes

Renita Okon owns a busy costume hire business in West London. The business has a computer and Renita uses Microsoft Office to help run her business. She uses Excel to produce cash flow forecasts every four months. A forecast for a four month period in 2005 is shown in Table 5. Renita also has a database to keep a record of the stock of costumes and customer details. She uses the customer database to identify regular customers. Each month she prints off a report to identify such customers. If a customer spends more then £200 in a six month period she sends them a gift voucher for £20. The voucher is a standard document which Renita designed using a word processing programme. The voucher can be personalised and has resulted in additional sales when used.

Mark Band 1 *Provide basic knowledge and understanding of business software. Identify and describe some software packages used by the business.*

Renita uses a computer to help run her business. In particular she uses spreadsheets, databases and word processing applications. She uses spreadsheets to produce cash flow forecasts. A spreadsheet allows a user to enter, store and present information in a grid on a computer screen. It can be programmed to calculate the receipts, total payments, net cash flow and closing balance automatically. Renita also uses a database to store customer information. A database is really an electronic filing system. It allows huge quantities of data to be stored cheaply and efficiently. Renita uses the database to identify customers who hire costumes regularly. She can do this because the database holds a record of every single customer

Meeting the assessment criteria

Table 5 *A four month cash flow forecast for Renita's Costumes*

	A	B	C	D	F
1		March	April	May	June
2	Receipts				
3	Cash sales	20,300	25,300	37,400	41,500
4	Total receipts	20,300	25,300	37,400	41,500
5	Payments				
6	Shop overheads	12,500	41,500	17,000	20,000
7	Casual labour	3,000	3,000	4,000	3,000
8	Drawings	3,000	3,000	3,000	3,000
9	New costumes		2,600		
10	Total payments	18,500	50,100	24,000	26,000
11	Net cash flow	1,800	-24,800	13,400	15,500
12	Opening balance	1,200	3,000	-21,800	-8,400
13	Closing balance	3,000	-21,800	-8,400	7,100

transaction. Renita also uses a word processor. She has designed a standard gift voucher that can be personalised. These are sent to reward regular customers and encourage them to remain loyal.

Mark Band 2 *Provide sound knowledge and understanding of business software. Identify and describe some software packages used by the business and explain how efficiency might be improved.*
Renita's Costumes is a busy business and benefits from the use of a computer. She uses a programme called Excel to produce cash flow forecasts. One of the problems when preparing cash flow forecasts is that if one of the entries needs to be changed, a lot of other numbers in the forecast, such as the closing balances, have to be changed as well. However, when using a spreadsheet, when an entry is changed any other numbers that are affected will be changed automatically. Renita also uses databases and word processing applications to improve the efficiency of the business. For example, by using standard documents, such as the personalised gift voucher, a lot of time is saved. Renita can also keep track of customer purchases on her database. For example, she can recall a customer's full details at the press of a button. Generally, the use of computer software speeds up administration tasks and the preparation of financial statements, improves access to data and saves space. Computers are also more accurate and the programmes employed by Renita are easy to use.

Mark Band 3 *Provide comprehensive knowledge and understanding of business software. Identify and analyse some software packages used by the business and discuss how efficiency is improved.*
As Renita's Costumes expanded Renita decided to invest £1,100 in a computer to cope with the growing workload. She also spent £199.99 on some software called Microsoft Office and attended an ICT course at her local technical college. Renita had never used a computer before and felt that the £300 cost of the ICT training would be a good investment. She found the programmes surprisingly easy to use and soon got to grips with spreadsheets, for example. She used Excel to produce cash flow forecasts and found that a lot of time was saved, particularly when changing entries in the forecast. For example, if the amount spent on costumes in April was changed to £4,600 on the spreadsheet, the total payments, net cash flow and closing balance for April would all change automatically. So would the opening and closing balances for May and June. Renita also uses databases and word processing applications to improve the efficiency of the business. By using standard documents, such as the personalised gift voucher, a lot of time is saved. She also used Microsoft Word to write letters, design leaflets and produce order forms. Databases are used to store customer records, stock lists, staff records and financial transactions. Renita suggests that her investment and training has paid dividends. Generally, the use of computer software speeds up administration tasks and the preparation of financial statements, improves access to data and saves space. Computers are also more accurate and the programmes employed by Renita are easy to use. Renita now has a lot more time to deal with the creative aspects of the business.

26 Specialist software

Types of specialist software

Many businesses use specialist software to help improve efficiency. It is possible to buy 'off the shelf' software packages which can be used by a wide variety of businesses. However, some businesses have to buy specialist software that is written and installed by an IT expert. This type of software will be tailored to the exact needs of the user.

Management Information Systems (MIS)

A MIS converts data from internal and external sources into information that can be used by managers to aid decision making. The diagram in Figure 1 shows how an MIS operates.

- Internal sources of data are generated by the business – staff time sheets and sales invoices, for example.
- External sources of information come from outside the business – bank statements and purchase invoices from suppliers, for example.
- This data is processed by the MIS to produce information that can be used to make decisions. For example, a business MIS is likely to have information about how much money each customer owes. From this information it would be possible to compile a list of customers that have owed money for more than three months. Managers might decide to target these customers for collection.

Generally, the bigger the business the greater need for a MIS. Each day a large corporation will process huge quantities of datawhich are then recorded, sorted, classified, summarised and stored. Quite often the data on one source document have to be recorded in many different files. For example, the data contained on a purchase invoice may have to be recorded in a supplier account, a creditors list, a purchases list, a VAT account and a stock list. A computerised MIS will do this automatically. A number of companies supply computerised MIS, such as Sage, Misys and Microsoft.

Figure 1 *Management information systems*

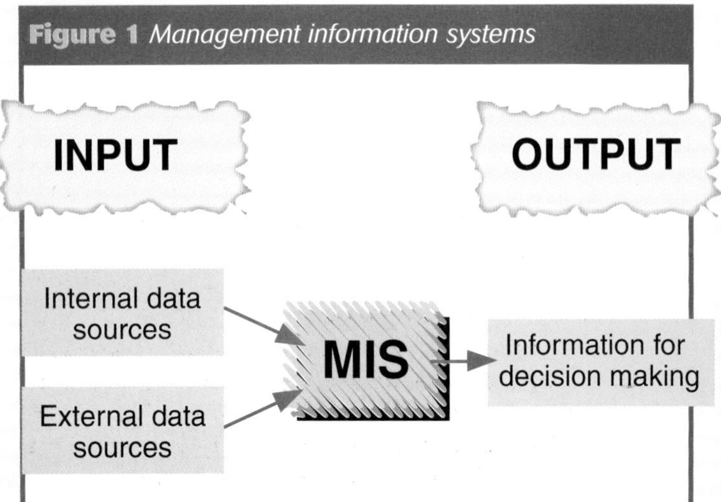

Accountancy software

Computerised accounts systems are very popular. They are used to record and store financial transactions and generate financial information such as creditors and debtors lists, profit and loss accounts and balance sheets. Many accountancy packages are integrated so that the different functions are linked. For example, if the details of a sales invoice are put into the system, both the customer account and the firm's sales ledger will be automatically updated. Then, when payment is made, the customer account, the sales ledger and the bank account will all be updated instantly. In financial accounting the most commonly used accounting applications include:

- invoicing;
- sales ledger with customer accounts;
- purchases ledger with supplier accounts;
- nominal ledger with sales;
- purchases, expenses and bank accounts;
- stock records;
- payroll records;
- profit and loss accounts;
- balance sheets.

Enterprise Resource Planning (ERP) software

ERP software helps a business to manage a number of activities, such as product planning, parts purchasing, maintaining stocks, communicating with suppliers, providing customer service and tracking orders. In recent years manufacturing companies in

Figure 2 *A computerised purchases ledger*

Suppliers

New | Record | Price List | Activity | Aged | Invoice | Credit | Dispute | Phone | Labels | Letters

A/C	Name	Balance	Credit Limit
AMSPLUMB	AMS Plumbing Supplies Ltd	0.00	0.00
BOCLTD	BOC Ltd	123.38	0.00
BRITISHT	British Telecom	0.00	0.00
CARLSBER	Carlsberg Tetley	4036.26	0.00
CHUBBFIR	Chubb Fire Ltd	0.00	0.00
EASYEQUI	Easy Equipment com	0.00	0.00
EFTSYSTE	EFT Systems Ltd	0.00	0.00
FROSCOLD	Froscold Refrigeration Ltd	0.00	0.00
HALLSCAT	Halls Catering Supplies	0.00	0.00
LEISUREL	Leisure Link	157.18	0.00
MEDWAYEN	Medway Engineering Ltd	0.00	0.00
PATHALAR	Path Alarms & Electrical Services	0.00	0.00
R&RBARSU	R & R Bar Supplies	39.74	0.00
REDROSER	Red Rose Rolls	0.00	0.00
RITAYLOR	RI Taylor Ltd	0.00	0.00
RSHARPLE	R Sharples Electrical & Building Maintenance L	0.00	0.00
SAWYERQU	Sawyer Quine & Co	-940.00	0.00
THURSTON	Thurston	54.10	0.00
TOSH	TOSH	642.67	0.00
UNITEDUT	United Utilities	-20.40	0.00
WESTLANC	West Lancashire Flooring Ltd	0.00	0.00

Figure 3 *Benefits of computer aided design*

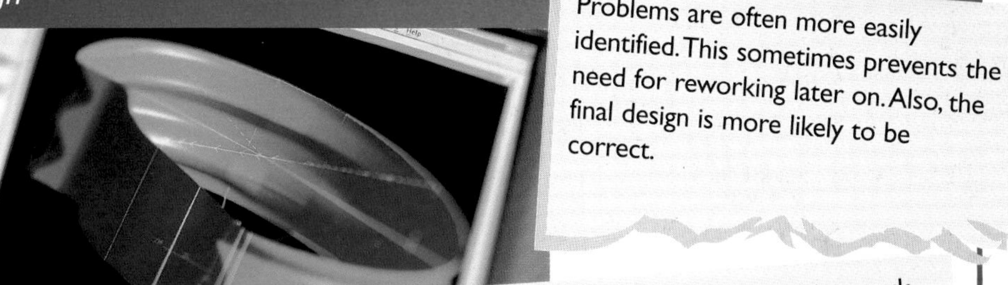

industries ranging from aerospace to bicycle parts and circuit boards to boat docks have used ERP software to reduce costs, improve productivity, and enable new business strategies within their organizations. Many ERP systems are used to improve stock control. For example, Jerrard Bros plc, a lighting specialist, enjoyed stock savings in excess of 30% after implementing an ERP system. With space at a premium at its Croydon factory, efficient warehousing and stockholdings are extremely important and K3 Business Technology's ERP system reduced stock levels from £900,000 to £600,000. Since installing the system Jerrard's product lines expanded, but stock levels have remained constant. Without the extra products, stocks would have dropped even further to £500,000. Stock obsolescence and stock-outs have also dramatically reduced.

Computer Aided Design (CAD) software

CAD is an interactive computer system which is capable of generating, storing, and using geometric and computer graphics. It helps design engineers to solve design problems and is used in a wide variety of industries. Computer aided design has a number of benefits for a business. These are shown in Figure 3.

The Internet

The Internet provides a huge source of information and can be accessed using a computer and a modem. With the introduction of broadband, which has speeded up access to information, the use of the Internet has grown significantly. The Internet can be used by a business in a number of ways.

Accessing information Information can be accessed to help decision making. For example, a business could visit the websites of competitors to find out what products are being offered for sale and what prices are being charged. Businesses might also make use of economic, financial and news information. Some businesses are able to carry out market research using information on the Internet. For example, they may be able to analyse 'hits' on their own web pages or search for information on industry trends.

Providing company information Most businesses have their own website which can be used to give information about the company to the outside world. Business websites contain corporate and financial information for investors, general information, such as the history of the company for the public, and information for customers, such as details about the company's product range. Business websites will contain links to other useful websites and a communication facility which allows people to contact the business by e-mail.

Offering services Some businesses advertise job vacancies on their websites and provide electronic application forms. People can apply for jobs online. This helps to speed up the recruitment process.

Marketing and sales Businesses are increasingly using websites for marketing purposes. Whole product ranges can be advertised and information given. Banner headings can be place on other websites to attract customers. Sales via the Internet are also increasing. This is dealt with later.

E-mail and intranets

E-mail is where people send text messages and other images to people using computers. It has helped to improve both internal and external communications in business. Businesses, other organisations and individuals have e-mail addresses. Information sent from one e-mail address, via a computer, modem and telephone, to another address is stored by a 'server', a computer dedicated to storage and network facilities. It stays in that address until it is accessed by the receiver. One of the main advantages of e-mail is that information can be sent instantly to anywhere in the world. It is also possible to send lengthy documents such as business plans and reports, drawings, photographs, spreadsheets and other images, as an attachment to the e-mail.

Some large businesses have an **intranet**. This is a company-wide computer network that links all staff in the organisation. This means that standard information, such as a daily news bulletin for example, could be distributed instantly to every single employee. This is a very efficient way of communicating relatively confidential business information.

E-commerce

An increasing number of businesses have e-commerce operations. This means that customers can buy products online. Examples include selling tickets for the theatre, cinema and sports fixtures, CDs and DVDs, books, tickets for coach, train and air travel, groceries, holidays, fast food such as pizzas, consumer durables and cars. In fact there are few products that cannot be purchased online now. Many people have Internet bank accounts and companies such as Telco, the telephone company, use online billing. The advantages of e-commerce are huge for both the business and customers.

Business benefits Benefits to a business may include:

- a retailer does not need shop space to sell products online which reduces costs and an airline can issue tickets electronically saving on staffing, stationery, postage and other costs;
- being able to offer products online 24 hours a day, 365 days a year;
- advertising products by sending direct mail, using 'pop-up' ads and their own websites, for example.

Customer benefits Customers might benefit from:

- lower prices;
- shopping without travel in the comfort of their own homes;
- placing orders at their convenience 24 hours a day, 365 days a year;
- access to 'electronic shops' all over the world.

Data protection

Many people have become concerned that personal details are stored on lots of computers and could be misused. However, the government has passed legislation to control the collection, storage, processing, and distribution of data. For example, the **Data Protection Act, 1998** specifies eight conditions with which users must comply. These are shown in Table 1. There is also legislation which aims to prevent the misuse of computers and makes it an offence to access certain unauthorised information. Finally, some EU legislation prevents the downloading of copyright music and outlaws the sending of junk e-mail known as spam by businesses.

Computers and health and safety at work

The increased use of computers in the work place has led to worries that employees may suffer physical harm as a result of spending too much time sat in front of a VDU. Some people, such as home workers and call centre staff, spend all day in front of a VDU. The effects associated with the use of computer equipment may include the following.

Table 1 *Conditions of the Data Protection Act*

- Personal data should be obtained fairly and lawfully.
- Personal data can only be held for specified and lawful purposes.
- Personal data cannot be used or disclosed in any manner which is incompatible with the purpose for which it was held.
- The amount of data held should be adequate, relevant and not excessive.
- Personal data should be accurate and kept up to date.
- Personal data should not be kept for longer than is necessary;
- An individual should be entitled to:
  (a) be informed by any data user if he or she is the subject of personal data and also have access to that data;
  (b) where appropriate, have data corrected or erased.
- Security measures must be taken by data users to prevent unlawful access, destruction, or loss of personal data.

Eye damage and defective vision According to IMPACT, the largest public sector trade union in the Republic of Ireland, although VDUs do not cause eye damage, they can highlight problems that are already there. And they can lead to eye strain and eye fatigue if you don't take the necessary precautions.

Muscle and skeleton problems These may be caused either by overexertion, known as Repetitive Strain Injury (RSI), or by static posture – sitting in the same position for a long period.

Operator stress Working in the same position at a work station for a long period can be stressful. It may also be a relatively tedious activity.

Health problems There maybe problems which might be related to radiation, such as miscarriages and birth defects and face rashes and reddening.

Guidelines exist for businesses that require staff to spend long periods sat in front of a screen. **The Health and Safety (Display Screen Equipment) Regulations 1992** requires companies to comply as follows.

- All VDU user workstations must meet the minimum requirements of the Regulations and BS/EU Regulations.
- All VDU user workstations are assessed in order to reduce the risks of the potential adverse health effects.
- The user's work routine allows breaks or changes of activity. Eye tests and remedial spectacles are provided, where prescribed, for users.
- VDU users are provided with adequate information and training on the adverse health effects and how to avoid them.

Confidentiality and security

The Data Protection Act requires businesses to store personal details safely and ensure that only authorised users have access to them. There are certain ways of protecting data stored by computers.

Computer passwords Access to personal information about customers and staff and other sensitive information, such as financial details, can be restricted. In these circumstances the data can only be accessed by authorised users. They usually require a password and a user name to be issued and recognised before anyone can gain access to the information.

Anti-virus software Computer viruses, which can damage both the information stored on computers and the software that operates them, are created by computer 'hackers'. Many viruses enter computer systems via e-mails. Viruses are attached to e-mails and sent to individuals and businesses. Once the e-mails are opened, viruses attack systems doing damage and spreading quickly. However, it is possible to buy anti-virus software which can detect and destroy viruses before they enter the system or repair files and systems if they are affected by a virus. The software must be updated regularly because new viruses are being created all of the time.

System back-ups Businesses should make back-up copies of all information stored on a computer to prevent losses. It is possible for computers to 'crash' due to technical problems or viruses. If data and programmes are not backed-up they may be lost completely.

Choose a well known business that sells products online and visit its website that sells products online. Identify information on the site that might be used by:

- customers;
- investors;
- employees;
- competitors.

Explain the advantages to the business of e-commerce.

Research task

Portfolio practice • Wilky Group

Wilky Group supplies bathroom fittings to major UK house builders. Wilky deals with a large number of sub-contractors which used to result in a huge mountain of paper and endless opportunities for mistakes. As the business expanded in recent years, so did the number of difficulties in the warehouse, such as picking errors, stock losses and warehouse congestion. According to IT and Logistics Director Dave Seagrove, 'Pick errors cost us a fortune. We had to pacify angry customers, arrange collection of the incorrect deliveries, raise all the necessary paperwork, put the items back in stock and either credit or re-deliver the right products'.

To resolve these problems Wilky installed an Enterprise Resource Planning (ERP) system. With this new stock control system, all products are scanned in as they are unloaded off the lorries and then stored in the warehouse. If a product is delivered without a barcode, the warehouse team simply print off a customised barcode sticker on a dedicated bar coding printer located in the goods-in area. Then, when the product is picked, it is scanned again ensuring that the right item is picked and the stock records are updated automatically.

The introduction of the ERP system has been a success. Wilky is now making record profits every month. The business has real time stock control, no bottlenecks in the warehouse operation, virtually error free picking, greatly reduced stock losses, greater visibility and above all, happy customers who get exactly what they want, when they want it.

Source: adapted from company information.

(a) Describe briefly the purpose of an ERP package.

(b) Analyse the benefits to Wilky of using the ERP package.

(c) Discuss how Wilky might maintain confidentiality and security when holding information about customers on a computer.

Meeting the assessment criteria

In your investigation you need to explain how software can support a business and help it operate more efficiently, make reference to the types of software used and how it is relevant to your chosen business.

Business example – Gerhards

Gerhards is a bespoke tailors located in Bristol. When Michael Fell joined the company as Accounts Manager an existing Sage accounting package was in use. However, the software was not being used to its full potential. The old manual system was still being used in its entirety, consisting of a typewriter, ledger cards and massive daybooks. The system needed five people to run it and took up a lot of valuable time.

Michael decided to use the software to its full capacity. When asked how Sage has benefited the company Michael argues that there was an immediate saving on audit fees which were halved. Also, it used to take auditors two weeks at the business to carry out the audit, but now one person could do it in three/four days. Michael also stated that customers of the business are mainly individuals and not companies. The business has a large database to store information about these customers. So sorting facilities are particularly important. The business often arranges customers by country of residence for mail shots and debt identification. The speed at which Sage can do this and then produce a report is far quicker than by hand and invoices can also be customised.

Source: adapted from www.sage.co.uk

Mark Band 1 *Provide basic knowledge and understanding of business software. Identify and describe some software packages used by the business.*

Gerhards uses specialist software in accounting. Such packages are used to record and store financial transactions and generate useful financial information such as creditors and debtors lists, profit and loss accounts and balance sheets. Many accountancy packages are integrated so that the different functions are linked. For example, if the details of a sales invoice are put into the system, both the customer account and the firm's sales ledger will be automatically updated. Then, when payment is made, the customer account, the sales ledger and the bank account will all be updated instantly. Gerhards uses a Sage accounting package. It is relevant because customers are individuals and not businesses. The software uses a large database and has an effective sorting facility. This enables the business to sort customers according to country of residence for mail shots and debt identification, for example.

Mark Band 2 *Provide sound knowledge and understanding of business software. Identify and describe some software packages used by the business and explain how efficiency might be improved.*

Like a growing number of firms, Gerhards uses specialist software packages to help run its business. Gerhards uses a Sage accounting package. When a new accounts manager was appointed the business was already using the package, but not to its full potential. The old manual system was still being used, which consisted of a typewriter, ledger cards and large daybooks. This system needed five people to run it and took up a lot of time. By making better use of the existing Sage system Gerhards was able to improve the efficiency of the business. For example, auditing fees were reduced by one half and the amount of time it took for the accounts to be audited was reduced from two weeks to three/four days. Sage was also suitable for the type of customers served by the business. As a bespoke tailor Gerhards served individuals rather than companies. The Sage program provided a customer database which allowed Gerhards to sort customers according to country of residence, which helped the business to target customers for mail shots and identify debtors more easily.

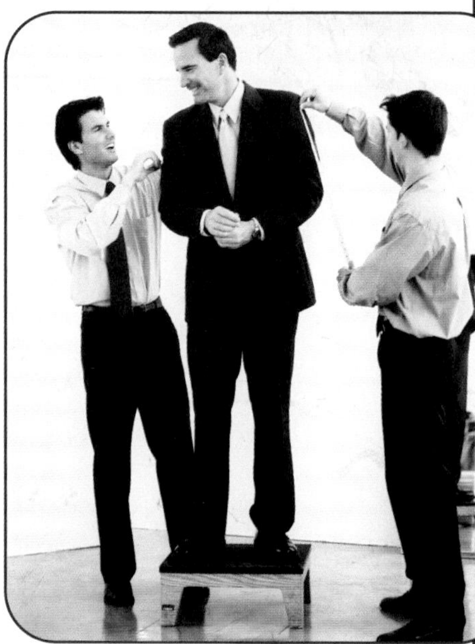

Mark Band 3 *Provide comprehensive knowledge and understanding of business software. Identify and analyse some software packages used by the business and discuss how efficiency is improved.*

Businesses use software packages for a range of activities such as design, stock control and internet selling. One common area of application is in finance and accounts. Accountancy packages are used to record and store financial transactions and produce financial information such as creditors and debtors lists, profit and loss accounts and balance sheets. Gerhards uses a Sage accountancy package. The system has been used for a while, but only when a new Accounts Manager was appointed was the system used to its full potential.

Before the appointment of Michael Fell, Gerhards used a combination of manual and computer systems. This was obviously inefficient. For example, the manual system consisted of a typewriter, ledger cards and massive daybooks. The system needed five people to run it and took up a lot of valuable time. It is possible that the people employed in the accounts department had not been trained properly to use the computer system.

Once the manual system was abandoned, efficiency improved. Gerhards benefited from lower auditing fees. Also, at one time it took the auditors two weeks on site to do their job, but now it only took one person three/four days. When questioned about the features of the Sage package which he finds useful Michael suggested that customers were individuals and not companies, so a large database was needed to store information. Sorting facilities were particularly important as the business often had to filter by country of residence for mail shots and debt identification. The speed at which Sage can do this and then produce a report was outstanding. The ability to customise statements and invoices also helped improve the efficiency of the system.

All this suggests that the software used by Gerhards is highly appropriate for the needs of the business.

27 Understanding customer needs and wants

Customers

Customers are individuals or organisations for which a product or service is provided. They have dealings with businesses and a variety of their stakeholders.

In personal terms, a customer is the person who asks for something. For example, if a teacher asks a student to write a report, the student will be the supplier and the teacher will be the customer. If a player is asked to play for a local team, the team manager and other team members are customers as the player is providing them with a service - the skills and willingness to play as part of the team.

In business terms, customers give others their business. Customers agree to buy or trade with others to provide them with an income. It is the customer that pays the money for the product or service that is provided.

Consumers

The consumer is the end user. Consumers are people or organisations at the 'end of the line'. Consumers use the product for its own sake, rather than just buying it as part of their own business activity. They may literally 'consume' the product if it is a food or drink. Or they might use it up as part of the production or development process for their own products, for example a raw material or a product from a service industry such as electrical power.

The consumer is not necessarily the person who purchases the product. For example, an adult may buy a toy in a shop, give it to a child who plays with the toy. In this example the adult is the **customer** of the shop, the child is the **consumer** of the entertainment and pleasure given by the toy.

A customer may also be the consumer, if they are dealt with directly and the product is a consumable item. For example, if instead of a toy the adult bought a ready to cook meal and ate it themselves, they would be both the customer of the shop and the consumer of the meal.

On a larger scale, a retail buyer may place orders and purchase goods in quantity and thus be the customer of the manufacturer or supplier. The retailer will then display the goods in its shop where they are bought by a shopper, the customer of the retailer, who may not be the consumer of the product from the point of view of the manufacturer. Their role as customer or consumer depends on what they do ultimately with what they buy. If the retail buyer in this example bought cleaning equipment from a cash and carry for use in the shop itself, then it would be both the customer (of the cash and carry) and the consumer, as the cleaning equipment is being used up by the retailer.

Internal customers

Internal customers are people who are provided with services within a business. For an employee they are likely to include the person to whom the employee reports directly, senior members of staff who ask the employee to do something, and members of the employee's immediate work team. Looking at other people in a business as customers can be very helpful for employees to establish standards of service, which may play an important part when it comes to performance reviews. Whilst internal customers may play an important role in the life of a member of a marketing team, the main focus of the work required for this unit is on external customers.

External customers

External customers are people or organisations (the buyers) outside of an organisation who are provided with products and services. They pay money for the products and services provided by a business or benefit from them in a material way. They include trade and retail buyers and consumers in some situations.

Why bother to understand customers?

For marketing planning purposes it is important to recognise the difference between the customer and the consumer. Having established who are the customers, the process of analysing and understanding their wants and needs can begin. Once this has been done, it is possible to identify where to aim the product and how to plan marketing activity effectively.

Customer needs

Customer needs are the basic requirements or desires at a given point in time that can be fulfilled by receiving or acquiring the right product. An example would be if you are thirsty you need a drink to satisfy your thirst. In a business context, if a shop has sold out of a particular line, it needs more stock to sell or will lose income.

It is often argued that satisfying customer needs is essentially a passive, quantitative activity, and that a pro-active marketing strategy, in a competitive market, should aim to meet customer wants in a qualitative way.

Customer wants

What a customer wants can be very broad and far-reaching. Wants are the customers' requirements in addition to just acquiring the product. They may include what the customer expects of a product and of the supplier in addition to just receiving the product itself. They are the reasons why a customer buys a particular product.

Using the example of thirst, a drink may satisfy the thirst (the need) but the customer may want the drink to have a nice taste, be cheap, be a well known brand, be packed in a can so that it can be drunk immediately and be stocked by many shops so that it can be bought easily,

In a business context, a shop may have sold out of a particular product. In addition to needing stock, its wants may include the product being at the right price, packed in the right quantity, delivered safely and on time, and a whole range of other customer service requirements.

Meeting customers' wants is sometimes referred to as adding value to a product. This is particularly important in competitive markets to make sure that that customers choose your product rather than those of competitors. It means that the customer is delighted rather than merely satisfied with your product.

A successful marketing strategy is based on meeting both the needs and the wants of your customers, in a profitable way. This means researching customers to identify the specific customer needs and wants that must be satisfied. If a business identifies needs and wants and decides which are the most important to the customer when making a buying decision, there is a good chance that customers will buy. Some examples of needs and wants for different products are shown in Table 1.

Table 1 *Needs and wants*

Product	Nike trainers
Need	To support and protect feet
Additional wants	Fashionable, hard wearing
Product	Taxi ride
Need	Transport
Additional wants	Arrive on time, safe and pleasant journey
Product	D&G coat
Need	Keep warm and dry
Additional wants	Fashionable, exclusive, eye-catching design
Product	Shredies breakfast cereal
Need	Satisfy hunger
Additional wants	Available at many supermarkets, low fat, add fibre to diet

Source: adapted from National Readership Survey Open Access data.

How does a business attempt to understand its customers?

Depending on the product, customer profile and method of distribution, there is a number of simple ways that a business can gain an understanding of its customers.

Talk to customers This can be:
- formally through the use of marketing research interviews or questionnaires in a customer survey to collect data on their needs, wants, opinions and motivation;
- informally by asking for advice or opinion before launching a marketing plan.

Observe customers This can be done directly by literally watching them, for example watching the way shoppers walk around a supermarket. It can also be indirectly, by using film of customers in a buying situation or analysing appropriate secondary research on customer behaviour. A business will try to find out:
- what they do;
- how they behave;
- what they buy;
- how they buy.

Measure and analyse customers This can be done by using:
- own sales data;
- primary research that collects customer purchasing data or information on product usage;
- analysing secondary research based on customer purchasing or product usage.

Analysing customers The process of analysing customers will involve:
- segmentation;
- profiling;
- targeting.

Customer segmentation

This means dividing customers into identifiable groups, which share common characteristics. Segmentation is covered in more detail in section 33. There are many different ways of segmenting customers. The three main ways are shown in Figure 1.

Figure 1 *Market segmentation*

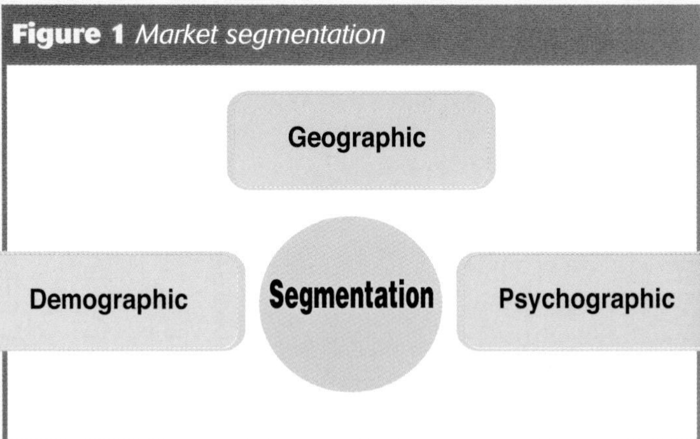

Geographic This involves analysing customers and dividing them into groups based on geographic factors, such as where they are located, where they live, where they work and where they shop including which towns or shopping centres and postcodes.

Demographic This involves analysing customers and dividing them into groups based on demographic factors, such as age, sex, socio-economic group or household type.

Psychographic This involves analysing customers and dividing them into groups based on psychographic factors, such as lifestyle, interests, attitude, opinion, values.

These three ways work well when segmenting people as customers and consumers. But what if the customer is a business or industry rather than an individual?
- Geographic segmentation of businesses can be done, as it is still important to know where they are located, the region or area and how far from the production unit deliveries must be made.
- Demographic segmentation of businesses could include company size, based on financial measures, how many outlets they may have, how many people are employed, how big are the orders that they place and how much they buy in total.

Figure 2 *Profiting of Saga Holiday's customers*

The profile of customers for SAGA Holidays could be:
- over 50 years old;
- sufficient income to be able to pay for a package holiday and healthy enough to take a holiday;
- interested in travel;
- attracted by direct marketing;
- interested in value-for-money.

Source: adapted from www.saga.co.uk.

- Psychographic segmentation is not so relevant when dealing with businesses and organisations. But even they will have attitudes and methods of operating based on company ethos.

Other ways of segmenting businesses could include by industry, by market or by status, e.g. new customers or old customers.

Profiling

Having achieved segmentation, attention can be turned to profiling. This is the creation of a description or profile of the customer, based on features of the segmentation. An example is shown in Figure 2. Profiling is important for assessing market potential, developing a profile of the main customer types for the product and then predicting potential sales and for targeting customers.

Targeting

The aim of segmentation is to identify the most important groupings and use this to target and tailor marketing activity that is likely to be the most effective on that particular group. A business must decide whether to put resources into targeting consumers, (consumer marketing) or targeting buyers, (trade marketing).

Portfolio practice • Merry Hill Retail Park

Today, Merry Hill is one of the region's most successful shopping destinations, attracting over 21 million visits every year, with over 200 stores, 10,000 free parking spaces, offering a wealth of high quality services and facilities. Unlike other comparable sized shopping centres, Merry Hill is located at the heart of a densely populated urban conurbation, and this dramatically affects its customer base. Whilst Merry Hill has great regional appeal, particularly at key sales periods, over 70% of visits to Merry Hill come from within a ten mile radius of the site. A high percentage of them shop weekly or more frequently, using Merry Hill as they would a traditional town centre.

The Merry Hill Retail Park is located in the Midlands between Stourbridge and Dudley. Among its many attractions it lists the following.

- Customer Service Team - over 250 staff to ensure that Merry Hill is kept clean, safe and secure at all times.
- Customer Service Points – a number of information points on the malls, including a Central Information Point. The information point offers Merry Hill, local tourism, public transport information and gift cheques.
- Customer Service Rovers – a team of Customer Service Rovers can be found out and about on the malls to assist with queries. Unlike traditional Customer Service, the Rovers won't be behind a desk, making it easier for them to offer help when required.
- Customer Service Charter Mark – includes a 10 day exchange policy.
- Tourist Information - Merry Hill has a Heart of England Tourist Board registered Tourist Information Centre.
- Travel Shop - to make arrival and departure convenient and pleasant for visitors.

- Services for disabled shoppers - including courtesy wheelchairs and scooters and specific parking spaces for disabled shoppers in all car parks close to Merry Hill mall entrances.
- A Bhs car park, a 5 storey award-winning car park which is well lit and has easy access via a bridge link to Next and TK Maxx as well as Bhs and the Tourist Information Centre.
- Child facilities including kiddy cars, a baby changing suite, buggy and wrist strap hire, parent and child parking spaces and Castle Hof play environment for children.
- Pamper Services including a therapy studio, wedding services and a hair salon.

Source: adapted from www.merryhill.co.uk.

(a) Identify THREE examples of how Merry Hill meets customer needs.

(b) Identify THREE examples of how Merry Hill meets customer wants.

(c) Explain, using examples, how the management of Merry Hill could segment customers.

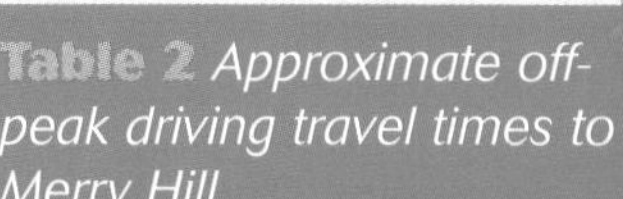

Table 2 *Approximate off-peak driving travel times to Merry Hill*

Birmingham	30 minutes
Bridgnorth	30 minutes
Kidderminster	30 minutes
Redditch	30 minutes
Solihull	45 minutes
Sutton Coldfield	40 minutes
Walsall	30 minutes
Worcester	40 minutes

Merry Hill is also serviced by buses and trains

For your chosen product, think about who are your customers.

- Make a list of the different types of customer, including family members, friends, teachers, other buyers and consumers.
- State what you provide and why they are your customers.

Consider situations where you are a customer.

- Make a list of each person or organisation which provides you with a product or service.
- State whether you are a customer, or a customer and consumer.
- Note what you think about the service that you receive. Is it what you want? Does it meet your needs? Could it be improved?

Considering your own needs and wants, identifying which are met and which are not, will help to identify the needs your own customers will be looking for.

Research task

Meeting the assessment criteria

You are required to produce an appropriate marketing mix for a new or existing product or service. Your work must include evidence of the identification of the wants and needs of customers and target markets.

Business example - Early Risers

The marketing mix for a 'wake-up' service, Early Risers, that will call mobile phones at times requested by subscribers as an alternative to using an alarm clock is being developed.

Oftel survey

According to the Oftel Residential Survey, 75 per cent of all adults in the United Kingdom owned or used a mobile phone in May 2003. Twenty one per cent used their mobile as their main method of telephony, with 8 per cent of homes only having a mobile, and no fixed line phone. Ownership of mobile phones varied with age. Nearly 90 per cent of people between the ages of 15 and 34 owned or used a mobile phone in February 2003. This proportion declined with age; less than a quarter of those aged 75 and over owned or used a mobile phone.

Source: adapted from *Social Trends*, Office for National Statistics.

Mark Band 1 *Description of the chosen product/service, basic description of the marketing objectives and the relevant segmentation and target market.*

From research, the basic need of customers was found to be the need to be woken from sleep each morning of the working week. In addition to being woken, potential customers had other wants, such as wake-up calls always being on time and that the calling should repeat until the phone is answered. The objective would be to provide a service that meets these needs and wants. The target market would be people who need to wake up early in the working week, who own mobile phones.

Mark Band 2 *Explanation of why the product/service has been chosen, what the marketing aims and objectives are and steps taken to identify the target market and segmentation.*

A survey was carried out to find the needs and wants of working people. A basic need to be woken on weekdays was found. But other wants, such as:

- calls on time;
- continuous ringing;
- a pleasant voice on the other end;

were identified. It was decided to have a marketing objective of providing this service. The target market would be mobile phone owners who worked in the week. Such people were interested in the service from the survey. Secondary research reports, such as those produced by Oftel, also backed this up. Mobile phone owners were continually seeking innovative uses for their phones, illustrated by the expanding market for new ringtones and the move to phones with built-in cameras.

Mark Band 3 *Comprehensive explanation illustrating depth of knowledge and understanding of the product/service, marketing aims and objectives, target market and segmentation.*

A survey was carried out to find the needs and wants of working people. A basic need to be woken on weekdays was found. But other wants were identified, such as calls being on time, continuous ringing, a pleasant voice on the other end and that it should cost no more than a basic call connection charge. It was decided to set a marketing objective of providing this service. Website research identified the main competitors for this service as O_2, Orange, T-Mobile, Tesco, Virgin and Vodafone.

The target market would be mobile phone owners who worked in the week. Such people were interested in the service from the survey. Secondary research reports, such as those produced by Oftel, also backed this up. But it was decided that not all owners of mobile phones would want this service, using data from the Oftel report. The most likely buyers and the target customers would be:

- males;
- aged 15-34;
- working;
- income in excess of £20,000 per annum;
- living in low-cost accommodation;
- owning a modern 'new generation' mobile phone;
- already subscribing to entertainment services on their mobile phone.

It was also decided that the service would be more successful in areas where ownership of mobile phones was highest, such as cities and large urban areas, rather than rural areas.

Before finalising the marketing mix, phone owners at a local college seen walking round the inside the canteen at lunchtimes were interviewed about the idea. Many thought an alarm clock would be far better. But it was concluded that most students surveyed were not in the target market, and although their opinions were valid, they should not be seen as a reason to deviate from the planned marketing mix.

28 Developing new products

What are new products?

'New products are the lifeblood of a business'. This is a cliché often repeated in business, but there is a lot of truth in this statement.

- Without new products a business will stagnate and be overtaken by competitors that have been developing and introducing new products.
- New products can give a boost and change the image from an old fashioned or slow-moving business to an innovator.
- New products can stimulate income and profit.
- New products can become the focus of activity, giving a sales team a good reason to talk to customers and a reason for customers to listen to the sales team.

A successful new product can rejuvenate a business and its workforce, moving the business forwards and overcoming competitors.

In reality very few genuine new products are ever introduced. There are few examples of a product that is so new that nothing like it ever existed before. Most 'new' products come about through ideas and innovation and are developments or changed versions of something that already exists. A product may be new:

- in the way it is presented, specified or used;
- in the way that it is perceived by customers and consumers;
- to a business or to a particular market.

Products which are totally and radically new however tend to be rare. Such new and original products are usually as a result of a new technological development, which consumers recognise as an advantage over old ways of doing something. Consumers are usually happy to adopt a new product based on new technology if it:

- allows them to do something quicker, easier or cheaper than before;
- allows them to do something they could not do;
- provides access to something they could not previously access.

New products fall into a number of different categories.

Genuine new products that did not exist before. It may be difficult to find examples, because as soon as they hit the market they are very quickly changed, modified and appear in different versions from other businesses. However, at the time of their introduction, it could be argued that products in this category were those shown in Table 1.

There have been many other examples and as breakthroughs take place, there are likely to be more in the future. The one feature that makes this category different is that the development and launch of such products is based entirely on risk. The risks are

Table 1 *New products at time of introduction*

Product	Reason
Televisions	Before the first television was developed nothing like it existed before. Televisions on sale today are in some way developments from the original concept.
Computers	Before computers analysis and computation was done by hand and brain power.
Digital technology	This is used for recording, photography, broadcasting, communication and other applications. It would have been genuinely new when it was introduced.
Genetically modified crops	Humans have selectively bred plants for centuries. But changing the genetic make-up of a plant and producing a plant that has characteristics deliberately added by a scientist was new.

Table 2 *Product improvements*

Product	Reason
Camera phones	Cameras and telephones existed before, but combining them into one unit created something new and different and changed the way that people communicate.
On-line ticketing agencies	Used for booking holidays, flights, theatres. The concept of booking agencies already existed. They were taken away from the high street and into the home through the use of the Internet.
Cars and road vehicles	New models are developed to bring improvements on past models by better performance, styling, comfort or safety. Improvements might include such things as new diesel engines and satellite tracking equipment.
Grocery deliveries	This service virtually ceased with the growth of supermarkets. In an attempt to improve their products and support websites, supermarkets have reintroduced home delivery after ordering on-line.
Washing powder	Most brands are re-launched regularly with new ingredients that claim to be an improvement over the old powders that are replaced.
Cat food in foil sachets	Instead of cat food sold in tins, the same brand and food is packed and sold in small, convenient foil sachets. Small sachets reduce the waste that occurs when a cat does not eat the full can.
Apple iPod and MP3 players	These use digital technology in a novel and effective way. It is a portable music player like a Sony Diskman, but stores thousands of tracks on a hard drive.

not only that the product is new, but that there may be no market for such a product, so the market may have to be created.

Product improvements This is the largest category of new products. These are improved or up-dated versions of existing products. It does not take a lot of changing for a business to bring about a small improvement in a product. Some examples are shown in Table 2.

A way of extending the life cycle of a product is to update constantly and bring out new improved versions of what is essentially the same product. This is dealt with later in this section.

New varieties of existing products This is also known as range extension. It is the introduction of additional flavours, colours, sizes of products that are currently in distribution and on sale. Some examples are shown in Table 3.

This approach to new product development is often used by a manufacturer to squeeze out competition, reducing the shelf-space in a shop that is available to competition by filling it with additional varieties of its own products.

Table 3 *New varieties of existing products*

Product	Reason
Emulsion paint	Manufacturers introduce new colours every year or season in an attempt to show consumers that they are up-to-date with current fashions. As far as consumers are concerned the paint remains the same.
Fruit drinks, ready meals and other food products	Manufacturers continuously introduce new flavours and withdraw flavours that do not sell well.
Deodorants	A brand may have a core range to which new fragrances are added every year.
Football replica kits	Details are changed each year and alternative versions are added to generate sales to fans, but the basic items that make up the kit remain the same.
Snack foods	The basic crisp remains the same, but the range of flavours grows. This form of product development can be seen in many food products.

Although not quite the same, this category could also include:

- promotional lines, such as multi-packs or larger sizes with a percentage extra free and products presented in other non-standard formats;
- me-too products, where businesses wait to see how a market develops before they introduce their own version of a product, usually when it is large enough. Examples are common in new or under-developed markets where risks are high. Small businesses often do the pioneering work to create a new market, then a large competitor enters with a similar product.

New uses for existing products Often marketing research will identify a gap in an existing market or a market that is not currently being supplied with a particular product. Sometimes it is the result of 'blue sky' thinking and consumer research that seeks to identify potential new markets. Some examples are shown in Table 4.

This can be a difficult way to introduce new products. Consumers are naturally conservative in their buying and usage of products. To re-present a product that is recognised and accepted in one area of use, in a new and different area may take a lot of convincing promotion.

Table 4 *New uses for existing products*

Product	Reason
Chocolates	Consumer research identified that chocolates were never eaten after a meal. A marketing team and an advertising agency created a chocolate specifically for eating after a meal. The market was created by promoting the idea that it was sophisticated to eat chocolates after a meal. The market for this type of confectionery is now huge.
Yoghurt	Yoghurt was sold for many years as a dessert. Recently manufacturers have introduced biological yoghurt containing 'healthy bacteria' in small 'singe dose' sizes. These products are marketed as health food supplements. They do not make specific claims, but the promotion suggests that it will improve the general health.
Sport Utility Vehicles	These were originally built for off-road activities. They have become popular for family use. Many brands are now targeted at this market rather than the smaller sporting vehicles market.

The product life cycle

This is an important factor in marketing and product development. It is based on the observation that all products pass through a series of stages from initial concept and development through to the time when they are withdrawn from the market. The main stages of the product life cycle are shown in Figure 1.

Some products, such as those based on fads and fashions, or those based on technologies that are quickly superseded and replaced, will have a relatively short and fast life cycle. They reach maturity

Figure 1 *The product life cycle*

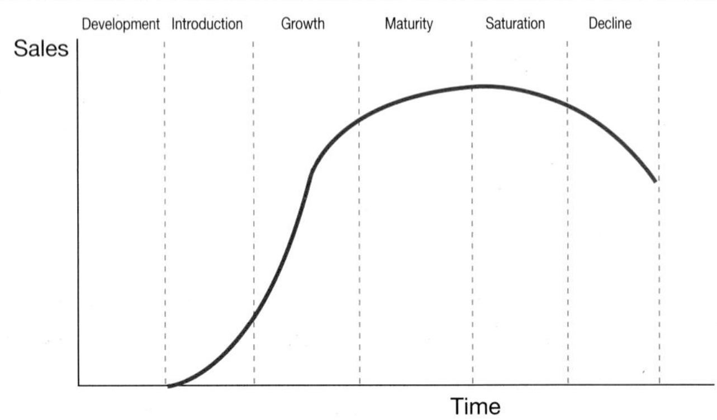

and peak quickly after launch and decline equally quickly. Others will have a long life cycle that extends the maturity stage through continuous marketing activity. This can maintain sales and keep a product profitable and prevent it from declining for many years. Examples of this are the Mars Bar and Coca-Cola. Both of these products receive regular marketing activity and both have enjoyed relatively long life cycles, which show no signs of declining. This illustrates that managing the life cycle of a product is an important skill in marketing.

Product re-launch

A relaunch is a way of taking an existing product, making any changes that are required to bring it up-to-date with the current market or customer expectations, and developing a new marketing plan that will promote it in the marketplace. The changes are likely to include:

- updating its specification, such as adding a 'magic ingredient' that can be used as the centrepiece of a new marketing campaign;
- changes to the design of the packaging, e.g. KitKat changed from paper and foil wrapper to a sealed wrapper;
- repackaging in a new style or format, e.g. Jif to Cif;
- producing new advertising and promotional material.

Re-launching is a relatively low cost way of creating interest around a product. A business may not face the high cost of developing a new product from scratch. It allows existing customers to look at a product in a new way and potential customers a reason to give the product a try.

The relaunch of a product is a useful way of extending the life cycle of a product if it is employed during the maturity-saturation stage, before it slips too far down the decline stage of its lifecycle. It is a technique that can be seen in regular use in highly competitive markets with strong brands, like confectionery, washing powders, magazines and newspapers. A relaunch can also be used if a product fails in a market. In this situation the product usually undergoes a radical change to overcome the reasons for its failure before it is re-launched.

Ansoff's product-market growth matrix

New product development is one of the options in Ansoff's product-market growth matrix. This is a tool that is used by businesses to identify which, of a number of options, a business could adopt to increase its sales. It is based on comparing the relative merits of selling existing products and new products in existing markets and new markets.

Depending on the aims and objectives of the business, and the strategy it wants to adopt, the Ansoff's matrix will suggest one of four options:

- **market penetration**, the safest option, based on selling more to existing customers, or taking sales from competition. It is the selling of existing products into existing markets.
- **market development**, seeking new channels of distribution or selling in different geographic areas, a slightly higher risk to the business. It is the selling of existing products into new markets.
- **product development**, selling new products into the existing market, with all of the risks associated with new products. It is the selling of new products into existing markets.
- **diversification**, the highest area of risk - almost like starting a new business, based on developing new products for new markets.

Product failure

Badly managed new products can drain a business of resources. It can also create a poor image from which the business struggles to recover and may never overcome. Customers have long memories when products fail or do not live up to their reputation.

Despite the importance of the thousands of new products launched each year, the level of failure is reported to be around 80%-90% or even higher in some markets. This is not surprising. If all the new products launched were to succeed, there would be no room on the shelves in shops and the road would be clogged with new vehicles delivering all of the new products.

Why might a new product be said to have failed?

- It may simply be a product that does not meet the needs of customers and which they do not buy.
- Failure may be relative. It may be that the product has a particularly short life cycle and that launch and swift decline is the nature of that product.
- The failure may be that it just did not achieve the aims and objectives in the marketing plan. If re-launched with a different marketing mix it may achieve some success or at least last longer before it is again deemed to be a failure.
- The marketing policy of some businesses is to introduce many products through the year because it reinforces its image of innovation. It may be satisfied if just a few are successful, provided it makes an overall profit from all products launched.

Reducing the high failure rate

The high failure rate for new products should not be ignored and a business can take steps to reduce the chances of new product failure through the use of a comprehensive marketing research programme:

Internal assessment and audit of the business Before developing a new product a business must analyse itself. It might consider a number of factors.

- The current level of technology, manufacturing and distribution capabilities and capacity. A new product that increases utilisation of plant and equipment may be more attractive than a new product that requires new investment, for example.
- The perception of the business in the market place. Some products may be considered inappropriate by customers no matter how attractive the new market, for example a chemical company making soup.
- The attitude of senior management. For example, the marketing team of a charity may recommend that it becomes more commercial to raise funds. This may conflict with the original ethos of the organisation.

Technical research The business must make sure that the product does what it should do, that it performs as required and that it will not fail technically when used by consumers. In-house testing of a product before it reaches the marketplace can save time, resources and reputations.

Consumer research This can measure and confirm that a

market is worthwhile and to check that consumers actually want the new product proposed.

Customer research This can check that customers will buy a new product and take it into distribution. This usually needs to incorporate consumer research to provide potential customers with evidence that a market for the new product exists.

Product research This involves testing the concept and actual product with consumers to confirm that it meets their needs. If not, the business must identify what changes need to be made to the product.

Market testing This is the piloting of sales in a small, controlled number of distribution outlets or restricting sales to a small geographic area to test the marketing mix before committing resources to an expensive national launch.

Pick two businesses that you are familiar with, that operate in different markets.

- List the main products or product ranges from each business.
- Divide the lists of products into core products that each business has marketed from the start or for more than three years and new products that each business has introduced in the past three years.
- Compare the lists and assess which business has been most active in new product development and introduction. Consider the reasons why.

Research task

Portfolio practice • Daily Bread

Sharon Dewell started *Daily Bread* when she left college. *Daily Bread* provides a range of fresh sandwiches for sale, which Sharon makes herself, first-thing every day. She sells the sandwiches by taking them round local offices during the morning in the boot of her car. Customers can buy fresh sandwiches for their lunch directly from her during her visits. She has built up a good reputation and a regular, local customer base. When she started the business, Sharon put a lot of effort into making sure that the bread and fillings were of the highest quality and that they looked good. Customers can also ring her to request bespoke sandwiches at particular times of the day and pre-book their delivery time.

(a) Explain TWO ways in which Daily Bread has improved the traditional sandwich sales service.

(b) Suggest ideas for:

(i) new products;

(ii) product development;

(iii) diversification;

by the business.

(c) Examine the possible risks involved and evaluate whether the business should attempt these.

Meeting the assessment criteria

For a chosen product or service you must be able to identify and explain the different marketing strategies used by businesses to achieve their marketing objectives and meet the needs of their target markets. This will involve a consideration of the marketing activities used when developing new products of re-launching existing products.

Business example - Jane Haralambos Permanent Cosmetics

Jane Haralambos operated a beauty consultant and service, providing beauty care and advice to clients. After training in London in permanent cosmetic enhancement she changed the focus of the service she provides to permanent cosmetic enhancement. This is a revolutionary beauty treatment used to define eyes, brows, lips and cheeks, for example. It gives a soft, natural finish that imitates applied make-up. The effect is achieved by infusing hypoallergenic pigments into the dermal layer of the skin where they remain, gradually fading over time. The results can be subtle or dramatic.

Jane offers a variety of other services from her own specialist treatment centre, which is part of a larger health and treatment centre in London. For example, she offers a tattoo removal service and the improvement of skin pigmentation. Jane has attracted a number of clients through word-of-mouth, people visiting the health centre and advertisements in specialist beauty magazines. She also hopes to gain more customers from her new website.

Source: company information, www.jane-permanent-cosmetics.co.uk

Mark Band 1 *Description of the chosen product/service, basic description of the marketing objectives and the relevant segmentation and target market.*

Jane Haralambos offers a revolutionary service to customers. Rather than simply applying make-up every time a person goes out or every day, a permanent, natural looking effect can be gained by treatment from Jane Haralambos Permanent Cosmetics. Other services include tattoo removal and skin pigmentation treatment. Jane changed her existing service to offer a specialist, different and targeted product. Her objective is to establish and then grow the business in the competitive beauty treatment market. Her target market is likely to be females looking for a permanently beautiful look or people looking for improvements in skin colour or tattoo removal.

Mark Band 2 *Explanation of why the product/service has been chosen, what the marketing aims and objectives are and steps taken to identify the target market and segmentation.*
Jane Haralambos's service was to provide beauty treatment such as make-up and beauty care. This is a competitive market with salons, home services and products that can be bought and used themselves by customers. Jane changed her service to offer a new, revolutionary service to customers. Rather than simply applying make-up every time a person goes out or every day, a permanent effect can be gained by treatment from Jane Haralambos Permanent Cosmetics. Other services, which are related, include tattoo removal and skin pigmentation treatment. This service is an improvement on existing beauty treatments. It saves time for people and gives a long lasting and visually appealing effect. Jane's objectives in launching this service would be to gain a market share in a competitive market and then grow the business by offering a specialist yet different product.

Her target market is likely to mainly be females looking for a more permanent look. It will also include males and females looking for improvements in skin colour and texture, plus those looking for tattoo removal. Jane researched the market before setting up. She chose a London base as more people in the capital could be looking for this service compared to, say, a rural location. She therefore stands a better chance of attracting her target market from a larger base of customers. Similar services are offered in the area, advertising in beauty magazines. But customers are attracted by quality products, standards and service. Jane trained with internationally recognised Dawn Cragg in Harley Street, London, which means that she is well qualified.

Mark Band 3 *Comprehensive explanation illustrating depth of knowledge and understanding of the product/service, marketing aims and objectives, target market and segmentation.*
Jane Haralambos's business offers a new, revolutionary service to customers. Beauty treatments are often time consuming. People pay large amounts for such treatment. It also takes up time to regularly apply make-up every time a person goes out or every day. Jane's business replaced her original beauty service. A permanent effect can be gained by treatment from Jane Haralambos Permanent Cosmetics, which specialises in providing permanent eyebrows, eyelines and lip enhancements, for example. Not only is time and money saved compared to non-permanent treatment, but it is more visually appealing. Other services, which are related, include tattoo removal and scar camouflage treatment.

Jane's objectives in launching this service would be to establish a market share in the competitive beauty market and then grow her customers. Offering a specialist product should help Jane's business to compete in the beauty treatment market, faced with the many salons, home services, tattoo parlors and products that can be bought and applied by customers themselves. Offering an additional range of services

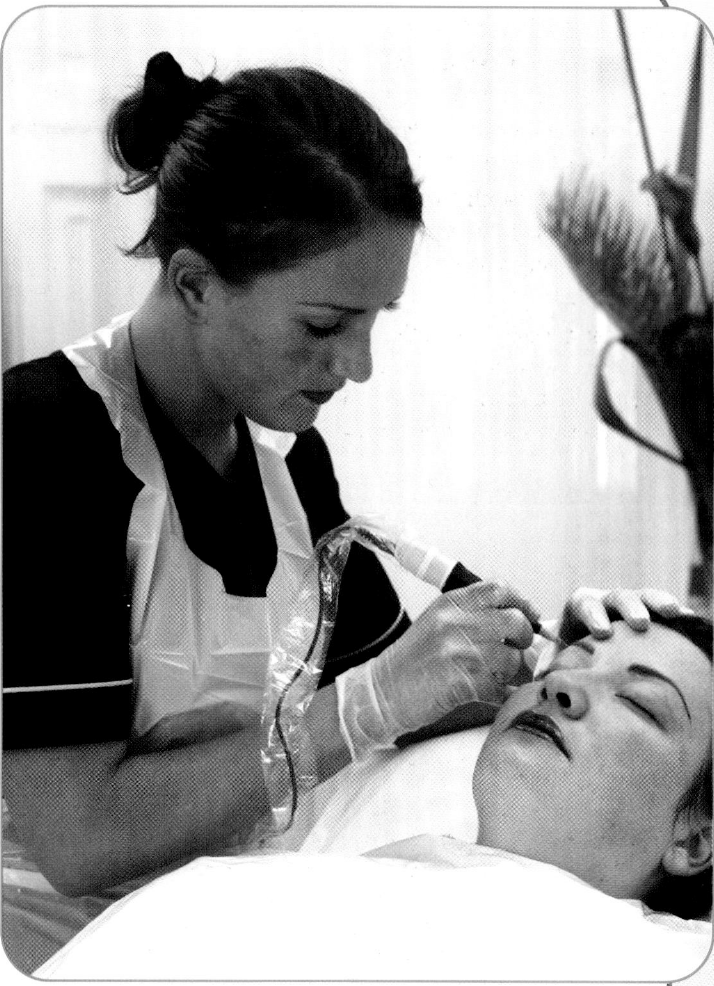

might also reduce some of the risks involved.

Jane carefully researched the market before setting up. Jane chose a London base as more people in the capital could be looking for this service compared to, say, a rural location. She therefore stands a better chance of attracting her target market from a larger base of potential customers. Similar services are offered in the area, advertising in beauty magazines. But customers are attracted by quality products, standards and service. Jane trained with internationally recognised Dawn Cragg at Harley Street in London, which means that she is well qualified. Her target market is likely to fall into a number of categories.

- Females in London looking for permanent eyeliner or lip colouring. This might be important for some clients in the capital, who eat out regularly or carry out functions. It might also appeal to actors or other people in the entertainment industry.
- Ageing men and women who want restore youth to their facial features. The UK has an ageing, yet active population. They have income to spend and may be attracted to such a service.
- People concerned about their appearance and who are looking to improve their skin's texture and colouring.
- Removing tattoos. Studies have suggested that they have a negative impact in interviews and other situations. People who had tattoos when they were younger may also be looking to remove them as they get older.

29 Improving profitability

Aims and objectives

There are many different marketing aims and objectives. Profitability is perhaps the most important for a business. Why? If a business is not profitable it will quickly run out of money to pay for materials, goods to sell or staff and other running costs. Further, it will not be able to build up retained profit for future investment. Profit is necessary for survival. Without profit the costs of the business will need to be paid from elsewhere, such as an overdraft, a bank loan, personal savings or investor's savings. Each of these will have a limit and will need to be repaid at some point.

Profitability is the measure of the level or proportion of profit compared to income from sales. It measures an organisation's ability to generate sales income in excess of the cost of producing that sales income.

Profitability alone is only useful as an indicator to the marketing and financial management teams in a business that the costing and pricing of a product is right. It can sometimes give an artificial indication that the marketing mix is right. But it is the actual profit generated that is important, as this will be real and can be banked or spent as required. The actual profit generated by an organisation will be the level of profitability multiplied by the rate of sales. It is no good having a high level of profitability if the product itself does not sell.

It is the responsibility of the marketing team to make sure that profitability is established, maintained and improved whenever possible.

What is profit?

The simple definition of profit is the excess of income over expenditure. Put even more simply, it is the money left from sales income after deducting the cost of producing the goods or services. Another way of calculating profit is the money added to the cost of goods or services to arrive at the selling price.

Profit can be expressed in absolute terms, such as an amount or a total cash figure, or in percentage terms, as a percentage of sales value or price.

Profit is sometimes referred to as a 'margin', as in 'a profit margin'. This is the same as expressing profit as a proportion of a sales value or price.

Profit is often calculated and measured in two basic ways - gross profit (GP) and net profit (NP). Examples are shown in Figures 1 and 2.

Gross profit

Gross profit is the basic raw measure of profit. It is the total sales value minus the cost of producing the good or providing the service. It does not take into account other overheads and operating costs such as tax, administration, distribution or marketing expenditure.

The gross profit is the money left from sales to cover the costs of marketing the product, operating the business and retaining some money in the business.

Gross profit can be calculated and expressed in two ways, as shown in Figure 1, which shows the gross profit of Alcom Ltd a manufacturer of buckets, and Hardware Stores, Lytham, a retailer.

Figure 1 *Gross profit of Alcom Ltd and Hardware Stores, Lytham*

Total amount

Gross profit = total sales value – production cost of goods

As percentage

$$\text{Gross profit margin} = \frac{\text{gross profit}}{\text{total sales value}} \times 100$$

EXAMPLE

A plastic bucket costs 10p to produce and is sold by Alcom Ltd to Hardware Stores, Lytham, for 50p.

The gross profit for Alcom Ltd

Gross profit = 50p – 10p = 40p per bucket

As a percentage

$$\text{Gross profit margin} = \frac{40\text{p}}{50\text{p}} \times 100 = 80\%$$

The bucket is sold by Hardware Stores, Lytham, to a consumer for £1.18.

The gross profit for Hardware Stores, Lytham,

Gross profit = 118p – 50p = 68p per bucket.

So, for example if 10,000 buckets were sold, Hardware Stores Lytham, would make an overall gross profit of £6,800 (68p × 10,000).

As a percentage

$$\text{Gross profit margin} = \frac{68\text{p}}{118\text{p}} \times 100 = 57.6\%$$

Net profit

This is the money that is left after all costs have been added up and the total cost is deducted from the money that is coming into the business from sales.

Net profit **does** take into account all the expenses or operating costs of running the business. These include overheads and operating costs such as tax, administration, distribution or marketing costs. Net profit is sometimes referred to as **operating profit** or **profit on ordinary activities** for companies.

Net profit can be calculated and expressed in a number of ways, as shown in Figure 2, which shows the net profit of Alcom Ltd a manufacturer of buckets, and Hardware Stores, Lytham, a retailer.

Figure 2 *Calculating net profit of Alcom Ltd and Hardware Stores, Lytham*

Total amount

Net profit = total sales value - cost of production - overhead costs

or

Net profit = gross profit - overhead costs

As a percentage

$$\text{Net profit margin} = \frac{\text{net profit}}{\text{total sales value}} \times 100$$

EXAMPLE

A plastic bucket costs 10p to produce and is sold by the manufacturer, Alcom Ltd, to a shop, Hardware Stores, Lytham, for 50p, which results in a 40p gross profit. Out of this 40p Alcom Ltd must pay (per bucket):

VAT	= 8.75p
Overheads	= 21.25p
Distribution costs	= 5.0p
Total	= 35p

The net profit for Alcom Ltd

Net profit = 40p - 35p = 5p per bucket.

As a percentage

$$\text{Net profit margin} = \frac{5\text{p}}{50\text{p}} \times 100 = 10\%$$

The bucket is sold by Hardware Stores, Lytham, to a consumer for £1.18. The plastic bucket costs 50p to buy and is sold to customers for £1.18 which results in a 68p gross profit. Out of this 68p Hardware Stores, Lytham must pay:

VAT	= 17.5p
Running costs	= 21.5p
Staff costs	= 10p
Advertising costs	= 5p
Total	= 54p

The net profit for Hardware Stores, Lytham

Net profit = 68p - 54p = 14p per bucket.

So, for example if 10,000 buckets were sold, Hardware Stores, Lytham would make an overall net profit of £1,400 (14p × 10,000)

As a percentage

$$\text{Net profit margin} = \frac{14\text{p}}{118\text{p}} \times 100 = 11.9\%$$

Improving profitability

One of the main objectives and responsibilities of the marketing team is to improve profitability. There can be three ways that the marketing team can improve profitability:

- raise prices;
- cut costs;
- change the product mix.

Before any improvement can be measured, the level of current profit needs to be confirmed by benchmarking, so that future levels of profit can be compared. Overall profit can be increased by selling more goods or services, but profitability is a function of the selling price and production cost.

Raising prices

Raising prices may be an option to increase profitability. Once the decision has been made to raise prices it should be done as quickly as possible to avoid losing income by selling at the old price. The only reasons to delay might be to inform customers and possibly to negotiate additional sales at the old price as a promotional incentive.

Market factors, such as competition, consumer expectations or willingness to pay raised prices, need to be investigated and taken into account before the price is actually raised. A rise may make a product uncompetitive and give competitors an advantage. Customers may have reached a limit for the price that they are prepared to pay and may buy a competitor's product as a lower price alternative if prices are raised. It is here that the strength of a brand and the strength of consumer loyalty become important.

Some businesses use **price leadership** as a factor in creating an identity for their brands. This is based on the idea that a most expensive brand is perceived to be the best and most desirable by some consumers. Certain products may have perceived 'price points', where retailers have an idea of where the price should be set for maximum consumer sales. However, retail price points can be moved and the retailer as well as the manufacturer can benefit from the increase in profitability produced by the price rise.

Financially, raising prices will also generate an increase in cash coming into the business so long as sales levels are maintained. Increased levels of cash are attractive to manufacturers, distributors and retailers.

Cutting costs

Cutting costs can be of great benefit to a manufacturer or supplier of the product. Any saving made would be 'invisible' to the distributors and retailers and, therefore, unlikely to be passed on.

Costs that might mostly easily be cut could be the production costs of the product. There are many areas where production costs may be cut to save money and thus increase profitability if the selling price is maintained. These include raw material costs, packaging costs, direct labour rates, machinery costs and other manufacturing costs.

Other than production costs, areas where costs could be cut may include distribution and transport. Also, there may be opportunities in the sales and marketing areas to cut costs that reduce the overheads in the business and thus improve profitability. These could include cutting staff or reducing wages and other employment costs. Care must be taken when considering the reduction of marketing budgets. Marketing expenditure is likely to come directly out of the profit generated by sales. If money is not spent on marketing it can be retained and contribute directly to the total profit that is made. However, cutting marketing expenditure may affect the organisation in other ways.

Profitability is the measure of the level or proportion of profit generated by sales compared to income from sales. On paper a product may appear to have a high level of profitability. But in absolute terms profitability is only useful if sales occur at a rate to generate sufficient income and total profit for the business, as set out in the business plan. Cutting marketing expenditure may result in consumer awareness and sales declining, competition getting ahead and distributors and retailers dropping the product because it is not being supported. It could result in a downward spiral from which sales never recover. Therefore it is no good having a product with high profitability that does not sell.

Changing the product mix

Changing the variables in the product mix can also lead to improvements in profitability. It is usually the responsibility of the marketing team to decide which products should be promoted and which customers should be targeted.

Products Having established the profitability of each product or product group within the current sales mix, the marketing team should be able to identify which product or group of products generate the highest level of profitability. If, overall, unit sales within a range of products remain stable, then selling more products with a higher percentage profit and fewer products with a lower percentage profit will improve the overall profitability of the business. The marketing team can do this through promotion, focusing on the products with the highest profitability at the expense of those with a lower level.

Customers Targeting the most profitable customers is another way of achieving improvement in profitability. Existing customers of a business will already know, buy and use the product. It will require relatively fewer resources, such as sales time and promotional spending, to service this group compared with trying to sell the same products to new customers. New customers are likely to require expensive promotion and incentives to convince them to buy a product. Thus profitability of sales to the new customers will be relatively lower. Similarly, it is likely to be more profitable to sell to local customers than to those in another country as sales, communication and transport costs are likely to be lower. In this situation profitability could be improved by focusing marketing activity on local customers.

The demographic profile of customers is another factor that may affect profitability. Branded goods manufacturers know that it is more profitable to market their products to higher income customers than those with relatively less to spend. Customers with more money are likely to buy higher cost items with a relatively higher level of profitability than consumers who, because they have a lower amount to spend, are forced to pay lower prices for products. The number of consumers is a factor that comes into this equation. A business may take a 'high value/low volume' or a 'low value/high volume' approach. Both can achieve a level of profitability. Which approach to take will be influenced by the overall aims and objectives of the business.

Make contact with the marketing team at a business that you are familiar with or where you have personal contacts. Explain that you are studying Applied Business and learning about profitability. Arrange to meet and interview a member of the marketing team and investigate:

- the main products or service that the business sells;
- how the business measures profitability;
- what targets are set for profitability;
- what are the main strategies used to maintain or improve its profitability;
- what changes have been made to the marketing mix to improve profitability.

This investigation should help increase the work relatedness of your learning.

Alternatively, use an Internet search engine to find news or financial reports on three businesses in different sectors that claim to have improved profitability. Analyse the reports and identify:

- the main products or service that each business sells;
- how each business measures profitability;
- what targets each business sets for profitability;
- the main strategies used by each business to maintain or improve its profitability;
- what changes each business has made to the marketing mix to improve profitability.

Compare your answers looking for common factors and try to explain any differences in approach to improving profitability.

Portfolio practice • Blacks Leisure Group plc

Blacks Leisure Group plc is a business that sells products to two specialist markets – outdoor wear and board wear. Its Blacks and Millets stores sell outdoor waterproof clothing and equipment for walking, hiking and camping. Its Free Spirit Boardwear stores sell clothing and equipment for skateboarding, surfing and skiboarding.

Table 1 *Gross and net profit, £000*

	2004	2003
Turnover	255,527	244,862
Gross profit	133,634	113,329
Net profit	16,070	13,108

Figure 3

'The mixed weather has held back sales of lightweight summer clothing ... This weakness has, however, been more than offset by the very strong performance of outdoor clothing, which once again demonstrates the benefits of the Group's balanced portfolio of products and stores.'

'Millets is positioned as a mid-market, family orientated, value proposition aimed, primarily at the everyday consumer ... Blacks is positioned as "The Outdoor Specialist", targeting the serious outdoor consumer ... Free Spirit appeals to the young aspirational consumer who is fashion conscious and attracted to the lifestyle of the Boardwear offer.'

'Our most significant marketing initiative in the year was a national advertising campaign for Millets. This comprised regular insertions in the main national press titles ... The aim is to attract new customers by emphasising what is different about Millets.'

'In developing new product ranges we have the benefit of our own exclusive brands which include Peter Storm ... and Alpine. The Group also has the UK Distribution Rights for O'Neill, which is one of the leading brands in the boardwear market worldwide.'

Source: adapted from Blacks Leisure Group, *Annual Report and Financial Statement*, 2004.

(a) Identify (i) the products offered by Blacks Leisure Group plc and (ii) the target markets.

(b) Calculate the profitability of the business in 2003 and 2004.

(c) Explain the reasons why the profitability may have changed between 2003 and 2004.

Meeting the assessment criteria

For a chosen product or service you must be able to identify and explain the different marketing strategies used by businesses to achieve their marketing objectives and meet the needs of their target markets. This will involve a consideration of the marketing activities used to improve the profitability of the business.

Business example - Greg Northam window cleaning services

Greg Northam is setting up in a local area to provide a window cleaning service. He has estimated the costs and income the service he is offering.

Mark Band 1 *Description of the chosen product/service, basic description of the marketing objectives and the relevant segmentation and target market.*

Greg Northam will offer a window cleaning service to the local area. He has a new business and must make a profit over a period of time to survive. Greg has decided to target larger houses hoping to be profitable. He has estimated the costs and income of cleaning the windows of a three-bedroom semi-detached house with 8 windows. The total cost of providing the service for this type of house is £3.70. Overheads, such as payments on a loan for a van and ladders, buckets and cloths will be taken out of profit generated. Greg will charge £5.00 for the service. So the gross profit per house is £5.00 - £3.70 = £1.30. Profitability is (1.30 ÷ 5.00) = 26% This is low and may not generate sufficient profit to pay overheads and retain any profit. He may have to consider changing prices or costs to make a profit.

Mark Band 2 *Explanation of why the product/service has been chosen, what the marketing aims and objectives are and steps taken to identify the target market and segmentation.*

Greg Northam will offer a window cleaning service to the local area. He has a new business and must make a profit over a period of time to survive. He has found that there are few competitors in the area offering a regular service after talking to potential customers. Larger houses will be targeted. These have more windows to clean. Both of these factors mean that Jeff hopes to stand a greater chance of being profitable.

His costs include labour costs of £3.30 per house and materials costs of 40p. So the total cost for this type of house is £3.70. Gross profit is £1.30. The profitability of a three-bedroom semi-detached house with 8 windows is 26%. This is not sufficient profit. So his marketing objective is to increase profitability. One option is to raise price to these customers to £7.00 and hope his target market will pay this. This will produce a gross profit per house of £7.00 - £3.70 = £3.30. Profitability will then be 3.30 ÷ 5.00 = 66%. An alternative is to reduce costs perhaps using fewer materials. Cutting costs will mean that the total cost per house could fall to £3.00. Gross profit per house will then be £5.00 - £3.00 = £2.00 and profitability will be (2.00 ÷ 5.00) = 40%.

Mark Band 3 *Comprehensive explanation illustrating depth of knowledge and understanding of the product/service, marketing aims and objectives, target market and segmentation.*

Greg Northam will offer a window cleaning service to the local area. Many new businesses fail within a short period of time. So Greg's main objective is to make a consistent and large enough retained profit to survive over a period of time to survive. Larger houses will be targeted. These have more windows to clean and he hopes to offer a high quality service geared to their needs, including cleaning conservatories and washing driveways. He has found that there are no competitors in the area offering such a unique service after talking to potential customers and looking at the operations of rivals. Both of these factors mean that Greg hopes to stand a greater chance of being profitable.

Initial costings have shown that profitability of a three-bedroom semi-detached house with 8 windows is 26%. This is based on a price of £5 and costs of £3.70, so gross profit is £1.30. This is not sufficient profit. So the marketing objective is to increase profitability without affecting the overall business in a negative way.

The business is considering two options to increase profitability. Option A is to raise the price to customer to £7.00 and hope that the target market will pay this. Option B is to reduce costs. Calculations show that raising price to customers to £7 will produce a gross profit per house of £7.00 - £3.70 = £3.30 and profitability will be 3.30 ÷ 5.00 = 66%. An alternative is to reduce costs. Cutting labour costs and reducing the amount of detergent will mean that the total costs per house will be cut to £3.00. Gross profit per house could then be £5.00 - £3.00 = £2.00 and profitability 2.00 ÷ 5.00 = 40%.

The results show that raising price will give the highest profitability. However, although Greg is offering a rather different service, competitors tend to charge no more than £6 for such houses. A small survey of customers said they would not pay £7 per house. Greg considered option B. He found that it would be relatively easy to cut his costs without reducing quality. He looked at ways in which work could be done more quickly so that his employees would not have to be paid overtime. Greg also looked at offering the same service to all houses. Smaller houses would use fewer materials, although there was a risk because they may not want the other services that Greg was offering and pay the price Greg needed to charge.

On reflection Greg decided that reducing costs would be the more effective option, even though profitability would not be as high as if prices were raised. Greg concluded that it is no use having high profitability if your service does not sell.

30 Improving market share

What is market share?

A business will use different marketing activities depending on the objectives it is aiming to achieve. One of these objectives is 'improving market share'. Market share is often used as an indicator of how well or not a business is doing. But it is not the figure itself that is important, but understanding what the figure means, how it is measured and how it is defined. A better understanding leads to the development and implementation of marketing plans that improve market share.

Market share is the proportion or part of a particular market that is accounted for by an organisation. Imagine the market as a round cake being cut into slices. The size of the slice will indicate the share of the market by a particular business. An example is shown in Figure 1.

Figure 1 *Market shares of magazine publishers and supermarkets*

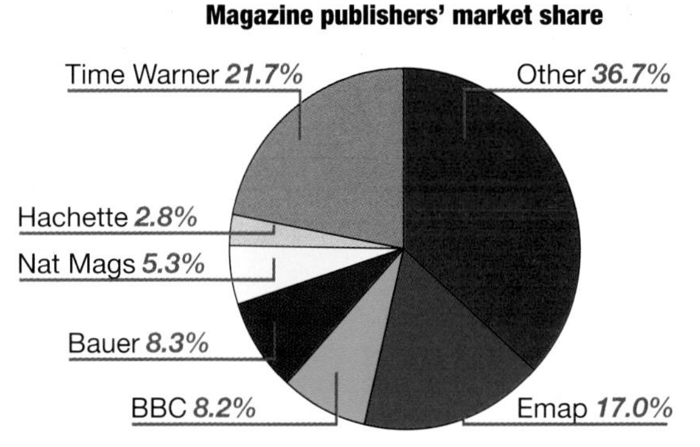

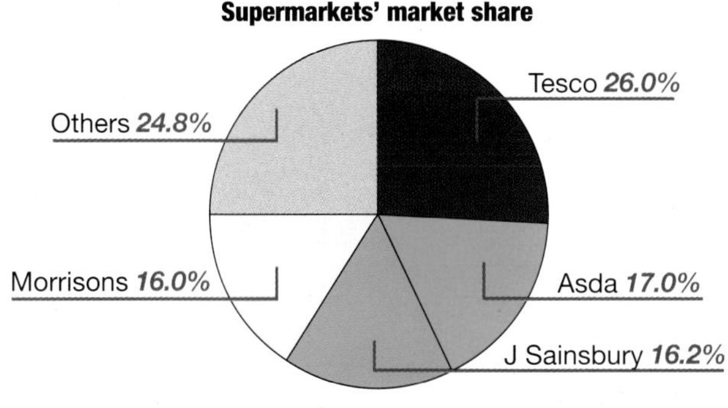

Source: adapted from Emap, 2004 and *The Guardian*.

Calculating market share

Market share is usually measured as a percentage of a total market. This can be expressed in different ways. For example a business:

- may claim to have a 25% share of its market;
- say that its sales account for £1 in every £4 spent in that market.

Market share can be calculated from the formula:

Market share % = organisation's sales ÷ total market sales x 100

Market share is likely to be rising or falling according to trends, activity within the market and the general economic situation. So it is important for a business to keep track of the market size and market share on a regular basis. Market size and market share can change rapidly and a business may need tactical marketing plans to protect and maintain its share.

How is the market measured?

A business may be able to measure its own sales based on its own data, such as deliveries. But determining the size of the total market and measuring competitors' sales can be difficult. There are many independent marketing research organisations such as GfK Marketing Services and AC Nielsen that conduct primary research to measure and monitor the size of markets. Government statistical data on production will give total market size in terms of output, which can be compared with export figures and import figures to arrive at a figure for UK consumption. Other organisations like Euromonitor, the *Financial Times* and Mintel measure markets and produce regular reports that are available to purchase or to read in some libraries. Some examples are given in Table 1.

Table 1 *Estimated market sizes, UK*

Market	Size	Date	Source
Cinema box office	£143m	2003	Nielson EDI
Video games	£1,152m	2003	www.elspa.com
Soft drinks	£49.5bn	2003	Key Note
Sports clothing market	£3.25bn	2004	Key Note
Footwear market	£1.5bn	2004	Key Note

What is the size of the market?

Defining the market and what is being measured is important when interpreting, understanding and making claims for market share. The market may be defined and expressed in different ways, the most common being sales volume and sales value.

- **Sales volume.** This is the number of units sold or the number of individual items. For example the milk market could be measured by the number of litres sold or by the number of bottles sold.
- **Sales value.** This is the revenue generated by sales in the market.

Sales value can be measured as retail sales, retail selling price (RSP) or as trade sales, sometimes called manufacturer's selling price (MSP) or 'factory gate' prices. For example, the retail sales value of the market for milk is how much money is produced by sales from shops and home deliveries to consumers. Sales value (MSP) is how much money is generated when producers sell the milk to retailers and the food industry. The value of a market at RSP will always be greater than the value at MSP because of the retail mark-up.

The market itself may be viewed in total or it may be segmented - split into smaller sections.

The total market The total market for milk in the UK will include all types of milk. A supplier could express its market share as a percentage of the total market.

Product type The market can be segmented into basic types of milk that are on retail sale, such as whole milk, semi-skimmed milk, skimmed milk, flavoured or organic milk. Measuring market share of one of these types could give a higher market share depending on the segment and product type.

Distribution The market could be segmented in terms of distribution through supermarkets, independent shops, and doorstep deliveries. A milk supplier that does not sell into supermarkets, but only has doorstep deliveries, could choose to measure its market share against the 'doorstep delivery market', rather than the milk market as a whole.

Geographic segmentation Looking at smaller markets defined by geographic area or region can be another important way of looking at market share. For example, Roys of Wroxham describes itself as 'the largest village store in the world'. In Wroxham itself, a small village in Norfolk, the retail market is dominated by Roys of Wroxham. Within East Anglia, Roys remains an important retail force with stores in Norwich, North Walsham, East Dereham, Thetford, Sudbury and Bury St Edmunds. Outside of East Anglia Roys is virtually unknown, except by people who holiday in Norfolk, and will only hold a relatively small share of the overall retail market in the UK. But in Wroxham, Roys is the market leader.

Statements and claims for market share should not be taken at face value. It is important to investigate and clarify what market is being referred to, how it is defined and measured and how market share is being measured within the market. Table 2 shows an example.

Other ways of measuring a market and market share

Sales volume and sales value are the most common ways to measure markets and market share. But this is not the only way to measure a market or express market share. Other ways include:
- the number of customers;
- the number of visitors;
- the number of shops that stock a firm's products;
- the size of a target market in terms of the number of consumers;
- the share of airtime that is filled by advertising by a particular organisation;
- the share of press coverage of a particular story;
- the best selling books or recordings in the sales charts.

Each of these measures of the market will allow a business to calculate its market share by adding its own figures into the formula. The aims and objectives of the organisation and how it wants to use market share information will determine how it chooses to measure the market, the units of measurement that are used, what is included and which segment is being measured. For example, Blackpool Pleasure Beach makes no claims for market share based on market value. But its website states that that Pleasure Beach, Blackpool is Britain's top tourist attraction with over 145 rides and attractions. This suggests that management has measured the market in terms of the number of tourist visitors, out of which it is the top attraction, the market leader. What is not clear is how 'tourist' is being defined. Is it all tourists making any visit in England? Tourists who visit seaside towns? Tourists who visit amusement parks? This illustrates why market share figures need to be examined carefully, so their meaning is clear.

Table 2 *Newspaper circulation (weekday)*

Popular national newspapers	
The Sun	3,095,993
Daily Mirror	1,604,975
Daily Star	728,794
Middle market national newspapers	
The Daily Mail	2,285,137
Daily Express	896,455
Quality national newspapers	
The Daily Telegraph	864,285
The Times	641,661
The Guardian	327,527
The Independent	220,939
Financial Times	132,989
The Herald	79,078
The Scotsman	69,791
Total	10,947,624

Source: adapted from ABC.

The Guardian is published by Guardian Newspapers. Based on these figures, it could be said to have:
- 2.99% of the weekday market for newspapers (327,527 ÷ 10,947,624 × 100);
- 14% of the weekday market for quality newspapers (327,527 ÷ 2,336,270 ×100).

Brand share

This is a particular measure that is used, as the name suggests, to measure the share held by a named brand within a market. It is often used in competitive markets that are segmented by many brands owned by few manufacturers, where different marketing teams may manage different brands owned by the same organisation. A business can add together the brand shares held by each of its brands to arrive at an overall market share. An example of this is the washing powder market, which is dominated in the UK by Procter & Gamble and Unilever, each with a range of different brands that compete with each other.

The importance of market share

All organisations are interested in their 'market share' for a number of reasons.

- It is a good way of judging how well a business is doing compared with its competitors.
- It can help to compare the relative strengths of businesses that operate in that market.
- Market share can reassure management, show strength or dominance to stakeholders or to motivate a team by showing how much the business has to catch up to beat competition.

The same market share figure can be used in different ways depending on its intended audience. For example, a business with a 50% share of retail sales may promote this figure in the trade and to shareholders as an example of how well it is doing. Management may use this same figure to show how poorly it is doing and how much harder the business will have to work to grow to the 75% share that has been set as an objective.

Niche suppliers or larger suppliers with niche products may be satisfied with a small share of a large market. Mass-market suppliers will be looking for a large share or dominance of every market that they supply. These are covered in section 33.

Market share over time

A single measure of market share may be an interesting 'snapshot' at a point in time. But in a dynamic market it is important for a business to keep track of its market share and those of competitors because the market situation could change. A business needs to be up-to-date with the current market situation so that changes to the marketing mix can be made and tactical marketing plans can be implemented.

Measuring market size and market share over time is very important.

Trends It can show trends and highlight problems that may affect a business. The trend data can be reassuring and if it shows that a market has declined it can help explain why sales are lower for a given period. Equally, trend data can show up weaknesses in sales strategy if the market is growing faster than reported sales. For example, the management of a business may be quite pleased that its sales are growing at 10% each year. But it will be less pleased if the market is growing at 20% a year, double its own sales increase.

Prevents misleading figures A one-off figure can hide a slow decline in market share. A business could be losing 0.5% every 3 months. Each time the market share is reviewed management may think that the figure is satisfactory as it has only slipped a small amount. It is only by looking over time and making comparisons that large movements in market size and market share can be identified. If the business was declining at 0.5% every 3 months, this is still 2.0% a year. Over a five year period a business my have lost 10% and it may be too late to reverse the trend.

Figure 2 *Improving market share*

In 2003 marketing intelligence firm IDC reported that Apple Computers shipped 25% more Macs in the UK in the fourth quarter of 2003 than in the previous year. It was suggested that consumer interest in Apple's iPod portable music player helped to spotlight its Macintosh computer and benefited sales. For the full year, Apple had a 7.5% growth, giving the company a 2.3% market share overall in the UK. Desktop shipments declined 8% but notebook shipments of the PowerBook and iBook grew 40%.

Improving market share

Improving market share is a common business objective. Management that sets the objective of improving market share is being positive and it is a good measure for the success, or not, of its marketing strategy. The variables of the marketing mix can be used and changed as part of the marketing strategy for improving

Figure 3 *Supermarket strategies to increase market share, 1995-2005*

- Wal-Mart entered the UK market by buying Asda in 1999. Its formula is based on low prices and selling non-food products.
- Supermarkets have responded to the increase in the number of people 'eating out' by increasing prepared foods, especially luxury own-brand ready meals. Some supermarkets are developing in-store juice and sushi bars. Sainsbury's has Starbucks coffee outlets in some stores.
- In September 2001, tesco.com announced it was on the verge of profitability. At the start of 2004, Tesco became the biggest online grocer worldwide, with sales of £500m worldwide.
- To challenge the potential threat from home shopping, shopping as an enjoyable leisure activity has been promoted. Asda has in-store chaplains, MP's surgeries, nail-polishing and pizza spinning. It has also hired trained actors to work as store greeters.
- Some supermarkets have introduced 'singles nights', such as Tesco in its city centre Metro stores, to attract single customers.

Source: adapted from www.corporatewatch.org.uk.

market share.

Product The product specification, features and benefits can be changed to provide added value to the customer and attract customers away from competitors. Market segmentation and the introduction of new products can also result in increased market share.

Price Price-cutting is a direct way of attracting customers away from competition, which could result in a short-term gain in market share.

Distribution Setting a target to increase the number of places that stock a product will increase share of distribution and could result in increased market share if wider distribution leads to an increase in sales overall. Targeting a completely new channel of distribution to stock a product is another way of increasing market share.

Promotion Raising promotional activity and advertising expenditure can increase market share by increasing awareness and increasing demand.

Figures 2 and 3 show methods of improving market share in different markets.

Research task

Make contact with the marketing team at a business that you are familiar with or where you have personal contacts. Explain that you are studying Applied Business and learning about market share. Arrange to meet and interview a member of the marketing team and investigate:

- the market in which this business trades;
- how the business measures the market, including any primary research used;
- what units the business uses to measure the size of the market;
- how the business measures its market share;
- where this market share places the business in the market – market leader, in the middle, or only a small share;
- whether this share has changed and if so why;
- what has happened to make the market share change;
- what targets are set for improving market share;
- how the marketing mix is changed to help improve market share.

In addition to learning about improving market share, this investigation should help increase the work relatedness of your learning.

Alternatively, use reports in the business press or on Internet websites to find examples of three different businesses, each trading in a different market and claiming market share. Analyse what you find and identify:

- the market in which this business trades;
- how the business measures the market, including any source of primary research used;
- what units the business uses to measure the size of the market;
- how the business measures its market share;
- where this market share places the business in the market – market leader, in the middle, or only a small share;
- any targets that have been set for improving market share;
- how the marketing mix has changed to help improve market share.

Compare your answers, looking for common factors and try to explain any differences in approach to improving market share.

Portfolio practice • The UK broadband market

On 7 April 2005 *Computing Magazine* reported data from a survey conducted by Forrester Research. It showed that UK households with broadband access had grown from 2.7million in 2003, to 5.9million in 2005, and was forecast to reach 11.4million by 2010 as in Figure 4.

(a) How is UK broadband market measured in this research?

(b) Which broadband provider is the market leader?

(c) Examine how the broadband providers might use their marketing mix to try to increase their market share.

Figure 4 *UK broadband market share*

%

Provider	%
[illegible]	24
NTL	22
Telewest	12
[illegible]	10
Wanadoo	8
Tiscali	7
[illegible]	17

Source: adapted from *Computing Magazine*, 7.4.2005.

Meeting the assessment criteria

For a chosen product or service you must be able to identify and explain the different marketing strategies used by businesses to achieve their marketing objectives and meet the needs of their target markets. This will involve a consideration of the marketing activities used to improve the market share of the business.

Business example - BlancDent

A new toothpaste is being launched called BlancDent. This toothpaste will aim to clean and whiten teeth at the same time. There is a certain amount of competition that already exists in this market from large companies with major brands. So it will be important to target an appropriate market in order to achieve market share.

Mark Band 1 *Description of the chosen product/service, basic description of the marketing objectives and the relevant segmentation and target market.*

The product launched by the business is BlancDent, a whitening toothpaste to be sold in the Republic of Ireland. The Irish market for toothpaste is worth an estimated €29 million. The main companies supplying this market are Colgate-Palmolive and GlaxoSmithKline. Colgate has 50.4% of the market. At present BlancDent could only gain 1.0% of the overall toothpaste market. But specialist whitening toothpaste holds about 10% of the overall market. So BlancDent could claim to hold 10% of the market for specialist whitening toothpaste, its target market. An objective is to double BlancDent's share of the overall market for toothpaste within the next year.

Mark Band 2 *Explanation of why the product/service has been chosen, what the marketing aims and objectives are and steps taken to identify the target market and segmentation.*

The product launched by the business is BlancDent, a whitening toothpaste to be sold in the Republic of Ireland. The overall market for toothpaste in Ireland is large at €29 million and Ireland's oral care market is valued at €48.8 million. It is also growing at 4% each year. Studies and figures from the industry have shown that growth is partly due to consumers trading-up to higher priced premium and specialist toothpaste such as whitening toothpaste. This is therefore the target market for the product. Competition is very strong between the two main suppliers, Colgate-Palmolive and GlaxoSmithKline. Colgate has 50.4% of the market. This has stimulated the growth in the whitening toothpaste segment. At present BlancDent could only gain 1.0% of the overall market, but 10% of the whitening market. Management's main objective is to achieve a 2% market share of the overall market and sales of €580,000 within a year. Growth in sales by the target market supports the choice of BlancDent whitening toothpaste as a dynamic product within a growing segment that is part of a large and well supported market.

Mark Band 3 *Comprehensive explanation illustrating depth of knowledge and understanding of the product/service, marketing aims and objectives, target market and segmentation.*

The product launched by the business is BlancDent a whitening toothpaste to be sold in the Republic of Ireland. The oral care market is worth €48.8 million and the toothpaste market an estimated €29 million. It is also growing at 4%. Studies and industry figures have shown that consumers have increasingly been 'trading-up' and buying specialist products, a major factor in increasing sales. The growth in the market for specialist whitening toothpaste suggests this to be a suitable target market. Market research conducted by BlancDent also shows that these consumers like the product and once they try it, they would continue to buy and use it.

Two large multinational companies dominate the market, Palmolive and GlaxoSmithKline. Colgate has 50.4% of the market and it has proved difficult for BlancDent to achieve distribution in the supermarkets where Colgate-Palmolive and GlaxoSmithKline are particularly strong. Both the leading suppliers have their own whitening toothpaste product, which competes directly with BlancDent.

At present BlancDent could only gain 1.0% of the overall market, but 10% of the whitening market. A major objective is therefore to achieve a 2% market share of the toothpaste market and sales of €580,000. To meet this objective of doubling market share in a year, BlancDent has produced marketing plans, which include:

- product – the introduction of a smaller 'trial' size;
- price – the smaller 'trial' size will be priced low enough to attract consumers, whilst still allowing retail customers to make sufficient return to stock the product;
- place – plans to boost distribution by targeting the sales force at independent pharmacies;
- promotion – plans for a new TV campaign and the use of outdoor media (posters) to promote the BlancDent brand.

The management of BlancDent plans to buy continuous retail audit data to monitor changes in the market for toothpaste and to keep track of the BlancDent market share to see if the marketing plans meet the objective of doubling market share.

Source: adapted from www.checkout.ie/marketprofile.asp?ID=140

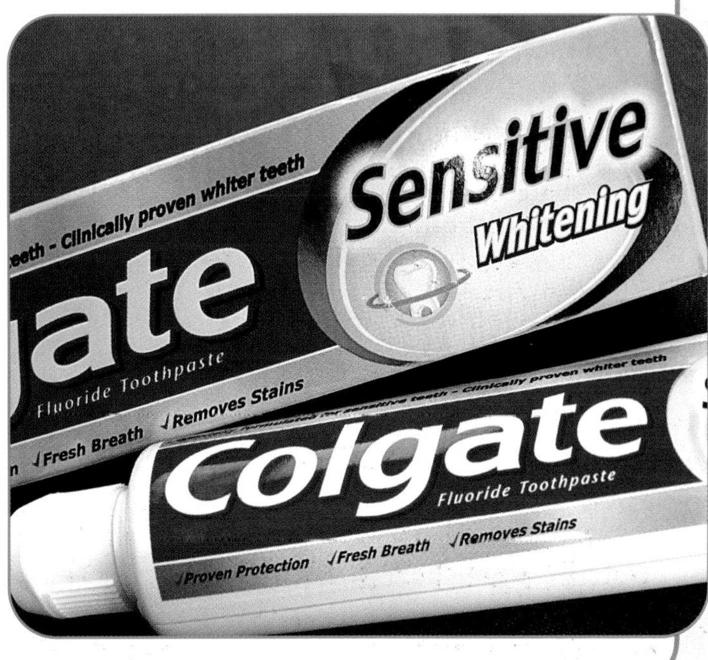

31 Diversification

What is diversification?

Diversification is where a business is prepared to change and move from its core market and enter totally new markets, with new products. The main objective of diversification is usually to expand the business in new and different markets without risking its core business. There are many examples of diversification in business.

Cafés that change to Internet cafés Here the core business has been based on selling food and drink. This market is crowded and sales are limited by the price of food available and the appetite of customers. Café businesses have diversified by moving into the communications market, providing Internet access for customers. The businesses are using established premises and services and adding a potential business for new customers who want to use the Internet. Internet access is charged by the length of time it is used. This produces sales in addition to income of food and drink.

Petrol stations that start selling groceries Here the core business is selling fuel and other goods associated with motor vehicles. Petrol stations have diversified into the retail food market with the addition of grocery products for sale. Businesses use their premises that are already paid for by sales of fuel to offer a new range of products to customers. Consumers who buy petrol may also buy grocery products rather than make another trip to a food shop. The reverse of this has also happened. Some food supermarkets have diversified into selling petrol from the same site as the food store.

Diversification in food supermarkets As food supermarkets groups grow and become increasingly competitive, they have used diversification to add to the portfolio of products in different markets that can be purchased under the name of the supermarket. Consumers can buy products from different markets under the same brand name under the same roof. Examples of this diversification has seen food supermarkets develop products for a range of different markets including clothing, pharmacy, dry cleaning, photo processing, banking, insurance and post office services. An example is shown in Figure 1.

The importance of a strong brand name

When diversifying, it helps a business to have a strong brand name that is recognised by consumers for:

- the image it projects;
- the generic qualities associated with its products and services.

It could be more difficult if the brand is linked exclusively to one product or market.

A good example of a brand that crosses markets and has enabled the business to diversify is Virgin. Originally a single independent music shop, then a music label and multiple retailer, Virgin has diversified over the years and brought new products bearing the Virgin name to many different markets, as shown in Figure 2. The Virgin business has kept music and entertainment at its core. But it has moved from market to market seeking potential for growth and development. Part of its success has been that it is willing to pull out of a market if it fails to meet its objectives and find another market which may be more successful.

There are other examples of how a strong brand name has enabled a business to diversify successfully, including Tesco, Sainsbury's and Nike.

Figure 1 *Asda's George range*

In 2004 it was reported that Britain's biggest clothing retailer was the UK supermarket Asda, owned by US firm Wal-Mart. The figures from retail market researcher Taylor Nelson Sofres underlined the growing power of supermarkets. For the 12 weeks to July 25, Asda raised its market share from 7.3% to 9.4%, compared with the same period last year. Asda's success has come on the back of its George range launched in 1990. The brand has five 'standalone' George stores in the UK. George at Asda is also sold in Wal-Mart stores in the US and Germany, helping to give it annual sales of more than £1bn.

Source: adapted from *The Guardian*, 23,8.2004.

Figure 2 *Virgin diversification*

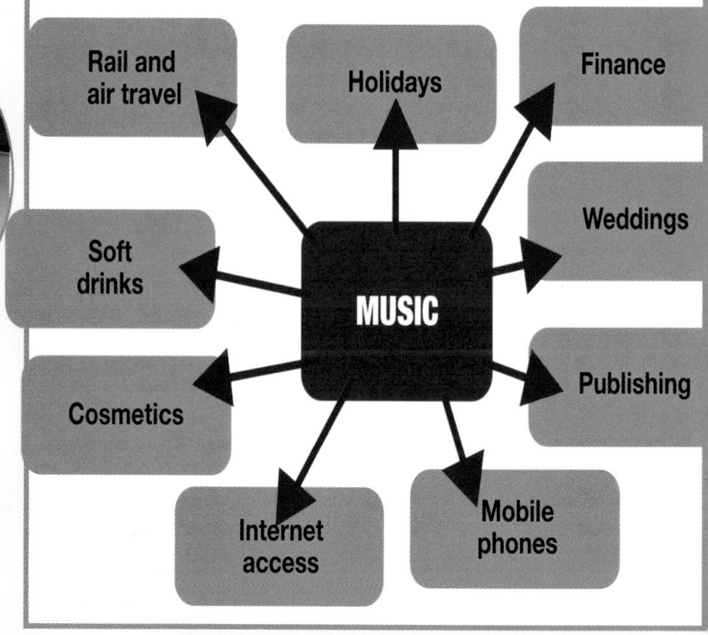

Reasons for diversification

There is a number of reasons why diversification is a strategy that is attractive to businesses.

Not putting all your eggs in one basket A business can spread its risks across different markets. If one fails, the other markets in which it operates will hopefully protect the business from collapse. It reduces dependence on one product and one market.

Potentially high returns There may be large markets which offer huge opportunities and returns. It is attractive to expand the business by moving into these large potential markets.

Failure will not threaten the core business directly If sufficient resources are available, a business may be in a position to take a risk and try new products in new markets because failure will not affect its core business.

A business can use its skills and expertise in one market and apply them to another market If a business has been successful and has developed a model for success, this could be applied to another market.

It can give a new focus and direction to a business If a business has become stale and complacent, the challenge of entering a new market with a new product, may reinvigorate a business. It can also demonstrate to stakeholders that it is a business that has firm future plans and objectives.

It makes good use of resources by utilising them for new developments A business with an existing production facility or distribution network could use the strengths of these resources and maximise utilisation by making products for different markets or distributing new products to different markets.

Risks involved in diversification

Businesses need to be wary when pursuing diversification as an objective for a number of reasons.

- Entering the unknown is always risky.
- Diversification will require increased investment and resources. It can be expensive to develop new products and distribution systems for diversification.
- There is a risk that the business may find that new markets and new products do not operate in the same way as its core business where it has expertise.
- A business can lose sight of what is happening to its core business because it concentrates too much on diversification. This often occurs because the business is complacent about its core business and forgets that customers need to be looked after and competitors need to be monitored all the time to make sure that the core business is protected.
- It may become a drain on resources if the business does not set clear objectives for the point at which it will pull out of the new market or halt the diversification if it fails. There is little point in throwing good money away, just to try to save face and protect failed products.
- Failure creates a bad reputation for investors and consumers. Customers and the industry will be aware of diversification that a business is making. This will be watched carefully and examined critically if the business fails. There is also the danger that the business may get a reputation for reckless diversification and failure. This could harm the core business, its reputation and its relationship with customers.

It may be possible to minimise these risks by:

- researching new markets before new products are launched;
- researching the needs of customers before new products are launched;
- test marketing products before they are launched;
- careful consideration of funds that are allocated;
- careful consideration of the effects of diversification and careful planning of its operation;
- contingency plans in case the diversification fails.

Diversification and growth

Diversification is one of the options in Ansoff's product-market growth matrix, covered in section 28. This is a tool that is used by businesses to identify which, of a number of options, a business could adopt to increase its sales. It is based on comparing the relative merits of selling existing products and new products in existing markets and new markets.

Depending on the aims and objectives of the business, and the strategy it wants to adopt, Ansoff's matrix will suggest one of four options.

Market penetration This the safest option, based on selling more to existing customers or taking sales from competition. It is the selling of existing products into existing markets.

Market development This is seeking new channels of distribution or selling in different geographic areas, a slightly higher risk to the business. It is the selling of existing products into new markets.

Product development This is selling new products into the existing markets, with all of the risks associated with new products. It is the selling of new products into existing markets.

Diversification This is the highest area of risk. It is almost like starting a new business, based on developing new products for new markets.

Visit a local garden centre.

- Note the time of the year and the market it appears to be trading in.
- List the main product groups that it sells and identify what would be considered to be its core business. You can do this by comparing the space devoted to different product groups.
- Identify any examples of diversification from its core business.
- Make contact with a senior member of the management team at the garden centre. Explain that you are studying Applied Business and learning about diversification. Interview the manager to investigate how its business changes each season and identify any diversification that occurs.

Portfolio practice • Milk Round, Wakefield

Geoff Coleman delivers milk door-to-door in a defined geographic area of roads and residential areas within Wakefield from a purpose-built milk delivery vehicle. Although Geoff is a self-employed sole trader, the business is a franchise in that it bears the brand name of a dairy, which supplies the milk and provides marketing support. The core market of the business is the supply and delivery of milk to consumer's homes. Although the supply of milk and branding is from the dairy franchise, Geoff is allowed to sell and market any other products that he feels are appropriate.

(a) Given this business:
(i) identify THREE realistic ways that Geoff could diversify;
(ii) suggest reasons why the business might diversify.
(b) Examine how Geoff could limit the risk of any diversification.

Meeting the assessment criteria

For a chosen product or service you must be able to identify and explain the different marketing strategies used by businesses to achieve their marketing objectives and meet the needs of their target markets. This will involve a consideration of the marketing activities used to achieve diversification.

Business example - Sports and Stars Bar

Café Life owns a number of number of cafés in the Tyne and Wear area of the North East. It had become aware in newspaper articles of two increasing trends in the area.

- People like to eat out and watch sports at the same time.
- There was an increase in the number of women parties and groups going out in the town areas.

It faced a considerable amount of competition in these areas from a variety of restaurants, bars and cafés. Its business plan identified that it needs to move into new areas to expand. It has decided to open a new establishment, The Sports and Stars Bar. The bar will be circular, with screens around the walls so customers can watch and eat. There will also be theme nights including, sports and fashion events and key episodes of 'soaps'.

Source: adapted from company information.

Mark Band 1 *Description of the chosen product/service, basic description of the marketing objectives and the relevant segmentation and target market.*
Café Life's core service is offering food and drinks for sale. To expand it needs to find new ways to meet customers' needs, given the strong competition it faces. So it has decided to diversify its core operation into the entertainment market. Customers can eat and view at the same time. Its main target markets will be sports fans, women's parties and television fans.

Mark Band 2 *Explanation of why the product/service has been chosen, what the marketing aims and objectives are and steps taken to identify the target market and segmentation.*
Café Life's core service is offering food and drinks for sale. The market was chosen because of the nightlife in cities like Newcastle and the culture of people 'going' out. There is also a large concentration of population. To expand it needs to find new ways to meet customers' needs, given the strong competition it faces. So it has decided to diversify its core operation into the entertainment market, so customers can eat and view at the same time. This market has been chosen because of the growing trends identified in newspapers and television about women's 'nights out' and also people going to the pub for a meal to watch football. A survey carried out by the business also confirmed this. The main target markets will be therefore be sports fans, women's parties and television fans.

Mark Band 3 *Comprehensive explanation illustrating depth of knowledge and understanding of the product/service, marketing aims and objectives, target market and segmentation.*
Café Life's core service is offering food and drinks for sale. The market was chosen because of the nightlife in cities like Newcastle and the culture of people 'going' out. There is also a large concentration of population. It faces a large amount of competition in the area. There is a variety of restaurants, cafés, pubs and other eating establishments. And there are also cinemas and theatres. But perhaps the combination of the two might give the business a unique selling point to customers. So to expand it needs to find new ways to meet these customer needs. The new Sports and Stars Bar is a diversification from its core market of food and drink sales into the entertainment market. Customers can eat and view at the same time. This market has been chosen because of the growing trends identified in newspapers and television about women's 'nights out' and also people going to the pub for a meal to watch football, confirmed by its own survey results. The main target markets have been identified for a number of reasons.

- Sports fans often like to watch the build up to the event. They may stay in the café for a long time both before and after a match, for example. So potentially earnings could be high.
- Women's parties are likely to have many customers at once, again increasing revenue.
- Television fans may want to eat out but not miss their favourite soap or other programme. They could record it for later, but there may be an incentive to watch with a group of friends. Again, many people may visit at once and may 'make a night of it'.

32 Increasing brand awareness

Brands

A brand is a set of criteria, features, specifications, attributes or values that:

- identify a product or product group; and
- differentiate it from competitors.

It is what makes the product different and identifiable in the eyes of customers. Examples might be the product name, design, term or any other feature of the product. The term 'brand' can also be applied to a trademark or logo that is used to identify a business.

A brand is a valuable commodity that reflects the perception that customers have about a business and its products. It can have a monetary value which represents its worth to the business and its stakeholders.

A brand can change a lower value product into something for which customers are prepared to pay a higher price. Also, a brand may become so strong that customers refuse to buy alternative products. Businesses, therefore, go to great lengths and great cost to create, maintain and protect the brand.

Brand image

Branding is about the creation and maintenance of an image that appeals to groups of customers. For example, petrol is a product which is technically similar wherever it is bought. However, some drivers will only buy Esso or BP petrol. Why, given that a car will work with petrol supplied by any company? Branding is likely to play a part in the decision of the customer. This situation can be analysed using the marketing mix, as in Table 1.

These variables will contribute to the images associated with different petrol suppliers. It is these images that customers relate to and will influence their choice of petrol. Psychologically, the choice of one brand of petrol rather than another will be affected by brand values and the image associated with a brand.

It is psychology and customer perception that help to explain the strength of branding in markets such as leisure clothing. Consider t-shirts made by different businesses. They may all be made from quality cotton, but the image associated with each t-shirt may be different. Figure 1 shows the images sometimes associated with different brands.

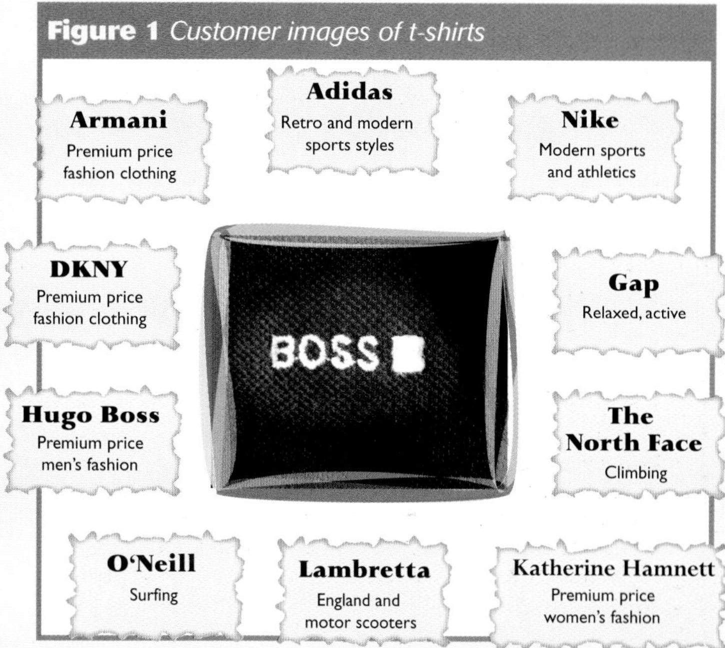

Figure 1 *Customer images of t-shirts*

Table 1 *Branding of petrol using the marketing mix*

Product Petrol is basically the same raw material, but each business will have product features that appeal to different drivers.

- Petrol types – premium unleaded or superunleaded.
- Filling stations – style, layout of buildings, goods sold, lighting, signage, corporate colours.

Price The retail price of petrol is similar as most of the price is accounted for by tax and international oil markets set the raw material cost. Within the retail price there is some room for manoeuvre for businesses.

- Some try to be the cheapest in an area.
- Some maintain an image of 'quality' by being a little more expensive.

Place The location of a filling station will affect driver choice of which petrol to buy. Stations may be sited:

- on main roads;
- in housing estates;
- next to supermarkets;
- in out-of-town shopping centres;
- near to motorways.

Promotion Petrol companies do not want price wars. So they often use non-price competition in the form of promotion. This can include:

- sponsorship and advertising of motor sports and high performance of cars using their petrol;
- being associated with environmental issues to attract customers who share these values.

Brand awareness

Having or creating high brand awareness is an important objective in most marketing strategies. It is a key marketing objective, a target and a very important measure in marketing. High brand awareness means that an organisation or its products are recognised in the market. It is a strength that can be used to promote associated products with the same brand name. This will hopefully lead to high sales when the target market is ready to purchase.

A business may have the best technically performing product in the world. But if consumers are not aware of the brand, then they will not buy it given the many alternatives that are available. Brand awareness is the measure of what proportion of customers have heard of a brand or are conscious of its existence. It is created by a marketing team through promotion and application of the marketing mix.

Brand awareness is usually measured as a percentage of a given market, based on marketing research designed to measure awareness. A brand may have a high or low brand awareness. Decisions can then be made as to whether the level of brand awareness is acceptable or needs to be increased, as a marketing objective.

There are two ways of measuring and reporting brand awareness:

- un-prompted brand awareness;
- prompted brand awareness.

Un-prompted brand awareness This is the proportion of people in the target market that remember a brand without being given any clues. An example of measuring un-prompted brand awareness from market research in the paint industry is shown in Figure 2. Un-prompted brand awareness figures are often lower than expected as few people remember all the brand names of all the products that they buy or use.

Prompted brand awareness This is the proportion of people in the target market that say that they have heard of a brand when the name is mentioned. An example of measuring prompted brand awareness from market research in the paint industry is shown in Figure 2. Prompted brand awareness figures are usually high relative to un-prompted awareness figures, as people will often reply 'yes' to questions such as 'Have you heard of...?' because they do not want to look foolish for not having heard of the brand.

Despite this reservation prompted figures are considered realistic. This is because consumers are usually presented with a choice of brands when shopping and are likely to respond positively, i.e. buy a brand they have heard of and like rather than one they know little or nothing about.

Figure 2 *Un-promoted and promoted brand awareness for paint*

Un-prompted

EXAMPLE
'Please give me the name of a manufacturer of paint that you have heard of.'

RESPONSE
Crown 35%
Dulux 35%
Retailer brands 20%
Other makes 9%
Don't know any 1%

BRAND AWARENESS
High for two brands in particular

Prompted

EXAMPLE
'Have you heard of Dulux paint?'

RESPONSE
Yes 98% No 2%

BRAND AWARENESS
High for Dulux

The need to maintain brand awareness

Coca-Cola has one of the strongest brand names in the world. It is certainly one of the strongest brands in the beverages market. Yet it continues to spend many millions of pounds each year promoting its brand. Why? Coca-Cola recognises the strength of its brand and that it needs to be maintained and protected to ensure that in future it will generate sales and profits for the business. A strong brand name will help sell the current range of products and the reputation of the brand name will help when introducing new products.

The marketing world has a history of famous brand names that were strong in the past, but for a variety of reasons are virtually unknown today. Ratners, for example, was the leading chain of high street jewellery shops in Britain in the 1970s and 1980s. It enjoyed high brand awareness and had a brand image based on low prices and good value products. This led to mass-market appeal. A negative remark, made in 1991 by the owner of the Ratners chain about the quality of its goods, changed its image overnight. Its customers no longer wanted to be associated with the brand and its image collapsed, followed soon after by the business itself.

Brands can be 're-made' by changing their image and associations. For many years Lucozade, a fizzy drink, was bought as an aid to recovery from illness. Its brand image was based on this and as a consequence sales opportunities were limited. Today, Lucozade is marketed as a sports drink. It has an image associated with providing energy and high performance for people engaged in sporting activities. This change has been brought about through the creative use of the marketing mix.

Other reasons for increasing brand awareness

In addition to the reasons already given, other reasons for wanting a strong brand and high brand awareness include the following.

Competition Customer perceptions and understanding of one brand compared to another is an important factor in competitive markets. It can be the reason why consumers choose to buy one product rather than another that may be similar. The more competitive the market, the more important it is for organisations to establish a strong image for their product. There are many examples of this situation, including the washing powder market, pet foods and chocolate bars.

Segmentation Some organisations use the brand name to compete through segmentation. This is the dividing up of a market into groups or segments and the exploitation of gaps in a market as explained in section 33. The key is to develop a product for every segment or gap to keep out competition. This can be done effectively by using a strong brand name in each segment. Good examples of this approach can be seen in the retail industry where retailers use their own brand for segmentation. Baked beans in supermarkets is an example, as shown in Table 2.

Table 2 *Ways of segmenting the baked beans market*

Manufacturers' brands	Heinz, HP,
Own brands	Tesco, Sainsbury, Morrisons
Own brand segmentation	
	Premium priced beans
	Value beans
	Organic beans
	Slimmers' beans

Launching new products It is easier to launch a new product with a brand name that customers and consumers have already heard of. If a new product can be associated with a brand that already has a strong name and reputation this can reduce the need to promote and explain the image and strengths of a product. A good example of this is the Sony brand name that can be applied to many new products. The high awareness and good reputation of the Sony brand means that customers who have a positive image of one Sony product are likely to try other Sony products when they are new to the market.

Entering new markets Trying to enter a new market with an unknown brand name is very difficult. Customers will have no reference points upon which to base their decision to buy. Faced with a choice between a familiar brand name and a brand that has never been heard of, most will buy the name they know, unless there is a strong reason to switch, such as low price. But any change in brand carries a risk that the new brand may not be as good as the familiar brand. Rather than take the risk, the familiar brand is the safe option. However, if a brand name is so strong and has such high awareness that it is known beyond its original market, then it can be used to help a business enter a new market. A good example of this is the Virgin brand name. Virgin has been applied to many different products in diverse markets, including music, rail and air travel and finance. The Virgin brand values are based on an image created and maintained by entrepreneur Richard Branson.

Investigate the brands which exist in the confectionery market by looking in a local store or supermarket.

- Which brands exist?
- Which companies produce these brands?
- What are likely to be the aims of the businesses in branding products?

Use a questionnaire to find out the level of brand awareness amongst people you know.

Portfolio practice · Dyson DC15 'The Ball'

In 2005 James Dyson, the inventor of the famous vacuum cleaner without a bag, combined this with another of his inventions. He had also invented 'The Ballbarrow', a wheelbarrow with a ball at the front to make steering easy. These two creations provided the inspiration for the launch in the latest in the line of innovative branded products.

The DC15 known as 'The Ball' went on sale in March 2005. It is a Dyson vacuum cleaner with a single large nylon ball at the front instead of wheels. It is designed to make steering easy, 'at the flick of a wrist', rather than the pushing and pulling of other vacuum cleaners.

It sells for around £320-£350, a relatively high price. But the business argues that there is more technology involved and that cleaning will be 30% quicker. James Dyson suggested that companies would try to produce their own versions of the 'The Ball' but would find it difficult because the product had 182 patents preventing the copying of designs.

The Dyson vacuum cleaner had become the market leader in the UK by 1995. By 2005 the business had 17.3% of the UK market by volume and 40% by value. In 2004, however, a Consumers' Association report suggested that the Dyson cleaner was less reliable than other branded products sold by Hoover, Panasonic and Electrolux. The business had also been criticised two years earlier for moving production to Malaysia, a low cost production area, making 500 staff redundant.

Source: adapted from *The Daily Mail*, 15.3.2005.

(a) Identify aspects of branding mentioned in the article.

(b) Explain how any of the variables in the marketing mix may have been affected by branding.

(c) Identify reasons why Dyson products need high brand awareness.

(d) Examine why consumer attitude to the Dyson brand is important.

(e) Discuss the importance of brands and branding in the market for electrical household goods.

Meeting the assessment criteria

For a chosen product or service you must be able to identify and explain the different marketing strategies used by businesses to achieve their marketing objectives and meet the needs of their target markets. This will involve a consideration of the activities used to achieve brand awareness.

Business example - Nestlé's KitKat

Nestlé is a multinational company that manufactures a range of products. These include breakfast cereals, ice cream, beverages, baby products and chocolate and confectionery. It has many branded products. These include the company name, Nestlé. But it also has branded products in the chocolate range such as Crunch, Smarties and KitKat.

Source: adapted from www.Nestle.com and www.confectionerynews.com.

Mark Band 1 *Description of the chosen product/service, basic description of the marketing objectives and the relevant segmentation and target market.*

The KitKat chocolate and wafer bar is manufactured by Nestlé. It is aimed at customers in confectionery markets. KitKat is one of the UK's best selling confectionery brands, with a very high brand awareness. The KitKat brand has been used since 1937. Over the years it has established a good reputation and an excellent brand image. Nestlé owns many famous brand names, but KitKat is likely to be one of the most famous, with the high level of brand awareness. One of Nestlé's marketing objectives is likely to be to maintain the position of KitKat in the highly competitive confectionery market. To do this it launches different versions for different market segments – people with different tastes. Each carries the Nestlé and KitKat brand names.

Mark Band 2 *Explanation of why the product/service has been chosen, what the marketing aims and objectives are and steps taken to identify the target market and segmentation.*

The UK has one of the largest confectionary markets in the world. According to a Euromonitor report the UK market amounted to over £10 million per annum in the early 21st century. KitKat is one of the UK's best selling confectionery brands, with a well known and established brand name since 1937. There are many competitors in the confectionery market. Nestlés objective will be to maintain the market position of KitKat. The KitKat brand keeps competition at bay and the market interested by high levels of promotion and a continuous programme of new product introductions. The brand is advertised regularly on television, on posters and in other media, which help to maintain the high level of brand awareness. The Nestlé and KitKat brands are used to launch new products. Recent introductions have been flavoured KitKat such as plain chocolate, mint and orange. 2004 saw the launch of various KitKat limited editions, such as lemon & yoghurt, luscious lime, KitKat white (covered in white chocolate), KitKat dark (dark chocolate) and a Christmas Pudding flavour for Christmas. Each of these will be aimed at a different market segment. Each segment will have customers with particular tastes.

Mark Band 3 *Comprehensive explanation illustrating depth of knowledge and understanding of the product/service, marketing aims and objectives, target market and segmentation.*

The UK market for confectionery products has been estimated to be one of the largest in the world. In the early 21st century Euromonitor estimated that over £5.5 billion per annum was spent on confectionery. Other research suggests that each person eats around 14kg of confectionery per year. In this large market Nestlé's KitKat has become a well know established brand since its introduction in 1937. Brand awareness is high. However, competition from manufacturers such as Mars and Cadbury means that Nestlé's objective will be to ensure the strength of its brand is maintained. This will give it a competitive advantage over its rivals. Over the years the Nestlé and KitKat brand names have been used in a number of ways.

- Segmentation. KitKat is available in a range of sizes and packaging formats aimed at different segments of the market. Each segment is likely to have different tastes. The business has also launched limited editions such as lemon & yoghurt, luscious lime, KitKat white (covered in white chocolate), KitKat dark (dark chocolate) and a Christmas pudding flavour for Christmas.
- To launch new products. KitKat Chunky was launched in 1999, a large, single-finger version of the familiar chocolate and wafer finger bar. KitKat Low-Carb was launched in July 2004. It is the result of years of research and development. It meets the needs of people with a low carbohydrate lifestyle whilst keeping the look, taste, and reputation for quality associated with the classic KitKat product.
- To enter new markets. Nestlé launched KitKat Kubes, bite sized chunks packed loose in a bag. There is also a KitKat Easter egg for this seasonal market.

The KitKat website claims that there are at least 23 basic pack formats for KitKat. This demonstrates how Nestlé has the marketing objective to use the strength of the KitKat brand name to maintain its position at the top of the UK confectionery market. Nestlé aims to have a product for all the important segments and gaps in the market and to expand the business by using the KitKat brand name to enter new markets.

33 Market segmentation

What is market segmentation?

Market segmentation is the practice of dividing a market into discrete, identifiable groups of customers or consumers that have common characteristics and motivations. There are reasons why a business might segment its market.

- Each group can be treated independently and a business can tailor the marketing mix or develop products to meet the needs of each segment.
- Opportunities, such as niche markets, that have not yet been exploited and new product opportunities can be highlighted.
- It can show which segments are performing well and which segments need additional marketing support.
- Decisions can be made about which segments are likely to be profitable and worth pursuing and which segments should be ignored.

Segmenting a market

A business needs access to up-to-date market research data in order to segment a market. This may be from primary research conducted specifically to see how a market is segmented or from secondary research that has already been conducted. Segmentation can involve analysing marketing data and using different criteria to split the data in pre-determined groups. Another method of segmentation is to see which groupings form naturally within the data. Market segmentation will identify which segments of a market are large or small, strong or weak and already supplied with products or if there are gaps that are ready for product development and introduction.

The three main ways used to segment a market are shown in Figure 1.

Geographic segmentation

Geographic segmentation involves analysing markets and dividing them into groups based on geographic factors. These factors are usually physical, such as country region, but could include economic factors, such as population density. Some examples are shown in Table 1.

Figure 1 *Methods of market segmentation*

- SEGMENTATION
  - Geographic
  - Demographic
  - Psychographic

Table 1 *Examples of geographic segmentation*

Method By region.
Examples Regions such as Europe, Asia, North America, Africa, areas within a country, e.g. England, Scotland, Wales and Northern Ireland.
Method By country.
Examples Within national boundaries, e.g. UK, Republic of Ireland, France, China.
Method By local authority area within a country.
Examples Categorised by size, development or membership of geographic region, e.g. Department of Trade and Industry (DTI) regions.
Method City or town
Examples Population within ranges or above a certain level. e.g. towns with over 100,000 people.
Method By population density.
Examples High/low density, urban/suburban population, rural/semi-rural population.

Geographic segmentation means that each market can be treated individually, taking into account regional differences and requirements. This is useful for different types of business.

- Multi-national businesses can take into account the needs of different countries or regions in their overall marketing plans. An example is shown in Figure 2.
- National businesses can tailor the needs of particular areas

Figure 2 *Geographic segmentation at McDonald's*

The McDonald's business is managed as distinct geographic segments: United States; Europe; Asia/Pacific, Middle East and Africa (APMEA); Latin America and Canada.

It also tailors its food to individual countries. For example, McDonald's India has developed a special menu with vegetarian selections to suit Indian tastes and preferences. McDonald's does not offer any beef or pork items in India. The business says that 'Only the freshest chicken, fish and vegetable products find their way into our Indian restaurants'.

Source: adapted from www.djia-valuation.com and www.mcdonaldsindia.com.

within a country in their plans.

- A small business may only advertise its products or services within a geographic area that it can reach effectively. A local Newcastle taxi service, for example, would not advertise in London.

Geographic segmentation and the marketing mix

The geographic segmentation of markets can affect the marketing mix of a business. Table 2 shows some examples.

Table 2 *Geographical segmentation and the marketing mix*

Part of mix	Effect	Example
Product	Nature of the product	Paint sold in Mediterranean markets needs to withstand sun and heat, but paint sold in Scandinavian markets needs to resist cold.
	Packaging	Some markets require full contents listed, others require nutritional information. Ready-to-drink coffee is available in cans in the Netherlands but not in the UK.
Price	Lower	Consumer goods sell at lower prices in Eastern European countries than they do in the West as incomes are lower.
	Higher	A UK manufacturer selling into the US will charge a higher price in the US than in the UK to cover transport costs.
Place	Availability	Products may not be sold in some countries due to regional differences, for example digital radios will not be sold in countries with only analogue wavelengths.
Promotion	Type of advertising	A small business such as a local car repair service can advertise in a local paper, use local radio and distribute leaflets in a local area using post codes.

Demographic segmentation

Demographic segmentation is where a market is analysed and divided into groups based on demographic factors. These factors relate to the economic and social features and characteristics of the market being segmented.

Age The UK Census 2001 provides broad examples of age groups. These are people aged 0 to 15, aged 16 to 74 and aged 75 and over. A more detailed breakdown may be 5 year age bands, e.g. ranges 0-4, 5-9, 10-14 up to 85-89, then 90 years and over. It may be more useful for a marketing plan to segment using larger age bands of say 10 years. Which bands are used will depend on the market and what the business wants to do with the different age segments.

Sex A market can be segmented into males and females. Many markets and products have a bias towards one sex or the other. This type of segmentation can be useful when the bias is extreme. For example, neck ties are worn almost exclusively by men, but bought by both men and women (as gifts). Segmentation will help plan promotion towards men (for wearing as well as buying) and women (for buying).

Socio-economic group Various methods are used to segment the market by socio-economic group. A widely used method in the media is shown in Table 3.

Table 3 *Social economic groups, National Readership Survey (NRS) social grade definitions (UK)*

Socio-economic grade	Social status	Occupation
A	upper middle class	higher managerial, administrative or professional
B	middle class	intermediate managerial, administrative or professional
C1	lower middle class	supervisory or clerical, junior managerial, administrative or professional
C2	skilled working class	skilled manual workers
D	working class	semi and unskilled manual workers
E	those at lowest level of subsistence	state pensioners or widows (no other earner), casual or lowest grade workers

Although still widely used, this classification can be unsophisticated and may not reflect modern society. Links between occupation and economic power are not so direct, so a number of other systems have been developed which reflect factors such as discretionary income, lifestage and working patterns.

- ACORN. This stands for 'A Classification Of Residential Neighbourhoods'. It is based on types of housing and the people that live there. This classification is linked to postcodes and is therefore a valuable tool when it comes to geographical targeting.
- Income. Like age, the bands used for segmentation by income can be tailored to meet the needs of the market or the current economic situation. Typical bands for annual income could be

under £10,000, £11,000 to £20,000, £21,000 to £30,000. Income bands are usually selected to be appropriate for the range of incomes in the market being segmented.

- Occupation. This segmentation assumes that different occupations have different levels of income which have an effect on the market. It can also be an indicator of social status or linked to behaviour factors which may be useful for marketing purposes.
- Marital status. The Census 2001 breaks down the population into single people (never married), married or re-married people, separated or divorced, and widowed.

Since 2001 the National Statistics Socio-economic Classification (NS-SEC) has been used for all official statistics and surveys in the UK as shown in Table 4. The Census 2001 website www.statistics.gov.uk/census2001 is a good source to see demographic segmentation in use.

Table 4 *The National Statistics Socio-economic Classification*

1	Higher managerial and professional occupations
	1.1 Large employers and higher managerial occupations
	1.2 Higher professional occupations
2	Lower managerial and professional occupations
3	Intermediate occupations
4	Small employers and own account workers
5	Lower supervisory and technical occupations
6	Semi-routine occupations
7	Routine occupations
8	Never worked and long-term unemployed

Demographic segmentation and the marketing mix

The demographic segmentation of markets can affect the market mix of a business. Table 5 shows some examples. Demographic segmentation is linked closely to branding, as explained in section 32. It is the use of different brand named products from the same organisation, each aimed at different demographic segments of the market.

Table 5 *Demographic segmentation and the marketing mix*

Part of mix	Effect	Example
Product	Nature of the product	Deodorants have different scents whether aimed at men or women users, as different sexes associate different scents with personal hygiene.
	Packaging	Cans of soft drinks are sold singly for younger or unmarried consumers and in packs for consumers buying for a family.
	Branding	Higher priced brands of canned vegetables are stocked alongside supermarket own brand goods, segmented in premium, standard and budget brands, each priced at a different level for different income groups.
Price	Higher	Higher prices may be charged in food halls of Harrods or Harvey Nichols aimed at higher income groups and category ABC1 consumers.
	Lower	Lower prices may be charged by supermarkets such as Netto, Aldi and Lidl, aimed at lower income groups or categories C2, D and E.
Place	Availability	Some clothes and accessories are sold in high street designer shops such as Hugo Boss, Gucci and Vivienne Westwood in London or other cities aimed at higher income groups and ABC1s. Clothes aimed at lower income groups or categories C2, D and E may be found in markets.
Promotion	Types of advertising	PR campaigns can appeal to particular segments. Prada or Gucci advertising may take place in magazines aimed at ABC1s. A product aimed at young males, such as football boots, would not be advertised in a magazine that has a high readership of older married women, such as *Lancashire Life*.

Psychographic segmentation

Psychographic segmentation is where a market is analysed and divided into groups based on psychographic factors. These factors relate to subjective personality features, such as attitudes, ideas and opinions. Psychographic segmentation is particularly useful for identifying new or niche markets.

Lifestyle Lifestyles may fall into different categories. For example they may be:

- modern and trend-setting or traditional with few changes;
- expansive and willing to spend money in pursuit of pleasure or cautious with money and unwilling to spend more than is necessary.

Often, these segmentations are based as much on perception much as actual lifestyle differences.

Interests These would include sports, leisure activities and hobbies.

Attitudes Markets can be analysed and segmented by attitude to politics, lifestyles, certain products. For example, some consumers will wear clothes that are made from real animal fur but others will not.

Opinions Groups with similar opinions of politics and social issues can be identified. Opinion polls are a widely used method of primary research to identify the mood or feelings within a target market. Products can be tailored to appeal to the attitudes of a segment. For example, the supermarket chain Iceland promotes the claim that none of the products that it stocks contain genetically modified (GM) ingredients.

Values These are often influenced by upbringing and family attitudes as well as social conditioning. Once formed, values are hard to change. Products can be changed and adapted to reflect the values of market segments. For example, the 'Fair Trade' product ranges for tea and coffee may appeal to ethical customers.

Taste People may see products as being in 'good or bad taste'. For example, some films have 'gross out' images and storylines and deliberate 'bad taste' designed to offend older people, but appeal to younger audiences where 'bad taste' is perceived as being amusing and entertaining.

Table 6 *Psychographic segmentation and the marketing mix*

Part of mix	Effect	Example
Product	Nature of the product	Magazines are geared towards different readerships, e.g. *Horse and Ride*, *FHM*, *Glamour*, *Hello*, *Kerrang*, *Men's Health* and *Art and Antiques* and niche markets can be targeted.
Price	Higher price	Crystal champagne sells for £100-£300 a bottle to consumers that embrace the hip hop lifestyle and to some star footballers. Tools and materials can sell for premium prices for some hobbies, e.g. carpentry.
Place	Availability	Retailers offer specialist products in particular shops geared to lifestyles, e.g. sports shops, 'new age' shops, American comic shops.
Promotion	Type of advertising	Some lifestyles might react better to visual advertisements such as fast cars. Radio and newspaper advertisements may be used for solicitors' services to appear 'serious and concerned'.

Psychographic segmentation and the marketing mix

The psychographic segmentation of markets can affect the marketing mix of a business. Some examples are shown in Table 6.

Other methods of segmentation

Sometimes businesses find that one method of segmenting markets is inflexible, not subtle enough or does not meet particular market situations. As a result, segmentation based on combinations of factors are used. For example, geo-economic segmentation that combines factors from both areas to identify, say, high-income families in a particular town or region can be used. ACORN, linked to postcode based marketing or promotional activity, can also be effective.

In some markets, such as trade or industrial markets, other ways of segmentation may be more appropriate. Examples could include segmentation by industry and by status, e.g. new customer/old customer.

Benefits and problems of segmentation

Market segmentation is a powerful tool in marketing. Each variable of the marketing mix can play a role in segmentation by tailoring products to meet the needs of each segment.

- New businesses can enter a market by targeting a particular segment.
- Established businesses can strengthen market share by producing new products to meet the needs of every segment.
- Niche markets can be identified and filled by existing or new products as appropriate.
- Competition can be kept out of a market by having a product for each segment and leaving no room for a competitor to enter.

However, there can be dangers associated with over-segmentation.

- Individual products can be picked off by competitors. If a market leader moves into smaller segments, a competitor that is particularly strong in one of those segments stands a better chance of beating the market leader as it knows the segment better and is already established.
- The finance department may argue that a highly segmented niche product may not be as profitable as it wants. But the marketing team may argue that it serves another purpose, such as keeping competitors out of a segment or showing that the business has a complete range or products.
- Range proliferation. Some businesses add products to a range for different segments just to keep competitors out of a market. This can have a negative effect on customers. They may become frustrated if all the available space is filled by products from one manufacturer.

Niche marketing

This is the development of a segmentation strategy. Niche marketing is based upon supplying a product that meets the needs of a small, discrete, specialist market or filling a small gap in the market.

Marketing research may identify a gap in the market or a group of consumers whose needs are not being met. The business must then decide whether it is worth specialising and concentrating marketing activity on the gap or the niche that has been identified. The niche must be large enough to be worth concentrating on based on the objectives of the business, such as profitability or the requirement to keep competition out of that niche.

A niche marketing strategy has a number of advantages for a business.

- Costs can be kept low.
- Relatively low sales can account for a big share of the market niche.
- A business can become a major player within the niche.
- Competition may be less. it could be ignored by mass marketing organisations.
- Customers can be satisfied by providing the product that is right for them.
- Marketing communication message can be focused.
- A business can become a specialist.
- A business can exploit specialism through higher prices which can increase profitability.

Large businesses can sometimes target niche markets. For example the UK paint market has both mass market products and highly specialised products aimed at niche markets. Smaller businesses can also successfully exploit niches. Some examples of niche providers are shown in Table 7.

Mass marketing

This is perhaps the opposite to niche marketing. A mass marketing strategy is based on providing a product that has wide appeal to a great number of consumers in a market that is very large in itself. There are many examples, including:

- vanilla ice cream, the most popular flavour within the large ice cream market;
- white paint, the top selling colour in the vast overall market;
- bedding plants in Spring will have mass market appeal as they will be the top selling plants in the garden plant market which is large.

Table 7 *Market niche providers*

Business	Niche
I Love Liquorice Ltd	An independent specialist retailer of traditional sweets.
Becker Underwood Ltd	Manufactures and markets a range of specialist niche products for the garden and horticulture markets.
Gecko Headgear	A specialist helmet manufacturer of lightweight headgear for extreme sports.
Artel Rubber	Manufactures high quality silicone rubber products for prestige motor vehicles.

Mass markets also have their own mass market brands, usually brands that have become household names or generic names. Some examples include;

- Hoover, a mass market brand of electrical household appliances that is associated with vacuum cleaners to the point that many people use Hoover to describe any brand of vacuum cleaner;
- Google has become the mass market brand name associated with Internet search engines to the point that it has become a verb and people talk about 'Googling' or say 'I will Google it.' when they mean search for it.

The attraction of mass markets to a business is that they are large, sell products in high volume and generate high levels of revenue and profit. Even a small share of a large market may be worth having. On the other hand there is a danger in achieving mass-market status. Consumers can be unpredictable and what is popular with the mass market this year may not be so next year.

Products for mass markets need a high level of marketing expenditure to enter the market and even more expenditure to remain in the market. Sometimes a short but profitable excursion into a mass market may be the objective a business has set. For example popular mass market ringtones can make a huge impact on the market, but have only a short product life cycle as there will be another popular ringtone along soon after. A mass market brand or product is also vulnerable to attack from smaller competitors that can pick-off small parts of the market with niche products.

Despite these reservations, many large organisations make high profits from being mass market providers.

Look in a copy of your local *Yellow Pages* directory. Identify three examples of:

- local businesses that have segmented their market geographically;
- national businesses that have segmented their market locally;
- businesses that have used demographic segmentation.

OR

Magazines often carry out surveys to find out more about their readers. Questions are asked to find out a variety of information about readers' characteristics. Find a magazine survey questionnaire from back issues of a magazine. Identify which questions in the survey are designed to find out about:

- geographic segmentation;
- demographic segmentation;
- psychographic segmentation.

Research task

Portfolio practice · Kuoni Group

One of the major businesses operating in the UK market for leisure travel is the international Kuoni Group. Its 2004 Annual Report stated that the Kuoni brand is 'positioned in the upper-to-middle pricing segments'. In the UK the business offers different holiday packages at different price bands under two different brand names.

Voyages Jules Verne Ltd. (VJV) 2005 brochures.
Country brochures include America Latina, China & Beyond, Travels in Italy and Dreaming of India.

Theme brochures include Journeys of Scientific Interest, World of Wonders, Le Weekend Extraordinaire, Travels through Ancient Lands, Great Journeys and Cruises of Discovery 2005.

Kuoni 2005 brochures.
Country brochures include Italy, Southern Africa, Australia, New Zealand & South Pacific, Morocco, Dubai, USA & Canada, India & Nepal, Swiss Winter and Swiss Summer.

Brochures based on 'what is important to you...' include Worldwide Our A to Z of long-haul travel covering 60 exotic countries, Family Worldwide 2005, World Class Luxury holidays from £2,500 per person, Selections Special Offers to Sri Lanka, the Maldives, Thailand and Indonesia in 2005, Limited Editions April to July Special Offers. Escorted Tours 2005/6, Sandals & Beaches, Weddings and Florida Sun.

Source: adapted from Kuoni, *Annual Report and Accounts, 2004* and author research.

(a) Identify using examples THREE ways in which the business might segment the market.
(b) Using ONE of these methods, suggest how it might affect the marketing mix of the business.
(c) (i) Examine the reasons why Kuoni might segment its market and (ii) discuss whether the benefits will outweigh any problems.

Meeting the assessment criteria

When producing the marketing mix for your product you need to have considered segmentation in your market and what this means to the marketing mix that you develop.

Business example - Great Windows Ltd

Made in Heaven is a made-to-measure curtain service, which is provided by Great Windows Ltd, a business that operates in the Harlow area of Essex.

A representative from the company measures a customer's windows and calculates how much fabric is required. The customer then chooses and buys the fabric they want and the team at Great Windows Ltd makes the curtains.

Table 8 shows a profile of all people planning to buy curtains in the next twelve months and a profile of those people who say that they will buy made-to-measure curtains. This is information downloaded from various sites on the Internet.

Mark Band 1 *Description of the chosen product/service, basic description of the marketing objectives and the relevant segmentation and target market.*
Great Windows Ltd is a business that operates in the Harlow area of Essex providing a made-to-measure curtain service. Its objective is to target market segments that want this service to be successful. Geographically, it will operate only in the Harlow area. Using the information in Table 8, demographic segmentation suggests that the basic target market is women, aged 45-64, in the AB socio-economic group, who are married, working full-time and living in a home that they own. Psychographic segmentation suggests that only 5% of people planning to buy curtains in the next twelve months are likely to choose made-to-measure curtains. This suggests that made-to-measure curtains is a niche market.

Mark Band 2 *Explanation of why the product/service has been chosen, what the marketing aims and objectives are and steps taken to identify the target market and segmentation.*
Great Windows Ltd is a business that operates in the Harlow area of Essex providing a made-to-measure curtain service. Its objective is to target market segments who want this service to be successful. Searching the Internet did produce some data, as shown in Table 8. This suggests a niche market, sold in the local area, targeted at women aged 45-64, who are ABs, married, working full-time, who own their own home. But more information was needed before developing a marketing mix. Great Windows Ltd contacted a similar business in Scotland

Table 8 *Buyers of curtains*

All figures %	Total sample profile. All planning to buy curtains in next twelve months	Profile of people who say they will buy made-to-measure curtains
All buyers	100	5
Sex of buyer		
Male	48	44
Female	52	56
Age of buyer		
15-24	18	13
25.34	19	30
35-44	17	15
45-64	26	32
65+	19	10
Socio-economic classification		
AB	17	28
C1	25	23
C2	26	22
DE	32	27
Marital status		
Married	61	77
Single	24	13
Widowed, divorced or separated	15	10
Working status		
Full-time	37	45
Part-time	9	15
Not working	54	40
Household tenure		
Mortgage	44	65
Owned outright	23	17
Rented	33	18

that was not competing and was prepared to share customer information, as shown in Figure 3. This information reassured Great Windows Ltd that although only 5% of people planning to buy curtains in the next twelve months said they would buy made-to-measure, most of the money spent on curtains went to the independent specialist segment, businesses like Great Windows Ltd. Because of the profile of buyers of made-to-measure curtains, it is important that Great Windows Ltd presents the right image. It must appeal to the profile of customers targeted. The image must be of quality and reliability, which should appeal to the target market, women who are working full time. The business might also charge a premium price to demonstrate the value and quality of the service. Customers buy their own fabric so Great Windows will not need to carry stocks.

Mark Band 3 *A comprehensive marketing mix which is clearly linked to the research and segmentation evidence and shows depth of knowledge and understanding of the relevant Ps.*

Great Windows Ltd is a business that operates in the Harlow area of Essex, providing a made-to-measure curtain service. Its objective is to target market segments that want this service to be successful and grow in the long term. Searching the Internet produced some helpful data. This suggested a niche market, sold in the local area, targeted at women aged 45-64, who are ABs, married, working full-time and who own their own home. Further information from a Scottish business about buyers confirms that although it is selling to a niche market, most people buy from independent businesses like Great Windows Ltd. In addition to targeting women aged 45-64, 32% of potential customers, it may also be worthwhile targeting women aged 25-34 as they represent 30% of target customers, another sizeable part of the market. The lifestyle and motivation of this latter group to buy made-to-measure curtains may be different to the older group, so the media used for promotion must be considered carefully.

The needs of the target groups must be taken into account in the marketing mix.

Product The business needs to make sure that the service is first class and appeals to women in the AB socio-economic group. For the same reasons, the quality of the finished curtains must be high. Added value features such as home delivery and curtain hanging in customers' windows might also be used.

Price Great Windows Ltd plans to adopt a premium pricing strategy. This should be in keeping with the expectations of the core socio-economic group.

Place There is little opportunity for varying the place element of the marketing mix as Great Windows Ltd only operates in the Harlow area of Essex. However, it may be useful to target the service at areas of the town where most of the houses are owner-occupied and lived in by people in the higher socio-economic groups.

Promotion The business is only operating in the Harlow area. So the media used for promotion must circulate, be read, and be listened to and watched by people in the local or nearby areas as some customers may be prepared to travel if the service is good enough. The following promotional strategy is suggested.

- Placement in the Harlow area *Yellow Pages* as it is used by all socio-economic groups to access local services.
- Press releases on a regular basis to the monthly Essex county magazine. This has an up-market readership profile that matches the profile of buyers of made-to-measure curtains. Consider advertising in the future if it proves to be worthwhile.
- Direct mail to owner-occupied households in higher socio-economic areas of the town and surrounding areas.

The following are not recommended.

- Local newspapers and free sheets - the readership profile means that there will be a lot of wastage as only a minority of the target market read these.
- Local radio and television as these have too wide a catchment area and could attract enquiries from a distance, which will be too far for Great Windows to service to the high standards set.

Figure 3 *Sales of curtains by outlet type, % share by value 2005*

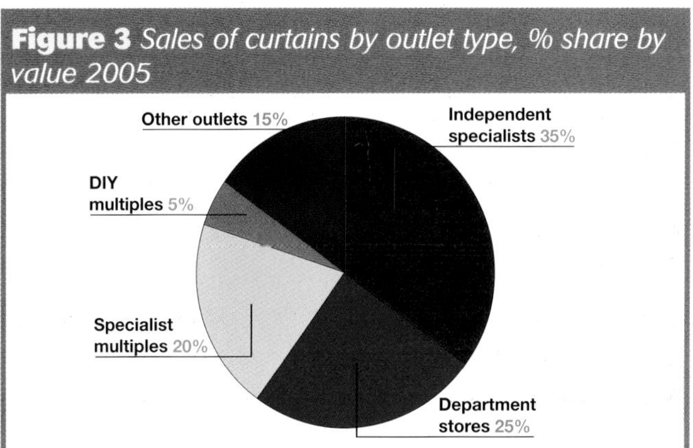

34 Primary research

What is primary research?

Primary research is used to collect original data and information for the first time. This is known as primary data. It is 'raw' data as it has not yet been analysed or interpreted. Because it is new and original, primary research can be designed to meet the precise needs of a research project.

Primary research is sometimes called **field research** because the activity is conducted 'in the field' or the marketplace. It can be referred to as a **survey** when primary research is carried out to find data about a large number of people, known as a 'population'. All mean the same thing, that primary research is about collecting data, facts or opinions, direct from the original source of the information. People who take part in primary research and supply data are known as **respondents**.

Conducted properly, primary research should be able to provide data which can be interpreted to give answers to particular questions or to support plans, ideas or decision making.

Planning and organising primary research

Like all marketing activity, primary research needs to be planned to be effective. There is a number of steps that the researcher must take.

- Identify the problem and decide what they want to know, what to ask, what needs to be researched, when answers are needed and how much to spend (the budget for the project). A marketing research project needs objectives and a time plan or it could be a waste of resources and produce misleading information. A budget is important so that the cost does not increase out of proportion to the research.
- Decide how to collect the data in the most effective way. This involves choosing the most appropriate primary research method.
- Decide on the respondents to survey and the style and content of the questions.
- Decide how to analyse and present the findings, what the data means and what conclusions can be drawn. This information will form a basic marketing plan for the research.

Quantitative and qualitative data

Depending on the way it is conducted and what questions are asked, primary research can be designed to collect quantitative or qualitative data.

- **Quantitative data** is objective numbers, facts and figures such as how many, how much, how often;
- **Qualitative data** is subjective views, opinions, attitudes and motivations.

Quantitative data is usually produced by counting the number of times an answer is given, based on a set list of questions in a questionnaire or the number of times an observed action occurs. Quantitative data can be analysed statistically. Qualitative data is usually produced from open-ended questions, where the respondent is asked for their own words, description or opinion, rather than answer from a set list. Focus groups, where respondents join in a discussion about an idea or topic, also produce qualitative data. This kind of data usually needs to be interpreted by an expert, such as a psychologist, rather than analysed statistically.

Uses of primary research

Primary research has many uses in business. These are shown in Figure 1.

Figure 1 *Uses of primary research*

USES

Testing new ideas and opinions
- Who would buy a new product?
- Would people stop buying if a product changed?
- What do people think about a product or service?
- Do people think that the retail price is too high?

Facts about a market
- What is the target market?
- Who is buying most?
- What are the common characteristics of these people?
- How big is a market?
- How much do people spend?
- What share of the market do the main brands enjoy?

Provide data on how often something happens
- How many people walk past a shop?
- How often do people use a supermarket?
- How many people enter the shop to buy something?
- How many products are returned to a manufacturer as faulty?
- How many people complain about the faulty product?

Marketing mix
- Primary research might help to:
- confirm what colour product or packaging style is preferred;
- suggest how much consumers are prepared to pay;
- show the type of shop where consumers would expect to buy a product.
- identify which magazines are read by the target market and are best for advertising a product.

How is primary research carried out?

There are many different primary research methods.

Observation Here data is collected by looking and recording findings rather than by asking questions. Observations can be open. For example, a respondent may be given a task such as following instructions on how to use a product. The researcher then watches and records how well they accomplish the task and what problems they find. Observation could also be used to count how many people visit a stand in an exhibition. Secret observation could be used to find out the way that most customers turn when they enter a shop. This will help the shop management plan the layout according to which way most people turn. A 'mystery shopper' is another common method of secret observational research. The behaviour of shoppers or shop staff is watched without them knowing and observations recorded.

Direct questioning Probably the most widely recognised method of primary research is the direct questioning of respondents in an interview situation, often with the aid of a questionnaire. A questionnaire helps to guide the flow of questions and records the answers from people being interviewed. Direct questioning can

Figure 2 *Types of primary research*

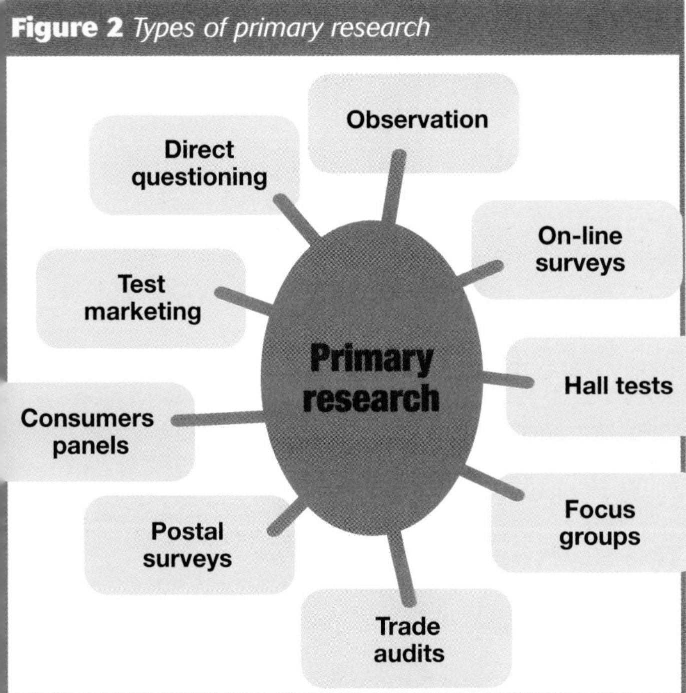

take place face-to-face, such as in the common street survey or one-to-one over the telephone (a telephone survey). Skilled interviewers can achieve high quality results from telephone surveys, which have the advantage that respondents are likely to be in the more relaxed surroundings of their own home. Against this, there can be a lot of wasted calls as respondents are not in when telephoned. Even when they are in, respondents may be distracted by what is going on in the home. Direct questioning is used for mass surveys, for example interviewing lots of people in the street or over the telephone and for individual in-depth interviews.

Another research method that uses direct questioning is omnibus surveys. These are surveys run on a regular basis, such as the first weekend of every month. A number of clients contribute questions to the overall survey and so the cost of setting up the research is shared.

Direct questioning has the advantage that if a respondent does not fully understand a question, it can be explained by the interviewer. There are likely to be fewer wasted questionnaires and the quality of the research is likely to be improved as a result.

Postal surveys This is an alternative to interviews. A self-completion questionnaire is prepared and mailed by the research organisation to respondents, together with a reply-paid envelope. A small incentive is often used to encourage respondents to complete the questionnaire and return it. Postal surveys have the advantage of being able to target households and respondents fairly precisely using postal code or to cover a wide geographic area. They can be based on mailing to an organisation's own database of customers or potential customers. They can also be longer than questionnaires used in face-to-face interviews as respondents are less likely to be under a time pressure to complete the questionnaire. Although the cost of printing and mailing postal questionnaires is relatively low on an individual basis, there is usually a high degree of wastage because questionnaires are not returned.

On-line surveys Increasingly, on-line resources are being used for marketing research. Although the method of delivery is different, on-line surveys are similar to postal surveys. Respondents are sent an e-mail to invite them to log on to the website of a research organisation. Using a discrete and secure website address, respondents are guided to an on-line questionnaire which is completed on screen and submitted directly upon completion. On-line surveys can range from straightforward reproductions of written questionnaires to surveys including photographs or moving images. A problem with on-line surveys is consumer mistrust of the Internet, particularly regarding security. People may also be concerned that completing an on-line survey will result in being bombarded with advertising and spam e-mails.

Hall test A hall test is an alternative to conducting street interviews. The research organisation books a hall or room to interview respondents rather than in the street. This has the advantage that respondents are more comfortable and secure and are more likely to provide better quality answers. As the environment is relatively confidential, respondents can be shown new products or advertisements or asked to sample new flavours and give their opinions.

Focus groups Focus groups are sometimes referred to as 'group discussion'. This is another form of direct questioning, but carried out with a number of respondents in a group, all being interviewed together. Focus groups are particularly useful for researching opinions and attitudes and uncovering ideas that the researcher may not have thought of in the first place. They usually take place in a quiet room in a hotel or a house and run for around 1-2 hours. The focus group is usually led by a trained psychologist. They aim to find out the feelings from the group that may not be expressed if interviewed one-to-one. Discussions will follow a 'pre-planned' route to make sure that the aim of the research is met.

Focus groups may be recorded on audio or video equipment, so that results can be analysed in great detail and individual quotes can be identified. To be effective, focus groups are usually 8-10 people. Any more and the group could become unmanageable and break up into several smaller groups. Any fewer and one person may become dominant, with others in the group not giving their opinions.

Focus groups are used widely to check current thinking and ideas, to monitor changes in social attitudes, to generate ideas for new product developments, to create stories for marketing, promotion and for public relations purposes. They are popular because they can be set-up quickly, results are generated immediately and they are relatively low cost to run.

Test marketing This is a form of primary research that is aimed at reproducing a national sales situation in a small controlled area before launching a product to the whole country. By selecting the right area for the test market, an organisation can test sales techniques, consumer purchases and acceptance of a new product, advertising styles and levels and other forms of promotion without the high cost of a full national launch. If a product is successful in a test market, marketing plans can be reproduced nationally. Conversely, if a test market is not successful, marketing plans can be changed and tested again, or the product may not be launched on a wider scale.

Consumer panels When research is required to measure changing attitudes or behaviour over a period of time researchers will often establish a consumer panel. This is a fixed group of respondents who are interviewed regularly. By recording any changes between each interview, researchers can see how attitudes or purchase levels have changed. These changes can be correlated against marketing campaigns to see what has been successful. Another way of using consumer panels is to establish a panel of experts or enthusiasts who will try out and test a product and report back to the business as part of a new product development programme. This method of using consumer panels is common with computer software and computer games designers.

Trade audits These are carried out with panels of shops or businesses in the same industry. Researchers will visit the premises of businesses on the trade audit panel regularly depending on the rate of sale of products in the market being audited. The researcher will measure stock levels and deliveries and from this calculate sales across the audit period. Trade audits are important for measuring market share or brand share and for showing seasonal trends. Trade audits can also show up long-term trends that are often missed by ad-hoc research surveys.

Who to survey – sampling and population

Having decided on the method of primary research that may be appropriate for meeting the objectives of the research, the researcher must decide who to survey, how to take a sample of people from the **population** and the **sample size**. This is known as the sampling plan. A **sample** of people to survey needs to be chosen. This is a number of people who are likely to be representative of the whole population. The population in a business survey might be every potential customer of the business or everyone in the market for its product.

For most primary research projects the total population that could be surveyed is likely to be large. It would be difficult and unnecessary to survey 100% of a population. Statistical evidence shows that it is only necessary to sample a percentage of a total population to get similar results to the total population to get similar results to the total population within acceptable levels of confidence.

The actual decision about how many people to include in the sample will depend on how much is in the budget to spend on the research, traded off against the level of accuracy required. In practice it is better to sample as many people as can be afforded. The higher the number, the more chance of the research being reliable. Whilst a low number will produce some data, the danger is that it will not be representative of the population. It might be suggested to survey at least 100 for a mini survey, up to 10% of a population or as many as can be afforded.

Questionnaires

A questionnaire is a structured document that contains all of the questions required to collect data. It is basically a list of questions that make up a survey. Although questionnaires are likely to be different for different surveys, some common features may include:

- an identification of what survey it relates to, a title or reference number;
- a control question to confirm if the respondent is suitable to interview, e.g. asking 'Have you taken a holiday outside of the UK in the past year?' (Yes = continue, No = end interview) may be used for a survey on foreign holidays;
- a means of classifying the respondent, usually based on basic demographic criteria such as age, gender, work status, income, socio-economic group;
- the questions themselves.

In addition it is important to include instructions on how the respondent should complete each question and how the interviewer should complete the questionnaire. Self-completion questionnaires will also need easy to understand introductions which explain the reasons for conducting the research, a sincere 'thank you' for completing the questionnaire and full details about how to return the questionnaire - address and 'when by' date. This should be supported by the self-addressed envelope.

The questions themselves

Certain basic types of question are commonly used in questionnaires.

Simple dichotomous questions These give the respondent a choice of two possible answers as in Figure 3.

Figure 3 *Simple dichotomous questions*

(a) Do you drink fruit juice? ☐ Yes ☐ No

(b) Which of these two advertisements do you like the most?

☐ A ☐ B

Multiple-choice questions These give the respondent a choice from a limited, pre-determined range as in Figure 4. An 'other' option is given in case a response that has not been considered proves to be the most popular answer. Sometimes a 'don't know' alternative is more appropriate. This enables respondents who genuinely have no opinion or cannot pick an answer from the given range to tick a box and complete the question. Without a 'don't know' option the survey would be incomplete, as this section of the population would not be represented. Multiple-choice questions enable the researcher to control the range of answers to a degree, which keeps the survey focused. This type of question is simple to ask, simple to answer and the answers will be relatively easy to analyse.

Open-ended questions These are designed to enable respondents to answer freely, without being restricted by the pre-determined choices of the researcher. Examples are questions (f) and (g) in Figure 5. Open-ended questions are very useful for assessing attitudes and opinions. But they can be more difficult to analyse because of the wide range of possible answers or because of the need to group similar answers so that conclusions can be drawn.

Scaling questions These questions are designed to measure the subjective attitude of a respondent to a given statement. There is

Figure 4 *Multiple-choice questions*

(c) Where did you take your last holiday of more than two nights away?
In the UK ☐
In Europe ☐
In the USA ☐
In the Far East ☐
Other (please state) ______

(d) What is your working situation?
Employed full-time ☐
Employed part-time ☐
Self-employed ☐
Not working ☐
Retired ☐
No job ☐
Full-time housekeeper ☐
Other (please write in) ______

(e) How many years should there be before a new edition of a travel book?
2 years ☐
3 years ☐
4 years ☐
5 years ☐
6 years ☐
Don't know ☐

a number of different ways that scaling questions can be constructed. One of the most commonly used is the Likert scale, which consists of five degrees of agreement, or not, with a statement. This is shown in question (h) in Figure 6. Another way of asking a scaling question is to use a semantic differential technique. In this type of question respondents given with a question and asked where along the scale their opinion would fit, as in question (i). The same question could be asked using a scale as in question (j). The point of a semantic differential scale is that it runs between two distinct alternatives, in this case very important or not very important. Scaling questions may also be presented in other ways.

Figure 5 *Open-ended questions*

(f) What do you think about being offered genetically modified (GM) foods to eat? (Write your answer here)
______

(g) Why have you visited this town today? (Write your answer here)
______

Figure 6 *Scaling questions*

(h) Fried egg sandwiches are a healthy alternative for breakfast (Please tick box that is closest to your opinion)

5 Agree strongly	4 Agree	3 Uncertain	2 Disagree	1 Disagree strongly

(i) Our sales assistants have been asked to smile when they serve customers. Do you think that this is: (Please tick box that is closest to your opinion)

Very important	Important	Somewhat important	Unimportant	Very unimportant

(j) Our sales assistants have been asked to smile when they serve customers. Do you think that this is: (Please tick box that is closest to your opinion)

Very important						Very unimportant

Planning the questionnaire

Although a questionnaire may appear to be just a list of questions, the order in which they are asked can make a big difference to the quality of the data produced. In general it is better to start with simple short questions, which are easy to answer, and follow a sensible and logical order. If any questions are likely to be personal, difficult or challenging they should be placed towards the end. Also, the questionnaire should not be too long. It could be tested first on a volunteer to see how long it is before they get bored. This will give an idea of the maximum length the questionnaire should be. It may be necessary to cut out some questions, but sticking to the most important questions should produce the required data. The recommended maximum length for:

- a face-to-face interview in the home is 45 minutes;
- a telephone interview is 20 minutes or less;
- a street an interview is 5 – 10 minutes.

These recommendations will limit the length of the questionnaire.

Piloting the questionnaire

Before finalising a questionnaire it is worth testing the questions by trying them out on a small number of people. In this way, any problems with the wording or the kind of answer you get for some questions can be checked. Any changes or improvements can be made before the survey goes into the field and it is too late to make any changes.

What to do with the findings

All of the examples of questions shown in this section are capable of producing quantitative data. This is data based on numbers that can be analysed statistically. Even the responses to the open-ended question can be grouped and counted as quantitative data. How much analysis is done will depend on what the research is designed to find out and the needs of the audience receiving the research. Marketing research professionals, especially statisticians, will demand higher levels of analysis than, say, a marketing manager who just wants a measure of market share, or a PR executive who wants a single fact upon which can develop a press release. The presentation of the results also depends on the audience. Computer spreadsheet programmes make the presentation of data easy to change to suit people's requirements.

Professional standards

Primary research is usually carried out by well-trained and often highly qualified experts in marketing research. They may be employed in this role within an organisation or they may operate as an independent agency that provides a specialist market research service. Market research should not be used as a guise for selling. This is considered to be very bad practice within the industry. Even inexperienced market researchers should follow professional standards for conducting research. All marketing research should be carried out within the professional and ethical standards and guidelines of the Market Research Society.

Research task

Write a questionnaire that will produce primary data about the soft drinks that people buy.
Typical questions may include the following:

- What type of drink do you prefer?
- Which brand(s) do you buy?
- Which flavour do you buy?
- Where do you buy your drinks?
- How often do you buy drinks?

In addition, you need to conduct local research in a range of shops to identify the selling price of drinks and any promotions that are running in-store.
Analyse the findings and draw some conclusions based on the aims of the research.

- What is the profile of people buying the drinks?
- How is the drinks market segmented?
- How can the marketing mix variables be applied to a new drink being launched?

Portfolio practice • Printview

Printview is a printer which provides local print services. These include leaflets for small businesses, small magazines advertising the services of local companies and business cards. It has been successful by targeting business customers in the local area. But it finds that paper printing is only a limited market. So it is considering offering a new bespoke service. It will scan in people's favourite pictures, such as their children, pets or holiday photos and print them onto personal items. Before it attempts to move into this new market it has decided to carry out some primary research. Table 1 shows the results of part of the primary research of 100 people surveyed.

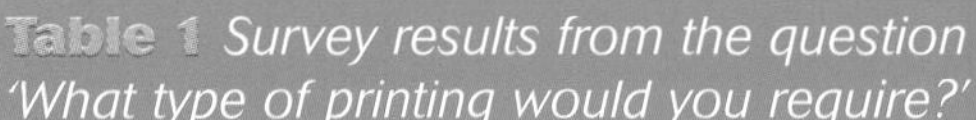

Table 1 *Survey results from the question 'What type of printing would you require?'*

T-shirts	37
Mugs and cups	18
Place mats	14
Key rings	7
Caps	24

(a) What does the information in Table 1 suggest to the business?
(b) What other types of questions should the business ask in the questionnaire?
(c) How might the information from these questions help the business to plan its marketing mix?

Meeting the assessment criteria

For your chosen product or service you must identify and carry out appropriate marketing research and produce a marketing mix. When planning and using primary research you must consider the factors that will help ensure the primary research is relevant and appropriate. Once you have carried out the primary research you will need to analyse the results and use it to provide information that will help in the development of your marketing mix.

Business example - Cat Whisk

Cat whisk is a new cat food product. Primary research has been carried out by the manufacturer to consider the current market. The results are shown in Table 2. The data was found by interviewing 100 people who were cat owners.

Table 2 *Cat food survey results – age profile and income group*

Numbers of people surveyed =100	
Sex	
Males	38
Females	62
Age profile	
Under 15	0
16-19	12
20-29	20
30-44	36
45-59	22
60 and over	10
Socio-economic groups of cat owners	
AB	19
C1	23
C2	48
DE	10

Table 3 *Cat food survey results – type of product purchased*

What type of food do you feed your cat and in which form of packaging do you buy your cat food
Numbers of people surveyed = 100

	Cans	Pouches	Trays	Box	Bag
Wet	26	18	10	n/a	n/a
Dry	n/a	n/a	n/a	28	18

Which brand of cat food do you buy?
Numbers of people surveyed = 100

Whiskas	27
Felix	23
Friskies	14
Arthurs	12
Others	8
Shops own brand	16

Which flavour cat food do you buy?
Numbers of people surveyed = 100

Chicken	26
Beef	22
Rabbit	16
Fish	20
Others	16

Table 4 *Cat food survey results – place of purchase*

Where do you buy your cat food?
Numbers of people surveyed = 100

Supermarket	64
Pet shop	18
Garden centre	8
Other shops	8
The Internet	2

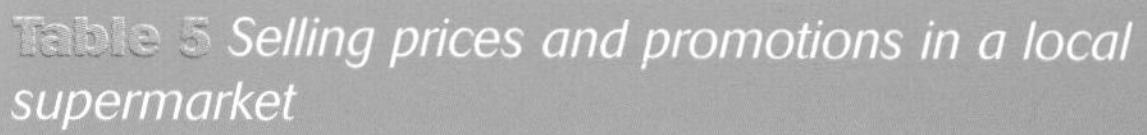

Table 5 *Selling prices and promotions in a local supermarket*

	Can	Pouch	Promotions
Whiskas	47p	29p	4 cans for the price of 3
Felix	47p	29p	15 pouches in special price pack
Friskies	38p	24p	None seen
Arthurs	40p	25p	None seen
Others	30p-49p	21p-30p	Prices cuts on some brands
Shop's own brand	45p	25p	Buy 4 get one free

Source: adapted from author research.

Mark Band 1 *Carry out and produce evidence of basic primary marketing research from a limited range of sources for your chosen product or service. There will be some attempt made at basic analysis of the information.*

Primary research from 100 cat owners has provided data in Table 2. More females in the survey own cats than males. The age group that owns most cats are people aged 30-44 who are neither teenagers nor very old people. The income group with the highest proportion of cats is people from the C2 band. The business might plan the marketing mix of Cat Whisk taking this data into account. It might advertise in magazines aimed at people older than teenagers or in women's magazines. Its price must not be too high as the C2 band is the second lowest income group.

Mark Band 2 *Carry out and produce evidence of sound primary market research, evidenced by a good range of relevant sources. There will be analysis of the primary research and extraction of the relevant information for your chosen product or service.*

Primary research from 100 cat owners has provided data in Tables 2-5. An analysis of the data in these tables could help the business to plan the marketing mix for Cat Whisk.

- Product. The survey results suggest that cat owners feed their pets a wide range of different products. Most people, 26%, bought chicken, although beef and fish were also bought by over 20% of people. 54% of people bought wet food and 46% dry food. This means that the business might need to offer Cat Whisk in different flavours and different packaging.
- Price. Only 19% of cat owners were in the highest income group, AB. The largest proportion was in income group C2. This might suggest that prices may need to be relatively low to be competitive.
- Promotion. Over half of all cats, 58%, were owned by people aged 30-59. This group of people are neither young nor very old. Promoting to magazines aimed at home owners might be useful. As more females own cats than males, promoting in magazines geared at females might also be a useful strategy.
- Place. Over half of all people buy pet food from supermarkets, 64%. This will be an important outlet for sales.

Mark Band 3 *There will be comprehensive primary research evidenced from a wide range of relevant sources, together with comprehensive original analysis.*

Primary research from 100 cat owners has provided data in Tables 2–5. An analysis of the data in these tables might help the business to plan a detailed marketing mix for Cat Whisk.

- Product. The survey results suggest that cat owners feed their pets a wide range of different products. Three flavours in particular, chicken beef and fish were also bought by over 20% or more people. 54% of people bough wet food and 46% dry food. The business is likely to face competition from four main brands in particular which account for 76% of the survey result. There will also be competition from own brands. This means that the business might need to offer Cat Whisk in different flavours and different packaging. Perhaps it might start by offering the three most popular flavours and then expanding its range.
- Price. Only 19% of cat owners were in the highest income group, AB. The largest proportion was in income group C2. ABC1s accounted for only 42% of cat owners. This might suggest that prices may need to be relatively low to be competitive, especially given the branded competition. The business might consider a price of say 38p per can to match Friskies, one of the cheaper brands.
- Promotion. 58% of cats were owned by people aged 30-59 and more cats were owned by females than males. Advertising in magazines geared at these target audiences might be a useful strategy. The business might attempt to establish a brand geared at this group by using a well known female aged around 30 to appear in advertising. However, the business must also consider promotions such as discounts offered by competitors. These often involve offering 'extra free' products with a certain quantity bought.
- Place. Over half of all people buy pet food from supermarkets, 64%. This is likely to be by far the most important outlet for sales. It may be worth concentrating on getting the product on sale in these outlets before moving into others.

The business must be wary about the extent to which this data is representative of the total population of cat owners. Comparisons must be made. Only 100 people were surveyed. National Statistics show that there are 7.5 million cat owners in the UK. So the business might conclude that the sample is not particularly representative. On the other hand a national survey suggested that 30% of cat owners in the UK are aged 35-44. So the business might argue that the survey might be a reasonable estimate for the age group.

35 Secondary research

What is secondary research?

Data that has been collected, analysed and presented for use in a project or report is called secondary data. It is any data that already exists and has been collected for another purpose. Investigating, analysing and using secondary data is known as secondary research. Secondary data may be **quantitative**, providing numbers, facts and figures. It may also be **qualitative**, providing views and opinions.

Sometimes secondary research is called **desk research** because the activity can be carried out at a desk or workstation as opposed to field research, which is the collection of primary data and usually takes place away from the desk.

Secondary research can be as important as primary research so long as the data is valid, is used in context and its limitations are understood.

Uses of secondary research

Secondary research has a number of uses.

Backgound It can be an important way of obtaining background information for a marketing project. For example, a market report might identify the growth in sales of mobile phones.

Issues It is often carried out at the start of a project to identify the main issues that need to be addressed. For example, a newspaper article might outline a growing awareness by customers of environmentally friendly products.

Evidence It can be useful for providing examples of statistics and supporting evidence in a report. For example, it might show trends that are taking place, such as growing sales of DVDs, or market shares of supermarkets.

Marketing mix It can be used to inform and to produce evidence for the marketing mix. For example, it might help:

- to influence the type of product, using information in journals about new technical innovations;
- to set the price of a product, using price lists in catalogues;
- to influence place, using information on the Internet about the growth of sales in different shops;
- to influence promotion, using data on advertising spending by businesses in reports.

The starting point for secondary research is the aims and objectives of the research. Questions such as 'Why am I doing it?' and 'What do I want to find out?' must be asked. Once aims and objectives have been set, the next questions are 'What sources of data are available?' and 'Where can they be found?'.

Sources of secondary data - internal

Secondary data can be found within an organisation itself. Most organisations will collect and hold a wide range of data, which is then analysed and presented to different teams or departments within the organisation.

Internal business data This could include sales records showing how much has been sold in a given period, how much these sales are worth and who has bought the goods. Sales may have been analysed by product, by area, by customer or by a member of a sales team. This data is likely to be used first by the senior management in an organisation and then stored for future use and analysis.

Accounts and financial reports Most internal business data will start with sales, particularly the value of revenue that these sales generate. The financial analysis of this data will result in one part of the business accounts. Other parts will include payments from customers, payments to suppliers, wages and other running costs.

Figure 1 *Secondary data*

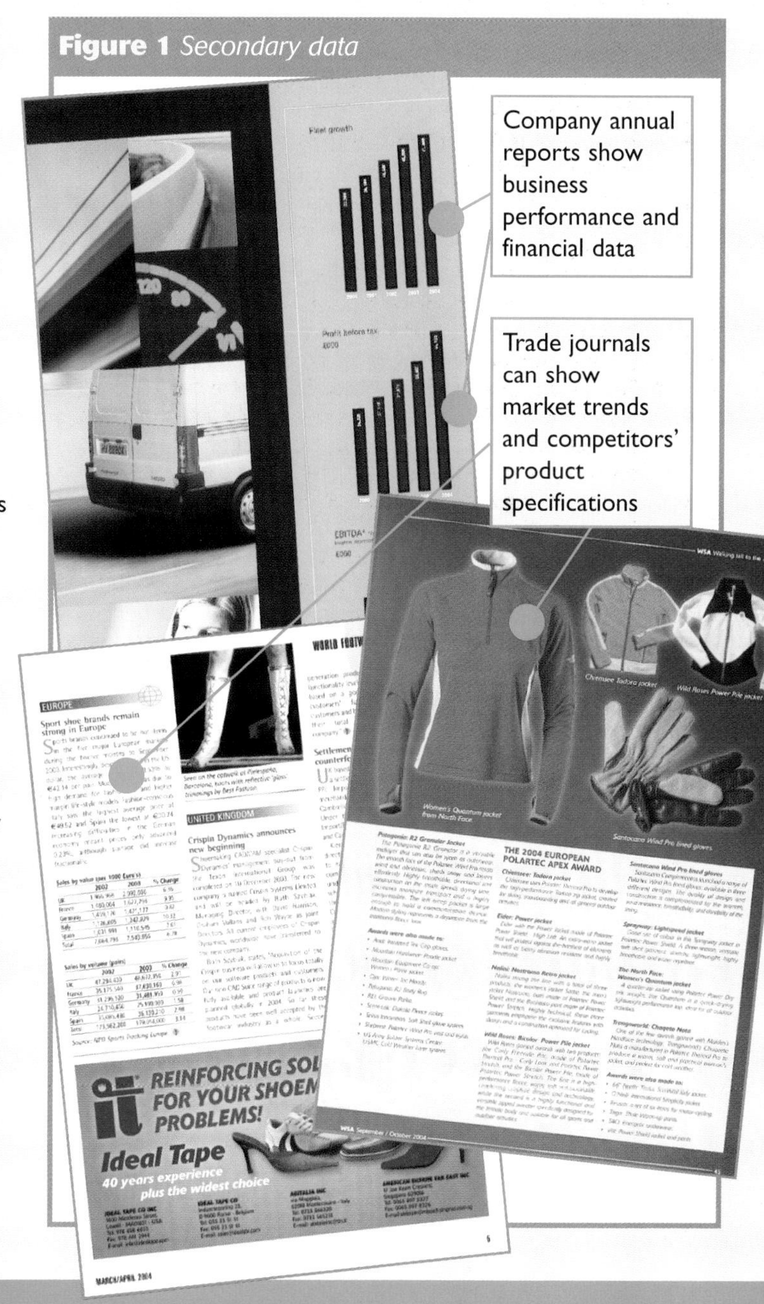

Most organisations will be able to use ICT resources to analyse and present financial data in a variety of ways to suit the needs of research users. The information can sometimes be found in company annual reports and accounts, as shown in Figure 1.

Customer data This could range from basic financial data, showing sales or deliveries to trade customers such as wholesalers or retailers, through to specific data about the buying habits of individual domestic customers and consumers. Data on trade customers will come directly from internal sales records. Information about consumers may have been collected from primary research, questioning consumers directly, or may be in a database produced from loyalty cards or credit card transactions.

Reports Over time most organisations will create a collection of research surveys and reports that were produced and used in the past for previous research projects. These can be a great source for secondary research, providing background against which to measure new findings or plan further research.

Sources of secondary data - external

Secondary data can also be found in material produced by other organisations.

Government published data Government departments and agencies collect a great deal of data. The information is sometimes referred to as 'official statistics' as it presents a picture of the country itself. This could include:

- population and demographic statistics (how many people);
- social statistics (what are the living conditions of the population);
- health statistics (what are the most common health problems);
- economic statistics (how much money is generated and where it is spent);
- industrial statistics (the structure and make-up of an industry).

To make this wealth of data easier to access, government statistics are usually grouped together and presented in easy to read reports. The 2001 Census, for example, contains demographic and geographic data about the entire UK population on a particular date in 2001. The data in the Census can be analysed for the entire population of the country, for a region, or to give a population breakdown for a specific town or district. There are many other ways in which government statistics are presented and reported. Most government statistics can be accessed at no charge, at libraries or from the Internet, although there may be a cost for individual reports if they are purchased outright. The Office for National Statistics (ONS) is the government agency responsible for collecting, analysing and disseminating UK statistics.

Commercial research reports These are produced independently by market research organisations and made available for sale. They cover a wide range of different products, markets and industries on a regular basis. They aim to provide a comprehensive background upon which business organisations can base their marketing plans. For example, a report on the ice cream market in the UK will include data such as the market size, value, main suppliers, main customers, a snapshot of the current situation in the marketplace, market trends from the past, and forecasts for the future. Organisations that publish such reports include the Euromonitor, Key Note, the Financial Times and Mintel. Some manufacturers produce business reports containing secondary data about their trade sector for stakeholders or PR purposes. Industries also produce reports containing statistical data about their own industry, for example the Engineering Council and the Institute of Grocery Distribution.

Trade journals These provide a valuable source of secondary information on specific markets, industries or trade sectors. Trade journals often include reports on the state of the industry, supported by a wealth of data and research information as shown in Figure 1. This data may have been generated by the journal itself or may have been supplied by an organisation from within the industry or trade sector, such as a leading manufacturer.

Other media The business pages in national newspapers and business programmes on TV and radio will often include secondary research to support or illustrate a particular report that is being presented. Most libraries hold a wide range of secondary data in the reference and business sections. In some areas there will be a specialist business library that collects together a wide range of secondary data and may buy commercial reports or trade journals and make them available for public access. These libraries may also hold reports from manufacturers or industry groups. Some manufacturers or industry bodies provide their own reports.

The Internet Using the Internet and search engines is an easy way to start looking for secondary data. Examples of information that could be obtained include:

- British government statistics from National Statistics Online www.statistics.gov.uk;
- statistics and reports on EU members at www.europa.eu.int/comm/eurostat;
- foreign government websites provide data about a country, such as www.fedstats.gov and www.stat-usa.gov (USA), www.china.org.cn/english (People's Republic of China);
- commercial publishers provide limited access to their data, for example www.euromonitor.com, but access to all information may require a subscription;
- business sites such as www.virgin.com or www.boots.com will provide data about individual businesses.

Benefits of secondary research

Ease of access Access is quick as the collection of original data has already been done. It is usually easy to find because there can be many sources to choose from. Data may have been published, be in the public domain and be available in libraries, on the Internet or in the press. Data can also be easy to read, interpret or understand as it will have already been analysed and presented in a way that it is easily accessible for the original audience.

Relatively low cost The costs of collecting and analysing data will have been paid for by the organisation that commissioned the original primary research. This applies particularly to secondary research data that is already in the public domain, for example a survey in a newspaper article about the buying habits of people who are about to go on holiday. In contrast, research reports are produced and then sold by specialist publishers such as Mintel. To buy them direct from the publisher can cost many thousands of pounds. However, they can be available in business libraries where the cost is lower.

Flexibility Research can be done in your own time, as and when you can get to a library, Internet or other source.

Limitations of secondary research

Whilst secondary research may have been precisely right when it was carried out and used for its original purpose, certain limitations can reduce its usefulness in any current research project.

Relevance The data has already been collected and analysed for some other purpose. This means that it may not meet the precise needs of the current research project. This could limit its usefulness for the current project. For example, 2001 Census Key Statistics may provide total population data for a particular town. However, it may not say how many of the people in that town order take away pizzas on a regular basis because pizza consumption was not the original aim of the 2001 Census.

Bias The source of the data needs to be considered. Also, the reasons for collecting the data and presenting it in the way it appears must be taken into account. There can be bias. The originators of the research will have their own aims, objectives and motivation for conducting research and for interpreting and presenting it in a certain way. For example, a pro-smoking lobby group may publish research that shows that the majority of people they have polled do not object to smoking in restaurants. Before accepting this research, the secondary researcher must consider who the lobby group has polled (smokers or non-smokers), the size of the sample and the motivation for publishing the research (to show that anti-smoking legislation is not necessary). This is likely to be less of a problem for data from internal sources.

Age Secondary research may not be up-to-date as it will have been collected and used by its originator before it becomes available for wider access. For example, manufacturers and marketing organisations will often make their research findings available once the data is no longer commercially sensitive or confidential.

Comprehensive The data may be partial rather than comprehensive. It could also be data that is presented in such a way as to meet marketing aims or communicate a particular message. For example, for many years Pedigree Petfoods promoted the claim that '(in research) 9 out of 10 cats preferred Whiskas cat food to any other brand'. This marketing claim could have been backed up by research findings. However, it does not provide any information about how the research was conducted, how many cats or their owners were sampled, what else they liked to eat, and did not take into account the many cats that are fed other brands.

Portfolio practice • E-Shoes

The marketing team at E-Shoes, a manufacturer of trainers, has obtained a copy of the Executive Summary from the commercial research report, *Euromonitor Footwear in the UK*, 2004. Some of the information in the report is shown below.

(a) State three pieces of information about the footwear market in the UK.

(b) Identify the largest target group of consumers in the market and how this is changing.

(c) Analyse (i) the level of competition and (ii) distribution in the market.

(d) Discuss other sources of secondary research that could help to research this market and how they would be useful.

Table 1 *The UK footwear market*

MARKET SIZE. The UK market for footwear has grown by 1.9% since 2002 to reach a value of £5.1 bn in 2003.
MARKET SECTORS. Women's footwear was the largest sector of the UK market, with 47.7% of the market, representing a value of £2.4 bn in 2003.
SHARE OF MARKET. C&J Clark has remained the market leader with more than 12% of value sales due to its successful positioning and its high brand awareness.
MARKETING ACTIVITY. In 2003, the leading advertiser in the footwear market was Nike, with a total adspend of more than £6 m.
CORPORATE OVERVIEW. C&J Clark has remained market leader in 2003 with more than 12% of sales, combined with a strong three-year growth performance of 5.9%.
NIKE INC. Turnover increased by 8.1% in 2003 to reach US$10.7 bn.
MARKS & SPENCER PLC. Turnover decreased by 0.7% in 2003 to £8.1 bn.
C&J CLARK LTD. Turnover grew by 7% to £937 m in 2002 from £875 m in 2001.
STYLO PLC. Group turnover figures reached £232 m in 2003, up by 11.4% on the previous year.
DISTRIBUTION. Accounting for 39% of the market in value terms in 2003, specialist shoe shops remain the dominant retail channels in the UK footwear market.
CONSUMER PROFILE. The most popular type of shoes sold in the UK in 2003 were formal footwear, with 65% of all shoe sales.
MARKET FORECASTS. The market is forecast to grow by nearly 7.6% between the forecast period to reach a value of £5.5 bn in 2008.
SECTOR FORECASTS. The women's sector is forecast to continue dominating the market with a value share of 46.3% by 2008.

Source: adapted from *Euromonitor Footwear in the UK*, Euromonitor, June 2004.

Meeting the assessment criteria

For your chosen product or service you are required to identify and carry out appropriate market research to help produce an appropriate marketing mix. When selecting and using secondary research you will need to consider the guidance shown above, that will help to ensure that the secondary research you use is relevant, appropriate and as up-to-date as possible. Once you have found the secondary research you will need to analyse and use it to provide information that will help in the development of your marketing mix.

Business example - 'The Mirrors Live'

Four students at college have formed a band called 'The Mirrors'. They have a live recording from a gig that they want to sell in summer 2004 as a CD album. They have looked for secondary research data to help plan the marketing mix.

Table 2 *Value of music sales*, UK, (£000)*

Quarterly totals	April/June 03	April/June 04	%change
7" singles	166	307	+84.9
12" singles	2,709	2,876	+6.2
Cassette singles	268	-	-100
CD singles	9,751	10,541	+8.1
Total singles	**12,894**	**13,724**	**+6.4**
LP	1,606	1,175	-26.8
Cassette	721	417	-42.2
CD	200,568	208,516	+4.1
Total album	**202,568**	**210,108**	**+3.7**
Music DVD	6,419	7,103	+10.7
Total value	**221,881**	**230,935**	**+4.1**
Annual totals	**Year to June 03**	**Year to June 04**	**%change**
7" singles	544	924	+69.9
12" singles	12,477	11,186	10.3
Cassette singles	3,435	154	-95.5
CD singles	58,606	48,248	-17.7
Total singles	**75,062**	**60,512**	**-19.4**
LP	6,028	5,442	-9.7
Cassette	4,301	2,728	-36.6
CD	1,068,050	1,105,318	+3.5
Total album	**1,078,430**	**1,113,490**	**+3.3**
Music Video/DVD	28,734	48,591	+69.1
Total value	**1,182,226**	**1,222,593**	**+3.0**

* Shipments to all distributors and retailers from record companies.
Source: adapted from BPI website.

Mark Band 1 *Carry out and produce evidence from a limited range of sources and do a simple analysis of the information. Information from secondary data should give some market information about the chosen product.*

Annual totals show that the market for recordings is large, at £1,222 million for the year to June 2004. The market has grown +3.0%, from £1,182 million for the year to June 2003. The quarterly totals show that for the most recent quarter, April/June 2004, the total value of the market has grown at a greater rate, +4.1%, compared to the same quarter in 2003. Both sets of data suggest that the market for recordings is worth trying to enter to obtain a share in the form of sales of the live recording. The annual totals show that the product generating the greatest sales value is the CD album. So a CD album could be a suitable format for the recording.

Mark Band 2 *Use a combination of research to determine the characteristics of the target group or size of market or competition, with some indication as to the most relevant information. Draw some specific conclusion from the research.*

Annual totals show that single sales fell over two years. But they increased by 6.4% in April/June 2004 compared to 2003. So this may be a good time to release a single to help promote a CD album sold in summer 2004. A CD single would be an appropriate format. The type of single generating the most sales is the CD single. It had nearly 90% of the singles market in 2004. Although sales of 7" singles hold a small share of the market, 0.075% in the year to June 2004, this format has shown the greatest change in sales between June 2003-04, an increase of +69.9%. Quarterly totals show that the growth in the most recent quarter April/June 2004 has been even greater, at +84.9% and that the share of the market for 7" singles has nearly doubled to 0.13%. Although 7" remains a small part of the overall single market formats, it might also be a useful as an unusual 'novelty' format for promoting a live CD album.

Figure 2 *Products bought over the Internet, 12 months to July 2003, survey results and CD prices*

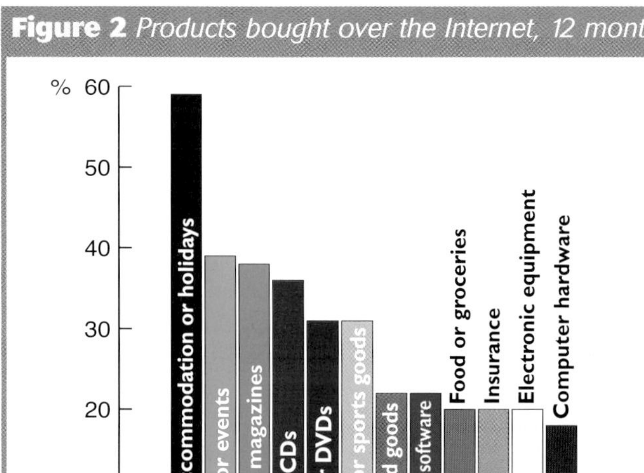

Source: adapted from *Social Trends*, 2004, Office for National Statistics.

Retail prices for CD albums, November 2004

HMV - 'chart' CDs £9.99
Tesco - most 'chart' CDs £8.39, reissues £4.97
Virgin Megastore - chart CDs £9.99, reissues £7.99
Woolworths - most 'chart' CDs £12.99, reissues £6.99
SPIN Compact Discs retail website - new releases £10.99-11.99, specialist reissues £7-8.99
Mute record label website - new releases £9.99-10.99

Mark Band 3 *Use a comprehensive range of secondary research from a wide range of relevant sources. There must be real application of the data to your chosen product, service or target group.*

The data in Table 2 and Figure 2 can help develop part of the marketing mix for the CD album. For example, the format of the product should be a CD. This has by far the largest sales in 2004 and was the only format showing an increase since 2003. Table 2 shows the extent of music sales through the retail trade. Sales through shops and to distributors are likely to be an effective way of distributing the CD. Figure 2 shows that in the 12 months to July 2003, 36% of people surveyed bought CDs over the Internet. So using the Internet could be another way of selling the CD, especially as downloading of music increases. However, CD sales will face strong competition from spending on 'Tickets for events' and 'Books/magazines and e-learning/training material' which are purchased by a higher proportion of people than CDs. The list of retail prices gives a good indication of current retail selling prices in high street shops, from Internet retailers and direct from a record label itself. It may be better to sell the CD album at a low price such as £7.99. This might help to attract people to take a chance to listen to a new band that is only just starting out. However, the list only covers 6 of many outlets selling CDs. More secondary data may be needed on prices of CDs as this may not be representative. Also, CD prices fluctuate. So prices need to be checked regularly to keep up-to-date.

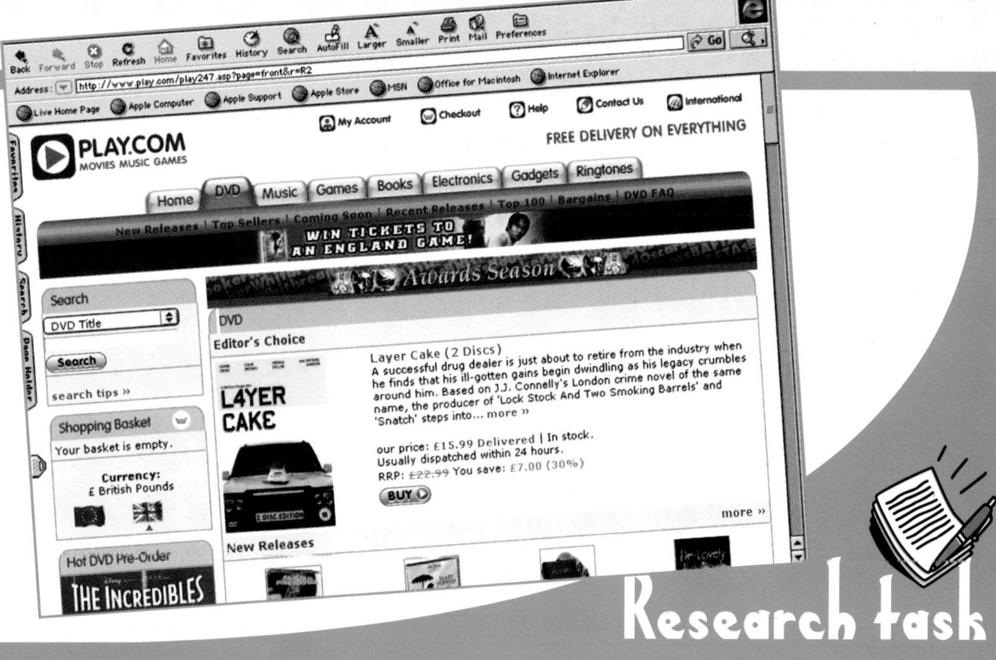

Use secondary data to research the price of DVDs.

- Think about the aims and objectives a business might have had when setting the price.
- Think about where the information can be found. Try to collect information from three sources.
- State how the prices of DVDs are different.
- Explain why these prices might be different.
- Suggest how these prices might affect the price of a new DVD being launched.

36 The marketing mix

What is the marketing mix?

The marketing mix is a term that is used a lot by individuals and businesses engaged in marketing activities. It refers to the combination of main variables that make up the marketing strategy and marketing plans. The main variables of the marketing mix are **product, price, place** and **promotion**, known as the 4Ps. Sometimes the marketing mix of services also includes the **people, processes** or activities and **physical evidence** or environment involved in delivering the service.

These variables can be viewed as decisions that must be made when bringing a product to market. The marketing mix is usually designed to achieve the marketing aims and objectives of the business, to meet or influence the needs and wants of customers and in most cases to attract customers to generate sales.

Product

This is the part of the marketing mix that specifies what it is that has to be marketed. A product can be either a physical good from manufacturers or a service from a provider. The way the product is defined may vary according to the resources available, the objectives of the business and the target market that the product is aimed at. Figure 1 shows important questions that a business must consider when deciding the nature of the product to be marketed. The marketing of a product is covered in section 37.

Price

This is the part of the marketing mix that establishes how much the product will sell for and as a result the potential income and profit from the product. Each of the questions in Figure 2 needs to be addressed before deciding on the pricing strategy and price structure of a product. The pricing of a product is covered in section 38.

Place

This is the part of the marketing mix that plans where and how the customer sees and buys the product. It is about how products are distributed to customers. The optimum 'place' for a product needs to be considered when developing a marketing mix. In the business world decisions about distribution can be outside the control of the manufacturer unless the manufacturer also sells directly to customers. Important place questions are considered in Figure 3. The distribution of a product is covered in section 39.

Promotion

This is the part of the marketing mix that creates awareness and desire for the product. Important promotion questions are considered in Figure 4. The promotion of a product is covered in section 40.

Figure 1 *Important product questions*

What is it? What do we call the product? How is it positioned?
Is it a good like a BMW car or a service like a taxi ride in London? Is it an Apple ipod or a Sony MP3 player? Is it a Christian Dior evening bag or an adidas sports bag?

How do customers experience the product?
Do they buy, use it and dispose of it, like a Duracell battery? Do they buy it, eat it and dispose of the packaging like a Domino's take-away pizza? Do they use it again and again like a Miele washing machine? Do they walk into it, look around and learn from their experience like a museum or art gallery?

How should it be packaged and presented to customers?
Should it be in a jar, bottle, bucket, plastic bag? If it's in a bottle, should the bottle be glass or PET? Should the bottle be clear, opaque or coloured? Should it be labelled or printed? Should the bottles be sold singly and/or packed in boxes of four like Ribena light, or sixes like Tizer?

What shape, size, material, colour should be chosen?
Should it be a formal pin striped suit or a beige summer suit? Should a domestic iron be made from black plastic and chromed metal or in many different colours of plastic to match current decorative styles, with the metal coloured to co-ordinate with the overall design?

What do customers think that they are buying?
Are they buying a ticket to the theatre or are they buying an evening's entertainment? Is it a jar of honey or is it a healthy natural sweetener?

What materials or ingredients?
Should a unique flavour be used, such as Coca-Cola or Heinz baked beans, or should many flavours be offered such as Innocent smoothies? Should the basic raw material be used and the product changed to appeal to different customers or different markets, such as buttered popcorn or a salty, savoury popcorn?

What if it is a service?
How should it be recognised by potential customers as something that they want to buy? How should it be packaged and presented? For example, should a flight be off-peak air travel, business travel, long or short haul, early, last minute booking or stand-by?

Figure 2 *Important pricing questions*

at should it sell for?
uld it be a relatively high price like a sche car or a lower price like a Smart ? Can the price by set by the business a can of paint or is it influenced by the rket such as vegetable prices?

What pricing strategy?
Should the business lead on pricing like pharmaceuticals companies or mirror what competitors charge like magazines?

hat is the price perception for this roduct within the target market?
this product thought to be a high price roduct like a Rolex watch or a low rice product like Aldi margarine?

What does a low price say about a product?
Is it seen as a good value product like supermarket own brands or washing powders? Is it seen as a 'bargain' or is it seen as having low quality?

What price will cover costs and make the profit margin required by the manufacturer and all the links in the supply chain?
Does a high price need to be charged to cover higher costs of production like a gourmet meal? Can a relatively low price be set if average costs are reduced by producing large quantities like BIC pens?

How much to charge distributors?
Is it the same for a wholesaler or cash and carry customer like Costco as it would be for a major retailer like Tesco?

Will tax influence the price?
Will there be VAT like on CDs or no VAT like on children's clothes?

Who makes the choices and decisions about the marketing mix?

Depending on the size and structure of an organisation, different people or teams of people will be responsible for making decisions about elements of the marketing mix. For example, in a large organisation like Nike there may be a team of international marketing professionals that make up a marketing department, supported by extensive marketing research on the markets in which they trade. Individual markets, such as soccer or basketball, may have dedicated marketing teams, each responsible for making decisions that are right for that market or sector, within the overall aims of the company as a whole.

In contrast, in most small organisations marketing will be the responsibility of the owner or a director. In this type of organisation the marketing decisions are no less important. If you were to launch your own product, it is likely that you would have to make all of the decisions about the marketing mix yourself. There are organisations that will support companies that do not have sufficient marketing expertise in-house. These include marketing and market research agencies, some banks, trade and industry bodies and government organisations such as Business Link.

How are choices and decisions about the marketing mix made?

Decisions about elements of the marketing mix are most likely to be made from a combination of marketing research data and individual knowledge or expertise. The availability of resources is another important factor.

Decisions based on marketing research data are more likely to be objective and supported by information rather than opinion. However, subjective opinion based on personal knowledge or expertise built-up from real-life experience in the marketplace can also be important.

Each marketing decision must be viewed within the context of overall aims and objectives for the organisation. The appropriate ideas or supporting data should then be used to help make the decision.

Figure 3 *Important place questions*

at is the supply chain for the product?
it be sold via a retailer like Dixons selling trical goods, a market stall like flowers, door-to- r like household goods sold through Lakeland logues, direct from an advertisement in a magazine Saga holidays or direct off the screen from a osite like Amazon selling books, CDs and DVDs?

Direct from the producer?
Is the producer equipped to sell and deliver direct to customers like take-aways or Dell computers? Do consumers expect to receive the product direct like hairdressing services?

re do customers look for the product now and e future?
traditional outlets be used like retailers or others the Internet? Will there be a growth in out-of-town il shopping centres at the expense of town centres? ere do they buy currently and is this changing like growth of non-food products sold from ermarkets?

first direct
banking mortgages loans credit cards save / invest travel / foreign insure firstdirectory
we've built our service to revolve around you
£25 when you apply online and transfer your banking
apply on-line now

What influence can the manufacturer or service provider really have over how and where the product is placed in the market?
How can they maintain their place? What are the opportunities like the growth of town centre living, leading to high value shops and entertainment? What are the threats like the Internet leading to increasing sales from abroad? What factors are outside the control of the manufacturer or service provider like the ageing of the population?

What role can the Internet play in selling and distribution?
Is the product suitable for selling from a website like a book? Are target customers ready to buy from a website like the growth of downloading music or financial services from First Direct?

Indirect via wholesalers or retail distributors?
What is the role of wholesalers, cash & carry's, and retailers? How much influence does the manufacturer or service provider have over retailers?

Figure 4 *Important promotion questions*

Which promotional tools should be used?
What methods will be used? These include advertising like McDonald's 'I'm lovin' it', sales promotions, public relations, direct marketing or sponsorship like Virgin's sponsorship of the Formula 1 BMW team? Which are appropriate for the product and target market?

How much promotion?
Is there a large budget like Nestlé or a small budget like a local tanning centre? What is the competitive position of the business and its aims and objectives?

Which media to choose?
What media will be used? These could include newspapers used by insurance companies, magazines used by clothes or perfume companies, posters used by Nike, leaflets and magazines used by Orange, audio, such as radio and recordings used by solicitors, moving images including television and cinema advertisements, ambient media such as stickers or printed carrier bags with the Tesco name, branded display items like Nestlé chiller cabinets in shops or product placement in films and on television by Sony and new media, including texts, screen pop-ups, and other web-based opportunities used by Google.

How long should a promotional campaign run?
Is it long-term and strategic like Coca-Cola advertisements or is it tactical to meet a short-term objective like the launch of a new film?

The importance of resources

Resources can have a major influence on the choice of marketing mix. A large organisation with a significant marketing budget is in a position to spend considerably more on its marketing mix than a smaller organisation with only a small amount of money to spend.

There is a direct link between the size and scope of the marketing mix developed for a product and the size of the budget available, together with the willingness to spend that budget. An example is shown in Figure 5.

Research task

Watch an ad-break on a commercial television channel. Pick one of the products being advertised. Identify as much as you can of the marketing mix that has been created for that product.

- Note the product - what is it? What are the main features that make it a distinctive 'product'?
- Price – is price mentioned? If so how much? How does this compare with the price of similar, competitor products?
- Place – based on the information in the television commercial where can you buy the product? What are the different places you can buy the product? If 'place' is stated clearly consider why and what customers must do to buy the product.
- Promotion – you have seen the product being advertised on television. How frequently does the advertisement appear? How does this compare with other products being advertised during the ad-break? What, if any, other promotional activity is being applied to the product?
- What is the target market? Who is the product aimed at? Who is the advertising aimed at? Is there a difference? If so, why is there a difference?

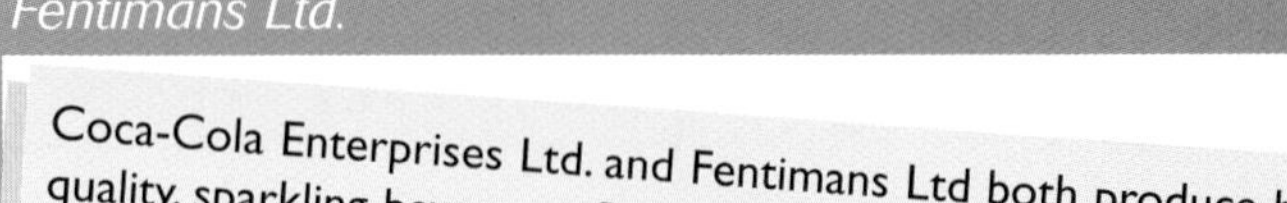

Figure 5 *Marketing at Coca-Cola Enterprises Ltd. and Fentimans Ltd.*

Coca-Cola Enterprises Ltd. and Fentimans Ltd both produce high quality, sparkling beverages flavoured with cola. Both companies have products distributed in British supermarkets, and both compete for sales in the soft drinks market. Despite some apparent similarities of product and objectives, the marketing mix for Coca-Cola Enterprises Ltd. is far greater and more extensive than the marketing mix for Fentimans Ltd.

One of the main factors for this difference will be the size of the marketing budget. As part of one of the largest multinational food manufacturing organisations in the world, Coca-Cola Enterprises Ltd. has a very famous brand to support and some major international competitors. As a consequence its marketing budget is huge in comparison to Fentimans Ltd. and it is more likely that people will see Coca-Cola advertising than Fentiman's advertising. However, within its own budget constraints Fentimans Ltd. will have developed its own marketing mix which meets the objectives of the business, is right for its products and creates awareness amongst its target customers.

Portfolio practice • Ambrosia Devon Custard

Premier Foods plc is a UK manufacturer and marketer of shelf-stable (ambient) grocery products. The company manufactures and markets grocery products for the retail grocery and out-of-home markets ... Branded products include Ambrosia (custard and milk puddings).

Source: adapted from http://today.reuters.co.uk/stocks/companyprofile.

Premier Foods, the maker of Branston pickle and Typhoo tea, said it hoped to pull free of tough trading conditions as winter creeps in and consumers turn to brands such as its Ambrosia custard. 'We're into the busy period now and goods like our custard and tea are biased towards the colder weather' said chief executive, Robert Schofield.

Source: adapted from *The Guardian*, 11.9.2004.

Figure 6 *Ambrosia Devon Custard advertisement*

SAVE 50p

Ambrosia Rice Pudding/ Custard pots

4x135g

~~£1.49~~ **99p**

(a) Using Figure 6, identify features of the marketing mix (price, promotion, product and place) of Ambrosia Devon Custard using examples.

(b) Examine ONE way in which each of the '4Ps' of the marketing mix for Ambrosia might be changed and how this might affect the product.

Meeting the assessment criteria

To meet the assessment objective for this unit you are required to produce an appropriate marketing mix for a new or existing product or service.

Business example - Beta Garden Tools Ltd

Beta Garden Tools Ltd is a business that manufactures plastic buckets. To use up scrap material it has designed and developed a lightweight hand-fork, made from recycled plastic, for weeding the garden. The company is based in Swansea and has received a Regional Innovation Grant of £25,000 to help market the new product. Although experienced in producing and selling plastic buckets to the packaging trade it has little experience of marketing consumer products. It needs advice on developing a marketing mix for the new fork. Some basic marketing research is available.

Selling prices for hand forks

Large DIY store: steel £6.58; stainless steel £7.98

Garden centre: steel £6.99; stainless steel £8.99

Table 1 *Percentage of people who are interested in Gardening*

Total		60%
Male		53%
Female		67%
Age group	15-24	30%
	25-34	47%
	35-54	64%
	55+	77%
Socio-economic group	AB	64%
	C1, C2	62%
	DE	54%

Source: adapted from RHS report, *The Good Life Factor*, April-May 2004.

Table 2 *Gardening magazines*

Readership of gardening magazines - 12 m to Sept 2004

All figures %	Socio-economic group		Age		Gender	
Title	ABC1	C2DE	15-44	45+	Men	Women
Amateur Gardening	51.6	48.4	18.3	81.7	42.0	58.0
Garden News	49.5	50.5	16.2	83.8	50.8	49.2
BBC Gardeners World	64.5	35.5	28.7	71.3	36.8	63.2
Garden Answers	54.4	45.6	28.9	71.1	42.5	57.5

Source: adapted from National Readership Survey, Open Access data.

Mark Band 1 *Creation of a basic marketing mix for your specified product/service that covers all the relevant Ps.*

Based on the available market research, a basic marketing mix has been created.

Product A lightweight hand-fork for weeding the garden will be produced.

Price Local retail selling prices for metal hand-forks range from £6.58 to £8.99. Beta hand-fork could be priced within this range to be competitive.

Place Local research shows that hand forks are bought mainly from large DIY stores. This is an area of distribution that could be appropriate for the Beta hand-fork.

Promotion Females aged over 55 and in the ABC1 socio-economic group appear to be the largest groups of people interested in gardening in magazines. These could be target markets.

Mark Band 2 *Creation of a detailed marketing mix for your product/service, which shows a good understanding and knowledge of the relevant Ps.*

Product The product is a lightweight hand-fork for weeding the garden. But there are other aspects of the product that need to be considered. For example, the product will be manufactured in green to fit in with consumers' views of environmental products.

Price The local research on price is limited. Further research has shown that consumers may be willing to pay a premium for metal garden tools, but are reluctant to pay much for plastic tools. Given that plastic is the only material that Beta can use, it may be better to charge a lower price than the band range £6.58 to £8.99.

Place In conversation with family members it becomes clear that there are many other places where garden hand-forks can be purchased. The business might consider selling through large DIY stores and garden centres, for example.

Promotion The fork needs promotion in two areas:

- to the retail trade, in order to get the product into distribution;
- to consumers, to raise awareness. Females aged over 55 and in the ABC1 socio-economic group appear to be the largest groups of people interested in gardening. Advertisements in gardening magazines may be effective.

Mark Band 3 *Creation of a comprehensive marketing mix which is clearly linked to the research and segmentation evidence and shows depth of knowledge and understanding of the relevant Ps.*

Product The product is a lightweight hand-fork for weeding the garden. A different way of describing the product could be as follows.

- Function. The product could be marketed as 'an easy way to a weed-free garden without the effort of using traditionally heavy garden tools'.
- Colour. As the product is made from plastic it can be made in any colour. The business may choose a colour traditionally associated with the garden, such as green or black. It may also produce some in bright colours that will show up easily if laid on the ground.
- Packaging. The product could be sold simply with just a bar-coded label. However, given the profile of the target market value could be added by packing it in a card carton with a clear plastic window on the front to display the fork.

Price Local research reveals the following retail selling prices for hand forks.

- Large DIY store: steel £6.58; stainless steel £7.98.
- Garden centre: steel £6.99; stainless steel £8.99.

But local research is limited. Further research has shown that people may not be prepared to pay a high price. Given the product is made from plastic (a material perceived to be cheaper than metals) but is packed in a box (which should add value), Beta Garden Tools Ltd has decided the new fork will sell at £5.99. An investigation of costs has shown that this price is sufficient to generate profit for Beta Garden Tools Ltd and the retail distributors.

Place As a business Beta Garden Tools Ltd has only limited experience with supplying the retail trade. It needs to consider if selling through retailers, such as DIY and garden centres, is the best place for the new fork. It has also investigated selling:

- through independent garden centres via wholesalers;
- direct to gardeners via magazine advertisements;
- via an Internet site.

The business has decided that selling through retailers will reach a larger market, but it will also sell some directly as this will not increase costs too greatly.

Promotion The business will sell to both the retail trade and directly. Discounts and other 'bulk buy' deals will be offered to DIY shops and garden centres to help increase sales. When selling directly to gardeners via magazine advertisements Beta Garden Tools Ltd needs to decide which magazines to use for the advertising. Beta Garden Tools Ltd has compared the readership profiles of the magazines with the profile of their target market - females, aged over 55, in the ABC1 socio-economic group. It has decided that the profile of readers for BBC *Gardeners' World* magazine comes closest to the profile of the target market.

37 Product

What is a product?

The term 'product' it can apply to:

- physical goods bought by customers and used by consumers;
- services that are bought, received or experienced by customers or consumers.

'Product' is often considered the most important of the four 'P's' as it is the product which defines and identifies what has to be sold - it is the one that will make money. Your 'product' is what you create, produce, manufacture or acquire to market and sell. Sections 28 and 31 look at the development of new products and diversification of businesses into other products.

Product specifications

Many people have bright ideas for products. Not all of these ideas are realistic or can be developed into something that sells and makes money. 'Product' in the marketing mix is about specifying and defining precisely what is for sale.

An example of a product specification for a shirt is shown in Figure 1. Similar information will be included in any product specification, whatever the product, although the materials used will vary according to the product itself. Services also need specifications, to make sure that nothing is missed and consumers know precisely what is being marketed and what service they will receive.

A product may be bought and used by consumers in a number of different forms. Most importantly, however, the customer must know precisely what it is that they are buying. If they are unsure, this could be a reason not to buy the product or to buy a competitor's product which may be clearer to understand and easier to identify.

A simple test to check if a product can be identified and understood clearly by potential customers is to:

- describe it in as few words as possible to someone who is not familiar with the product;
- confirm that they understand the product clearly by asking them to explain back what they think the product is all about.

In this way a business can make sure that customers recognise products for sale.

Figure 1 *Examples of information that could be included in a product specification for a shirt*

All features of the design, e.g. how many buttons, width of cuffs and angle of the point on the collar.

The fabric to use from the wide range available, e.g. the basic material, the weight/ thickness and wash and wear characteristics.

The shape to cut the fabric and make into a shirt.

The thread to use for sewing up and stitching.

The size or range of sizes to produce.

How much it should cost to produce.

The colours to make it in.

The price it will sell for.

How it is packaged for the consumer, e.g. the material, the look of the packaging, branding, labels, product identification number and bar code.

How it is packaged for delivery to customers, e.g. how many in a case or shipping unit.

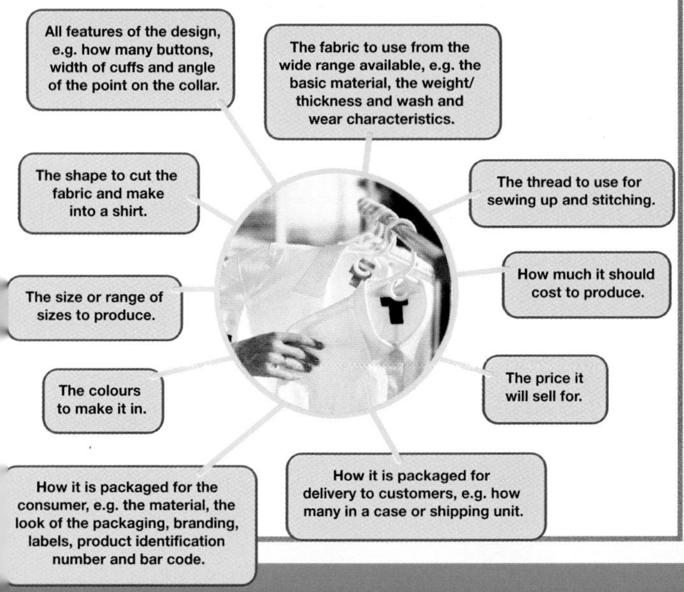

Product strategy

A business must plan its product strategy based on its overall aims and objectives. It may have narrow or wide product range or somewhere in between.

Narrow product range Some businesses are content to limit their products to a narrow product range that can be produced easily, to a good standard, and at a price that returns a satisfactory profit. Products may be aimed at a particular market or even a small niche market. Small businesses are often limited in their product ranges due to limited finance or the use of specialist skills.

Wide product range A business may be in markets that are growing, have many innovative competitors and survival depends on producing and launching a stream of new products to keep up with market developments. Businesses sometimes launch new products when some of their products are reaching the saturation stage of their product life cycle. This allows them to maintain revenue. As sales of some older products fall, they are replaced by sales of newer products.

Different businesses in different markets will need to adopt different product strategies that meet the needs of:

- the market;
- its own stakeholders;
- its own capacity.

Figures 2 and 3 show some examples.

Figure 2 *Cellect Executive Chauffeurs (narrow product range)*

Cellect Executive Chauffeurs specialises in providing high quality private transportation services for business and leisure use in London and the surrounding areas. It includes chauffeuring to and from airports, seaports, helipads or train stations, sightseeing, shopping trips and dining and special events, such as Royal Ascot, The Wimbledon Tennis Championship, and Chelsea Flower Show. Services also include diplomatic and VIP services, anti-surveillance and protection and booking of accommodation, restaurants and theatres.

Source: adapted from www.cellect.net.

Figure 3 *Unilever's product range (wide product range)*

Unilever is one of the world's leading suppliers of fast-moving consumer goods. It has a number of product areas and many brands with variations.

Product areas	**Examples**
Cooking and eating	Colman's mustard Carte D'Or ice cream Birds Eye frozen foods Flora pro-active spread Boursin cheese PG Tips tea Cornetto ice cream Bertolli pasta Bovril drink
Beauty and style	Dove soap Lux soap Timoteo shampoo Vaseline products Lynx deodorant
Around the house	Domestos cleaner Persil washing powder Surf washing liquid Comfort washing conditioner

Source: adapted from www.unilever.co.uk/ourbrands.

Developing a product

There are various stages in the development of a product. They apply to the development of both goods and services.

Product brief In many businesses the starting point for a product will be a descriptive 'brief' from the marketing team. This will outline what they believe will have appeal and therefore sell in the market. This brief is likely to be based on marketing research or other data, such as sales information or customer requests. The product development brief will be more or less detailed depending on the business, but is likely to include some of the features in Figure 4.

Prototypes and samples It is usually the responsibility of a product development team working with members of the production team to produce a prototype or samples of the product. These early versions of a product can be used by the marketing team to check that they meet the product development brief.

Market research Prototypes and samples can also be used for marketing research. They allow a business to check that the product being developed meets the needs of customers and consumers.

Launch Once the marketing team has agreed that the sample product meets the needs of the market and that it will be a viable and profitable addition to the business, plans can be made for full production and its launch.

Figure 4 *Product development brief*

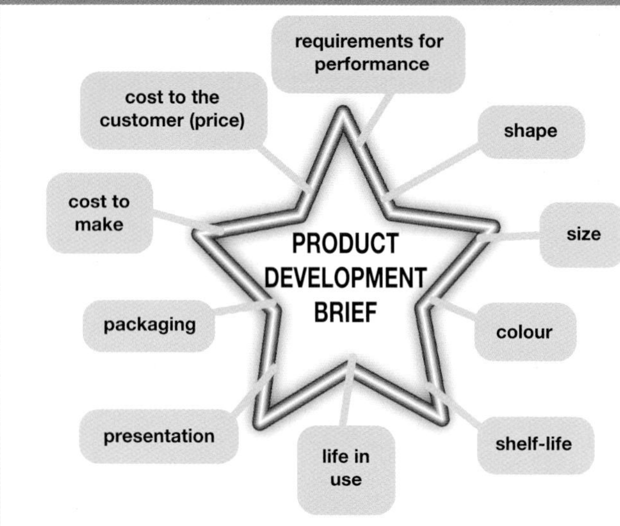

Customer driven and technology driven approaches

Businesses often take different approaches to the development of products.

Customer driven If the reason behind the development of a product is based on customer requests or meeting the needs of customers, as identified from marketing research, this is known as customer driven approach. It can also be referred to as being **market orientated** or having a **market oriented** approach as it takes into account the needs of customers in the market. It can be very successful, as meeting customer needs is key to the successful marketing of a product.

Technology driven Some businesses approach the market in a different way. They first develop and produce a product, often based on an idea or concept, and then they look for a market for the product. This is a way of working that is often adopted by businesses that are at the leading edge of technological development. It is a **product orientated/oriented approach**. This can be a risky strategy. It may turn out that there is only a small, limited market or even no market at all and the business will have already spent time and money on developing the product.

When developing a product it is easy for a business to get locked into what they can do from a technical or manufacturing point-of-view rather than what they should do because there is a viable market. Businesses therefore often use marketing research to identify a market or to confirm that a market exists for a product. Then, when the product has been developed, they use research to confirm that the product does actually meet the needs of customers and consumers. A business may develop the best product in the world, but if there is no market for it all the development work will have been a waste of resources. The business may have incurred unnecessary expenditure or investment which could have a disastrous effect on the business through over expenditure.

However, a technology driven approach is often used successfully in markets where the products are of a highly technical nature, such as pharmaceuticals or computer technology. New products may come about as a result of a technical development that could not have been foreseen by the marketing team or from marketing research.

Product management

It is the responsibility of the marketing team to manage the product. It must create a successful and profitable business out of selling the product and attracting customers to buy the product. This involves:

- managing a product and monitoring its sales and the marketplace through the use of research data;
- monitoring and adjusting costs and pricing to ensure profitability;
- creating the right marketing mix and implementing effective marketing plans to increase awareness of the product in the market so that it continues to generate sales;
- planning marketing research and product development to make sure that the product on sale remains right for the market.

Research task

Look for product specifications of two different goods and two different services. Depending on the product, you may find them in a number of different places. Look in instruction manuals, technical operating manuals, terms and conditions documents produced when setting up a business relationship and charter documents produced by service organisations. Specifications available for consumers are produced for many products, including pharmaceuticals, building products or motor vehicles.

Compare the product specifications that you find. Consider why some information is common to most of the specifications and why some pieces of information are exclusive to individual products or markets.

Alternatively, make contact with the marketing team at a business that you are familiar with or where you have personal contacts. Explain that you are studying Applied Business and learning about product management. Arrange to meet and interview a member of the marketing team who is responsible for product management and investigate:

- how they see their role in the business;
- their main responsibilities;
- their day-to-day activities;
- the main contribution that they make to the business.

Portfolio practice • Copella

Tropicana UK is a leading producer of fruit drinks, including the Copella juices range. The Copella range, is positioned at the top end of the market, usually at a premium price.

With its expertise and resources Tropicana UK could produce a huge range of juices with the Copella brand name, but it has chosen to limit the range to seven. At some point a decision has been made about which flavours to choose and how it should it be packaged and presented to customers.

The Copella website states:

'There have been many changes to Copella over the years, including new flavours such as Apple & Cranberry and Orchard Fruits. In October 2002 Copella was given a new look with a new logo and bottle redesign. Copella Apple is now available in a larger size 1.75 litre bottle. However, despite the changes, you can be assured the juice is as good as it's always been. Simple, natural, honest and true – Copella still reflects the timeless values of the Suffolk countryside.'

Source: adapted from www.copellafruitjuices.co.uk.

(a) Identify THREE different decisions that may have been made about the packaging of Copella juices.

(b) Suggest reasons why Tropicana UK may have limited the Copella range to just seven flavours.

(c) Suggest ideas for primary market research that Copella might carry out if it wanted to develop new products.

(d) Discuss to what extent the development of Copella was likely to have been customer or technology driven.

Meeting the assessment criteria

You are required to produce an appropriate marketing mix for a new or existing product or service. You must justify all aspects of your devised marketing mix for your product or service.

This section, 37, deals with just one aspect of the marketing mix – Product. The suggestions below only cover the mark bands in terms of this aspect of the marketing mix. To cover the mark bands effectively you will need to take into account 'meeting the assessment criteria' in sections 36 to 40 which cover the marketing mix.

Business example - Helpcraft

Helpcraft manufactures products suitable for people with mobility difficulties. The product range is:
- rubber moulded grippers that can be pushed onto the ends of cutlery or tools;
- extended 'arms' with a moving grab mechanism to pick things up;
- plastic handles to attach to telephones.

It has decided to expand its product range into other areas. These include electronic moving chairs which help to lift people from the chair when they stand up.

Figures 5 and 6 show some information about this market.

Source: adapted from company information.

Figure 5 *UK population aged under 16 and over 65*

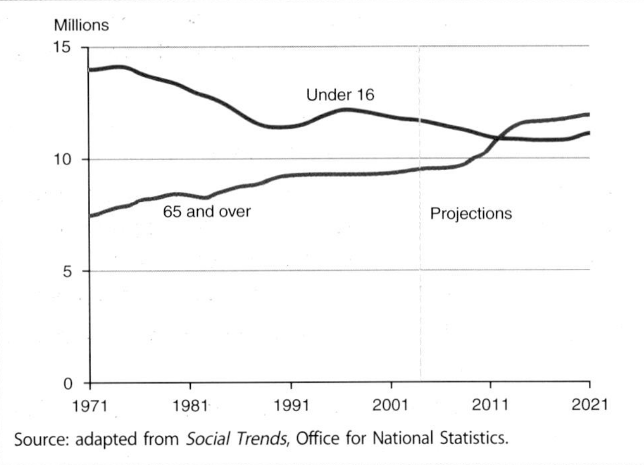

Source: adapted from *Social Trends*, Office for National Statistics.

Figure 6 *Great Britain population aged 90 and over*

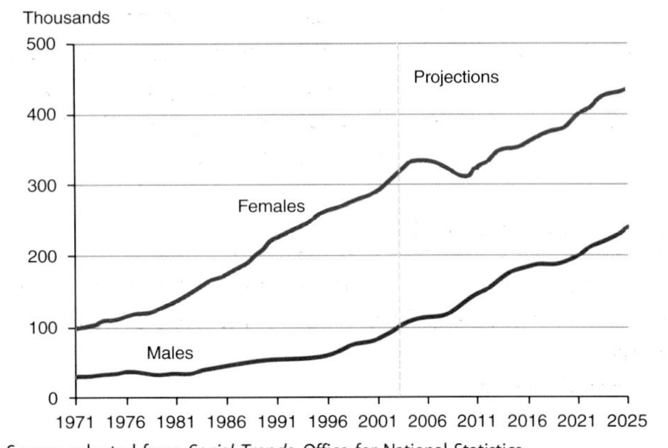

Source: adapted from *Social Trends*, Office for National Statistics.

Mark Band 1 *Creation of a simple marketing mix and a simple evaluation of the marketing mix and conclusions made without supporting evidence.*

Helpcraft makes products to help people with mobility difficulties. The product range includes rubber grips, extended plastic arms and plastic handles. It is a limited product range, geared at a particular market. The specifications are simple and the products are relatively easy to make, all from plastic. The target market is growing and likely to do so in future. So the choice of product in the marketing mix is a likely to be profitable for the business.

Mark Band 2 *Creation of a detailed mix showing an understanding of the 4Ps and a justification of the marketing mix, showing a range of supported evidence, arguments and conclusions.*

Products manufactured by Helpcraft are designed to help people with mobility difficulties. The product range is limited to simple designs and specifications that can be made from plastic, including rubber grips, extended plastic arms and plastic handles. The products are geared at a particular market – people who have mobility difficulties who are often elderly. The target market is growing and likely to do so in future. The UK has an ageing population. Figure 6 shows that the number of males and females aged over 90 is likely to rise. But perhaps also importantly, Figure 5 shows that the number of people over retirement age, 65+ is growing. So the choice of product in the range is a likely to prove profitable for the business. Costs must be controlled and sales should rise.

Mark Band 3 *Creation of a comprehensive mix linked to research and segmentation evidence and a comprehensive and fully justified account of all aspects of the marketing mix.*

The products manufactured by Helpcraft are designed to help people with a range of mobility difficulties. The product range is limited to simple designs and specifications that can be made from plastic. They include rubber grips, extended plastic arms and plastic handles. The products are geared at a particular market – people who have mobility difficulties - many who are often elderly. The target market is growing and likely to do so in future. The UK has an ageing population. Figure 6 shows that the number of males and females aged over 90 are likely to rise. But perhaps also importantly, Figure 5 shows that people over retirement age, 65+ are growing. There are also fewer younger people to look after them.

The choice of gerontic products in the marketing mix is a likely to be profitable for the business.
- Costs can be controlled due to the limited range produced and the simple yet standardised specifications.
- Sales should rise. The products only sells to a niche market. But it is one with particular needs which the products meet. The market is growing. The market for people aged 65+ is predicted to increase by around 50% in the next 15 years.

The expansion of the range could be a problem. Although they are related products, they may require different production techniques, different marketing and increased costs. Perhaps the business should find more simple ways to expand its product range, such as its range of plastic accessories.

Price

What is price?

Once consumers have seen a product, decided that it meets their needs and that they want it, the price is often the next thing they consider. Price is the charge made to purchasers of the product by a business or what customers have to pay to buy the product. This section considers where the price a business charges fits in the marketing mix, how a business determines the price of its products and the factors that go towards determining the price of a product.

Cost price

This is how much it costs a business to produce or acquire its product. Determining the cost price of a product is one of the most important management controls in marketing. Some businesses have specialist cost accountants that work with the product development and marketing teams so the cost of the product is measured and monitored at every stage in the development.

Knowing the cost price is important for the marketing team because any change in the cost price will directly affect the profitability of the product and will need to be addressed to protect profit margins. The most direct way of doing this is by reducing costs.

In every business, costs will be different. So depending on the product, different factors will be included in the cost price. In most businesses, the total cost price can be split into direct costs and indirect costs. Again, what is included in direct costs and indirect costs can vary depending on how a business wants to analyse its costs.

Direct costs These are all costs that can be related directly to the production of the product, such as:

- direct materials – the raw materials, bought-in components and
- packaging that are used to produce the product;
- direct labour – the wages and other costs of the workforce that is employed to make the product;
- direct production cost – the cost of the process, which may include energy, power and other fuel used directly in the manufacturing process.

Indirect costs Indirect costs, also called overheads, are the fixed costs that a business has to pay whether or not there is any production output, such as:

- indirect labour – the cost of employees not directly involved in the production process, including management, sales, marketing, quality assurance and other activities involved in the business;
- warehousing and distribution costs;
- rent, business rates, insurance and other business costs.

The total cost of these elements, added to the direct manufacturing costs, will give the total cost of the product. The total cost is usually divided by the quantity of products being produced to give the cost of a single product or unit of production, such as the cost per litre or kilo.

The cost price of a service can be calculated in much the same way, although the materials will be what are used in the provision of the service rather than in the production of goods.

Selling price

This is the price applied to the product when it is offered to the market. It is usually the price at which the business sells its products to distributors, such as wholesalers or retailers. It is sometimes known as the trade price. If a business deals directly with consumers, the selling price is what the consumers pay for the product.

The selling price has to meet the objectives of the business, including meeting sales and profit targets and allowing the product to perform in the market.

The difference between the total cost of the product and the selling price gives the business its gross profit margin. It is the gross profit that is retained by the business to:

- pay stakeholders;
- provide funds for investment in new machinery;
- pay for research and development;
- pay for advertising and promotions.

Gross profit will also be used to fund any discounting off the selling price or refunds that are given to trade customers. If the business sells the product for a figure below the total cost price it will make a loss.

How does a business decide what will be the selling price? It may take into account a number of factors.

Profit level This includes how much or what level of gross profit the business needs to survive and to pay for its planned investments. This is usually set as an objective by senior management within the business on advice from accountants.

Market place pricing This is how much similar products sell for - the price of competition.

Customer expectations Most customers will have an idea of the market price and what they are prepared to pay for a product. If a business charges too much, it may choose competition. If it charges too little it may raise questions over quality.

Distributor margins Each business in the supply chain (producers, wholesalers or retailers) will expect to make a margin when the product passes through their business. Distributor margins need to be considered in the costing equation because these additional costs to the cost price may raise the retail price beyond consumer and marketplace expectations.

Reducing costs

If the gross margin is not sufficient to meet the objectives or needs of the business, there are two ways that this can be addressed:

- raise the selling price;
- reduce costs.

Raising the selling price may not be an option because of market and competitor pressures. So the business may have to look carefully at reducing prices. There is a number of ways this can be done, but the most direct include:

- raw materials – buy cheaper, ask for a reduction from the supplier, find a new lower cost supplier or reduce the quantity used, as if less material is used then the cost price will fall;
- direct labour – cut wages or cut the number of employees engaged in production without reducing output;
- direct production cost – use the production equipment more efficiently to increase output within a given production time or use different equipment with a higher output and lower unit cost
- indirect costs – cut by buying services more cost effectively or cut the wage bill by reducing the number of employees not engaged in direct production.

Retail selling price (RSP)

This is the price paid at the end of the supply chain, usually by the consumer. If a business sells directly to consumers then the selling price and the retail price are the same. In this situation the producer has direct control over the retail price.

However, many businesses sell via a distributor, such as a retailer, that will set its own retail price for the product based on its own objectives. The producer may suggest what it believes is the optimum retail selling price for its product in the market. But it will have no direct control over the actual retail price that is charged.

Deciding on the retail selling price can be arrived at by taking into account factors such as:

- market place pricing – how much similar products sell for;
- customer/consumer expectations – what they expect to pay based on previous purchases and competitor pricing;
- distributor expectations – retailers will have their own objectives for gross profit on sales and this may be used to determine the retail selling price;
- profit at each point of distribution – as mentioned under selling price, each business in the supply chain will expect to make a margin when the product passes through its business. Distributor margins need to be considered because they may raise the retail price beyond consumer and marketplace expectations or reduce the profit margin for the manufacturer;
- VAT – this is added at the current rate to most products sold in the UK and EU countries. Rates vary and some products may be zero-rated;
- marketing strategy – depending on its marketing objectives a business may adopt a particular pricing strategy for its retail selling price. The strategy may be to price low for market penetration, price high to skim the market or for price leadership, or to price in the same range as similar products, known as market-based competitive pricing.

Table 1 shows the prices of different women's perfumes.

Table 1 *Women's perfume retail prices, 50ml bottles, Eau de Parfum*

Perfume	Price
Agent Provocateur	£36-37
Coty Exclamation	£5-£11
Dolce & Gabbana for Women	£18-£38
Burberry Touch for Women	£17
Vivienne Westwood Boudoir	£40-£42
Sisley Eau Du Soir	£55

Source: adapted from www.kelkoo.co.uk, 2005.

Determining the optimum price

It is important that the selling price of a product is set within a range that is right for the market.

- Setting too low a price may not maximise the profit potential for the business.
- Setting too high a price may limit sales and could make competitor products appear more attractive to consumers.

If a price is set too high it can always be adjusted down until it i right for the market, using promotions, discounting or adding

Figure 1 *How the price of a product is made up*

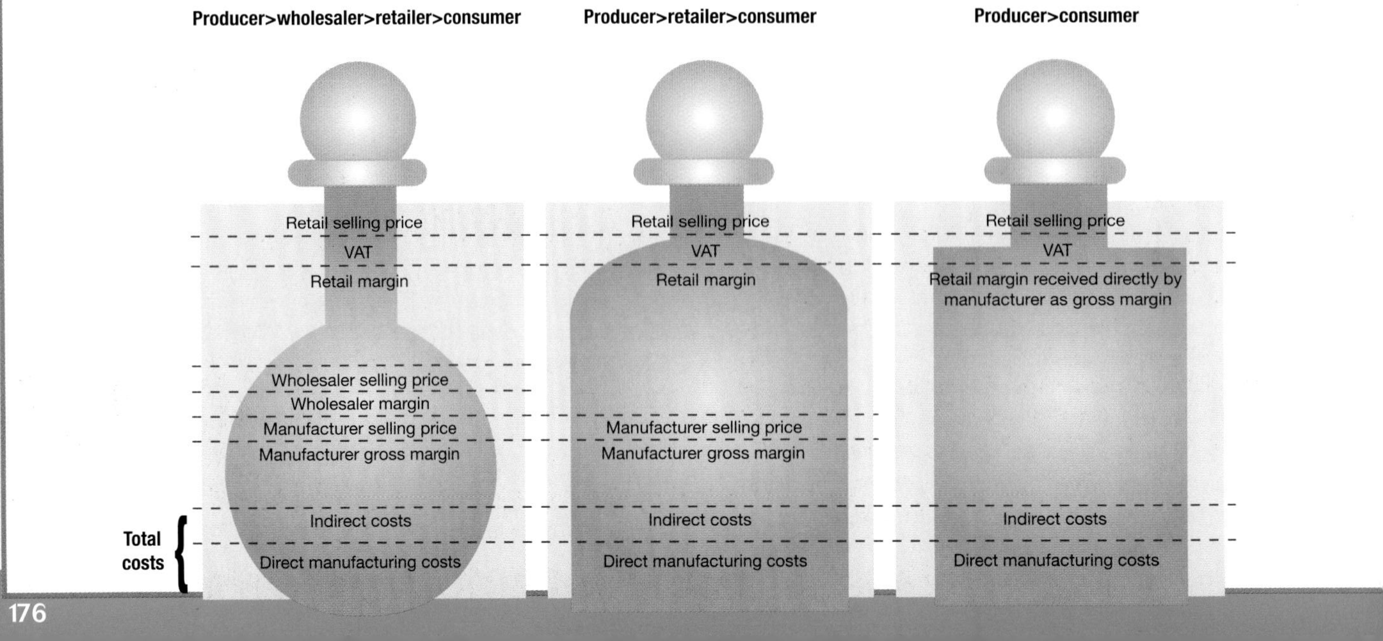

Producer>wholesaler>retailer>consumer
Retail selling price
VAT
Retail margin
Wholesaler selling price
Wholesaler margin
Manufacturer selling price
Manufacturer gross margin
Indirect costs
Direct manufacturing costs

Producer>retailer>consumer
Retail selling price
VAT
Retail margin
Manufacturer selling price
Manufacturer gross margin
Indirect costs
Direct manufacturing costs

Producer>consumer
Retail selling price
VAT
Retail margin received directly by manufacturer as gross margin
Indirect costs
Direct manufacturing costs

Total costs

value. But if a price is set too low it can lead quickly to losing money on a product as costs increase. Once set too low, it is very hard to raise the price because there will be resistance from customers and other market factors. However, no matter how low a price a business charges there will always be a competitor somewhere that will undercut this price to meet its own objectives.

Figure 1 shows how the price of a product, such as perfume, might be made up when sold using different distribution methods.

Supply and demand and the effect on price

Price is affected directly by levels of supply and demand. The supply and demand model of the economy describes how prices vary depending on the balance between:

- supply - the availability of product and;
- demand - how much the market wants to acquire of the product.

Demand If supply remains steady, then generally:

- the more that consumers demand of a product the higher the price that can be charged;
- the less consumers demand the lower the price that can be charged.

Various factors may affect demand by consumers including:

- incomes - the more people earn the more they are likely to buy;
- tastes - if something becomes fashionable people might buy it;
- other goods - if products become more expensive or less attractive consumers might switch to buy a different product;
- population - a rise in population might increase demand;
- advertising - promotion might encourage people to buy products;
- laws - legislation can encourage or discourage buying of certain products.

Supply If consumer demand remains steady, then generally:

- the more that businesses supply of a product the lower the price that can be charged;
- the less businesses supply the higher the price that can be charged.

If consumer demand for a product remains steady and more of the same product comes into the market than is being bought, then the price is likely to fall. Manufacturers may try to make it more attractive to consumers to buy, by lowering the price. Conversely, if less of the product is available than consumers want to buy, the price will increase as it becomes more scarce and consumers become willing to pay more to buy what they want. Figure 2 shows an example.

Figure 2 *The price of seasonal fruit*

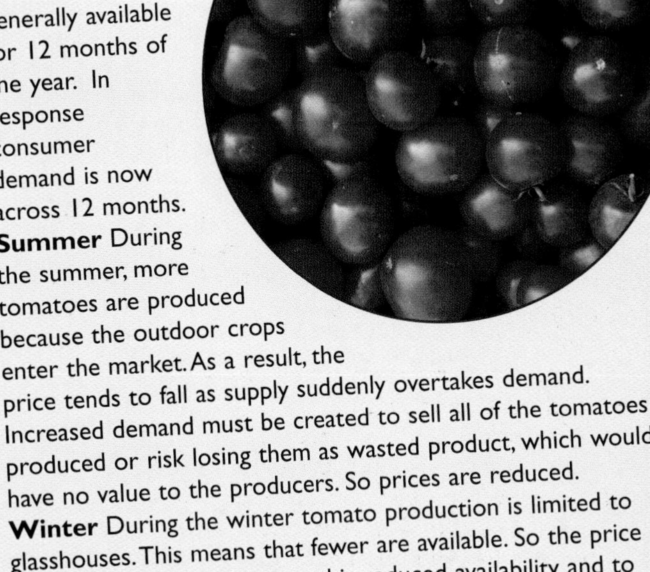

Modern glasshouse growing and supermarket management techniques mean that tomatoes are generally available for 12 months of the year. In response consumer demand is now across 12 months.

Summer During the summer, more tomatoes are produced because the outdoor crops enter the market. As a result, the price tends to fall as supply suddenly overtakes demand. Increased demand must be created to sell all of the tomatoes produced or risk losing them as wasted product, which would have no value to the producers. So prices are reduced.

Winter During the winter tomato production is limited to glasshouses. This means that fewer are available. So the price tends to rise to capitalise on this reduced availability and to moderate demand to a level that can be met.

Identify a product that is sold to consumers:

- directly from the business;
- through retailers.

The product you choose should be the same brand in each supply chain. Examples could include CDs, computer games, confectionery, clothing.

- Identify the retail selling price in each supply chain.
- Consider reasons why the prices are the same or different when the product is retailed through the different supply chains

OR

Make contact with the marketing team at a business that you are familiar with or where you have personal contacts. Explain that you are studying Applied Business and learning about pricing. Arrange to meet and interview a member of the marketing team or an accountant who is responsible for pricing and investigate:

- how they cost their products;
- what they include in direct costs;
- what they include in indirect costs;
- how they set the selling price.

Research task

Portfolio practice • The price of shampoo

Figure 3 shows a basic costing sheet that has been produced by the accounts team at Extra Cosmetics Ltd. for a new shampoo product Shinee.

(a) (i) Calculate the direct cost involved in the production of one 250ml bottle of Shinee.
(ii) Calculate the total cost for the production of one 250ml bottle of Shinee.
(iii) Calculate the selling price if Extra Cosmetics Ltd. wants to make 50% gross margin.

(b) Similar shampoo products have a retail selling price of £2.19 including VAT @ 17.5%. Suggest how Extra Cosmetics Ltd. could increase the profit that it makes on selling Shinee shampoo.

Figure 3 *Costs for Shinee shampoo*

Raw materials
surfactant, colour, scent = £1.00 per litre

Packaging
1 x 250ml bottle 10p
1 bottle cap 2p
printed label 2p

Labour for running filling machine for Shinee bottles, £10.00 per hour. The machine fills 1,000 bottles each hour.

Factory overheads Estimated to be £1,000 per day, each da[y] 10,000 bottles of Shinee can be filled.

Meeting the assessment criteria

You are required to produce an appropriate marketing mix for a new or existing product or service. You must justify all aspects of your devised marketing mix for your product or service.

This section, 38, deals with just one aspect of the marketing mix – Price. The suggestions below only cover the mark bands in terms of this aspect of the marketing mix. To cover the mark bands effectively you will need to take into account 'meeting the assessment criteria' in sections 36 to 40 which cover the marketing mix.

Business example - Concert tickets

In 2005 Cream, the rock supergroup of the 1960s featuring Eric Clapton, Jack Bruce and Ginger Baker, reformed for four shows at The Royal Albert Hall in London on May 2nd, 3rd, 5th, 6th 2005. Face value tickets for the concert were priced at £50, £75 and £125, although they were exchanging at many times that value on some Internet sites. *The Guardian* reported that 'The first live show for 36 years by Eric Clapton's blues/rock 'power trio' may have attracted the attentions of the media, but it has had difficulty snaring anyone under 40; young people are conspicuous by their absence from the bars and foyers of the Royal Albert Hall.'

Between 2-7 July 2005 Destiny's Child toured Great Britain, performing five dates, the first time since 2003. The face value of ticket prices at Earl's Court ranged from £27.50 to £40. Other venues included The Manchester MEN Arena.

Source: adapted from Guardian Unlimited, Ticketmaster, Albert Hall website.

Mark Band 1 *Creation of a simple marketing mix and a simple evaluation of the marketing mix and conclusions made without supporting evidence.*

Businesses involved in the pricing of concert tickets must decide what prices to charge. The prices must take into account certain factors. Prices must cover the direct and indirect costs involved in setting up the concert and the profit that the businesses involved want to make. But prices must also take into account the supply of tickets and the demand for the tickets. The prices charged for Cream and Destiny's Child tickets are likely to be appropriate and effective prices. The prices are relatively high enough to cover costs. They also take into account that there is limited supply of tickets and high demand. This allows high prices to be charged.

Mark Band 2 *Creation of a detailed mix showing an understanding of the 4Ps and a justification of the marketing mix, showing a range of supported evidence, arguments and conclusions.*

Businesses involved in the pricing of concert tickets must decide what prices to charge. The prices must take into account certain factors. A low price will not cover costs, but a high price may deter customers. Prices must be high enough to cover the direct and indirect costs involved in setting up the concert, including wage costs, hire of equipment and transport and promotion costs. The price must also be high enough to make the profit that all businesses involved want to make. Prices must also take into account the supply of tickets and the demand for the tickets. The prices charged for Cream and Destiny's Child tickets are likely to be appropriate and effective prices. The prices are relatively high enough to cover costs. They also take into account the supply of tickets and the demand for tickets. Supply is limited to the number of seats in the theatres and the number of concerts. In both cases supply is relatively limited. Demand is likely to be very high. Cream have not toured for 37 years. Destiny's Child are popular current artists with a large younger fan base. High demand and limited supply will allow high prices to be charged.

Mark Band 3 *Creation of a comprehensive mix linked to research and segmentation evidence and a comprehensive and fully justified account of all aspects of the marketing mix.*

Businesses involved in the pricing of concert tickets must decide on an effective pricing strategy. The prices charged are likely to be influenced by a number of factors. If prices are set too low they will not cover costs. Setting too high a price will deter customers. The price of concert tickets must be high enough to cover the direct and indirect costs involved in setting up the concert, including wage costs, hire of equipment and transport and promotion costs. The price must also be high enough to make the profit that all businesses involved want to make. The relative prices charged are fairly high. These should be enough to cover the costs of venues, promoters and agents involved in the tour.

Prices must also take into account the supply of tickets and the demand for the tickets. Supply is limited to the number of seats in the theatres and the number of concerts. In both cases there are no more than 5 gigs. So supply is relatively limited. Demand is likely to be very high. Cream have not toured for 37 years. They have a large fan base over many years who will want to see concerts. Destiny's Child are popular current artists with a large younger fan base. The relative prices of Cream tickets are able to be set higher because fans are older and likely to have higher income to spend. They have also waited a long time to see the group and may be prepared to pay higher prices. Younger fans may not be able to afford relatively higher priced tickets. There may also be more seats available for Destiny's Child tickets so supply is higher.

High demand and limited supply means that charging high prices is likely to be effective for these concerts. The price charged for Cream tickets could have been higher.

39 Place

What is place?

In the marketing mix 'place' refers to where a customer or consumer can buy or access the product. In practice this means the point of distribution, the end of the supply chain that is used to get the product from the producer to the consumer. Figure 1 shows some examples of the different methods of distribution which producers may use to get products to the consumer.

Figure 1 *Supply chains - methods used to get the product from producer to consumer*

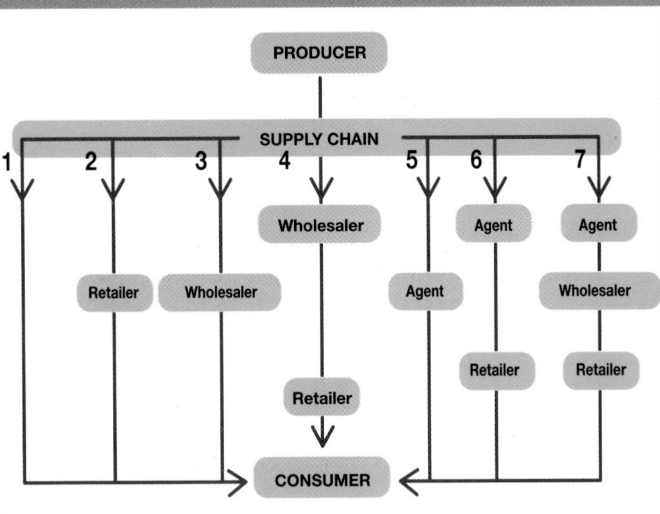

Direct selling This is where the producer sells goods directly to consumers without the use of intermediaries or distributors, such as wholesalers or retailers. Services are often sold directly to consumers. This is method 1 in Figure 1. Direct selling can reduce costs and also be used to target customers. But it can be a limit on the coverage of the market.

Through wholesalers Wholesalers are businesses that 'break-bulk'. They buy large quantities from manufacturers and then sell to consumers via retailers or directly to consumers. Methods 3, 4 and 7 use wholesalers in Figure 1. Wholesalers take large quantities and can bargain for lower prices.

Through retailers There are many varieties of retail outlets in high street shops and shopping centres and on out-of-town shopping estates. They buy directly from producers or wholesalers and then sell to consumers. Methods 2, 4, 6 and 7 use retailers in Figure 1. Retailers can give a business a wide scope of distribution, but again may increase costs for a business. Businesses may also lose control of distribution, as explained later.

Through agents Agents are individuals or businesses that are often specialists in selling into particular markets. They can be effective if a business is selling to a specialist market or into an unknown market.

Some examples of these methods are shown in Table 1.

Table 1 *Distribution methods*

Method	Example
Direct selling	Pick your own strawberries at Garden Farm in Norwich. Avon Cosmetics Ltd sells products from its website and through party plans.
Wholesalers	Barnsley Footwear Distributors Ltd which deals in footwear brands such as Nike, Puma, Lacoste and Timberland selling to the trade only.
Retailer	Specsavers which sells Hugo Boss, Storm, Red or Dead and Monsoon frames.
Agents	Kinnersley Brothers Limited, an international importer / exporter and manufacturer's agent based in Bristol, UK, that specialises in fruit juices and oils & fats.

Using distribution methods

Using different distributions methods may require a different approach from producers or providers.

Direct selling A business may deal directly with consumers. This could include

- setting up it own retail outlets;
- using a mail-order catalogue;
- direct sell leaflets and advertisements;
- creating a website that consumers can buy from;
- selling door-to-door or running a party-plan scheme that brings together potential consumers to look at and try the product before their buy.

Any of these examples would be possible sales and marketing plans so long as the business has sufficient skills and resources to setup and run these schemes and resources to create awareness amongst consumers through promotion and advertising.

Retailers and wholesalers To meet place objectives when dealing with distributors and retailers, requires a different approach.

First, the business needs to research the market to establish how its product could be distributed by investigating similar and competitor products. This research should identify the most important distributors to target.

Next, the business will need to prepare a case to take to the target distributors to convince them that it is in their interests to stock and sell the product being marketed. This should be a combination of:

- product specification details, e.g. what it is, what it does, why it does it better than competitor products and the price;
- market research that supports the manufacturer's case, e.g. data on the size and dynamics of the market and market data that proves the product will be in demand;

- consumer research that shows that the product is right for consumers in the market;
- the package of promotional support that the product will receive to create awareness and demand which should help it sell.

The business will then need to maintain the distribution that it has gained. This will require constant monitoring through marketing research and a package of marketing plans and promotion to keep the product selling.

Control over distribution

'Place' in the marketing mix can be the factor that the producer has least control over. A producer or provider may set certain objectives for distribution and availability for consumers in most markets. But place is often controlled by retailers and other distributors that make decisions about whether or not to stock and sell a product. There are situations, however, where the producer may have some control over distribution.

Direct selling A producer may have control if it sells directly to consumers from its own outlets, its factory or via ordering on the Internet. Businesses selling services directly to consumers can have a great deal of control.

Branding and promotion If a brand is very strong or if there is heavy promotion, wholesalers and retailers may be 'forced' to stock the product. Also, consumers may expect certain top brands of beans or cereal to be stocked. Newly released DVDs and CDs are often heavily promoted and become ' must stock' items.

Consumer demand If demand is so strong, not stocking a product could put a business at a competitive disadvantage because the range it offers range is incomplete. For example, most consumers would consider that a newsagent would have an incomplete range if it did not sell most national daily newspapers.

Positioning Place can refer to precisely where the product is located within a retail store. This is something that the producer can advise on, but the decision will be up to retailers. This is dealt with later.

Even then, a powerful retailer may not stock or may withdraw a product because it has a disagreement with the producer over the cost, image or the level of marketing support given. Also, some retailers, particularly the food supermarket chains known as 'discounters', base their own brand image on the fact that they do not stock branded goods. Instead, they make up their complete product range from smaller, lesser-known or imported brands that can be sold at low prices compared with well known branded goods.

Place and consumers' tastes

During product development, businesses must carry out research to identify where consumers expect the product to be available and sold. If a product is in the wrong place or if consumers cannot find it easily, sales may suffer. Certain characteristics of consumers must be taken into account when setting place objectives.

Consumer behaviour can change Until recently grocery supermarket businesses traded exclusively from large retail outlets. Consumers had to visit the supermarket to buy what they wanted. The Internet and the worldwide web have changed all that. Many supermarkets now have an on-line shopping website. Consumers with computers and Internet access expect to be able to buy groceries from a website as an option to visiting the supermarket itself.

Consumer expectations If a business launches and promotes a new product, consumers will expect it to be available where they normally buy similar, competitor products. For example, they will expect to find a new mobile phone in mobile phone shops, electrical stores and other places that sell mobile phones. If the new phone was only stocked in newsagents it would miss a huge section of the market looking in traditional outlets.

If a new national dry cleaning service is launched, sited on an industrial estate, consumers may look for it in the high street. Unless promotion is clear, they will not expect to have to visit industrial estates, where there may be plenty of properties at lower costs than in the high street. Even so, consumers may not be comfortable about visiting an industrial area to get their clothes cleaned.

Place within a retail outlet

Part of setting place objectives may include advising where the product should be located within the retail outlet to maximise sales. This could include recommending:

- the product is placed alongside those of competitors;
- the product is placed in a different product section, with non-competing but complementary products;
- the space required;
- the number of shelves;
- the height at which the product should be positioned in order to catch the eye of consumers;
- products are located at checkouts to create an impulse purchase, rather than tucked away on a shelf amongst other products competing for consumer attention.

Place and price

Marketing objectives for price may have a place element.

- If a business believes that its product should command a higher,

Figure 2 *Dell distribution*

Dell is one of the most successful suppliers of computers in the world and all of its business is conducted direct with its customers, consumers of the computer equipment. By not relying on retailers to stock, distribute and sell its goods, Dell can control the selling price, setting the price according to the competitive market and its own profit requirements. It sells its products directly in two ways;

- contacting the company directly;
- Internet sales.

Source: adapted from ww.dell.com.

premium price when sold it needs to target retailers that are less likely to discount the selling price.
- If the objective is to sell the product at a low, competitive price, then it would be no good targeting retailers that have an up-market image and try to sell goods at the maximum price their customers will stand.

But businesses that sell via distributors and retailers do not have the final say over the prices that are charged for their products. It is often the retailer's decision, based on its own objectives. Direct selling can bring control of 'place' and 'price' back to the manufacturer. An example is shown in Figure 2.

Place and promotion

Marketing objectives for promotion may also have a place element.
- Place can affect the decision about the geographical area where the advertisement is shown or distributed – national, regional, local.
- Place can affect the precise location for promotion, such as handing out leaflets outside a particular shopping centre or club, or showing the advertisement in a particular cinema, depending on the product, the target market and the marketing objectives.
- Place can affect the choice of promotional medium. For example, it is recognised in the magazine industry that an advertisement on a right-hand page has more impact than on a left-hand page and that the top of a page has more impact than the foot of the page. In television, advertisements placed between popular programmes will be seen by more viewers than if placed between less popular programmes.

Research task

Choose a popular product with a strong brand, such as Coca-Cola and a specialist market such as railway tickets.
- Identify how many different places these products are sold.
- Give as many reasons as you can why the products are sold at each place you have identified.

Then interview people in the street.
- Ask where they usually buy the popular product and where they usually buy the specialist product.
- Compare the answers you get from consumers with your own investigation into where each product is actually stocked.
- Draw conclusions from your findings. This should help you understand how businesses set objectives for place and how consumer expectations affect place.

Portfolio practice • BGO Records

Figure 3 shows a section from a full-page advertisement placed by BGO Records to promote its new releases.

(a) Identify TWO 'places'/distribution methods that BGO Records may use for its new releases.

(b) Suggest ONE expectation that consumers may have about this product from Figure 3 and explain how it might affect distribution.

(c) (i) Explain which distribution method might allow the business to control its distribution better.
(ii) Discuss whether this should be the only method the business should use.

Figure 3 *BGO Records advertisement*

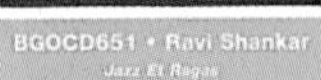

All BGO new releases and catalogue available from good record shops everywhere or buy online at www.bgo-records.com

For a FREE 2005/06 BGO catalogue send a large (A4) sae to:
BGO Records, PO Box 22, Bury St. Edmunds, Suffolk IP28 6XQ

Meeting the assessment criteria

You are required to produce an appropriate marketing mix for a new or existing product or service. You must justify all aspects of your devised marketing mix for your product or service.

This section, 39, deals with just one aspect of the marketing mix – Place. The suggestions below only cover the mark bands in terms of this aspect of the marketing mix. To cover the mark bands effectively you will need to take into account 'meeting the assessment criteria' in sections 36 to 40 which cover the marketing mix.

Business example - Killer Kits/Model Mayhem

Killer Kits is a business that manufactures resin figure kits that can be made up into models of characters from sci-fi and horror films and television, such as Austin Powers, Batman and Basil Fawlty. It sells kits from its website www.killerkits.net and also at trade fairs, such collectors fairs at the NEC, in Birmingham. On 2 May 2005 it branched out by opening its own shop, Model Mayhem, in Liverpool. The shop is part of Gostens, a retail shopping centre in a converted warehouse on Hanover Street. Shoppers can buy the kits or arrange for them to be made up and painted.

Source: adapted from company information.

Mark Band 1 *Creation of a simple marketing mix and a simple evaluation of the marketing mix and conclusions made without supporting evidence.*
Killer Kits manufactures resin figure kits. It distributes them in three ways. One is directly to the public though trade fairs at centres such as the Birmingham NEC. Another is directly to the public through the use of the Internet website and online ordering. A further method is through its own retail shop in Liverpool. This is likely to be an effective distribution mix. A number of methods are being used and customers are likely to be more effectively targeted using these methods, particularly direct selling.

Mark Band 2 *Creation of a detailed mix showing an understanding of the 4Ps and a justification of the marketing mix, showing a range of supported evidence, arguments and conclusions.*
Killer Kits manufactures resin figure kits. It distributes them, the part of the marketing mix that deals with 'place', in three ways. One is directly to the public though trade fairs at centres such as the Birmingham NEC. This method is likely to be effective because it targets people who are interested in collectables. They can buy kits having viewed them at the trade fair. Another is directly to the public through the use of the Internet website and online ordering. Again this will be effective. People can see the products and read information by clicking on thumbnails. Products can then be delivered directly to homes. It is a relatively cheap way of reaching the target market.
A further method is through its own retail shop in Liverpool. Running a shop will incur costs, although they have been minimised by being part of a complex. Stocks can be kept elsewhere and sent out as required. Using a variety of direct methods of distribution is likely to be effective for such a specialist market.

Mark Band 3 *Creation of a comprehensive mix linked to research and segmentation evidence and a comprehensive and fully justified account of all aspects of the marketing mix.*
Killer Kits manufactures resin figure kits. It distributes them, the part of the marketing mix that deals with 'place', in a number of ways. One is directly to the public though trade fairs at centres such as the Birmingham NEC. This method is likely to be effective to some extent. It targets people who are interested in collectables. They can buy kits having viewed them at the trade fair. However, there is the cost of getting to the event and hiring a stand. Also, it only takes place a few times a year. In itself, this method of distribution would not be sufficient.

Another is directly to the public through the use of the Internet website and online ordering. People can see the products and read information by clicking on thumbnails. Products can then be delivered directly to homes. It is a relatively cheap way of reaching the target market and proved effective in establishing the business.

A further method is through its own retail shop in Liverpool. Running a shop will incur costs. Choosing a site with relatively low overheads, which is part of a larger retail complex, will help. Stocks can be kept elsewhere and sent out as required. Choosing a city centre location such as Liverpool, with a large number of students and younger people, will also be effective for reaching the target market.

The distribution method used by the business allows targeted customers to be given information effectively and products delivered quickly. The business uses direct methods rather than selling to other retailers, such as comic shops, which may only want built models. Also they are likely to take part of the profit of the business. It may be possible to sell kits through other model shops, though they may not be specialists. In conclusion, it could be argued that using a variety of direct methods of distribution is likely to be effective for such a specialist market.

40 Promotion

What is promotion?

Promotion is how businesses make customers aware of their products or services. A variety of promotional methods can be used. They are designed to:

- attract new customers to buy new products of the business;
- ensure that existing customers keep buying the products of a business;
- attract customers away from buying the products of other businesses using comparisons;
- improve the image of products in the eyes of customers;
- attract customers to the business itself so that they buy other products;
- support customers that they have bought products.

Advertising

Advertising is a very popular method of promotion used by businesses. It is the use of paid-for space in the media to raise awareness of a product and communicate with a target market. Advertising is designed to sell or to carry a message to an audience. It is carried out in many highly creative ways, in a range of different media, as shown in Figure 1. Examples of advertising can be seen on television, in newspapers and magazines, in the street, in shops and in town centres, in fact anywhere where there is space to carry a message.

Decisions about which form of advertising to use in the marketing mix will depend on:

- what is appropriate for the product;
- the market it is aimed at;
- availability;
- access;
- the budget available.

Some examples of the most commonly used advertising media are shown in Table 1.

Before deciding which method of advertising to use, or whether to advertise at all, a business must set its marketing aims and objectives. Then it must make a decision, based on what advertising is appropriate and what is most likely to achieve the objectives set.

Another important factor in the decision making process is the budget available for advertising. Advertising space and time in different media cost different amounts, depending on the price of producing the advertisement and the size of the audience the medium will reach. The bigger the audience the more expensive the cost of advertising in that medium. For example, a page in *The Sun* newspaper, which has a huge circulation, is likely to cost more than a page in a newspaper with relatively fewer readers. Some specialist media which can reach a small but hard to contact group of consumers may also be expensive. For example, on a per reader basis it may cost more to advertise in a specialist magazine like *The Plantsman* than it does in a more general gardening title magazine which has a relatively large circulation and readership.

Figure 1 *Advertising media*

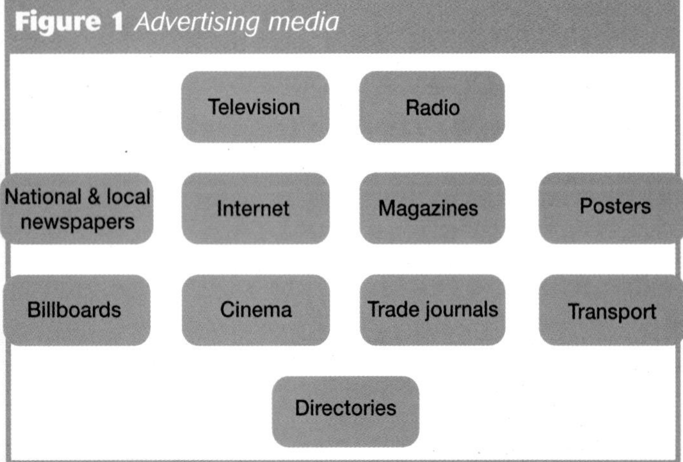

Sales promotion

This covers a range of methods and techniques that are used as an alternative to or in addition to advertising to persuade customers

Table 1 *Advertising media*

Media	Examples
Television	McDonald's 'I'm lovin' it' campaign with a catchy jingle to remember and images of youngsters enjoying themselves.
Radio	Paul Rooney solicitors, explaining verbally what services are offered.
National newspaper	The Travelodge national chain of hotels advertising in *The Guardian* national newspaper.
Local newspaper	Local Conlons opticians branches in Ormskirk, St Helens and Formby advertising in the *Ormskirk Champion*.
Internet	A banner headline for Orange mobile phones appearing on the *Yellow Pages* search engine to attract a large number of customers.
Magazines	A Cuprinol advert for treating fences appearing for target audiences in *The Gardener*.
Cinema	A Lord of the Rings trailer before other similar action/adventure films with the same age certificate.
Transport	Capital Gold London radio or Thomson directory adverts on London taxis.
Directories	The Barrowland theatre appearing in the Glasgow *Yellow Pages*.

and the target market to buy products. Commonly used and effective methods of sales promotion include those shown in Table 2.

Sales promotion often takes the form of an incentive that is offered to customers or consumers to buy the product. This is an inducement to try the product. It is usually only applied to the product for a limited time to act as a tactical marketing plan designed to:

- get consumers to try a new product;
- boost sales of a product when sales have slowed;
- clear stocks of a product that is over-stocked or out of date.

Just like advertising, before deciding on which method to use, or whether sales promotion is required at all, a business must set its marketing aims and objectives. Then it must decide what type of sales promotion is appropriate and what is most likely to achieve the objectives set.

It is important to consider aims and objectives carefully before deciding which method of sales promotion to choose. If the method chosen is not appropriate for the product and the market it could cost a lot of money and affect the reputation of the product. For example, a poorly chosen promotion by Hoover vacuum cleaners gave free flight vouchers to anyone buying a Hoover vacuum cleaner. The vouchers were worth more than the cost of the cleaners themselves and the business was inundated with consumers that bought the relatively low-cost cleaners and then demanded their holiday. This cost the business much more than it had budgeted. It also affected its reputation in the short term because of the poor publicity it received when it tried to limit the number of holiday vouchers claimed by consumers.

Public relations

This is the use of media and events to raise awareness of a product, to communicate a message or to change public opinion. The main difference between public relations and advertising is that, whilst advertising relies on communication through paid-for media space, public relations is based on the use of editorial space and broadcast time that is not paid for directly.

Table 2 *Sales promotion methods*

Method	Examples
Coupons	Coupons given away by magazines to save up and exchange for products.
Loyalty cards	Boots Advantage Card which builds up points to exchange for goods.
Competitions	Travel companies hold competitions and give holidays as prizes.
Product endorsements	Samsung signed to sponsor Chelsea football club in 2005 for five years.
Special terms	Buy now pay later or interest free credit offered by DFS on sofas or Currys on electrical goods.
Product placing	Nokia mobile phones in Charlie's Angels films.
Free or value offers	'10% or 20% extra free' used on confectionery products or cereals.
Money off purchases	Buy One Get One Free offers (BOGOF) used by supermarkets.
Free gifts	CDs or DVDs given with the *News of the World* Sunday newspaper.

For example, when a business launches a new product it may send a press release about the product and a photograph to newspapers and news programmes on the radio and television. The media want the information provided by the business to report on the new product. The business will hope that reports in the media will generate awareness of the new product and encourage consumers to buy the new product.

The use of press releases is just one of the tools that public relations experts use to create awareness without it appearing to be explicit advertising. Public relations techniques can be used for all kinds of promotion and publicity and include press and customer receptions, open days and other publicity generating events. In addition to creating awareness, public relations can be used to change the image and perception of a product.

Figure 2 shows an example of public relations in action to generate publicity in the airline industry.

Direct marketing

This is the use of marketing media to communicate directly with customers and consumers. It may be in the form of leaflets and promotional material that is mailed directly to potential customers and consumers. Sometimes it is in the form of what appears to be a 'personal letter' direct from the business to the customer. Increasingly direct e-mail is also being used.

An important factor in direct mailing is the use of databases. They are used to manage information about customers, so that the direct mail can be sent to precisely the person who is in the market for the product at that time. Direct mail organisations

Figure 2 *Airbus A380 superjumbo launch*

In January 2005 Airbus threw a spectacular party for the A380 superjumbo, the largest civil airliner ever built. 5,000 guests including Eurpean Presidents, Chancellors and Prime Ministers watched a theatrical ceremony at the final assembly plant in Toulouse, France. Airbus chief Noel Forgeard predicted Airbus would sell 700 to 750 of the planes, which cost $260 million to buy and has a 15 per cent gain in costs per seat-mile compared to the Boeing 747-400. It already had 149 orders or commitments from 14 airlines. The A380 has room for 70 cars to park on its wings and looks similar to the Boeing 747, but with the top deck stretching all the way back to the tail.

This type of promotion is often used by airline manufacturers because:

- of the need for airline sales around the world;
- similar methods used by other airlines;
- to make an impact for a new product;
- the size and cost of the project.

Source: adapted from news.airwise.com.

spend a lot of money on market research to build up databases that can be analysed and segmented to fit the target market as precisely as possible.

Sponsorship

This is when a business supports an event, an activity or an organisation, such as a sports team, in exchange for having its name or product brand name linked directly with the event, activity or the organisation being sponsored. Sponsorship is usually in the form of money, but it can also be in the form of donations of products, equipment or resources.

Examples of sponsorship can be seen by looking at the company and brand names on the shirts of many sports teams. Individual sportspeople often benefit from sponsorship and wear the sponsor's logo on their clothes when they are competing. Some television programmes also have sponsorship. This can be seen by watching television and looking for examples of brand names and logos that appear before the programme starts or between commercial breaks. Examples of this include The Simpsons on Sky One television being sponsored by Domino's Pizza and Coronation Street being sponsored by Cadbury.

Sponsorship can also be seen when businesses support major events. Examples could include the Glastonbury music festival, whose sponsors include mobile phone network Orange and Formula 1 motor racing, whose sponsors include high-tech sponsor LG Electronics.

Sponsorship can be a good way of increasing brand awareness with targeted groups, by linking the sponsor's name with the activity or event. It can also have positive benefits by creating an association in the audience's mind between the team or the event and the sponsor. For example, if fans of a particular team see that the team is being sponsored, they may have positive feelings towards the sponsor for also supporting their team. The sponsor will hope that the positive feelings translate into increased awareness, a positive image and increased sales.

However, sponsorship can sometimes work in reverse. Using the earlier example, consider what fans from an opposing team think about the business that sponsors their rivals. Their thoughts may not be positive and it could result in a section of the market boycotting the business that sponsors and supports their rivals. Similarly, if a business sponsors an event that receives poor publicity, this may reflect on the sponsor and its product sales.

Before a business decides to add sponsorship to its promotional plans it needs to think carefully and decide whether such sponsorship really helps the business to meet its marketing aims and objectives.

Factors influencing choice of promotion method

A business must ensure that it chooses promotion methods that are appropriate if promotion is to be successful. A number of factors might influence the choice of promotion method used by a business.

Objectives of the business The marketing mix of a business will be influenced by its overall corporate and marketing objectives. For example, a business that wants to expand sales quickly might use a method of promotion which has a large impact instantly, such as a national television campaign.

Market research Primary and secondary research by a business provides information about the market that might help a business decide the most suitable method of promotion. For example, an article in a trade journal might tell a manufacturer of golf equipment that exhibiting at trade fairs or golf competitions would be effective.

Nature of the business Some types of marketing might be more suitable to certain businesses. Trade journals are often valuable for technical products sold to other businesses, for example.

Target customers Certain types of promotion might be very effective in appealing to the target audience, whereas others might not. For example, if customers are not willing to travel far to use a service, then local promotion methods might be appropriate.

Size of the business Small businesses have limited budgets and markets. Larger businesses with larger markets may be able to spend a great deal more on promotion. For example, a local tanning salon might use a local newspaper to advertise its service but a chain of salons might use a cinema advertisement.

Nature of the product The type of product might affect promotion. For example, a product with moving parts might use a visual advertisement on television rather than on radio.

Competition Businesses in competitive markets often use similar promotion methods to their competitors. For example, large amounts are spent to launch new films, both in advertising, merchandising and other forms of promotion.

Impact Some promotions have greater impact than others. However, this does not mean that large, noisy promotions are most effective. It will depend on the target markets and the nature of the product.

Cost and budget Some promotions, such as television advertisements during peak time sporting events, can be extremely expensive. Others, such as leaflets, can be relatively cheap.

Law Legislation affects certain aspects of advertising, such as information that can be stated in adverts about products. This is dealt with in section 15.

External constraints Some pressure groups can constrain promotion. The Advertising Standards Authority, for example, is responsible for making sure that adverts are legal, decent, honest, truthful and responsible.

Select a large business and identify the methods of promotion that it uses. Compare these methods to promotion being carried out by a small business in your local area.

Use a search engine on the Internet, back issues of newspapers and magazines, and other media for your research. Identify the aims and objectives of the businesses that explain why each business has used particular promotional methods.

Research task

Portfolio practice · Keys

Vernon Keys runs a roofing and building business in Southport, Merseyside. He has built up contacts over the years both in the building trade and amongst customers. But he now wants to concentrate on interior renovation work. He has read reports in newspapers that the DIY boom was over in 2005. People who had previously thought about DIY, encouraged by makeover programmes, were now paying for work to be done.

Vernon decided to sell his specialist roofing equipment and scaffolding. He wanted to advertise his services within a 50 mile radius of Southport. He considered a number of alternatives to help him promote this change in business activity and decided on the following methods.

- To advertise in *The Southport Visitor*, a local newspaper.
- To place his name in the local *Yellow Pages*.
- To sponsor a local drama society where he had friends.
- To visit trade fairs in London each year to develop the prestige of his business.
- To place an advertisement on Capital Radio London. He could get this station on his DAB radio at home and thought that there would be many other people who would be attracted to such a popular station.
- To produce a glossy leaflet to distribute in the local area.

Source: adapted from company information.

(a) Examine the advantages and disadvantages of each method which Vernon is using to promote the new business.

(b) Using your analysis in (a), evaluate the likely success of Vernon's promotion methods.

Meeting the assessment criteria

You are required to produce an appropriate marketing mix for a new or existing product or service. You must justify all aspects of your devised marketing mix for your product or service.

This section, 40, deals with just one aspect of the marketing mix – Promotion. The suggestions below only cover the mark bands in terms of this aspect of the marketing mix. To cover the mark bands effectively you will need to take into account 'meeting the assessment criteria' in sections 36 to 40 which cover the marketing mix.

Business example - Blueyonder sponsorship of show on Virgin Radio

In 2002 Blueyonder, Telewest Broadband's high speed Internet service, signed a deal to sponsor the award-winning Pete & Geoff Show on Virgin Radio. It has a cult follolwing with a history of web links. Telewest would advertise on a banner campaign on the Virgin website. The Telewest Broadband service allowed people to surf the Internet ten times faster than a standard dial up modem. People can browse the web, download music and have video streaming and online gaming. The show would also include give-away prizes and promotional trials and on-air credits for phone users.

On 1st May the company also launched a 3 month broadband taster campaign, aimed at homes with BT, AOL, Freeserve and other dial-up services. New customers paid £13.48 a month for their first 3 months of broadband, lower than the average cost of dial-up services in the UK. Customers could claim back the installation fee if they didn't want to continue with the service at the standard price.

Source: adapted from mediacentre.telewest.co.uk.

Mark Band 1 *Creation of a simple marketing mix and a simple evaluation of the marketing mix and conclusions made without supporting evidence.*

Promotion forms an important part of the marketing mix of a business such as Telewest Broadband. It used a number of methods to promote its fast broadband service. These included banner advertising on the Virgin website and the sponsorship of a radio programme on Virgin Radio. It also gave away free gifts and credits for phones and trials, forms of sale promotions. These methods are all likely to be effective in attracting customers. A large business in a competitive market such as mobile phones must have a number of promotions. It must also choose methods which attract its target market effectively, encourage people to buy the product and promote the name of the business and its products. The methods it has chosen are likely to do this.

Mark Band 2 *Creation of a detailed mix showing an understanding of the 4Ps and a justification of the marketing mix, showing a range of supported evidence, arguments and conclusions.*

Promotion forms an important part of the marketing mix of a business such as Telewest Broadband. The business used a number of methods to promote its fast broadband service. These included banner advertising on the Virgin website and sponsorship of the award winning Pete & Geoff Show on Virgin Radio, a form of public relations. The free gifts and credits for phones and trials are forms of sale promotions. A large business in a competitive market such as mobile phones must have a number of promotions. It must also choose methods which attract its target market effectively, encourage people to buy the product and promote the name of the business and its products. The methods it has chosen are likely to do this for a number of reasons. The programme sponsored has a reputation and a following, particularly amongst those customers who are likely to want to buy broadband service and make use of its facilities, such as downloading music. So the market is being targeted effectively. Further, offering free trails is a useful way of attracting custom. It is perhaps more difficult to stop using a service once installed than it is not to use it in the first place.

Mark Band 3 *Creation of a comprehensive mix linked to research and segmentation evidence and a comprehensive and fully justified account of all aspects of the marketing mix.*

Promotion forms an important part of the marketing mix of a business such as Telewest Broadband. The business used a number of methods of promotion. These included:

- an advertising banner campaign on the Virgin Radio website;
- sponsorship of the award winning Pete & Geoff Show on Virgin Radio, a form of public relations;
- free gifts and credits for phones and trials, all sales promotions.

A large business in a competitive market such as mobile phones has to have a number of promotions. It will face competition from other broadband providers such as BT as well as cable. They will make use of advertising media and other promotions which Telewest must combat.

It must also choose methods which attract its target market effectively, encourage people to buy the product and promote the name of the business and its products. The methods it has chosen are likely to do this. The programme sponsored has a reputation and a following, particularly amongst those customers who are likely to want to buy broadband service and make use of its facilities, such as downloading music. So the market is being targeted effectively.

Elizabeth Sheard the Sponsorship Manager at Virgin Radio said that Virgin Radio had over a million ABC1 adults between the ages of 25 & 44 tuning in each week and this is the key market for Blueyonder. She also said that Virgin was the most listened to online radio station in the world with the average online listener tuning in for approximately 20 minutes each session. This suggests that the choice of sponsorship and advertising will be very effective. John Orriss, head of marketing for Blueyonder said the campaign would enable the business to 'create further awareness within our key audience, of our broadband Internet service' and 'allow us to highlight the many benefits of high speed Internet access for music and film fans and anyone who uses the Internet at home'.

Offering free trails is a useful way of attracting custom. It is perhaps more difficult to stop using a service once installed than it is not to use it in the first place. Once the audience has been attracted by free trials, it may remain loyal.

41 Other constraints on the marketing mix

Constraints

The marketing mix selected will be affected by both internal and external constraints. Constraints are like brakes being applied to marketing plans or to the business. They are limits that exist or parameters that are set, producing guidelines within which the plan has to operate. Constraints might:

- slow down a project;
- result in plans being changed;
- even lead to a plan being cancelled.

The marketing team may have some control or influence over some constraints. Other constraints are likely to be outside or beyond their control. But each may affect the marketing mix to some degree.

Some constraints can be avoided or reduced. Others may need to be overcome through the use of tactical plans to counter their effect. Although constraints may appear to be completely negative at first, they can result in a rethink that leads to a better marketing mix or a more creative, productive and profitable set of plans than originally thought.

Figure 1 *Internal constraints*

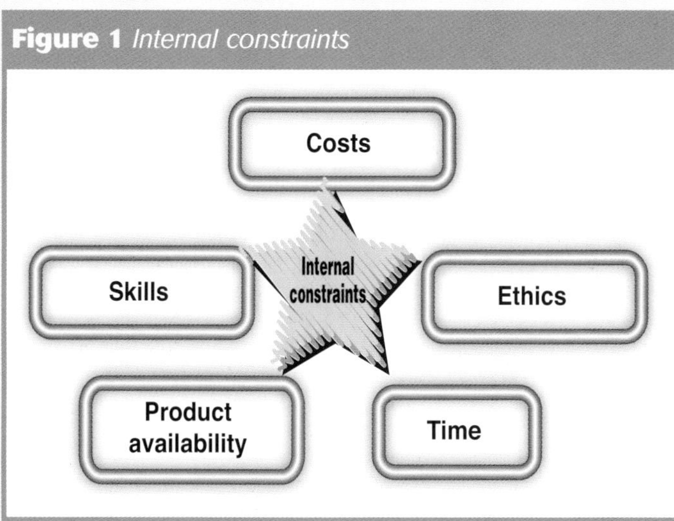

Internal constraints

These constraints exist within the structure and operating procedure of a business. They are likely to be set, applied and controlled by the senior management or influential stakeholders of the business.

Financial constraints These are perhaps the main internal constraint. They are usually set in the form of a budget. This is the amount of money that is allocated to a project. A budget can be based on real, market based costs required to be spent on a project, how much an organisation can afford to spend without hurting investors or damaging its viability, or an estimate of investment expenditure required for a forecast return on expenditure. Whichever way a budget is set, it will feel like a constraint on the marketing mix as there is always a reason to spend more money than the budget will allow.

Sometimes a financial constraint may be perceived to be external. For example, a supplier may raise its prices or the cost of a service may be higher than the budget allows. However, even though higher prices or costs may feel like the constraint is external, the real constraining factor is access to financial resources, the internally set budget.

Financial constraints can be changed or overcome by reassessing the situation and presenting the case for a change of budget, supported by marketing research, to senior management or the budget controller in the organisation.

Time Timing can affect marketing plans. For example, when a major new film is launched by Dreamworks or Warner Bros., it is preceded by trailers advertising the film for a certain period. Promoting too early or too late may lose impact on potential cinema goers.

Skills and expertise of staff Skills can affect marketing plans. For example, if a UK business is launching a new product abroad, such as in India, it may need to recruit an agent or a specialist marketing agency with knowledge of the market to promote, sell and distribute the product. Its current staff may lack this expertise.

Ethical standards These are the values and beliefs which influence a business. Ethical trading can mean taking into account social justice issues in business. Figure 2 shows how ethical standards can affect marketing decisions.

Product availability The availability of products can affect marketing plans. For example, car manufacturers often launch new models each year. They cannot be marketed until they are designed and manufactured.

External constraints

These are constraints that are usually beyond the direct control of an organisation, yet still affect the marketing plans. They may be set, applied and controlled by a range of organisations, such as the government, the European Union (EU), or a non-government organisation (NGO) such as a trade or industry association.

Political and economic factors

One of the main functions of government is to create and maintain economic conditions that allow the population to enjoy a

Figure 2 *Ethical standards at Ethical Wares*

Ethical Wares is an ethically-based mail order company run by vegans who seek to trade in a manner which does not exploit animals, humans or the wider environment. It states ' By the sale of these vegan products we hope to play our part in the promotion of a cruelty-free lifestyle'. Products include shoes, jewellery, bags, rugs and other accessories.

Source: adapted from www.ethicalwares.com.

Figure 3 *External constraints*

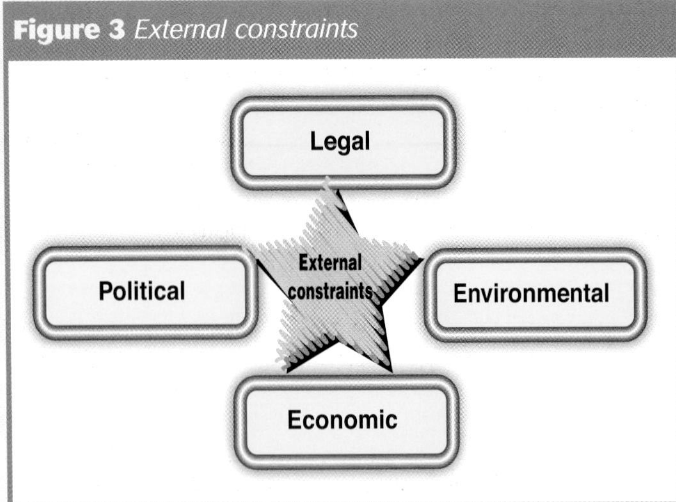

good and improving standard of living. Part of this includes protection from extremes or changes in the world economy that could affect the economic situation in a country. Governments also have a duty to protect consumers. This usually happens through changes in licensing or legislation. These factors will have an effect on marketing plans and can sometimes constrain marketing activity.

Political factors These are factors relating to government which affect businesses. An example of how political factors have affected the marketing mix is the way that the Sunday Trading Act 1994 has changed shopping patterns and marketing opportunities. The Act regulates opening by large shops on Sundays. Before the Act, large shops in England and Wales were required to give prior written notification to the local authority of their Sunday opening hours or changes in these hours. The retail industry lobbied government to deregulate Sunday opening to provide additional marketing opportunities, i.e. an additional day of the week for consumers to shop. Thus one constraint on retail marketing was removed, although it did introduce other constraints as it limited opening times to 6 continual hours between certain times.

Another way that political factors can affect the marketing mix can be seen in a run-up to a general election. Advertising media such as posters will be bought by political parties for promotion. This leaves fewer poster sites for advertising consumer products. The availability of poster sites could constrain where advertising occurs and the remaining poster sites will be priced at a premium, thus placing a financial constraint on potential advertisers.

Other political factors could include the effects of the Competition Commission rulings on marketing plans and the government establishment of regulatory bodies such as the Office of Water Services (Ofwat) which affect the marketing mix of suppliers of important public services. The Office of Communications (Ofcom) and the Advertising Standards Authority (ASA) can have a particular constraint on marketing plans as they control advertising and promotion in most media.

Economic factors These are factors relating to the operation of the economy. A variety of economic factors can affect businesses. Some are shown in Table 1. For example, interest rates may be lowered or raised to warm up or slow down the economy. As interest rates change, so does the amount of money available for investment in industry and for consumers to spend. If interest rates are high, it will cost a business more to invest in a new production line. High interest rates mean that consumers have higher mortgage or loan repayments and less to spend on consumer goods and services. Conversely, low interest rates will encourage a 'feel good' factor among consumers. They will have relatively more income to spend, opening up marketing opportunities for suppliers of goods and services.

Table 1 *How economic factors might affect a business*

Factor	Effect
Rising inflation	Raise costs
Rising unemployment	Greater pool of labour
Trade restrictions	Fewer imports
Falling exchange rate	Exports cheaper and imports more expensive
Economic growth	More consumer spending

Legal factors

Legal constraints on the marketing mix and on marketing plans are the result of legislation. There is a great deal of legislation that could affect marketing plans. Most legislation affecting marketing has resulted from the objective of protecting consumers. The Trading Standards Central website www.tradingstandards.gov.uk is a good place to look to get some idea of just how much legislation exists to protect consumers.

There is no need to learn every part of every piece of legislation. But it is useful to understand how the principal pieces of consumer protection legislation can constrain the marketing mix. Some examples are shown in Figure 4. The Office of Fair Trading provides useful general advice on consumer rights in the UK. It also provides information relating to businesses and markets.

Before any marketing plans are put into practice it is always worth checking them against current legislation to make sure that no offences are likely to occur and no legislation is broken as a result of the plan. Once a potential constraint has been identified, steps can be taken and plans can be changed to avoid or reduce the effect of any constraint and reduce the chance of breaking the law.

Other legislation that could constrain and have an impact on the marketing mix include Sex, Race and Disability Discrimination and Equal Opportunities Acts. These are also dealt within sections 8 and 15.

Environmental and ecological factors

This is another group of external factors that could constrain marketing plans and activity. It could include environmental standards, environmental protection and voluntary codes and agreements that have been established to reduce the impact of commercial activity on the environment.

Examples of environmental standards include:

- the Montreal Protocol, concerned with substances that deplete the ozone layer, such as propellants and gases used in aerosols,

Figure 4 *Examples of legal constraints*

LEGAL CONSTRAINTS

[CO]NSUMER PROTECTION [AC]T 1987. Prohibits the supply [of g]oods not in accordance with general safety requirement or unsafe and provides for the [saf]ety and protection of [con]sumers by enabling [reg]ulations or orders to be made [co]ntrolling consumer goods.

HEALTH AND SAFETY AT WORK ACT 1974. Controls the classification, packaging, labelling, carriage and storage of dangerous substances.

TRADE DESCRIPTIONS ACT 1968. Prohibits the misdescription on the supply of goods and prohibits false claims for services, accommodation and facilities.

[SU]PPLY OF [G]OODS AND [SE]RVICES ACT [19]82. Details [th]e rights of [pur]chasers and [the] duties of [sup]pliers of [serv]ices.

SALE OF GOODS ACT 1979 and SALE AND SUPPLY OF GOODS 1994 and SALE OF GOODS (AMENDMENT) ACT 1995. Details the rights of purchasers and the duties of sellers in the sale of goods.

fire extinguishers, and refrigerators;

- the Kyoto Agreement, a framework laid down by 38 developed countries to reduce their emission of greenhouse gases to prevent global warming.

There are others and likely to be more in the future. The effect and constraint on the marketing mix may not be felt directly by every business. But all businesses will be affected indirectly as different industries have to find ways of reducing emissions. This in turn could affect the cost and supply of some materials used in production.

The environmental and ecological standards that are established by a business can also affect other businesses. Such standards are likely to affect the way that a business expects suppliers to operate. This could constrain some aspects of the marketing mix, particularly when it comes to the sourcing of raw materials and the use of renewable resources for production. A decision to reduce air pollution by airlines, might affect the marketing mix of airline manufacturers.

Other external constraints in this area would be voluntary and industry codes, competition, customer standards and requests. These are also dealt with in section 13.

Research task

Use newspaper articles to investigate how internal or external factors have affected the activities of a business over a period of time. Choose a well known business that is likely to have had a number of articles written about it, such as a car company, supermarket or a fashion clothing business. Identify the factors that have affected a business and how they have had an impact.

OR

Identify a business that could be affected by the ASA and legislation. Investigate how the ASA's activities and legislation could constrain the development of the marketing mix of this business.

OR

Design a questionnaire to identify and investigate the effects of both internal and external factors on a small business organisation.

Portfolio practice · Selling paint to B&Q

B&Q China in 2003 developed an educational promotion on water-based paints to inform its customers of the benefits. Operating companies will continue to be encouraged to give their customers the products and information to help enhance the quality of their home whilst making them more energy-efficient and environmentally sound. It is not our role to tell our customers how to live their lives, but as the debates around sustainable consumption and sustainable development evolve, we as a retailer need to be ready to respond through the products we offer and the information we provide.

Case study

Paint

Paint is core to home improvement. The story starts with its various raw materials, most of which are composed of hydrocarbons or titanium dioxide. Although these raw materials cause concern, the most significant issues surround product use. As paint dries, volatile organic compounds (VOCs) are emitted into the air, causing unpleasant smells and headaches. This is why B&Q UK has been reformulating paint to reduce its dependency on the solvents and VOCs. To help customer choice, the VOCs label was introduced in 1995. In 2004 this label will be reviewed to ensure compliance with the proposed EU paint directive, while the Asian businesses will look into rationalising the environmental labels on their paint ranges.

Source: adapted from *Growth, Returns ... and Responsibility*, Corporate social responsibility summary report from Kingfisher plc, 2003.

(i) Identify the constraints placed on the marketing mix of a paint company wishing to sell its products in B&Q stores.

(ii) Examine how these constraints might affect the marketing mix of a paint company.

Meeting the assessment criteria

You are required to produce an appropriate marketing mix for a new or existing product or service. Your work must include evidence on how the mix selected has been affected by both internal and external constraints.

Business example - CDRack

Students have chosen a vacuum formed CD holder as their product. The product, named the CDRack, will be produced in their D&T department.

Mark Band 1 *Basic evaluation of the marketing mix evidenced by conclusions made without supporting evidence or reasons.*
During the development stage it was decided that a simple design for the CDRack could be made without the need for additional equipment, which would prevent any extra cost. It was also decided to use a plastic that was suitable for vacuum forming and was within the agreed budget for the production cost of the CDRack. Looking around the town centre, the best places to achieve greatest sales for the CDRack were a local music shop and hardware stores. The best place to promote the CDRack would be in local media, such as newspapers. Economic conditions could affect price, so it would be best to keep it low.

Mark Band 2 *Justification of marketing mix showing a range of supported relevant evidence, arguments and conclusions.*
During development of the CDRack a simple prototype was made and shown to people. Some thought it was too big, but were told that the size was constrained by the size of the 'jewel case' used for CDs and to be worthwhile it had to hold ten CDs. A local supplier of plastic suitable for vacuum forming was found. A price was negotiated based on an initial forecast and a lower price for repeat sales if the product took off. This would improve profitability, as the retail selling price has an upper limit determined by the price of similar products. The best places to achieve greatest sales for the CDRack were a local music shop and hardware stores. They were close to the town centre. Selling further away might limit shoppers and sales. In addition, it was thought that the CDRack could be sold direct to consumers from a website. This was supported by a report on television, which said that increasing numbers of consumers were using the Internet for buying household goods. Special packaging for the mail order sales was needed. This was a constraint which was not costed into the original product, and could thus affect profitability. Packaging would be recyclable, which may help to take into account ethical considerations. The local newspaper would be a suitable media to advertise the CDRack. It was decided to spend most of the marketing budget on newspaper advertising, constraining other forms of promotion. This was justified as sales were likely to be in the local area. Prices were kept as low as possible as confidence in the economy had not recovered yet.

Mark Band 3 *Comprehensive and fully justified account of all aspects of the selected marketing mix showing originality of thought.*
During the development stage a simple prototype was designed. It was shown to two groups. Some consumers felt it was too big, but reducing size was rejected. Although this might save costs, the CDRack had to be large enough to hold ten CDs in a 'jewel case'. It was also shown to the local Trading Standards office which stated that the design chosen was suitable for sale to consumers and did not break any consumer protection legislation. The Trading Standards office also checked that wording used on the labelling was acceptable.

A local supplier was found to provide plastic suitable for vacuum forming. An initial price was agreed along with a reduced price for repeat sales which would improve profitability. An Internet survey was used to make sure this was the best price they could get, which it was. However, the supplier was also found to meet certain criteria laid down about ethical trading, such as good employee conditions and not buying materials from countries with oppressive political regimes.

Before the CDRack was launched the owner of a hardware store was interviewed to gauge her reaction and to check that the business had made the right conclusions about how suitable it was to sell in the shops in the town centre. She agreed that the town centre would be the most effective place to maximise sales. The positive comments on the product and location were used as part of their sales presentation to other shopkeepers. The business also decided to sell via the Internet. Television and newspaper reports, as well as surveys from the Office of National Statistics, indicated growing sales via the Internet by consumers.

Before committing to advertising in the local newspaper, the students sought opinion from the local shopkeepers about how effective this method of advertising was likely to be. After their comments confirmed this would be effective, most of the budget would be spent in local newspapers. However, another cost effective method was posters hung in shops that stocked the CDRack. The posters were carefully worded to comply with advertising legislation.

A local survey was carried out to check the retail selling prices of CD racks. Economic conditions were stable at the time. Inflation was low and interest rates had not been increased. But there was still a view that confidence had not yet recovered. Based on this, it was decided that keeping the selling price as low as possible was the correct strategy. It was also decided that, although special packaging was not included in the initial cost, it would be used. This is because it was recyclable and would appeal to ethical customers. Details of plastic waste disposal sites would be included on the packaging to fit in with the business's ethical stance.

Index

A

B

D

E

F

G

I

J

K

L

M

P

Q

R

S

T

U

V